A Strange Kind of Glory

Eamon Dunphy is an Irish writer and broadcaster. He played professional football in England for seventeen years (five of them for Manchester United) and is the author of the classic football book *Only a Game?* and the hugely successful Roy Keane autobiography. He also wrote the international bestseller *Unforgettable Fire: the Story of U2*. He lives in Dublin.

Praise for *A Strange Kind of Glory*

'A brilliant biography' *Observer*

'The sports book of the year – by a distance' Frank Keating

'Vividly authentic . . .' Brian Glanville, Sunday Times

'The best, most readable football book of the year' *Mail on Sunday*

'Eamon Dunphy's *A Strange Kind of Glory* is certainly the major football biography of the year. Several years in the writing, it succeeds in capturing, for the first time, the essence of this enigmatic and intensely charismatic figure, who had such a huge impact on the game and the way it was managed and played.' *Daily Telegraph*

'If there is a better football book this year, it would have to be astonishing' *Guardian*

'Dunphy pulls no punches on the most glamorous club in Britain, exposing all football's double standards in the most intriguing football book of the year.' *Sun*

'The most appealing football book of the year.' *The Times*

'Eamon Dunphy has written the big football book on the big subject – Sir Mat̶   passionately, with fine writing and

an acute eye for the sweep of professional football history in which Busby played such a vast and illuminating role. But what we have in *A Strange Kind of Glory* is no plaster saint. Dunphy gives us a big and complex man who . . . didn't so much beat off his rivals as transcend them . . . Dunphy's recreation of the pre-Munich years, the swelling of great ambition, great teams, is wonderfully fresh and long before the final page there is more than enough evidence for Dunphy's claim that Busby was "the last great football man".' James Lawton, *Daily Express*

'For Man Utd fans, I'd say it's a must.' Mick McCarthy, *Sunday Tribune*

'Eamon Dunphy, whose 1970s diary as a Millwall player produced the superb *Only A Game?*, has brought his insight to *A Strange Kind of Glory* which is an immensely engaging analysis of Sir Matt Busby and Manchester United.' *Independent on Sunday*

'Sports writing of the highest order' *Time Out*

'The Munich air disaster of 1958, the greatest tragedy to hit an English football team and the event that made Manchester United forever something more than just another club, is inevitably the bleak centrepiece of Eamon Dunphy's tale of Sir Matt Busby and Manchester United. But Dunphy, with a terrific cast of characters at his disposal, reveals many other chilling dramas in the Old Trafford tapestry.' Tim Rice, *Sunday Express*

'A fascinating and absorbing story.' *Irish Times*

'A fascinating insight into one of the key figures of yesteryear and a riveting, comprehensive read for all those who believe the golden age of British soccer lies in the past and not the future.' *Today*

'Busby's story has lain untold for far too long. Finally his life story, warts and all, is revealed in the 396 pages of *A Strange Kind of Glory* ... This had to be a great book. It does not disappoint.' *Birmingham Post*

'Anyone who loves the "beautiful game" will find *A Strange Kind of Glory* an essential part of their football library.' *Irish Press*

A Strange Kind of Glory

Sir Matt Busby
& Manchester United

Eamon Dunphy

For my father Paddy and my brother Kevin

First published in this new edition
2007 by Aurum Press Ltd,
7 Greenland Street, London, NW1 0ND
www.aurumpress.co.uk

A catalogue record for this book is available from the British Library.

ISBN-13: 978 1 84513 255 2

10 9 8 7 6 5 4 3 2
2011 2010 2009 2008

Printed in Great Britain by Bookmarque, Croydon, Surrey

Contents

Introduction to 2007 Edition

Busby was the first great football man. Anybody reading his story may conclude that what he achieved for his football club, and the wider game, would not be possible today. When Matt Busby joined Manchester United as manager in 1945, Old Trafford was, literally, a bomb site, and United was an undistinguished club, familiar with mid-table mediocrity. When Sir Matt Busby retired 24 years later, Manchester United was one of the world's most renowned sporting institutions.

Before Busby, football managers were little more than glorified office boys. Yes, they selected the team and organised matters on the training ground, but real power resided with the directors and the club secretary. Hiring and firing was somebody else's business, not the manager's.

The manager was a figurehead, his purpose to obey orders. Some clubs wouldn't even trust a former professional player as a stooge. In English football's caste system men who played the game for money were the lowest of the low. Any contemporary player who feels a *frisson* of guilt at the allegedly 'obscene' amount of money he is paid can turn to the chapter devoted to Billy Meredith, a great player and founder of the Professional Footballers Association. This principled sportsman was crucified by English football's pre-war ruling class. His crime? Being honourable and professional, and articulating his justified grievances.

Those looking at the modern game, where wealthy young princes earn fortunes, might usefully reflect on the way it used to be. Before the Second World War, when Busby played with distinction for Manchester City and Liverpool, many footballers lived down to their bosses' low expectations. Badly paid, feckless, unfit and resentful, many of the best players spent their spare time gambling, drinking and womanising. On account of their deeds on Saturday afternoons the players were local, sometimes national, heroes. But fame was fleeting and fickle. Even the most distinguished player was cast out by his early to mid-thirties.

But Matt Busby was different from Billy Meredith. He kept quiet. He was cunning. Of course he knew what kind of business he was in, but he also knew that actions spoke louder than words, an attitude he took into management. Aware that many older pros were soured by resentment, he was determined to recruit a new breed of man. Young, fearless, gifted and committed to him and to his vision of how the game should be played. It took Busby time to achieve these goals.

Time, of course, is a commodity in short supply in the modern game. Another reason why Busby's story still resonates today. Busby won his first Championship in 1952 in the seventh year of his managerial career. Winning the F.A. Cup in 1948 helped buy that time. Yet the triumph in '52 still left Busby disenchanted. He was some distance from where he wanted to be, his vision not yet reality.

Still, victory conferred more power upon him, which he used to break up that winning side and begin building his dream team of young warriors. The Busby Babes would soon emerge to dominate the English game, playing football of inspiring beauty, grace and power.

Europe was also part of Busby's grand vision. Alone, he possessed the courage to defy English insularity and arrogance, the belief that what happened elsewhere was irrelevant and that the English scene was 'the greatest game in the world'. That deluded conviction had been undermined in 1953 when a brilliant Hungarian team came to Wembley to demolish England by six goals to three. But this humiliation changed nothing as far as the clowns who ran English football were concerned.

So Busby's was a dissenting voice. He was eager to engage with the European game. When Chelsea qualified for the European Cup by winning the 1954–55 Championship, the Football League refused to sanction its participation in the following year's European Cup. Chelsea accepted this ruling.

When Manchester United qualified 12 months later, Busby refused to succumb to Football League threats. This act, borne of the deepest conviction, was courageous. He refused to be intimidated. However, the threat that League points would be docked if European involvement compromised the Football League fixture list was potent.

Hence the anxiety Busby felt when United's British European Airways flight was delayed by bad weather at Munich Airport. United was returning from a European Cup engagement in Belgrade when tragedy struck. The team had to get back to England to play Wolves away on Saturday. Some present at Munich Airport still believe that Busby's anxiety was conveyed to the airline, which may, as a result, have opted for a risky departure.

6 February 1958: The Day A Team Died. Those words echoed across the world, causing feelings of unprecedented grief, not just in Manchester, or, indeed, in England, but around the globe. Eight of the Busby Babes died in the Munich air crash, while Busby would fight for his life for weeks in hospital.

Busby set out to build another great team. Ten years later at Wembley, Manchester United became the first English club to win the European Cup. Matt Busby's life work was done. The following year he retired. There was, however, no happy ending. Venality, bitterness and disillusion would linger around this great man to the end.

When *A Strange Kind of Glory* first published in 1991, Sir Matt Busby was 82 (he would die just three years later). Always wary of the media, which on the whole he effortlessly controlled, Sir Matt agreed somewhat reluctantly to co-operate with my endeavours to research his story. He relented only because I had spent five years at Old Trafford as a journeyman dreamer. I wanted to tell Busby's story because it was an opportunity to portray an extraordinarily large character – ruthless, tolerant, visionary and naive – and also because in tracing his life one could explore the history of English soccer, learning in that process much about the game today.

But, more importantly, his life is a parable for a game that is corrupt in body and spirit. *A Strange Kind of Glory* tells a sad story of a very great man, whose fate is a brutal indictment of English football and all who wield power within it.

Eamon Dunphy, July 2007

Introduction

He insisted that we meet in his office at Old Trafford. He had, reluctantly, agreed to have his story told, but there would be no easy intimacy on this our first meeting. Sir Matt Busby is eighty-two. He still goes to Old Trafford every day to his small office on the first floor of the Executive Suite. Kath, the receptionist, is a bespectacled middle-aged lady, warm, unpretentious, a comfort amid the Habitat gloss of the Executive Suite. She dials the first floor.

'Sir Matt, Eamon Dunphy's here to see you. Shall I send him up luv?'

The lift takes me up. Sir Matt is waiting for me when the doors open. He is immensely charming. I am an undistinguished Old Boy, a reserve and youth team player for five years –1960 to 1965. 'How are you, Eamon, lad?' he greets me. The handshake is firm, the welcoming smile practised, breaking through his remarkable face, large features, handsome as a knight should be. His is a strong and imposing physical presence. Except for a certain deliberation in his gait, Sir Matt could be a man of sixtysomething.

For all the sense of bodily strength and spiritual power, there is something graceful, almost feline about him as we walk down the short, carpeted corridor to his office. Sir Matt is affable as always, yet eye contact is fleeting, he remains distant in a way that is hard to define.

Sir Matt Busby's gift for leadership owed much to his mystique, the elusive force men imagined lay behind the façade of genial composure. Old players, even the greatest of them, who shared extraordinary days and nights with Busby, remain in awe of him. They speak of always wanting to please him. Long after they were famous, universally adored and in all worldly ways secure, it was Sir Matt's attention and affection men like Bobby Charlton, Johnny Carey, Denis Law, George Best and Harry Gregg craved. Great athletes felt inadequate in his presence, although he had ostensibly done nothing to induce the feeling.

This he understood. He remained in control. Always. There was no lilting rhetoric or heated condemnation in Manchester United's dressing-room. Words were not his means of inspiring others or rebuking them.

Journalists, biographers and ghosts purporting to tell His Own Story, those seeking to reveal more than he wanted known, have found Sir Matt a daunting subject. The renowned qualities which inspired great footballers could be redeployed to form a barricade against intrusion. He was modest, declaring that the only memorial he wanted was the football played by his teams. Everything else was irrevelant, he humbly insisted. Because potential inquisitors also wanted to please Busby they invariably settled for the carefully crafted anecdotes which, varying little, stud most accounts of his life. Sir Matt is prudent, access has always been strictly limited.

I spent several years patiently wooing Sir Matt and his family seeking his consent to write this book. He was wary of an Old Boy poking around. My intentions, however, were honourable. I felt that his was the great football story. No other English football club has given such glorious expression to the game on the field. Understanding how that was achieved seemed important, the more so given the wretchedness of the contemporary game, bereft as it is of heroes and values of a kind with which the names Busby and Manchester United are synonymous.

Once Sir Matt's imprimatur was on this project my task was eased. His family, friends and the great players who served him opened up and talked about Busby as never before.

Although Manchester United have not won the First Division Championship since 1967, the club's legend remains as strong as ever in the 1990s. Wherever football is played, the name

2

Manchester United is honoured, as are the names of Matt Busby, Bobby Charlton, George Best, Denis Law, Duncan Edwards, Roger Byrne, Eddie Colman and Tommy Taylor. This great English sporting institution has, uniquely, touched hearts and minds across the world. Tragedy is evoked as well as glorious football.

On 6 February 1958, eight Manchester United players died or were mortally injured in what people in Manchester simply call 'The Crash'. The Munich Air Disaster left twenty-three people dead. Many planes have crashed, costing many more lives since that day almost thirty-four years ago. Yet, the Munich Disaster lives poignantly in memory, an afternoon, like the one on which President Kennedy was assassinated, when a shadow fell across the world, when something was lost never to be replaced. Those who saw them claim this was the greatest team ever to grace the English League. The average age of that Busby side was twenty-one. Mere boys, they had won two successive First Division Championships, one of them by eleven points.

Triumphant at home, this brash, brilliant, outrageously confident football team from the industrial North set out to conquer Europe, where no other English club had dared to venture. The England they left in the Fifties was the drab place 'damned' by the playwright John Osborne as stultifying, reactionary, unimaginative and boring. Busby's 'Red Devils' were the antithesis of this. When they embarked on their European adventure, English football, reflecting the national mood, lacked confidence, stood in awe, or pitiful insularity, as the seemingly invincible Hungarians and Real Madrid lent new enchantment to the game England had taught the world to play. The quest for self-respect, restoration of England's pre-eminence, led by Busby's young team, had a resonance beyond football. Their adventure would tell England something about itself.

The omens were good. United played as magnificently in the European Champions Cups, with the same verve and irrepressible style, as in domestic competitions. The crusade looked likely to succeed when these daring young men perished on that cold Munich afternoon.

Matt Busby almost died from his multiple injuries. Two agonising weeks after the crash, Duncan Edwards did. He was twenty-one.

Busby's club was destroyed at Munich. Ten years later the next team he created, perhaps the greatest of the three, won the European Champions Cup at Wembley, a magical goal from another great player, yet another type, from yet another generation, Georgie Best securing the trophy the 'Red Devils' had died pursuing. Manchester United were the first English team to win the European Cup. A measure of Busby's achievement is that that statistic, historic though it is, is almost irrelevant to his story.

In the Sixties United won an FA Cup and two Championships. The style of Law, Best and Charlton will live in football folklore as long as the game is played.

Matt Busby was knighted in 1968. In a Gallup Poll in February 1969 he was voted Britains's seventh most popular man. Still the man himself remained an enigma. He had never been on a television chat-show or profiled in any depth in print. The books were full of football lore, triumphs and defeats, reports of matches won and lost, results and scorelines. Of him little was known. People responding to Gallup voted for an image, an idea about him as represented by the football played by his teams: gracious, courageous, poignant by virtue of Munich, glorious, stylish, a nobleman from the world of professional sport where such are rarely found.

This miner's son is the longest-serving professional in the English game. He started out a young player with Manchester City in 1928. Sixty-three years later he survives in a sport that casts off its servants with callous disregard, as of habit. As I write, in the summer of 1991, thirty professional managers have been sacked during the season past. Busby survives, the mystery intact, people still voting for an image.

Who knows Sir Matt Busby, the one great man, in the fullest sense of that phrase, to emerge from more than a century of professional soccer in Britain? Those closest to him, the smart, the best and brightest of their time, his friends and colleagues, all argue about him. How did he do it? What is he really like?

What is the truth, tantalisingly concealed, of Busby's Manchester United?

Busby changed the nature of England's national game. He was a revolutionary, entering management in 1945 to effect swift and radical change, taking control of Manchester United, and in the process defining the role of the manager as Boss rather than servant. Before that, as a player he had commanded respect beyond the aspirations of pre-war professional sportsmen. Matt the player was dignified and charismatic; Matt the manager was powerful, a paternalist in an age of authoritarianism. A man of action and a visionary, a football man to the core, with the bearing and political instinct of a cardinal.

On one level Manchester United is the greatest sports story in England's history. On another, more human, level the story of this great club is a saga of tragedy, betrayal, hurt, bitterness, ruined lives and careers. Wherever there is glory, power and wealth one finds such things. In that respect Matt Busby's story is no different from any other saga.

In his small office, sipping coffee, he is at eighty-two as immaculately dressed as always: light-brown suit, white shirt set off by rust coloured silk tie. The shoes, brown patent leather. Dignity personified. He would co-operate, as would his family and closest friends with more enthusiasm. They faced a contradiction, wanting at once to protect him and explain him.

Protect him from what? Those who love him most know how much Sir Matt hates intrusion, is content to be remembered for his extraordinary achievements, would wish to remain distant and dignified. Yet towards the end of a magnificent life there was disappointment and hurt. This too is part of his story, an important part, for enabling us to understand, through the life of English football's ultimate professional, the true nature of the game.

Those who wished to protect Sir Matt felt compelled to explain him because, being football men themselves, they understood that Busby was the last great football man, a genius who gifted greatness to his players, to more of them than any other man in the history of the game. Hence, the importance of separating myth from reality, of reconstructing the life as it was lived rather than as it may be imagined. Seen from inside,

5

Busby's life is even more substantial than the myth. There are few of whom that can truly be said.

1

Mattha

'The menace of the Irish Race to our
Scottish Nationality'

Title of pamphlet published by the
General Assembly of the Church of
Scotland in 1923

Matt Busby was born in the Lanarkshire mining village of
Orbiston on 26 May 1909. He was Alexander and Nellie
Busby's first child. 'A footballer has come into this house
today,' Dr Douglas told Nellie as she cradled her firstborn in
her arms. Matt's father was a notable footballer in a village
that was proud of its footballers. There were two things above
all in which the men of Orbiston took pride: playing football
and working on the coalface. The harsh unnatural work bred
tough men for whom danger was a fact of everyday life and at
the end of the week their leisure was consumed with appropriate lust. They felt themselves to be apart from other men,
better, more versed in life's realities, more deserving of the
good times in pubs and dancehalls where for a few hours on
Saturday night the filthy grime and physical stress of the pits
could be forgotten.

Recalling the harsh reality of life in a mining village many
years later, Matt Busby would tell an apocryphal story of two
miners walking to work on a bitterly cold January morning. As
they approached the pit-head a bird sang to greet the dawn.
One of the miners paused, stared at the bird and barked, 'Ye
wouldne be singing sae loud if ye had a pit bonnet on yir heid.'

Mining was filthy and dangerous. Football was one antidote,
an escape into daylight and fresh air. In the pit the men lived
like animals, but above ground life was often little better.
Money was a constant source of worry; illness a lingering fear.

If you lost your health you lost everything, most tormentingly the home you lived in. You belonged to the mining company – everything was theirs except your leisure time.

It was the same for every miner and his family. The most obvious and profound example of uniform dependence on The Company was the home you lived in. Matt Busby was born in a miner's cottage in Old Orbiston, three-quarters of a mile from the town of Bellshill. There were eight pits around the town. Each pit had its own community divided in sections of thirty-two cottages, called Miners Rows. There were sixteen dwellings in each row. When Matt was born the cottage the Busbys lived in was over a hundred years old. There were two rooms, a kitchen and a living-room-cum-bedroom, with a cold-water tap outside. The communal toilets were seventy-five yards away and on a cold night men didn't always feel inclined to make the journey. Most families were decent, some weren't. People lived close together, little things distinguished a family. Behaviour reflected on the household, mattered so much because it was so easily observed.

Individuality was most commonly the consequence of bad rather than good behaviour. A man would acquire a reputation as a fighter or a drinker, maybe as a womaniser. A large spirit, imprisoned by the uniformity of work and the social conventions of his row, would have no means, other than drink, aggression or romance, of breaking free of the constraints of village life, no means other than football of giving expression to his personality and imagination. Football was the decent man's flight from conformity, the way he was known and identified himself. Football was respectable. Hence, perhaps, Dr Douglas's encouraging words to Nellie Busby. The Busbys were respectable people, a footballer of local renown would be no more than they deserved.

While the way a man conducted himself in the village reflected on the family, the nature of life within the home was determined by his wife. Alexander Busby was a quiet, genial man, a big man who didn't throw his weight around. Nellie was a more vigorous character, a woman of some conviction. The Busbys were Catholics, Nellie the daughter of Jimmy Greer, an Irishman who'd come to Orbiston to work in the pit and who lived five cottages down the row from Alex and Nellie. Jimmy was a character. He liked a drink and though his fecklessness was largely redeemed by a generous nature, he was never entirely redeemed in Nellie's eyes. She resented the torment her mother had endured when Jimmy spent too much time and money in the public house. More deeply felt, as she grew up in Orbiston, was her sense of embarrassment as her father conformed to the stereotype of Irish Catholic behaviour which fuelled the racial and religious bigotry that was pervasive at all levels of Scottish life.

In the community around Bellshill, Catholics and Protestants lived and worked side by side. The profound philosophical and theological arguments that led to the Reformation were never an issue in a mixed working-class village like Orbiston. Sectarianism focused on everyday existence, on behaviour. The Reformation was not as bitter for Scottish Catholics as for their co-religionists in England. Only one person, a Jesuit priest named John Ogilvie, lost his life, executed at Glasgow Cross in 1615 for treasonable recognition of the Pope's spiritual jurisdiction in the King's land. Those Scots who remained loyal to Rome after the Reformation lived mainly in the Highlands and Isles and around Banff in the north-east of the country. In the seventeenth century hatred was about religion. Two hundred years later, when the Irish arrived in Scotland, race became the issue and anti-Catholicism gained a sinister new lease of life as the Irish, fleeing the poverty of home, came in search of work. In the mid-nineteenth century anti-Catholic riots were a feature of life in the Central Lowlands. The immigrants were accused of offering 'scab' labour, taking jobs from native Scots, and with their large and ever increasing families they were reviled as a burden on the Poor Rates.

The Irish immigrants had no rights – they couldn't vote or own property – until in the 1820s the Irish Catholic leader, Daniel O'Connell, began to campaign for civil rights for Catholics in the United Kingdom. Opposition to this campaign was most virulent in Scotland, yet, supported by moderate Protestants and, notably, by the liberal newspaper the *Scotsman*, O'Connell was successful, and in 1829 King George

III reluctantly signed the Emancipation Act, which allowed Catholics most of the civil rights enjoyed by other citizens.

In an essay published in 1973 the religious historian the Reverend Ian Muirhead pointed out that, had they been offered a referendum in 1829, the Scots would have emphatically rejected Catholic Emancipation. Hatred of Catholics was most intense north of the border, and worst of all on the west coast of Scotland where the Irish had settled. Emancipation was deemed a threat to the Protestant way of life. One of many popular anti-Popery broadsheets of the time felt obliged to warn its Protestant readers that: 'We shall have a Popish Government; a Popish Parliament; a Popish Provost, Popish Magistrates, Popish Lords of Session, Popish Patrons of Churches, Popish Professors in the colleges, Popish schoolmasters in every parish, if once we suffer the barriers of the Protestant Constitution to be broken down.'

In the decade following the Emancipation Act Anti-Romanism grew in intensity. The arrival of the Irish – men like Jimmy Greer – exacerbated the problems in Scotland. Another expert on Popular Protestantism in Victorian Britain, Professor Geoffrey Best, notes that once Parliament had lifted the restrictions on Catholics, Anglicans and Non-Conformists felt vulnerable and were therefore more ready to support a vigorous anti-Popery movement. The festering sore became uglier, more visible. In 1850 there were anti-Catholic riots in Greenock and elsewhere, provoked by John Sayers Orr, a notorious anti-Catholic demagogue, widely known as the Angel Gabriel for his histrionic performances. In a publication called Bulwark the Reverend James Begg, the author of a Handbook of Popery, attacked Catholics in verse:

> They say the clouds of Papal Rome
> Are rolling o'er our land
> But this we know our hearts are fixed
> And firm shall be our stand.

Fixed hearts begot clenched fists on the streets of Glasgow and in Bellshill, eight miles away. In the neighbouring town of Coatbridge there was a six-day riot between Protestants and Catholics in 1883. According to the Reverend Muirhead, 'Anti-

Catholicism was the anti-semitism of the liberal.' There were few liberals at street level. There, prejudice had little to do with liturgy, whether or not you were loyal to the King or to Rome. Loyalism and Catholicism were merely badges of identity reflecting differences of character rather than religious belief. In the Protestant psyche Papists were feckless, sly, weak, too fond of drink, unable to control themselves, least of all in the matter of sex. Catholics were uneducated, and irresponsible. They lived for the day. They could sin and gain easy forgiveness in confession. To Protestants this Holy Catholic Sacrament was a joke.

Catholics knew the Protestants to be a harder breed. Prods saved their pennies, worked harder, were neat and clean. And joyless.

Among devout Catholics a more malicious myth flourished, the notion that Protestants were to be pitied. The Prods have abandoned the one True Faith – we should pray for them. In 1886 Pope Leo XIII declared the Anglican rite of ordination, 'wholly invalid and null'. Three years later he issued a papal letter, Caritatis Studium, addressed to Scotland. Noting that the majority of Scots were Presbyterians, Leo regretted 'more and more the unhappy state of so many people who lack the Christian faith in its entirety'. He prayed that one day Protestants 'might be willing to join us in restoring the communion of one and the same faith'. Rescuing the fallen Prods was deemed by Leo to be 'the big project'.

Pope Leo was as irrelevant to everyday life in Bellshill as his extremist Protestant counterparts, the frenzied orators of the Orange Order. Ordinary decent Catholics had no mission to convert their Protestant neighbours while most Protestants were content to allow their Catholic neighbours to live free of persecution. As Stolther's 1911 edition of social life in Glasgow, Lanarkshire and Renfrew observed, sectarianism was not the only coinage of the day. Two years after Matt Busby was born, Stolther's, a Protestant publication, spoke of 'the laudable efforts, noble ambitions and high character' of the St Vincent De Paul Society and thanked Catholics involved in public bodies for their efforts to 'obliterate those differences and suspicions that, unfortunately, at one time prevailed'. Such men, Stolther's went on, were 'true patriotic citizens'. Men *and* women.

Nellie Busby had noble ambitions. Character, high and low, was formed in the home. Religion was a private matter. But there were other matters of importance, education being in her mind the most important of all. From education would flow enlightenment, respect for yourself and for your neighbour. Three daughters, Delia, Kathy and Margaret were born to Alex and Nellie between 1911 and the outbreak of the First World War in 1914.

The Busby's cottage was crowded, but a warm and tranquil refuge from the world outside. Nellie's father had little interest in football. Jimmy was expansive as only the Irish can be, the old live-for-the-day man, a product of his times. Alex took his pleasure in football, his home and his family. He shared Nellie's convictions about education. In this both the Busbys reflected the moderate, progressive aspirations of Catholics of their generation. The fecklessness of the past was rejected. From the 'pennies of the poor' the Church built its own elementary schools and paid for the training of its own teachers. Acknowledging this Stolthers Guide remarked upon the praiseworthy efforts of Catholics on schoolboards who 'receive nothing from the rates in support of their schools – their own people having to contribute to these rates – [yet] they support any expenditure well directed in the interest of education'.

Catholics were at this time Scotland's largest minority. By 1850 there were about 200,000 Irish residents in Scotland, most of them Catholic, the minority Protestant and therefore welcome. The Catholic descendents of those immigrants like Alex and Nellie Busby were faced with a critical choice, assimilate or agitate. Those who chose to do the latter uttered the Fenian rhetoric of Irish Republicanism. On a Saturday night in Glasgow or Bellshill drink would lead to rebel songs, then, from the opposite corner of the street, the Pope would be 'fucked'. Thus battle between 'Tim' and 'Blue Nose' would ensue. Prejudice would harden. To this tendency Jimmy Greer was sympathetic. Alex and Nellie Busby were not.

They sought a new life. Rejecting sectarianism, they wished

to assimilate. They and their children were Scots, proud of their origins but aware that self-respect – and the respect of the wider community – could not be won in hostile exchanges on street corners after the pubs closed on a Saturday night. Education offered the opportunity for real advancement; agitation was a blind alley. Nor did it make sense to a man like Alex Busby who worked alongside Protestants in the pit and played football with them at weekends.

In 1914 young Matt started school at Rothwell St Brides. He was a well-mannered and clever boy, and if his mother worried about her 'Mattha' it was because of the company he kept, in particular Frank Rogers, a wild young fellow whose family were notorious Fenian agitators. Football was the bond between Frank and Mattha, yet Nellie thought young Rogers a bit of a blackguard, and feared the influence he might have on her son. The imminent war was, however, a more profound source of worry. Alex had decided to volunteer to fight the Germans. Any doubts he and other Catholic men may have harboured about fighting for King and country, and such doubts were few for this was regarded as a just and popular conflict, dissolved when a letter from Archbishop John Maguire of Glasgow was read out at Mass one Sunday. Maguire urged his flock to 'go to the front against the evil Germans'.

Thus, with a mixture of pride and foreboding Nellie and her children saw Alex and his fellow villagers – Catholic and Protestant – off to war.

A consoling thought for Nellie was that the men would return as they left, together, for bigotry would be less profitable once victory had been achieved. That largely unspoken hope was voiced shortly after hostilities began by Professor J. S. Phillimore, a convert and one of the Catholic Church's leading intellectuals. Scottish Catholics would gain much from being loyal combatants, Phillimore claimed. When the war was over soldiers would come home bringing stories of what priests and nuns did on the battlefields. There would, he asserted, be a complete revolution of feeling in Scotland's attitude to Catholics.

Alex Busby was killed by a sniper's bullet at Arras in 1916.

Over forty years later Matt Busby would recall how 'unprotected' he felt at the loss of his father. There was, he reflected, 'a gap in the life of a boy without a father when all the other boys around him could talk about theirs and incessantly did'. He felt that the death of his father as he approached his seventh birthday induced in him 'some paternal, protective feeling to other unfortunate, sensitive young people'. Of the Busby men, only Matt and Jimmy Greer survived the First World War. The war that was to end all wars had claimed the lives of all the menfolk in the family. History would mock the claim that the Great War would end all wars. Nor was the Britain the fighting men returned to the land fit for heroes that had been promised. Economic depression led to unemployment, which, in Scotland, pitched young Catholics against Protestants in the search for scarce jobs. In those desperate circumstances another pre-war promise was shown to be hollow: the notion that by volunteering for the frontlines Catholics would still the clamour of the bigots. The Busbys, having sacrificed so much, remained members of a despised minority.

Perversely, after the war sectarianism increased and became respectable. In 1923 the General Assembly of the Church of Scotland published a pamphlet, 'The Menace of the Irish Race to our Scottish Nationality', which accepted that Orange or Protestant Irishmen could be assimilated but asserted that the Catholic immigrant stock 'cannot be assimilated or absorbed into the Scottish race. They remain a people by themselves, segregated by reason of their race, their customs, and are gradually and inevitably dividing Scotland racially, socially and ecclesiastically.'

Religious persecution was a fact of daily life for Nellie Busby and her family. If in later life Matt Busby felt protective to those vulnerable and sensitive and if, as he did, he came to detest bullying, his experiences of bigotry and intolerance in his formative years helps us understand why.

The swelling tide of Protestant bigotry touched all Catholic lives. Young unemployed Catholics seeking work would be weeded out by questions such as, 'What school did you go to?' 'Were you in the Boys Brigade?' and 'Who was your Sunday

School teacher?' Faced with this type of provocation Catholics responded in differing ways. In the Rogers family, along the row of cottages from the Busbys, bitterness was the self-defeating consequence of bigotry. Intolerance begot spite and hatred. Matt's friend Frank Rogers burned with rage, seeking any opportunity to confront the Blue Nosed bastards in his village. When they went looking for trouble, Frank and his equally belligerent brothers were as feared in their own community as they were by neighbouring Protestants. People stood aside when, usually on Saturday nights, the Rogers boys marched aggressively into Bellshill. Only one young man could reason with them.

When Matt Busby cautioned against bitterness Frank tended to listen. Don't play into their hands, Matt would plead with his friend, you're only letting yourself down. Coming from somebody else this advice would have carried little force. But Matt was different. The Busbys were respected on Miners Row. They were decent, generous neighbours. Nellie and her children had borne the loss of Alex and the other men with admirable stoicism. Nellie had been given a job at the pit-head to supplement her widow's pension. Respect was compounded by affection, this being due in no small measure to Jimmy Greer and Matt, the surviving male members of the family.

With Nellie working at the pit, Jimmy spent his days caring for Delia, Kathy and Margaret. He was still the rascal drinker, still the expansive character who would appear on the doorstep of his cottage in his long-johns and hail 'Mattha' to leave his football game and fetch a pitcher of beer from the village saloon. If Nellie represented the serious, responsible, conscientious face of Catholicism in Old Orbiston, Jimmy, tolerably dissolute, vouched for the family's street credibility, forming a human bridge between the Busbys and the Rogers. When as a teenager Matt remonstrated with Frank, the rough young diamond paid heed; Jimmy Greer's grandson was no goody-goody, no preacher talking for talking's sake. Respect was Jimmy's legacy to young Mattha.

The death of his father thrust new responsibilities on Matt. Some of the gaiety of childhood was gone. He was his mother's ally now, her partner as much as her son, so while other young

15

lads dallied after school Matt hurried back to the cottage to help Jimmy with his sisters and the household chores. He learned to cope around the house, to light a fire, shop, and soothe a young girl's cries. He had always looked older than his years, now he had to act that way too. Jimmy and Matt grew close those afternoons. At times an odd role reversal caused them to laugh, as the older man feigned irresponsibility to tease a rebuke from his earnest grandson. 'Och, come on wee Mattha, your mother willnae knoo,' Jimmy would chuckle as he proposed some conspiratorial short-cut around their domestic duties. Thus, gently, laughter returned to the Busbys' cottage to ease the pain of Alex's passing. A joke shared, the work done, Mattha would take off to play football with his pals. Later in his distinguished life Matt Busby would be accused of being too tolerant of rogues. He was, perhaps, acknowledging an important debt.

In 1919 Nellie married Harry Matthie whom she'd met while working at the Colliery. Although he never talked about it, except perhaps to Jimmy Greer, there was always a feeling in the family that Mattha resented the new presence in his cottage.

Matt had done well at St Brides. The school principal advised Nellie to send the boy to Motherwell Higher Grade, the best second level college within reach. Such a recommendation was not lightly made as sending a boy to college for five years entailed sacrifices for a family. Scarce money would have to be spent on clothes and books and there was the loss of the wage-packet most young men in Bellshill brought home when they started working at fourteen. It was almost certainly with the 1918 Education Act in mind that the teachers at St Brides chose Matt Busby for educational advancement. As part of that Act the State and the Catholic Church reached agreement on the controversial question of whether or not Catholics should be allowed to run their own schools. Non-denominational schooling would expose Catholics to an alien doctrine, the Hierarchy argued, and if the Catholic ethos was to be preserved, religious teaching must be part of the curriculum in schools and colleges. The Catholic school would become an extension of both the home and the parish in the formation of Catholic character.

Before the 1918 Act Catholics who progressed to second level education were at risk, exposed to the mores of the non-Catholic majority. The State's concession meant that the brightest young Catholics could now – with the Church's guidance – aspire to the professions and higher trades without losing their identity. The primary school teacher's task was to find the best and brightest children and urge their parents to make the necessary sacrifices to ensure that Catholics would climb the social ladder from the ghetto to the middle classes.

It was for this cause that twelve-year-old Matt set off from the cottage in Old Orbiston shortly after seven o'clock each weekday morning to walk the five miles to Motherwell. Every day for the next three years, except on precious holidays, Matt braved the elements, a pioneer for his class and his creed. Soon two more children were born to Nellie and Harry; a son, Jimmy, and a daughter, Ellen. As a nipper young Jimmy remembers running the two hundred yards to the turn off from the main Motherwell–Glasgow road every evening to wait for Matt who would hoist him on his shoulders and carry him home.

Matt was an unusual boy, composed and mature, serene almost at times, and he stood out at college. He was a diligent scholar, yet somehow distant in a way other pupils and teachers could never fathom. A popular, affable lad, Matt could, at the same time, seem detached in a way that some found intimidating, others simply curious. He was not what the more socially conscious teachers imagined a collier's son would be. He had, without the slightest sense of affectation, a certain quality, an élan, that was extraordinary in a teenage boy. The headmaster, Mr Bennett, took special note of this lad from Bellshill.

The aura around Matt Busby was natural. If there was within him any sense of being different it was due to football. The district of Bellshill was renowned for its footballers: by 1923 the names of Jimmy McMullen, Alex James and Hughie Gallacher were famous in the newspapers. All three came from Bellshill. McMullen, James and Gallacher would later play in the greatest Scottish team of all time, the Wee Wembley Wizards that beat England 5–2 at Wembley in 1928. Tales of their deeds, and memories, fresh and vivid, of seeing them play on the football pitch that lay in the shadow of the pit-bing in Old Orbiston, filled the villagers with more than pride. The bing, a large black mound of disused coal-slack, was the ugly symbol of this and all other mining villages. This filthy waste reminded them of what their lives were about, of the grime and squalor that governed village life.

Village pride was the memory of Alex James playing here, the thought that a rare beauty, which had resonance in the world far beyond this bleak terrain, had been conceived and nurtured beneath their own bing. Men like James, Gallacher and McMullen were more than heroes; they carved a space for Orbiston and Bellshill in the world, creating an identity for their community, a sense of pride, a sense of romance, a sense that what was precious was within reach, a rare exhilarating glimpse of something wonderful and glorious which was accessible to all who had known them or their families in a way that other things, perhaps equally desirable, were not.

To outsiders Old Orbiston was known as Cannibal Island, partly because of the fierceness of its men playing football, partly because of the stark landscape; the humble Miners Rows dwarfed by the dark sulking bings. Partly, too, because of the malevolent undercurrents of Catholic/Protestant hostility which could, on any drinking night, burst into a torrent of violence and hatred. To those who lived in the cottages, Old Orbiston was the place where Alex James, Jimmy McMullen and Hughie Gallacher created beauty. Beauty to which people responded. Even so that even those who couldn't play would be touched, spiritually, in a way few preachers of dogma could match, and would be better for the experience.

Young Matt Busby had never visited an art gallery, listened to Beethoven or Mozart, or read the poetry of Byron, but he knew what beauty was, knew what man was capable of, knew of the wonders of imagination, and knew that he could express himself through the delightful, accessible language of football. If there was an uncanny self-assurance about the boy from Cannibal Island, football was the source.

Like most young boys in mining villages and city ghettos, Matt discovered the ball almost as soon as he could walk. At first this piece of rubber was whimsical, elusive, teasing, a private challenge. It ran away and made you chase it, made a fool of you, seemed to have a mind of its own. There was life in this thing, mysterious, seductive life. Slowly you began to understand the mystery. You began to exercise control, you tasted power, perhaps, for the first time. You knew a certain

18

secret satisfaction. Then you joined the others, testing your power against theirs. In this way you learned about yourself and about them. You took communion without liturgy or dogma. The ball was more than a toy, it was a divine invention, an instrument that required of its players sensitivity and imagination. Naked aggression led only to torment. The brute was never rewarded, was indeed made to look foolish when he tried to bully the ball; the hero was the man who possessed wit and nerve, who harnessed his power to spirit and mind, creating the most wonderful theatre in the most unlikely setting.

Matt Busby fell in love with football when he first watched his father play. He quickly mastered the ball. Then he took the next steps; out to join the other boys on the street, a sense of belonging there, losing inhibitions, taking stock, measuring yourself against them in a way that transcended other ways of keeping the score like school, money, possessions, the way you looked, the clothes you wore. If you could play this game the hole in the arse of your trousers didn't matter, no more than your buck-teeth or the acne on your skin. To master football was to escape the material world, the uncertainties, the frustration, the pain.

For Matt Busby, the boy without a father, sensitive to the 'incessant' chatter of other boys about *their* dads, football was always more than a game.

Alex James was Matt's first hero. As a teenager James played for Old Orbiston Celtic when Matt was the team's hamper-boy, charged with looking after the stockings, knickers and jerseys, and the footballs, which were in those days a scarce, precious commodity. Before the match Matt would collect the gear and hand each player his strip. Afterwards the mucky, sweat-stained jerseys, shorts and stockings would be packed away and delivered to the lady who washed them. This was a dream assignment for a lad, a chance to get the feel of the glory game from the inside, to glimpse the heroes, smell the liniment, inhale the intoxicating mixture of apprehension and excitement in the dressing-room before a game. To be known by name to Alex James. One day, when James's boots got lost, Matt solved the problem by racing the two hundred yards to the cottage to fetch his own – they were a perfect fit for the little genius.

In almost every way James embodied football's magical attraction for the working man. In civies he looked ordinary; small at five feet five inches, unprepossessing, just another miner's son. He took the field wearing long, baggy shorts that billowed down around his knees. He was anything but athletic, an eccentric waif amid the purposeful muscularity of those around him. He was Everyman, the baggy shorts that looked too big for him made him seem more vulnerable and out of place. He was the little guy all could identify with. The pleasure of seeing him triumph was sublime. To the otherwise undistinguished gathering which massed on the touchlines to watch Old Orbiston Celtic, in the shadow of the black pit-head bing which stood as a monument to the harsh futility of their working lives, Alex James was an inspiring sight. For once the contest began he was no longer ordinary or frail. He was the master; audacious, elusive, seeing moves nobody else could see; here, a miraculous escape from the flailing boots of bigger men who, being so impressive when they'd confidently strolled out onto the pitch, were now left floundering desperately in the little guy's wake; there, a deadly pass delivered with cold precision into the path of a colleague racing free in open space. A feint, a drop of the shoulder, a teasing little shuffle of the hips and those apparently powerful opponents were confused, rendered impotent for all to see. Football played with such wit and grace by this unlikely hero aroused the deepest passions in those who witnessed it. For he was one of them, the hero Everyman in a parable about power and powerlessness which the watching men understood. His victory was theirs, his wit, daring and grace was theirs as well, the beauty that lay beneath the grimy surface of life in a mining village. Football was theatre and even those who couldn't play were part of the story. The line between hero and audience was thin. Only the ball separated James from those who worshipped him. Only the ball.

Small boys and grown men drifted away from the football ground to talk and dream about the wonder of the afternoon. James soon went on to fame with Preston North End, Arsenal and Scotland. Hughie Gallacher and Jimmy McMullen went as well. News of their deeds filtered back to Old Orbiston and Bellshill when, in the bitter years of the early Twenties which were the prelude to the Jarrow Hunger March and the General Strike of 1926, there was little else to be proud of. Fears of hunger and unemployment in those years were real, and Harry Matthie and Nellie began to think about emigrating to America. The widows of most of the Busby men had gone to the States after the war, and the news they sent back was encouraging: America offered opportunity. Where you came from, what religion you practised made no difference. This was a new country, free of bigotry and want. There seemed nothing to keep them back – but Mattha.

Matt didn't want to go. Nellie didn't want to leave him behind. He was fifteen. Although he was doing well at college he had no real academic ambition. His dreams were about football and he had more reason that most to dream. He and Frank Rogers were the two best young footballers in the district of Bellshill. As boys of eleven or twelve Matt and Frank had played with the men in the improvised games in the village. They were the two to watch according to Bellshill gossip, the two who would surely follow James, McMullen and Gallacher to glory – they were heroes-in-waiting who had already tasted local fame. They had moved from rubber ball to leather, from the street to the pitch with proper lines and goalposts, a referee and corner-flags.

The fantastic dreams, the imaginings of the pillow on which boys fell asleep at night were of goals scored and cunningly flighted passes, of heroic dribbling, the flawless performance in which ball and opposition were mastered as never before. Part of the magic was aesthetic; the feel of a jersey on your back, a proper jersey with colour, a collar and cuffs; the fresh white shorts, the clean stockings, the boots shining and neatly laced; the smell of leather off a real football. The move from rubber to leather, from street to pitch inspired other dreams; of Hampden Park, Wembley, of the great stadiums in cities like London, Manchester and Birmingham. America did not feature in Mattha's dreams. But as he fell asleep at night he heard the talk of emigration to a land that held no promise for him.

The first step towards the emigration ship was taken when it was decided that he would leave Motherwell Higher Grade. The alternative was to stay in college until he was eighteen and another three years on the road had no appeal for Matt. When he delivered the message to Mr Bennett, the headmaster travelled to Orbiston to plead with Nellie. This was a great mistake, he said. Matt would make a splendid teacher. His future was assured. But Nellie explained that the family had already applied for visas to the States. There was no future for them in Orbiston, she said, no way they could wait another three years while Matt finished his schooling. Football wasn't mentioned. The arguments were economic and unanswerable. But while Mr Bennett sadly accepted the inevitable, Nellie was less successful with her son. Matt didn't want to go to America –if money was the problem he would earn it down the pit. The US visas would take six months to come through and every pound would matter to pay for the trip, he reminded his mother. Knowing this was true, Nellie was forced, like Mr Bennett, to accept the inevitable. Matt had already bought time and the pit was the lesser of two evils. When, six months later, the family sat down to make the decision about emigration, Matt, the wage-earning coalface worker, was a much more formidable proposition than the reluctant schoolboy who had originally demurred. The trip into the unknown, always fraught with risk and heartache, was now indefinitely postponed. Matt's opposition proved decisive. Jimmy Greer, not wishing to lose another daughter, was once again his silent ally and Harry Matthie understood that the blood of family was thicker than the water of marital love. This unspoken truth widened the gap between step-father and son. Nellie had been loyal to her own, Mattha could now shape his own destiny.

At midnight on 3 May 1926 the General Strike began. The world fit for heroes for which Alex Busby and his comrades had died had not materialised, least of all for Britain's miners. A contemporary English magazine describes the standard of living of miners and their families as 'being little better than that of brow-beaten coolies in the colonies'. The squalor and filth which had at one time been tolerable grew less so in the Twenties when glimpses of a better, cleaner, brighter world filtered through to mining villages via newsreels, films and print media. Colour printing was common by the early Twenties, magazines like *Boy's Own Paper*, *Famous Novel Magazine* and *Popular Gardening* used colour extensively. *Popular Gardening*'s issue of October 1925 offered a 'beautiful art supplement' in colour. Comics proliferated, many from America. Their engaging heroes, like those in *Boy's Own*, a British paper for 'school-boys of all ages', were clean-limbed, well-dressed role models for the young lads in pit-villages who excitedly consumed these images of another world. Silent movie stars like Ronald Colman played their part in the awakening of the working classes. Romance and adventure seemed more accessible.

The role of advertising in creating a new consciousness of life's possibilities is, perhaps, the most ironic phenomenon of this period. H. H. Harris's advertising poster for Bovril in 1923 was to become a national institution. A contented, well-fed man was, in this colourful print, depicted sitting on a jar of Bovril riding the ocean waves. 'Bovril,' the caption read, 'prevents that sinking feeling.' The words *sinking feeling* were underlined. Other ads, for Nestlé's or Cadbury's Milk Chocolate touted other images of men and women contented by consumerism.

The contrast between this imagined world and the urban slums and Miners Rows never seemed more stark than in the bitter months before the General Strike was called. The British mining industry was suffering keen competition from Europe. Traditional markets were being captured by France, Germany and Poland. The Sankey Report of 1919 had recommended that British mine-owners spend more money modernising pits and investing in new machinery, but the owners ignored the Report, and by 1926 the mines were uncompetitive. A Royal Commission headed by Sir Herbert Samuel was appointed. It found that three-quarters of British coal was being produced at a loss; the miners were paid too much and the mine-owners were taking too much profit. Nationalisation was recommended. Tory Prime Minister Stanley Baldwin turned down nationalisation, ignored the mine-owners' profits and backed their claim that miners' wages be cut by thirteen and a half per cent. He also agreed with the owners that the miners should work longer hours to help solve the general economic problems of the country. The TUC responded by calling the General Strike. Arthur J. Cook, the miners' leader, declared 'not a minute on the day, not a penny off the pay'. He asked that miners be given safety in the pits, be allowed proper compensation, fair working hours and decent living conditions.

For a brief period before the fateful day in early May the air in Bellshill, as elsewhere, was heady with the scent of justice and victory through solidarity. Britain rang with the sound of great oratory which spoke seductively of freedom, equality, justice and vindication for the oppressed. The most oppressed, the miners, took heart as their fellow workers in other unions downed tools, declaring they would fight to the end. Industrial workers left the factories. Railwaymen and other transport workers ground their vehicles to a halt. Printers and other craftsmen joined the crusade.

The government, however, had made extensive preparations to counter what it described in newspaper notices as an 'Organised Attempt to Starve the Nation'. Troops, naval forces and thousands of special constables were placed on alert. A volunteer strike-breaking force was formed to maintain essential services. The government took various emergency powers which virtually amounted to martial law. Britain was polarised in a way that would have seemed unimaginable (except in the minds of revolutionaries) a year before. This was class war. When the TUC tried to ensure food supplies reached the strikers, particularly those isolated in mining villages, the government called out the Army. This show of force, ostensibly to keep power and communications going, was intimidating. Worse were the actions of the middle and upper classes who, in their tens of thousands, volunteered to do the strikers' jobs. Popular newspapers were used as propaganda sheets by the government. Truculent Churchill, editor of the government's own news sheet, the *British Gazette*, seemed to many of those who'd left their work to the clarion call for justice to be speaking for the nation when he depicted the strikers as 'the enemy' supported by 'Reds and all the other odds and sods within spitting distance'. The *British Gazette*'s invective was not simply directed at 'the enemy' but at the BBC whose news service under Reith seemed to be too impartial for Churchill – this despite the fact that the Corporation gave no radio time to the strike leaders.

24

Baldwin was, not surprisingly, confident and refused to negotiate. The General Strike, begun with such optimism, lasted nine days. It was a humiliating defeat.

The miners were deserted, the heady air of 3 May quickly evaporated. In its place a sour musk, the smell of stale, empty rhetoric, of promises broken, of solidarity pledged but not forthcoming. Alone, hungry and pitiful, the miners stayed on strike until November, easy prey for the government. The word went out; there would be no concessions, no pity, no mercy for the people in the mining villages. They would be driven back underground. Starved, their spirits broken, the men of Bellshill began to drift back to the pit-head, among them Mattha Busby. He had learned a lesson . . . about trust and loyalty, about rhetoric and promise, about family and community, most profoundly about power and powerlessness.

Football continued to sustain young Mattha. He had progressed from the village team to the best youth side in the district, Alpine Villa. Along with his pal Frank Rogers, Mattha helped Villa win the Scottish Under-18 Cup, a proud achievement even for a community as steeped as Bellshill was in soccer folklore.

The celebrations were held at the Bellshill Miners Club and it was here that Matt met and fell in love with Jean Menzies. Jean was a pretty, vivacious girl who stood out as Mattha himself did. They began walking out, and discovered they shared more than their love. Jean was a foster-child, born with the family name Macvie, who had been fostered to the Menzies as a baby. When her real parents decided they wanted her back Jean had chosen to stay with the Menzies, who became her adopted family. Neither Mattha nor Jean took family life for granted. The bond this created between them was more profound than teenage love. They knew the pain of loneliness and insecurity which could lie beneath the surface of a dashing young hero, Mattha the footballer, and a pretty, glad young girl, Jean. Each private, each vulnerable, their love deepened, their friendship grew, a rare empathy rapidly bound each to the other. But Matt and Jean's love was fraught with danger. The Menzies were Protestants. Worse, Jean's adoptive mother was the Secretary of the Bellshill Orange Lodge. She came from the Palace a bastion of the most intractable anti-Catholic Protestantism, and though her people were miners too, that fact didn't ease their fears. Bigotry was most intense among the Protestant working class. Some sense of Mattha and Jean's dread is gleaned from a scene in *No Mean City*, the classic early Twenties novel set in Glasgow's slumland.

Johnnie is Protestant, Bobbie Hurley a Catholic, Mary the object of their desire. Johnnie admits on the dance floor 'Ah'm no so good as Bobbie and you know it. But Hurley's a Catholic all the same, Mary. You and me are Protestants.'

'Too bliddy true, we are!' she fervently agrees.

'Catholics are awright but it's best to settle doon wi' one of your ain kind.'

And that was putting it mildly.

Mattha had made up his mind. His younger brother, Jimmy, remembers the atmosphere when Nellie was informed and asked to invite Jean to the cottage for tea. 'Matt was shaking,' Jimmy remembers. 'I've seen him before big football matches but believe me he was quaking that night. The house was cleaned from top to bottom and we were all togged out in our Sunday best.' This first hurdle was comfortably cleared. Nellie loved Jean whom she described as a 'right decent girl'. This was, nevertheless, a remarkable match for its times.

After Alpine Villa's triumph in the Scottish Under-18 Cup Frank Rogers and Mattha were invited to join the junior club, Denny Hibs, thus following their heroes Alex James and Jimmy McMullen. Junior football in Scotland was open-aged and highly competitive, the breeding ground which had produced the great Scottish players now distinguished in the game at home and in England. This, more than the money allowed in Junior football, excited Frank and Mattha and they shone brightly in the junior game, so brightly that within a couple of months both of them said farewell to Bellshill and headed for Manchester to try to emulate Jimmy McMullen, by then Manchester City's and Scotland's left-half. For Mattha the dream which had become a plan was now realised. The only ache in his heart was the leaving of Jean. He would, he promised, be back for her. She pledged to wait for that day.

Manchester

'This is a dispute between masters
and servants.'

C. E. Sutcliffe, FA Council member,
on attempts to form a Players' Union
in 1908

Matt Busby arrived in Manchester in February 1928. He had by
no means led a sheltered life, but was a mature eighteen-year-
old, hardened by life in Cannibal Island. Football had been a
romance, an escape from reality. That it would no longer be. As
a professional, football would be his reality. What had been a
release from obligation became a way of life to which all other
things must be subservient. The days of dreaming were over.

Professional soccer is a cruel, sometimes seedy game. Soccer
still delighted those who watched and was, to the citizens of
Manchester as to the crowds who packed the touchlines in
Orbiston, theatre, enriching and illuminating lives which were
otherwise drab. That was its glory. That was what the newspapers wrote about. Few dwelt on the shame that lay behind the
glorious façade. The truth, obscured if not altogether hidden
from public view, was to dawn on Matt Busby during his first
few months in Manchester, and the lessons he learned then
would be repeated in various forms throughout his playing
career. These facts of professional football life would be the
formative influence on Matt Busby. There was no place better
than Manchester to begin to understand England's national
game. The conventional wisdom of the 1990s is that money has
ruined soccer, that the greed of contemporary players and their
agents is a cancer that is destroying the game. The truth is that
professional football was deformed at birth. The game was
never honourable, never decent, never rational or just. Class

27

was the root of all professional football's evils: those who played the game for money, the heroes who drew the crowds, were working class; those who administered the game, the directors and football club shareholders, were, as the greatest player of the age, Billy Meredith, contemptuously described them, 'little shopkeepers who govern our destiny'. The conflict between heroes and shopkeepers was about the nature of the game which had captured the people's imagination. Was it a business or a sport? Or both? Could business and sport be reconciled? And, of most concern to Meredith and his fellow professionals, how should they be rewarded? Should footballers' wages be controlled, as the Football Association had decreed in 1900 when a ceiling of £4 a week, including bonuses, had been set, or should men who were obliged to dedicate their lives to this game be free as others were to offer their labour to the highest bidder? When they imposed the maximum wage, compounding the error with an accompanying clause in players' contracts which bound them to their employer for the duration of their sporting lives, the little shopkeepers committed football's Original Sin.

Billy Meredith's contempt was well deserved. He knew as well as those who governed football that the prohibitions placed on professional players were rendered even more hypocritical when set against the values preached by the entrepreneurial classes of Victorian and Edwardian Britain. The virtues of enterprise and free market forces, of sacrifice and hard work rewarded, were not, it seems, to extend to the business of football. And football *was* a business, theatre for the masses who packed the grounds, paying their hard earned money to do so. In Manchester the game aroused extraordinary passion. For men working in invariably harsh conditions, in engineering plants or railway yards, in the docks or the cotton mills, football was a heavenly respite from their daily toil. Whether they followed United or City these sons of immigrants were offered something less obvious but more precious than entertainment; a means of identifying with the city that was their home. Football enabled those who watched it in Manchester in the early years of the twentieth century to come together as Mancunians. They flocked from Salford, Ardwick, Chorlton,

Collyhurst, Gorton and Stretford, Denton and Longsight, from all corners of the city, seeking sport but finding something they needed even more – a sense of their own community. These men's fathers had come to Manchester to survive poverty and starvation. Success had meant a meal on the table and a roof over your family's heads. Squalor and desperation were old acquaintances. To be a Mancunian was to know these things. A certain humanity existed in this labouring city. You helped your neighbour when you could, and though nobody had much, what they had they tried to share. A family wasn't judged by what they possessed, rather by how they responded to the hardship next door. Poverty could turn hearts cold, but it hadn't in 'Cottonopolis', and the people were proud of that. They had survived. Together.

Mancunians were a special breed, circumstances had determined that. They were generous. Generosity had been a currency in each community, but each community was separate – until football drew the city together. Watching football the man from Gorton stood next to the man from Chorlton, docker stood beside mill-worker, the man from the locomotive works cheered as lustily as the fellow who made machine tools. For the sons of Irish immigrants and Scots, for those whose families had migrated to Manchester from the rural parishes of East Anglia, via London and the Ship Canal, for all who were unsure of what they were, who'd broken free of their roots in order to survive, and now, having done so, were desperate to *belong*, football offered a unique opportunity to discover and declare a sense of civic pride.

And no footballer generated greater civic pride than Billy Meredith, the Wizard, professional football's first great star. Born in the South Wales mining village of Chirk in 1874, he went to work on the coalface at the age of twelve. He joined Ardwick, later to become Manchester City, in 1894. From the outside-right position he both made and scored goals. He played until his fiftieth year, making 857 League appearances, scoring 281 goals. Over the course of this long career Meredith won fifty-one caps for Wales, scoring ten goals. The wizard of national renown, he appeared in films, on the stage and in advertisements endorsing everything from football boots to

Oxo and herbal remedies. He also ran various businesses, none of them with any great success. In Manchester he was a folk-hero, the tooth-pick that was always in his mouth his trademark in the game.

In 1904 when Billy Meredith led Manchester City to win the FA Cup, 20,000 Mancunians made the journey to Crystal Palace to see him score the winning goal. The city had never known such glorious excitement. Meredith was the inspiration. One 'Ode to the Will o' the Wisp' sent to a local newspaper ended with these lines:

> He's a darling, he's a duck, is Meredith
> And a mascot, too, for luck, is Meredith
> Though ten casualties we own
> Still we don't break down and moan
> He can play teams quite alone, can Meredith.

Poignant, too, were the songs sung on the terraces of Crystal Palace that glorious day when Manchester came to London town . . .

> Oh I wish I was you Billy Meredith
> I wish I was you, I envy you, indeed I do
> It ain't that you're tricky with your feet
> But it's those centres you send in
> Which Turnbull then heads in
> Oh I wish I was you
>   Indeed I do
>   Indeed I do.

Thus the men of Edwardian Manchester, machine-minders, factory apprentices, clerks, the flotsam and jetsam of the city's industrial sprawl acclaimed their hero on a day which would stand wondrously apart from all others in their lives. When the team brought the FA Cup back to Manchester the whole city turned out to pay tribute to their professional footballers. Manchester had never known anything like it. The scene was captured by *Athletic News*, the local sporting newspaper:

> The band struck up 'See the Conquering Hero Come'. As soon as the people caught sight of the trophy, trimmed with

blue and white ribbons, which Meredith now and then raised above his head, they gave vent to prodigious cheering. Most of the windows of the upper stories were packed with people whose plaudits, added to by the blowing of a bugle here and there, and the music of the band, made a deafening sound. To the accompaniment of incessant cheering, the procession made its way at walking-pace down Dale Street where what might be called the welcome of the middle-classes was exchanged for that of the proletariat. It came from rough working men and larrikins and beshawled women and children in arms and hand, and was as hearty if not heartier than had gone before.

Most of professional football's heroes have been content with their fifteen minutes of fame and glory. They have conformed, if not to the muddied oaf of boardroom stereotype, then to something as insidiously demeaning; the modest, shy, self-deprecating beneficiary of good fortune who had much for which to thank The Game and by implication those who ruled it. The great players – Stan Matthews and Tom Finney being two perfect examples – may have despised the shopkeepers and builders who ruled the professional game and may have bitterly resented the injustices and iniquities of which they were daily the victims, but in public they remained respectful cap-tippers, knowing their place, accepting ritual humiliation with a grateful smile. Privately such heroes would damn their directors and the Football Association as all professionals did. Publicly they tended to distance themselves from trouble.

Billy Meredith saw the absurdity of the professional player's lot from the beginning from a perspective that was unique and fascinating. His family were Welsh Methodists whose deepest convictions questioned the morality of playing sport for money. Meredith had been reluctant to turn pro, arguing that a man could play football at weekends *and* have a proper job during the week. Was it necessary to devote all your time to football, he wondered. The answer from the professional game, administered by the Football Association, was an emphatic *yes*. The very same contract that restricted players' earnings to £4 a week, and bound them to their clubs for life – unless the club

31

decided to get rid of them – insisted that professional footballers engage in no other occupation. Meredith accepted this definition of a player's obligations. He became a master craftsman, pursuing excellence and achieving it. Then, having attained the ultimate as a professional, Meredith demanded that he be respected and rewarded accordingly. He was branded a troublemaker.

Football was governed by a group of men, some of whom were little better than wealthy buffoons, some of whom saw themselves as the upholders of Corinthian values. The latter were concerned – many of them genuinely – that professionalism would corrupt sport. This fear was philosophically valid. It could not, however, be reconciled with the demand made of Meredith and his contemporaries that they devote their lives exclusively to football. Unable to reconcile a problem they themselves had created, the Football Association blustered arrogantly before producing the deadly fudge of 1900 which enslaved the professional player, institutionalised deceit, and encouraged a cynical disregard for authority which would, through the decades, right up to the present day, tarnish every decent man who entered the world of professional soccer.

Once football became a professional sport the Corinthian principle was set aside. Meredith, an honourable and courageous man, who was not initially unsympathetic to the Corinthian ideal, clearly understood better than most the consequences of enacting football legislation which had no basis in real law. He saw that the restrictive practices which were to govern the lives of professional players flew in the face of reason, and made no philosophical or moral sense, so he used his access to newspapers to challenge the Football Association. In books and articles he advocated reform, never missing a chance, however oblique, to expose absurdity. He made few friends. Asked in 1906 to contribute an article on The Art of Wingplay, for a publication entitled *Association Football and the Men Who Made It*, Meredith wrote briefly about how to become a good winger, but the thrust of his contribution was about the social and professional status of the player, not about the glory but about the *reality* of a professional life, about the sacrifices and injuries and the amount of dedication required of the hero. Footballers deserved respect, he reminded the readers of this semi-official publication. Reviewing Meredith's article, Jimmy Catton of *Athletic News*, an influential commentator, observed that the great man's contribution had not been 'as practical' as those of other famous players writing on their speciality. Quite.

In fact Meredith was a very practical man who had learned from bitter experience the consequences of enacting and attempting to enforce bad law. It couldn't be done. Ambitious clubs would flout the FA rules. Under-the-counter payments would become the norm. Deceit would be institutionalised. As he repeatedly challenged the notion that professional footballers should be denied the working conditions others were entitled to by law, Meredith sought to define professionalism and its logical consequences which he argued were inevitable and must be faced.

> What is more reasonable than our plea that the footballer, with his uncertain career, should have the best money he can earn? If I can earn £7 a week, should I be debarred from receiving it? I have devoted my life to football and I have become a better player than most men because I have denied myself much that men prize. A man who has taken the care of himself that I have done, and who fights the temptation of all that injures the system surely deserves some recognition and reward? They congratulate me and give me caps, but they will not give me a penny more than men are earning in the reserve team some of whom, perhaps, do not trouble themselves to improve and don't worry about taking care of their condition. If football is a man's livelihood and he does more than others for his employer why is he not entitled to better pay than others? So far as I can make out the sole reason why the best footballers in England are prevented from earning better pay than men of lesser ability and experience is purely sentimental.

The sentiments Meredith was referring to were those of the Football Association, which responded to his arguments by accusing him and other pros who thought like him of 'greed' and 'elitism'. Meredith's reply was that professionalism was, by its very nature, elitist.

It would be misleading to cast Meredith in the role of starry-eyed idealist. He was a hard man who stood to benefit more than most from the reforms he proposed. But by 1907, when he and a group of fellow Manchester professionals established the first Players' Union at a meeting in the city's Imperial Hotel, experience had deepened his conviction that football must face up to the facts of life, the most fundamental of which being that footballers were in business, had families to support and futures to provide for and that therefore the game must be subject to the conditions of the marketplace like any other commercial activity.

Although Manchester City's glorious FA Cup triumph of 1904 had delighted the citizens of 'Cottonopolis', it had not pleased the Football Association. The suspicion in official circles was that the ambitious Mancunians had broken the rules about wages and bonuses en route to glory. Meredith in particular was the focus of administrative frustration. They knew what he was like and sensed that the satisfied smile on his face as he held their precious trophy aloft reflected not just victory over Bolton Wanderers but defeat of the system he was known to despise. They were right. As Meredith would years later explain with characteristic insouciance:

> What was the secret of the success of the Manchester City team? In my opinion, the fact that the club put aside the rule that no player should receive more than £4 a week. From 1902 I had been paid £6 a week and Livingstone was paid ten shillings more than that in wages. I don't believe that any member of our team was paid less than I was, and the season we carried off the Cup I also received £53 in bonuses for games won and drawn. Some players drew more. McMahon, for example, received £61 in bonuses that season. Altogether the club paid in bonuses £654.12s.6d. The team delivered the goods and the club paid for the goods delivered, and both sides were satisfied.

Within two weeks of City's triumphant return to Manchester, F. J. Wall, the FA secretary and J. Lewis, a member of the FA General Council, were dispatched from London to examine the

34

club's books. The investigation, which lasted two months, found no evidence of illegal wages and bonuses. However, they did uncover discrepancies in the transfer of two men to the club. There were cheques that could not be accounted for and obviously forged receipts presented by City's financial director. The men from London judged that the missing money had been paid as a signing-on fee to persuade two players, Frank Norgrove and Irvine Thornley, to join the club. The law, FA law that is, permitted no signing-on fee in excess of £10. So Manchester City were criminalised, even though the 'crime' was to do nothing worse than apply the enterprising spirit of Edwardian England to professional football.

In October 1904 Manchester City were fined £250 and their ground was closed for a month. Three directors, Josh Parlby, John Chapman and Lawrence Furniss, were banned from football for three years. Mr Madders, director in charge of finance, was banned from the game for life. This was an unsatisfactory outcome for the Football Association. Meredith had eluded them, and the Wizard was the man they really wanted to get. The Northern clubs in general were known to be the most flagrant abusers of football law. In the matter of financial constraints it was, however, Manchester City and Billy Meredith who posed the deadliest threat to the new order. The club was enterprising and ambitious, Meredith, the heroic symbol of the merits of professionalism, a popular hero, willing to challenge those whose authority was based on foundations, which in the early years of this century, were beginning to seem rather shaky. The whiff of revolution was in the air, workers everywhere were questioning their masters who were fearful and uncertain, and nowhere more so than in Association Football, for nobody knew better than the game's adminstrators that professional football was a thoroughly amoral business.

The most damning example of official cant lay at the core of the Manchester City scandal. The Football Association knew what was going on because when many of those charged with upholding the laws of the game swopped their FA hats for their club favours they were sanctioning illegal payments themselves. The seeds of the Swindon Town Affair of 1989, that club being brought to its knees for committing a 'crime' everyone else was equally guilty of, were sown almost a century ago.

Meredith and his club remained in the frame. He was a marked man and within a few months the Football Association were back in Manchester. City's success continued the season after their FA Cup win. With four games left to play in the First Division Championship only two points separated City, Newcastle and Everton. Newcastle held the edge. In the event they went on to take the title. In the third last game of the season City travelled to play Everton at Goodison Park. After a scrappy, ill-tempered match a police escort was needed to protect the Manchester players as they left the field. City's final game was at Villa Park against a team fresh from winning the FA Cup. They had to win and hoped Newcastle would lose at Middlesborough. The two clubs were old and bitter rivals and Villa were in no mood to do any favours for their foes from Manchester. Another vicious struggle ensued. The ugliest confrontation of the afternoon took place between City's fiery centre-forward Sandy Turnbull and the Villa captain and England international Alec Leake. Blows were exchanged, and as Turnbull made his way to the dressing-room after the final whistle a group of Villa players dragged him into the home dressing-room where the Scot was kicked and beaten. Villa had won 3–2. Once again police were sent for. On the way from the ground the City coach was stoned by an angry mob.

This blackguardly end to the season offered the Football Association a pretext for yet another official inquiry. Rowdyism was not a new feature of the professional game, but the Association's concern, they claimed, was that 'professionalism' was getting out of hand. Stern action was needed to prevent the game descending into anarchy.

A desire to restore football's reputation, the public rationale for this latest investigation, was admirable. It was not, however, the whole truth. Of more compelling interest to the FA than on-field behaviour were events off the field which continued to take a radical turn. The hidden agenda had more to do with discrediting Manchester City, Aston Villa and Everton who were, together with League champions Newcastle, leading a campaign to have the maximum wage abolished at the forthcoming AGM of the Football Association. As they were being placed in the dock these clubs were preparing resolutions and issuing circulars challenging the FA's right to impose financial ceilings on earnings. Meredith was as usual agitating in his newspaper columns. The inquiry, which delivered its verdict on 5 August 1905, was headed by J. C. Clegg, chairman of the FA Council, a stern defender of Edwardian values who was, when not crusading against anarchic professionalism, the Official Receiver of Bankruptcy for the city of Sheffield.

By mid-afternoon on 5 August, the football world, its Manchester constituency in particular, was in a state of shock. Newspaper headlines were for once an inadequate reflection of the stunning story told on the page beneath them. 'SENSATION IN THE FOOTBALL WORLD', 'BOMBSHELL IN THE CITY CAMP', 'THE FOOTBALL WORLD SHOCKED'. Thus, the news of Billy Meredith's suspension for attempted bribery of another player was conveyed to a disbelieving public.

The Clegg Inquiry's findings were baffling. The fracas at Villa Park had nothing to do with Meredith, nor indeed the incidents at Goodison. How could an inquiry set up to investigate violence on the pitch suddenly pass down a sentence relating to bribery? The answer, evident if one studies the Clegg Report in full, was that the investigation was more concerned with tarnishing professionalism – and those who espoused it – than dealing with unseemly behaviour on the field of play. Manchester City and Billy Meredith were the real targets; both had been hit.

The violence, which was the ostensible reason for setting up the Clegg Inquiry in the first place, was dealt with summarily. The sentencing here was in itself revealing. Tom Booth, Everton's captain whose assault on City's 'Tabby' Booth had sparked the violence at Goodison Park, was given a suspended sentence. Alec Leake of Aston Villa, whose fight with Sandy Turnbull had been the catalyst for the Villa Park eruption, was found not guilty. Turnbull was suspended for a month for his part in the incidents on and off the field. The assaults on Turnbull in the Aston Villa dressing-room, to which Leake and other Villa players were party, drew no official rebuke. The burden of guilt – for all professional football's ills – would, it seemed, be borne by Manchester. This time the Football Association *had* got its man. Having exonerated all bar Sandy Turnbull and R. T. Johns who refereed the Everton game and was suspended for having failed to control it properly, the Clegg Report concluded: 'The Commissioners also reported on statements brought to their notice with regard to W. Meredith of Manchester having offered a sum of money to a player of Aston Villa to let Manchester City win the match. W. Meredith is suspended from football from August 4th until April 1906.'

A torrent of rumour and speculation engulfed professional football in the wake of the Meredith Scandal, but the sequel to this murky affair would prove to be even more sensational than the events now unfolding. Meredith immediately issued an emphatic and widely believed denial of guilt:

> I am entirely innocent and am suffering for others. Such an allegation as that of bribery is preposterous. I could never risk my reputation and future by such an action and I repeat that I never made such an offer. It is totally unjustified and grossly unfair. This sort of thing will totally demoralise Association Football. Manchester has not many friends among the Association officials and I doubt if the decision will be reversed or the suspension lessened if the whole case is reopened and enquired into.

This protestation of innocence sounds convincing enough. But as time would show, the words 'I am suffering for others' offered a significant portent of the truth of this affair which was never to be definitively established. The temptation to cast Meredith in the role of innocent victim, reflecting the popular mood of the time, can, with hindsight, easily be resisted: victim he undoubtedly was, innocent he almost certainly was not.

As the facts of the case began to emerge it became clear that there were no heroes, few who were innocent; almost all of those involved in the conduct of professional football were victims, caught in a web of cynicism and deception. None were as culpable as those who governed the game. J. C. Clegg, the expert on financial bankruptcy, seemed to care little for its moral equivalent.

The Clegg Inquiry had, it transpired, been acting on a tip-off regarding Meredith. The *Birmingham Sports Argus* revealed that the FA Commission had been 'impressed by what was told them by a disinterested witness who had overheard a most interesting conversation between Meredith and Alec Leake the Villa captain'. Meredith had, it was alleged, offered Leake £10 to throw the game. This attempted bribery was, the *Sports Argus* informed its readers, witnessed by 'a gentleman who holds a responsible position in Birmingham municipal life, and nobody would allege that he concocted the story, so the hysterics from Manchester about being condemned merely on the evidence of a rival player may be treated with contempt'.

Meredith admitted having the conversation with Leake, but he claimed that the offer was 'a joke'. Leake, who was, it must be remembered, facing charges himself, had indeed regarded the bribery offer as a joke and had not mentioned it at his original hearing. But he was called back to face Clegg and company and, he claimed, 'forced to admit' that the allegation levelled by the 'gentleman' who held a 'prominent position in Birmingham municipal life' was in fact true. Given the choice between the word of a *gentleman* and that of a *player* there was never any doubt about the outcome of the Clegg Inquiry. The issue was so clear-cut that the Commission never bothered to call Meredith to answer the charge against him. Justice as dispensed by the Football Association – in secret – resulted in professional football's most renowned player having his livelihood taken away from him on the hearsay evidence of a 'gentleman'.

Apart from the occasional caustic reference to official humbug, W. Meredith seemed surprisingly sanguine about his lot. Few people believed that he had tried to bribe the Villa captain. His local newspaper, the *Athletic News*, spoke for most in the game and outside: 'Anyone who has known the careful life and thrift which has characterised Meredith will feel confident that he never offered such a sum out of his own pocket. Where is the man who dare ask Meredith to try to purchase a victory and give him £10 for the nefarious bargain?' There was an air of mystery about the whole affair, a sense, heightened by official secrecy, that the whole truth had not been revealed.

Meredith was further reassured by a letter he had received from Tom Maley, City's secretary, which promised that he would not lose out financially during his period of suspension. Alas, as autumn gave way to the bitter winter of 1905, during which many Mancunians died of cold and malnutrition, Meredith grew increasingly disenchanted. During his frequent appearances at the City ground, his heated arguments with directors and the secretary became the talk of the club. Having been the victim of the FA's kangaroo justice, Billy now found his employers reneging on their promise to 'see him right'. No money was forthcoming. The club denied they had made any promise and asked the Football Association to mete out more punishment to the scapegoat who wouldn't lie down. City accused him of trying to illegally extract payments from them and informed the Association that 'the refusal of the board to lend itself to any illicit or illegal practices led to many threats by the player. The rigid observation of the rules has ultimately silenced the player, but nevertheless it has been for the board a very trying time.' Things were soon to become even more trying.

The deal Meredith had struck with City, backed up by the letter in his possession which informed him that he would 'not be the loser by his suspension', was that in return for wages paid during his absence from the game he would keep quiet about certain matters. The phrase in his original denial of bribery referring to 'suffering for others' now haunted his City masters. The words could mean either of two things – or indeed both: was he inferring that he had been framed because he was the most vocal advocate of illegal practices in vogue at City and elsewhere, or was he suggesting that he had in fact offered Leake a bribe but in doing so had merely acted as an intermediary for the Manchester City club? It was time for another FA Commission which was convened in March 1905. Meredith, pursuing a scorched earth policy in response to his club's betrayal of him, had decided to tell the unvarnished truth.

Meredith began by confessing that he had indeed broached the subject of selling the vital championship game with Alec Leake, but he claimed he had been acting as a spokesman for

City. Club secretary Maley had provided the £10 bribe and his team-mates had been aware of the proposed transaction. Manchester City had constantly breached the rules regarding wages and bonuses in their dealings with him and all the other players. The story he told the Inquiry was of utter venality, their rules counted for nothing at Hyde Road.

Within a month all the damning evidence was gathered. One by one Meredith's colleagues were summoned to Manchester's Grand Hotel where they were presented with incontrovertible evidence of their guilt. Most confessed, throwing themselves at the mercy of the Association. Club directors began typically by 'stoutly denying' their guilt and 'promising to prove their good faith'. Soon they too began to sing.

On 4 June the FA report was published. Manchester City had virtually ceased to exist. All the directors were suspended. Tom Maley and his chairman, Forest, were banned for life. The club was fined £250. None of the players involved was to be allowed to play for City again, several of them were fined a total of £900 and suspended for one year.

So, justice was served . . . or was it? The *Athletic News* thought so, castigating Meredith in uncomprising terms:

> The famous footballer determined not only to make an offer to Alec Leake – an offence which ought to have ended his football career – not only that, he had been most generously and lavishly paid by the club which ran dreadful risks to give him all they had except the goalposts, but dragged everyone else he could into the same mess. No sense of gratitude for all the managers who, over the years, remunerated him so that he became comparatively rich, no ideals of friendship for the men who, admitting his enviable playing skills, had done everything they could for him, and no feeling of loyalty for the comrades who had fought side by side with him in many a scrap in hard games restrained this man from divulging the secrets of his masters and colleagues. It would have been honourable to confess his own deeds, to express his sorrow and promise an amendment that he promised to fulfil, but he took a course that amounted to revenge after he had been simply killed by kindness by the club whose colours he wore.

41

This was self-righteous stuff based on some dubious premises, the most dubious being that otherwise good men had 'risked all' to satisfy Meredith's avarice. In fact, perhaps the most remarkable aspect of the Manchester City saga was that other players – Livingstone for example – had earned more than Meredith, the designated scapegoat. As for the view expressed by *Athletic News* that Meredith had betrayed his 'masters' by 'divulging their secrets', it was equally devoid of sense. This canard was, however, reflective of the official rationalisation of Manchester's wrongdoing. The buck should stop with the professionals. Or, as one member of the Football Association put it in *his* newspaper column: 'We cannot help feeling sorry that men of intelligence and of good reputation in the several walks of life (City's directors) should have driven a coach and four through the rules of the Association and been so generous to the players. The professionals have not been able to resist the impulse, the desire to obtain all they could from the club coffers.'

Meredith summed up the whole affair accurately and more succinctly: 'Clubs are not punished for breaking the law. They are punished for being found out.' Assessing his role in the scandal, one can see that he had been contaminated, not by greed, but by professional football's prevailing ethos, which was, simply put, to cheat and lie whilst proclaiming the loftiest of virtues. Understanding this, his colleagues retained their affection and respect for the man who allegedly betrayed them. Even though most were unwilling, as Billy Meredith was, to voice their contempt for their 'masters' the vast majority of players knew he was right about the gentlemen from the Football Association. New depths of administrative hypocrisy were reached in the wake of the Manchester scandal, as Meredith gleefully revealed: 'The League met and the representatives of each club voted in favour of the punishment meted out to us being enforced. And while their representatives were passing this pious resolution most of them had other representatives busy trying to persuade the "villains whose punishment had been so well deserved" to sign for them under conditions very much better in most cases than the ones we had been ruled by at City.'

Meredith's condemnation by the *Athletic News* was countered elsewhere. He remained an esteemed popular hero. The *Bolton Football Field* argued that he and his City colleagues ought not to be damned. The *Field*'s observer wrote: 'Let me remind you that Meredith is no cunning astute financier or a sleek diplomat. A village youth, an artist of football and delight to hundreds of thousands of football enthusiasts, a maker of thousands of pounds for League and other clubs and Associations, a sober and consistent performer. Is it right that the club he has made famous should seem to want to be rid of the trouble of him?'

Arguments condemning Meredith and his colleagues 'won't hold water', the *Field*'s correspondent concluded.

Billy Meredith was now thirty years of age. He had made Manchester City, and this shabby ending to what should have been a glorious story might have broken a lesser man. Meredith, having refused to be sacrificed, seemed to gain strength. The Football Association had decreed that the guilty players would be disposed of by the City club at an auction to be held in the Queens Hotel, Manchester in November. He had always despised the transfer system which he insisted 'treated the player as though he were a sensible machine or a trained animal'. He had cost City no fee and now refused to be auctioned to the highest bidder. After ten years' service, City owed him a benefit match and had signed a contract to that effect. This he now produced, agreeing to waive his rights in return for a free transfer to a club of his choosing. Thinking he was more or less finished anyway, City and the FA complied with his demands.

Ernest Mangnall, the shrewd manager of Manchester United, then the city's poor relations and newly promoted from the Second Division, moved swiftly to sign the Welsh Wizard. At the auction Mangnall also acquired Meredith's former City colleagues, Herbert Burgess, Sandy Turnbull and Jimmy Bannister. The foundations were thus laid for Manchester's second great team which, like City in 1904, would be inspired by Meredith and the source of extraordinary civic pride. The scene was also set for the final, decisive confrontation between Players and Gentlemen, the outcome of which would determine the character of professional football in England right up to the present day.

The trauma of the previous two years had radicalised Meredith and many others who saw beyond glory and the next pay-packet. Workers everywhere were uniting to seek freedom. There had been a revolution in Russia; at home the Labour Party was about to be formed; strikes were causing disruption the length and breadth of Britain; men's notions of fairness and justice were changing; miners rioted in Staffordshire; and Manchester was brought to a standstill by demonstrations of the unemployed and striking transport and municipal workers. Soon a reforming Liberal Government would be elected to office.

The time was ripe for Meredith to turn defiant rhetoric into decisive action. He found kindred spirits in the Manchester United dressing-room. Two men in particular shared his views, the club captain, Charlie Roberts and Herbert Bloomfield, United's reserve goalkeeper. Roberts, principled and intelligent, had himself tried to form a Players' Union in 1903. Now he conspired with Meredith to establish a representative body which would right the fundamental wrongs of the professional game once and for all.

The inaugural meeting of the Players' Union took place on 2 December 1907 at the Imperial Hotel in Manchester. Players from a dozen clubs attended. The following month at the King's Arms in Sheffield officers were elected and a manifesto issued which set out their three principal demands: an end to wage restraint; freedom of contract; and access to the laws of the land rather than the corrupting rules of professional football. Reaction was at first mixed. Later that year in a move that has ironic resonance today twenty-two top League clubs threatened to form their own Super-League if some measure of common sense was not applied to the professional game. Even the Football Association seemed to concede that some liberalisation of their laws was in order. But the voices of reactionaries were also heard, some predictable, some surprising. Responding to the players' assertions that complete freedom from all restraints was the only solution, *Athletic News* contended: 'We have no hesitation in saying that the sweeping aside of all restrictions with reference to money is solely the idea of a few rich clubs and a few players who are in a class by themselves.' This was an indirect swipe at Manchester, United in particular, which, under the influence of Mangnall and his enlightened chairman, J. J. Davies, understood the players' aspirations and shared the view that football business should be conducted honestly and above board. Davies, a Manchester businessman, agreed to become the Union's first president, with Jimmy Catton of *Athletic News* as one of the new vice- presidents. This latter appointment gives some indication of the moral confusion in the professional game of 1908. For while their distinguished correspondent was lending support to the players' cause, *Athletic News* was commenting disapprovingly: 'We now know the ultimate demands of the players. They may be crystalised into one sentence: Unlimited wages, with the right to move from clubs and share in the transfer fees. These are the dreams of visionaries.' It was not, it seemed, in football's interests for players to be either dreamers or visionaries.

Mr C. E. Sutcliffe, an FA Council member, was even more outraged – and outrageous – than the conservative sporting newspaper: 'The strong feature of the players' demands was self-interest.' This 'spirit of selfishness' had threatened to ruin the game before the maximum wage had been introduced, Sutcliffe claimed. He had wanted to help them, he went on, 'but I can play no part in helping the players to immoderate and unreasonable demands'. Meredith and and his cohorts were, Sutcliffe cautioned them, 'committing suicide', their resolutions were 'contemptible claptrap' and what was more, they were ignoring his, and his League's, wise counsel. 'We were running football years before some prominent players knew anything about it.' In conclusion, Sutcliffe, the archetypal Edwardian Gent, defined the struggle now raging as being between 'masters and servants'. The servants' demands for freedom were 'but the outward and visible sign of inward greed'.

The arguments continued and intensified over the next eighteen months before being resolved in the summer of 1909. The story of that ending is a pitiful parable of professional soccer in England; a handful of decent courageous men –

visionaries – drowning in a sea of apathy, intolerance and venality.

Manchester United won the FA Cup in 1909. Alas, the celebrations were blighted by the Players' Union controversy. Roberts and Meredith had urged their members to join with their fellow workers in the General Federation of Trades Unions and, if necessary, resort to strike action which the GFTU would support to win their rights under the law. The Players' Union's desire to seek refuge and justice in the law of the land was perceived by the Football Association as a deadly threat, all the more potent because those posing it were among the best footballers in the country. Rather than sue for peace through compromise, the FA warned those clubs sympathetic to the Union's cause that their power over their 'servants' was at stake. And to clubs wavering between right and wrong, between the shabby deceit of underhand dealings and the honest and enterprising future which 'visionaries' promised, the administration offered a deal that was, for such self-regarding men as C. E. Sutcliffe, astonishingly and audaciously venal. If all Football League clubs would insert a clause into their players' contracts for the following season 1909/10, which effectively disowned the Players' Union and pledged loyalty to the FA and its rules, the Association would declare an amnesty for all clubs which had hitherto breached the law in regard to wages and bonuses, excusing all previous misdemeanours. The clubs, many of them up to their necks in 'misdemeanours' and fearing that their players might turn King's evidence as Meredith had done, agreed.

An ultimatum was presented to the players: forfeit your rights under the law of England or face banishment from the game. With a rather sad mixture of sarcasm and naivity, *Athletic News* reflected: 'Until a week ago, the clubs, the employers were under the thumb of the players and the Union. But the FA offered a free pardon to the clubs if they refused to be dictated to by the players, if they would refuse to pay players sums of money in violation of the rules. The clubs consented to be honest and started with a clean slate. The players lost their power and ceased to be the real masters and now they have to rest content with a miserable pittance of £4 a week all the year through, many free meals and perquisites during training, and three months holiday every summer if they are not taken for a continental tour – miscalled a football tour. The plight of the football player is terrible.'

Jimmy Catton, the players' erstwhile friend, had returned from his off-side position. The signing-on process, with its disavowing clause, would be, Catton now claimed, 'an act of loyalty just as much as the enlistment of a soldier'.

The final act of this tragedy was now played out. During the close-season players dispersed to their home towns. Some were scared, some apathetic, many simply happy to be professional footballers belonging, they imagined, to a higher caste than the average working man. Meredith continued to proselytise, along with Roberts and Bloomfield, offering defiant leadership in the certainty that right was on the Union's side. Their Manchester United colleagues supported this stance and refused, en bloc, to sign the Rogues' Charter that would institutionalise perversity, deceit and injustice in the English professional game for all time. The coming of the new season saw the Manchester men isolated from their peers. The United players, the FA Cup heroes of three months before, were suspended *sine die*. Once more sensational headlines told the story:

'THE WHOLE OF THE ENGLISH CUP-WINNERS SUSPENDED SINE DIE',

'MANCHESTER UNITED WITHOUT A TEAM'.

For the second time in his career Billy Meredith – the cup-winning hero – experienced the strange kind of glory that was professional football; one day a hero, the next the victim of abject humiliation.

The United players were now football's self-proclaimed Outcasts, yet, as Charlie Roberts recalled in his memoirs:

> None of us had received any official intimation from the FA that we were suspended, so we turned up for our wages as usual the Friday after our suspension was announced.
>
> We waited and waited for our manager but he did not appear that morning and all we could get out of the office-boy was, 'There are no wages for you as the FA suspended you all.'
>
> 'Well something will have to be done,' said Sandy

Turnbull as he took a picture off the wall and walked out of the office with it under his arm. The rest of the boys followed suit, and looking-glasses, hairbrushes and several other things were for sale a few minutes after at a little hostelry at the corner of the ground.

I stayed behind a while with the office-boy, who was in a terrible state over the players taking things away and he was most anxious to get them back before the manager arrived. 'Come along with me and I will get them back for you,' I said, 'it's only one of their little jokes.' I soon recovered the lost property for him. But it was funny to see the players walking off the ground with the pictures etc. under their arms.

Two contrasting images from the summer of 1909 offer a poignant insight into the lives of professionals of that age: one, the glorious homecoming after winning the FA Cup; then, a couple of months later, the heroes pilfering from the Manchester United offices to try to scrape a few shillings together.

In the first week of November a ballot of players was held to decide the issue of affiliating to the GFTU. The alternative was to accept an FA compromise which allowed the Players' Union a token existence. The result was 470 against affiliation, 172 for. Meredith, Bloomfield and Roberts had lost their most important game. The struggle was over. The master/servant relationship would remain in existence for over fifty years, serving only to contaminate both.

W. Meredith was the last player to re-sign the Rogues' Charter. Reflecting on the struggle, Meredith ruefully acknowledged: 'I confess that the bulk of the players have not shown much pluck in the matter . . . but those who voted in favour of remaining within the GFTU have the satisfaction of knowing that they behaved like men. A man said to me the other day, "Ah, the players have not the pluck of the miners," and he was right, of course.'

Billy Meredith embodied and, perhaps more than any other, reflected professional soccer's wicked contradictions. His abiding conviction was that players ought not to be full-timers. Football should be a recreation, not a career. Yet, if professionalism was forced upon them footballers should be free as other men to earn as much as they could and organise themselves as they saw fit. The professionals had too much time on their hands and too many of them squandered their money and their talent on gambling and drink. Living thus as 'pampered idols' many professionals were reduced to a pitiful state of dependence, no matter how gifted they were. These convictions about behaviour, and the proper relationship between money and sport, suggest that Meredith's Methodist upbringing had left its mark upon him. What he sought, for himself and his peers, was dignity. To some extent, as we have seen, he failed in this regard. He was the victim of circumstances, the most profound of which was his love for a game run by masters and played by slaves. Of football, the game's first and most inspiring rebel would later write: 'My heart was always full of it.'

3

A Prince Among Pros

'I feel I am out of my sphere in
football.'

Matt Busby

Meredith had returned to City in 1921 as player/coach at the
behest of Ernest Mangnall who had signed him for United in
1906. Meredith was one of the first people Matt Busby
encountered when he arrived in Manchester in February 1928.
Now fifty-three, Meredith was coaching the younger players at
Maine Road. The Football Association had succeeded in
breaking the Players' Union in 1909 but not its founding
father. The taming of the Union had not shaken Meredith's
convictions. The emancipation of professionals apart, the most
fundamental of Meredith's convictions concerned fitness and
preparation for playing. Conventional wisdom about the lifespan of a professional footballer was resisted as fiercely as the
idea that he should be enslaved. If professionals wanted to be
respected they must, he believed, respect themselves. Self-
respect began with your body. Meredith was fastidious, almost
obsessive, about his own physical condition. In this, as in most
other matters, he was an enlightened man apart from this peers.
He was almost teetotal and never smoked. On match days he
would take a glass of port before the game and eat boiled
chicken afterwards. His grandmother had passed on her
extensive knowledge of herbal remedies, and comfrey was a
particular favourite of his for healing strains and other muscular
ailments. Meredith had regular massage, using various embrocations including a foul-smelling ointment he called 'dog-fat',
sometimes used on mining machinery, which he would smear
on his torso and legs. He paid the most meticulous attention to
injuries, however minor. When in doubt he consulted two of his

50

sisters who were nurses or his wife, Ellen, who had trained for nursing. His dressing-room colleagues were amused by his fads. They trusted to fate and the club doctor. Billy knew better. In 1902 Di Jones, City's captain, had fallen and cut his knee during a pre-season friendly match. He had been treated by the club doctor and had gone home to convalesce. The wound turned septic because it had not been properly treated. A week later Jones died.

Meredith understood that the better you looked after yourself, the longer you'd play. And, of course, the better you'd be while you were playing. This battle he didn't lose, and he continued playing until 1924 when he made his last appearance for Manchester City in the FA Cup semi-final. He was four months short of his fiftieth birthday.

Mangnall was, like Meredith, a singular man. A Bolton-born grammar-school boy, Mangnall had joined United in 1903 from Burnley where he had been club secretary. Mangnall was tough and well educated, with a penchant for straw boaters and Havana cigars. He was to become the prototype pre-Second World War football manager, concerned more with the wheeling and dealing of club administration than the finer points of the game on the field. Mangnall had rescued Burnley from dire financial circumstances and his immediate task at United was to do the same. This he did and much more. Having languished in the Second Division for nine years before Mangnall joined them, United narrowly missed promotion twice before he led them back to the First Division in 1906. When later that year he swooped to sign Billy Meredith, Mangnall demonstrated his understanding of, and contempt for, the cant that was endemic to the professional game. Manchester City's demand for a £600 transfer fee was resisted by Meredith, and City were forced to give him a free transfer in the end. In his memoirs Meredith revealed that 'a gentleman' had given him £500 to sign for United. Ernest Mangnall arranged that meeting between willing Gentleman and dissenting Player.

Mangnall and Meredith were congenial partners. They hadn't invented the rules that were supposed to govern all football transactions and neither man felt morally bound by their

51

constraints. When it came to steering a course between the smug self-serving illusions of those who ran football and the realities of the pro game, Mangnall and Meredith allowed pragmatism to be their guiding star.

Mangnall's bold acquisition of Meredith and his disgraced City colleagues, Turnbull, Bannister and Burgess, was soon rewarded. In 1907/8 United won their first championship. The following season the FA Cup came back to Manchester. Mangnall had transformed a struggling Second Division club by encouraging clever free-flowing football and added a new chapter to Manchester's burgeoning football tradition. United's pitch at Bank Street, Clayton, tended to turn into a quagmire in the winter months which was not conducive to the team's style. In 1909 Mangnall proposed a spectacular solution to this problem: capitalising on the team's achievements, he persuaded the club's directors to commission architect Archibald Leitch to design a new stadium with the best facilities in the land.

On Saturday 19 February 1910, Manchester United moved into their new 100,000 capacity home at Old Trafford. The press preview the previous day had taken journalists' breath away. This was a 'classic ground', one scribe wrote. The pitch was like 'a lush green carpet' and, the writer went on, 'the appurtenances of the ground are excellent in conception, construction and arrangement'. The first game against Liverpool attracted 50,000 paying Mancunians and another 5,000 were estimated to have sneaked in free of charge. The *Manchester Guardian* reported astonishing scenes in the city in the hours before the game. 'Such a crowd has never before been seen in Manchester.' Hordes of people swarmed up the Chester Road. Trams were barely able to move under the weight of passengers. Some travelled by cart, a few on horseback. All were awestruck by the stadium, which, it was generally agreed, was the finest in the world.

Old Trafford was a fitting monument to a team that had won the League and FA Cup in previous seasons, a symbol, also, of the pride Manchester's professionals had bestowed on the city and its citizens. The combination of success and defiance of the London-based football Establishment was enchanting.

Wizards on the field, rebels off it, United's professionals embodied the city's romantic sense of itself as a place apart from any other.

In 1911 Meredith and his men won the championship again. The following year Ernest Mangnall left the club to cross Manchester and join City. United's directors weren't unhappy to see him go. The construction of Old Trafford had emptied United's bank account. Mangnall had grown too big for his boots. City, still struggling to recover from the scandal of 1906, offered Mangnall the job of secretary/manager. Eighteen months later they were top of the First Division, while United were heading rapidly in the other direction. Then the Great War intervened. Meredith guested for Mangnall's City during the war. When hostilities ceased he sought a transfer from United, but, belligerent as ever, he refused to move if any fee changed hands. He held out for three years before United released him to rejoin City and Mangnall. He was forty-six years of age.

Mangnall had kept City solvent and the team had finished runners-up in the First Division in 1921. But, for both him and Meredith the great days had passed, and in 1924 City refused to renew their secretary/manager's contract. Manchester's first great football era had drawn to an end. Before being dismissed by City, Ernest Mangnall rendered Manchester football one final service when he commissioned the building of Maine Road which would, like Old Trafford, become one of the finest stadiums in the country.

Billy Meredith had no real vocation for coaching. He was too obsessed with himself to dwell on others' needs and imperfections. Coaching was a way of prolonging his football life, the only life he really understood or cared about. He had always had interests outside of football, but they were merely ways of making money, and sometimes losing it. Matt Busby and he passed like ships in the night. One the grand old man, the other a young prince. The young prince was confident, his life before him. The old man's best days were past. Like many great old players, Meredith was slightly sad, miscast in the marginal role now afforded to him.

The game was changing and he disapproved of the changes.

53

The off-side law had been altered in 1925. Herbert Chapman had emerged as a great manager at Huddersfield Town where his imaginative response to change, the introduction of a centre-half or 'stopper' around whom defensive play would pivot, had enabled his team to dominate the First Division which they won in three successive seasons between 1924 and '27. Meredith believed – and loudly proclaimed – that soccer's emphasis had shifted disastrously from skill to pace and strength. People listened but less attentively. Chapman was the hero of the new age. Billy eventually left football in 1930 to run a pub in Stretford. By then the young prince from Bellshill had discovered the pro game. It was nothing like his dream.

Professional football was a brutal business, Matt soon learned. In Bellshill he'd been renowned, a figure of note, the young man who was going places. Manchester City and other clubs, among them Glasgow Celtic, had wooed him. It would be hard of course, there were no guarantees, he'd been warned, but *he* would be all right. They wouldn't be taking him if they thought otherwise. The urgency of the club representatives' pleas vouched for their confidence in him. The fuss was gratifying.

Matt signed for City in the Bank Restaurant in Glasgow owned by Willie Maley, a famous former Celtic manager. It was an auspicious occasion. Arriving in Manchester, however, he quickly came down to earth. Nobody seemed to notice his coming. The fuss was over. He was anonymous, just another youngster who could play, and football was full of kids who could play – in their local town or village – but playing here for money was a different matter. The atmosphere at Maine Road was coarse and unforgiving. In those days clubs carried huge staffs of between forty and fifty pros, sometimes more. Only the eleven in the first team were contented, and not even all of them. Fear, discontent and disillusion were in the air. City was a typical professional football club, no place for dreamers, no place for kids who'd been big-time in their own village. The old pros knew how to sort them out, and they relished the job. Kids with talent and brio were an irritant. They reminded the old pros how *they'd* been when they thought the world revolved around *them*. This fucking game soon taught you otherwise. Naivety on or off the field was harshly treated. Mistakes made when playing earned you a bollocking and a withering look; in the dressing-room innocence was sneered at, the source of much contemptuous laughter. It was as if the senior players were reassuring themselves, eliminating potential challengers before the contest began.

To a youngster newly arrived in the pro game, the player you'd worshipped could turn out to be a foul-mouthed bastard with a heart of stone. The nobleman of Saturday afternoon was simply an identity he assumed; the real man was a shock. Many young dreamers never recovered from the reality.

For the first couple of years it seemed as if young Matt Busby would be one of professional football's casualties. After his first game at inside-forward in the Central League, against Preston North End at Deepdale, Matt realised how difficult things could be. He hardly got a kick. The pace of the game was beyond him. There seemed to be no time on the ball, no space in which to work. The young prince of Bellshill was irrevelant. City were well beaten. Alex James, then an established star with Preston, called into the dressing-room after the game to wish Matt well. This thoughtful gesture was as appreciated as it was rare. A few weeks later, City, chasing promotion from the Second Division, signed a complete forward line, Horne, Marshall, Tait, Tilson and Brook, a decision which left Matt in no doubt how far away he was from glory.

Matt's confidence evaporated as the months passed. He had always been the commanding figure on a football field. With a deft touch and his ability to distribute the ball accurately and imaginatively he could compensate for the one flaw in his game – a lack of pace. Speed of thought had always served to conceal his slowness, but now this deficiency was ruthlessly exposed. Like all touch players he depended on confidence; the nerveless pause where others would hurry; the daring flick where others would lunge and thrust; the chipped pass that floated tantalisingly, tempting an opponent to reach the ball which would surely elude him to find a colleague; feinting and shimmying past the aggressive foe to escape from the tightest corners, triumphant with just a hint of arrogance. All of this achieved by

55

instinct, an unerring sense of danger, where it was coming from, how to avoid it.

In Bellshill Matt had felt invincible. Now he discovered how wretchedly awkward the game could be when you lost confidence. He was now the lunger. Where once he escaped by a yard he was now trapped. That yard made all the difference between the pro game and the game played by dreamers. Anxiety disarmed the touch player. Self-doubt caused the passes to be overhit, the delicate flicks to be mistimed, your every feint to be anticipated and countered. Now the disdain was on your opponents' face, and your team-mates'. 'For fuck's sake, son.' The words, spat out with venom, began to haunt you. Your soul, once warmed by approving cheers, now chilled. You began to dread receiving the ball. The unexpressed anger, reflected in a look or gesture that hinted you were hardly worth rebuke, was worse than the oaths of impatience.

Matt Busby learned these bitter lessons in his first few months in the pro game. Once the season ended he caught the first available train home to Orbiston. Manchester City had won promotion. The celebrations only made his plight worse.

The three-month break restored his confidence. Playing in summer games with old friends, he rediscovered his touch and felt once more the comfort of being in control of the rhythm of a game. Back among his own folk he reflected on the differences between his new life and the one he'd eagerly left behind.

The most striking contrast between Matt's new world and life in the pits was in men's attitude to each other. The team ethos that was supposed to exist in football really *did* exist among miners. Once you were old enough to go down the mine you were deemed worthy of respect. Experienced miners made fun of youngsters. But it was gentle fun, designed not to wound or demean but simply to lighten the gloom of the day. Down on the coalface older men wanted younger men to learn; experience was a gift you passed on, knowing that your life might depend on the man next to you. He wasn't, as in football, a threat or a rival. He was part of your shift, taking the same risks for the same reward, serving the same master. You depended on each other. The camaraderie was real. There was no place

56

for vanity, selfishness or greed. Loyalty wasn't, as in football clubs, a rhetorical call to arms, rather the essence upon which your life depended. Team spirit was something more than an expedient on the road to glory.

Young Matt returned to Manchester determined to deal with football on its own terms. He was harder now, but, in the short term at least, things didn't improve. He was surprised to be selected for the first team when Eric Brooks and Tommy Johnson were claimed to represent the Football League. City's manager, Peter Hodge, took a calculated risk choosing Matt. The boy was impressive in his manner and bearing, he was reserved and impeccably behaved, a cut above the average; and he looked good in training, good enough to be a player. Training in those days was casual and disorganised. The senior players decided, by and large and they pleased themselves. If you were good enough you were fit enough. The converse was also deemed to be true. The manager was in the office most of the week, making deals, appeasing directors, keeping himself a respectful distance from the players – or so he imagined. Officers and men couldn't get too close, after all. It was the trainer's job to look after the training, but compared to the senior players his influence was marginal. Power was the ability to do the business on a Saturday afternoon. If you were in the first team the rest of the week was your own. If you were striving to get on that was your own business. Nobody would stop you – the men in possession would simply keep an amused eye on you.

To this haphazard norm the weekly practice match between first team and reserves was the presumed exception. Presumed that is by the reserves, and trainers and managers, naive enough to confuse Tuesday morning with Saturday afternoon.

Cynicism wasn't all pervasive, but those players tainted by it could be disproportionately influential. In this hard man's world the sceptic was king. Even the most enthusiastic first team player found it difficult to rise to the occasion of the practice match. The absence of a crowd made it hard to get the adrenalin flowing. The empty stadium added to the air of unreality; the hollow sound mocking this phoney war was the echo of your own voice rebounding eerily from the terraces.

This was artificial, football without pain and therefore devoid of pleasure and purpose. Except for the reserves striving to impress.

For the reserves the midweek practice match was more important than any Central League match. The manager was watching, *he* was the atmosphere. Very often the absence of spectators was a blessing; mistakes would not be greeted with derisive jeering. It was in such circumstances that young Matt Busby caught Peter Hodge's eye. With the senior players relaxed, he had time and space to display his talent. On the strength of his midweek performances Matt was given his chance in a home game against Middlesborough which City won 2–0. He did well but was back in the reserves the following week. There was to be no instant cure for his problems, indeed life got harder. He continued to mystify Peter Hodge and torment himself mixing midweek brilliance with weekend mediocrity. Switching positions from inside-left to outside-right and centre-forward was no solution. Injury to Tilson gave Matt another first team opportunity in an FA Cup replay against Spurs. City won 4–2, Matt scoring two of the goals. This time he kept his place for an away fixture against Bolton Wanderers but he had a nightmare game at Burnden Park and was dropped the following week.

Matt's despair deepened. Writing home to Jean he told her, 'I feel I am out of my sphere in football'. The truth, which he glimpsed in his more objective moments, was that he was the victim of circumstances. Matt was, like other young boys alone, left to fend for himself in a sport that was savage from top to bottom. Professional soccer was hierarchical; ninety per cent of those at the bottom were crushed, had their spirits broken by cruelty or indifference.

The trouble began at the top. The directors were either idiots or autocrats who contributed nothing to the club. Affectations of grandeur were their *raison d'être*. They preened themselves when things were good, searched for scapegoats when the results turned. The manager was their representative. He did their bidding, listened to their suggestions on team matters and then accepted responsibility for their mistakes. As the job was defined he could only be a wretch desperate for approval – for employment.

The players knew this, the older ones with talent at once sustained and undone by the manager's weakness. Their contempt for his attempts to lift them on match days was, in the case of the good players whose example was followed down the line, thinly veiled. They were slaves to *this* master? At the end of this inglorious trail the starry-eyed kid was either ignored or the focus of resentment. Everybody had their own problems, his were his alone.

Not all football clubs were like that, but most were. Occasionally an autocrat like Chapman or Mangnall would happen along, identify what needed to be done and enforce his will, but leadership was rare for it incurred great risks. The manager with strong opinions of his own – some kind of vision – better make it work – and quick. Sometimes, too, a group of good men ran a dressing-room, making the place less comfortable for bullies and vicious piss-takers, but this was rare, for as the fate of Charlie Roberts, Herbert Bloomfield and Billy Meredith illustrated, football was inhospitable to decency, unrewarding of justice, deaf to reason.

In this brutish environment Matt Busby was indeed 'out of his sphere'. Few were sensitive to his woes, which grew so intense during his second season at Maine Road that after yet another bleak day he returned to his lodgings, took out his suitcase and flung his few belongings into it with the intention of catching the next train to Glasgow. Fortunately his room-mate, a fellow Scot Phil McCloy, walked in on this scene. McCloy was a first team player who cared for the kids. He'd been through this, he recalled as he sat young Matt down to reconsider. 'Don't do this, kid,' McCloy advised. 'Give it a little longer. You can still make the grade.' Matt had never worn his heart on his sleeve, so the desperation beneath the sturdy self-possession surprised his room-mate. They discussed the situation into the small hours before Matt relented and unpacked his case.

Despite his footballing traumas Matt had retained the respect of all at Maine Road. He was reserved, but not priggish. He never used bad language, was a regular attender at Mass, yet he joined in the dressing-room banter with the more raucous characters. He dressed smartly. Barely twenty, he was mature beyond his years with an indefinable quality that set him apart from the others, a certain graciousness, almost feline, strange to see in a large, powerful, young man. Matt was a good listener and nobody impressed him more than Jimmy McMullen, Manchester City's veteran captain, who'd played in the great Scotland team that beat England at Wembley in '28. Shortly after Phil McCloy's sympathetic intervention, Matt contracted pneumonia. He was physically and psychologically at an all-time low when McMullen offered the hand of friendship that undoubtedly saved Matt's football life. The City captain invited the struggling young reserve to come and live with him and his family. Whether through a sense of responsibility or because, as a footballer of touch and vision like Matt, he empathised with his desperate young compatriot, McMullen became his mentor.

McMullen's generosity and advice did not produce instant results. Coming to the end of the 1929/30 season Matt was half expecting to be released by City. Life as a collier back in Orbiston beckoned and he wasn't sure he would grieve too much if this were to be his fate. To his surprise he was retained. It must have been a marginal decision, undoubtedly swayed by his behaviour and the ability he'd revealed in the midweek practice matches.

After a carefree summer in Orbiston he dreaded returning to Maine Road. By the autumn of 1930 his fortunes had further declined. He lost his place in the reserves. For a professional player of his experience this was the ultimate indignity. He later learned that around this time Manchester United's chief-scout, Louis Rocca, approached City to inquire about Matt's availability. Nobody was more available. Peter Hodge asked for the nominal sum of £150. Alas, United, very much Manchester's second club in those years, couldn't afford the fee. Had Matt been costing City any more than £5 a week he would certainly have been given a free transfer.

He was no more than a gap-filler for City's Central League side. Then one afternoon when he was hanging around the ground to watch City's third team play in a Northern Midweek game, a young amateur trialist failed to turn up and trainer Alex Bell asked Matt to fill in at right-half. Until now, thinking too much had been one of his downfalls; now with no time to confuse himself he simply went out and played.

This, he would later recall, was the first time he truly enjoyed a game of football since coming to England almost two years earlier. Manager Hodge enjoyed the performance as well. The following Saturday Matt played right-half for the reserves against Sheffield Wednesday at Hillsborough. When regular first team right-half, Matt Barrass, was injured a week later Matt Busby was selected to play in the first team away to Huddersfield. Barrass never regained his first team place.

Busby was a revelation as a wing-half. A forward needed pace to be really effective at the highest level. Not the devastating pace of a sprinter, more like a change of gears to accelerate through those vital first few yards once you had deceived your marker and made some space to work in. Matt had only one gear. Enough for Tuesday morning, but not for the quicker, adrenalin-driven rhythm of a First Division match day. But the most fundamental difference between his new role and the old one was that he now received the ball facing the way his team were playing. He had more time, more space, and, receiving the ball earlier in an attacking thrust, *he* could dictate the rhythm of the move. It was the difference between being the conductor and a mere player in the orchestra, more cerebral than physical. Technically and temperamentally Matt Busby was perfect for the part. The long severe apprenticeship was over, his life transformed within a few weeks.

Over the next few years Matt Busby established himself as one of the finest wing-halves in the game. His lack of pace and palpable absence of real aggression meant that greatness was denied him. But in possession of the ball he was always delightfully perceptive. Years later his contemporary and friend Joe Mercer, of Everton and England, remembered: 'What made Matt noticeable was the silkiness in possession, the way he drifted inside from the wing and then switched the ball back over the head of the full-back for his winger. He had this calm influence on events around him. He pin-pointed his passes uncannily like Paddy Crerand. I think Matt and Archie Macaulay were two of the most delicate strikers of a ball there have been.'

Of modern players, Jimmy Murphy, who played for West Brom and Wales in Matt's time, thought he was most like Jim

Baxter: 'He was the master of the reverse pass having this marvellous control with his inside foot. He was subtle and always seemed to do things at his own pace.'

Manchester City reached the FA Cup Final in successive years, 1933 and '34. In 1933 they lost to Everton 3−0, with the great Dixie Dean scoring one of Everton's goals. Cliff Britton, Everton's right-half, who would go on to be a leading club manager with Burnley, Everton, Preston and Hull City, had a hand in Everton's first two goals. The following season City returned to Wembley where a Tilson goal three minutes from time gave them victory over Portsmouth. City's regular goalkeeper, Len Langford, and his deputy, Barber, were both injured, allowing a virtually unknown nineteen-year-old, Frank Swift, to win an FA Cup winner's medal with less than a handful of first team games to his credit. Upon hearing the final whistle Swift fainted and had to be revived to receive his medal from King George V. In its match report of the final, the *Daily Telegraph* commented: 'Busby, the finest right-half ever seen at Wembley, and Brook inspired the whole side.'

Later in 1934 Matt won his first and only peacetime cap for Scotland, against Wales in the Home International series. That wonderful season was his finest as a player. He would never win another medal or, except for a few wartime internationals, be selected for Scotland again. City finished fourth in the First Division in 1935, their highest placing in his time with them. Early the following season he tore a hamstring and began a tormenting phase of his career which ended when he was tranferred to Liverpool for £8,000 in March 1936. As with most other things, injured players were left to fend for themselves. Treatment was rudimentary, not much improved since Billy Meredith's day. When you were of no use life went on without you. Soon even the man described in a *Guardian* profile of a year before as being 'at best [a player] who has no superior as an attacking half-back' began to feel dejected and isolated. In a desperate attempt to cure himself Matt went to Southport with a friend to consult a quack who, it was rumoured, could fix anything muscular. The method was to drop blocks of ice on the injured spot. It didn't work for Matt. Eventually he asked City for a transfer.

Matt's dissatisfaction with the game was more profound than the relatively simple matter of absence from the team through injury. He was twenty-six and had experienced professional football from top to bottom, from the anonymity of the reserve team dressing-room to the game's most coveted stage, the Royal Box at Wembley, where he had received his winner's medal from the King. But the game had disappointed him too often. Even the glory of Wembley that other men dreamed about, as he himself had done, was not as fulfilling as it might have been. What was missing was spiritual rather than material. Success had not blinded Matt, it had served only to accentuate his awareness of professional football's ills. The joy of Cup Final victory was brief. There followed the vanity and the squabbles about the spoils of victory. The slave culture had bred greed, mistrust and resentment. In an autobiography published almost forty years after the reality of the pre-war game crystallised in his mind Busby remarked: 'Long before I became established, before I moved from Manchester City to Liverpool I vowed that if I ever became a manager I would respect players as individuals.' There was, he recalled, 'a seemingly unbridgeable gulf between first team players and the rest, and an even wider gulf between players and management. I was appalled by these gulfs and about the indignities that were heaped on players. There are players, of course, who are too thick to understand that they are being got at. There are others who feel every stinging, sarcastic thrust, every bullying, scoffing, snide wisecrack.'

Like Billy Meredith before him, Matt Busby had understood his trade. The greatest evil was the absence of 'respect for the individual'. Unlike Meredith, Busby the player kept his own counsel. He was no crusader. He was no rebel either. 'I had decided that loud noises were not my forte and that strength was not measured in decibels,' he reflected, in a slightly different context, in his autobiography. By the time he was ready to leave Manchester City Busby knew what ailed the game he loved. He knew also that overt dissent earned one the tag of troublemaker, and football dealt ruthlessly with those who questioned its values too insistently. His manifesto, drawn up, as he put it, to imbue professional football with 'the essential qualities I felt had been missing from the game as I had known it' remained a secret document of his imagination. He understood that professional football was in essence a shabby replica of Britain's class-ridden society, snobbish, vain and deceitful, rewarding least those who invested most in it. In the game as he envisaged it 'everybody [was] important to himself –the director, the manager, the secretary, the players, the trainers, the coaches, the groundsmen, the tea-ladies, the lot. Their importance must not only be appreciated, it must be *seen* to be appreciated.' The emphasis was his.

Matt Busby's response to the disillusioning realities of the professional game was characteristically prudent. The sensitivity that prompted his concern for the individual also governed his reaction to what he clearly saw as football's most pervasive disease. Matt was a cautious man. There was no explosion, no angry agitation. He hated confrontation. He was, as all had remarked, a reserved man, loath to bare his inner self, to display his emotions in public. Many associates have remarked on Busby's need for privacy. 'Prudent . . . a very prudent man, intensely private,' thus, the painter Harold Riley, a close friend, described him. 'You could never push my dad,' his son Sandy would recall, 'he would reveal things in his own time with a little prompting. If he wanted to. If not . . .' There was a part of Matt that no one except Jean reached.

'He always kept you *there*,' remembers Charlie Mitten, outside-left in the first successful Busby team, his arm stretched out pointing just beyond touching distance. Privacy, his own and other people's, mattered deeply to Matt Busby. Respect for the individual was not just a footballing imperative, it covered everything, most of all the emotions. One's deepest feelings were one's own, intrusion beyond a certain point was a violation of trust. Displays of anger, the inevitable consequence of confrontation, meant exposing yourself. Life had taught him to value the privacy he had enjoyed so little of.

In the crowded, close-knit world of miners' cottages in which he'd grown up, privacy was virtually impossible to find. Even going to the toilet was, to a degree, a public act; bathing in the enamel tub in the kitchen on a Saturday night was, similarly, a violation of a kind, even if it took place within the sanctuary of the family home; he had slept in a room with seven other people. The distance this deeply sensitive man would always seek to keep between his inner self and the world outside was determined by the unnatural extent to which others had encroached upon his private world when he was young and vulnerable. His exposure had been physical *and* emotional. The loss of his father when he was six had left a void never satisfactorily filled. This space, too, had been invaded or, at least, occupied by a stranger, another violation, this time of the spirit, from which he recoiled. Football was Matt's way to his own private self. And as his world, small at first, grew larger, its imperatives became clearer to him. He learned the importance of controlling his emotions and so developed his own non-combative style.

Bullying offended him because it too was an attack on the spirit. 'There are players, of course, who are too thick to understand that they are being got at.' The pejorative use of the word thick is extremely uncharacteristic of Matt Busby. It indicates the strength of his feelings about the crude, often wounding, taunts to which young footballers were subjected in the dressing-room. What had been 'got at' was their private selves where doubt and anxiety mingled with hopes and desires, where young lads dreamed, where they could most easily be hurt. He resented bullying for the same reason he rejected confrontation as a means of righting football's wrongs.

In many respects being a professional footballer in 1936 was not unlike growing up as a Catholic in the Scotland of Matt Busby's youth. The slave footballer was despised by his so-called betters in much the same way as Scotland's Catholic immigrants were despised by their Protestant neighbours. Both were deemed untrustworthy, irresponsible and potentially disloyal. This was the game's administrators' view of Meredith, Roberts and Bloomfield, the early agitators for professional's rights. The lesson of the early struggle to emancipate professional footballers, as perceived by Matt Busby and his generation of players, was that agitation was doomed to failure. Confrontation was futile and ultimately demeaning, as much a waste of time for footballers in the Thirties as it had been for the

Catholics of Busby's youth who'd traded sectarian abuse on the street corners of Bellshill when drink had roused their emotions on a Saturday night.

Slaves who got involved in slanging matches let themselves down. Be they Catholics or footballers, their bitterness served only to undermine their cause, dignity was sacrificed when you behaved as the enemy expected you to. In Bellshill many Catholics had proved their persecutors right, lent substance to bigotry, proved that if power corrupts, powerlessness can be even more corrupting. Powerlessness could induce fecklessness, as happened in professional soccer. Unable to win justice, Billy Meredith and his contemporaries had traded their self-respect for under-the-counter payments and worse. In 1915, just before League football was suspended for the duration of the war, Meredith and his Manchester United colleagues had been involved in another match-fixing scandal. On Good Friday 1915 Liverpool visited Old Trafford for a game United had to win to avoid relegation. United duly won 2–0, but the Old Trafford crowd booed and jeered the two sides towards the end of the game. For days before the match rumours had circulated in Manchester that the result was 'squared'. The casual approach of both sides – Liverpool in particular – convinced many spectators that the rumours were correct. Later it was revealed that bookmakers throughout England had taken large bets predicting the 2–0 scoreline.

The subsequent Football Association inquiry found that there had indeed been skulduggery. Eight players, four from each club, were suspended for life, among them Meredith's close friend, Sandy Turnbull, who had scored the winning goal when United won the FA Cup in 1907.

Their United colleague, Enoch 'Knocker' West, denied his guilt and took the FA to court. Meredith was called as a witness. He denied being involved, although admitting that during the first half he had come to the conclusion that 'something was wrong'. West lost his case. John Harding, Meredith's biographer, concluded; '. . . his part in this shabby business seems to have been a peripheral one. Perhaps he watched the furtive arrangements going on from the corner of the dressing-room and simply turned a blind eye – he had seen it all before and suffered the consequences. Perhaps he no longer cared what went on among his colleagues.'

Enslaved and denied respect, even the best of professional football men could descend into fecklessness. Thus, men deemed to be a lesser breed became the creatures of their masters' bigoted mythology, a caste from whom nothing more than performing tricks was expected. Denied respect they lost self-respect. Denied responsibility they behaved irresponsibly.

Nothing in professional soccer had changed very much between 1915 and 1936. The maximum wage had risen from £4 to £8. Otherwise all was as it had been: the coarseness of the dressing-room, the suspicion between castes; the ritual abuse of the innocent; the isolation of those who sought reform. The most protected footballer was the one who played with the grace and courage of a hero whilst simultaneously knowing his place. The Modest Hero was popular in the boardroom and idealised by the sporting press. When directors and the public had no more use for him, the Hero, whether injured or too old, was supposed to fade away. Those who tried to fight the system invariably lost.

Matt Busby was allowed to join Liverpool for £8,000 in March 1936. His injury had responded slowly to treatment, but unfortunately too slowly for City, who thought he was finished, his best footballing days behind him. Throughout this difficult year he had, as always, behaved with dignity, experience having taught him that the alternatives to dignity – impotent rage or simmering resentment – were self-defeating. Now he knew that he was powerless in all respects except one: he could control himself. But this was not the only lesson his years at Manchester City had taught him: he had also learned that service rendered was soon forgotten. Another formative experience, to be stored with all the others in that private world of his which existed behind the façade of Genial Matt the Modest Hero. Behind the mask a different man had been born, a visionary rather different from those who'd gone before, a slave whose eyes had been opened, who understood that before you could effect change you had to aquire power, who saw clearly that if football's ills began at the top they couldn't be cured from the bottom.

'Perhaps my background had made me a little older than my years,' Busby modestly reflected in his autobiography, 'but long before I moved from Manchester City to Liverpool I vowed that if I ever became a manager I would respect players as individuals who needed individual treatment and thereby try to inspire respect from them.' Busby's background had done more than make him a 'little older' than his years. And there is every reason to believe that he had learned, from his own experiences and those of others, not just how to exercise power but how to acquire it. To this end the guise of Genial Matt the Modest Hero esteemed by all was of inestimable value.

4

The Man on the Tram

'Matt has always known what he is
and that has given him enormous
power.'

Harold Riley

Football was still a young sport in 1936 – the Football League
was barely twenty years older than Matt Busby – and the
professional game was still handicapped by its original
deformities. Great men had lent enchantment to the game by
their deeds on the field, and men like Billy Meredith and
Herbert Chapman had tried, with varying degrees of success, to
help their crippled love develop. But if Meredith's pre-
occupation had been the professional's identity, what he was,
how he should be treated and rewarded, Herbert Chapman's
vision was strictly tactical. He had been concerned to make the
players function more efficiently as a *team*, and it was he who, in
pursuing this end, put trophies in the boardrooms of
Huddersfield and Arsenal.

By the time Matt Busby left Manchester City for Liverpool in
the spring of 1936, he had identified a problem more fundamental than those that concerned Meredith and Chapman.
Busby's analysis went deeper than the individual pro and the
team to the womb in which both were conceived: *the club*. For
most people football happened on Saturday afternoon. The
professional, manager or player, was judged by results on the
field. But Busby understood that those results were determined
by what happened on the training ground during the week. As
things stood, the training ground, the place that ought to be a
university where skill and character were nurtured, was little
better than a playground for the senior pros, where they
amused themselves between performances. With the directors

69

away working at their businesses and professions, and the manager in his office, leadership was left to the trainer, whose status was considerably lower than head boy. Thus, the hours of the week which mattered most passed anarchically. In all playgrounds the bully is king, and so it was in football. The victims were the young, those professionals in embryo, whose talents withered as their dreams calloused, their spirits broken by angry words or, worse perhaps, indifference.

This was the club away from the gaze of public and directors, the club that was never written about in the newspapers and magazines. This was professional football. *This* was far more, far more real than the glorious atmosphere of a packed stadium on a Saturday afternoon. This was what Busby vowed to change. If he got the chance.

Some men see the world as it is and ask why, others dream of things that have never been and ask why not? When Busby thought about the 'gulfs' in football the one that bothered him most was between manager and players. Here, most critically, leadership was required. The vacuum on the training ground must be filled, for the training ground was the club, Saturday afternoons merely a reflection of the happenings of the week, good or, as was mostly the case, bad. The game on the field was fashioned by the game off the field, the character of a professional football club could no more be left to chance than the character of a family. Like a family, a football club had to have values, human values, a sense of fairness, decency and justice. Also a sense of responsibility more profound than the one Busby had known: the pithy call-to-arms ten minutes before kick-off on a Saturday afternoon.

The Manchester City club Matt Busby chose to leave was neither better nor worse than others. The most important things were left to chance. Since its inception professional football had been preoccupied with money, football had tended to be forgotten, and the club directors and the managers who were their hired hands expended most of their energy and imagination dealing with financial matters. This was particularly true in Manchester where both the city's Football League clubs had been tainted by scandal, and both had flirted with bankruptcy. Commerce, via the adroit manoeuvring of Ernest

Mangnall and Billy Meredith, had been the principal force at play when the success of its professional footballers had bestowed glory and a proud sense of its own identity on Manchester. Manchester's football clubs were, therefore, more commercial institutions engaged in the business of football than sporting academies of the kind Matt Busby envisaged. The law of the commercial jungle was more applicable than the values of family or university and the gifted footballer was just another valuable piece of merchandise.

Success was no insurance against the day your luck ran out – even Matt Busby, the hero of the 1934 Cup Final, was a disposable piece of merchandise little more than a year later. Success in the atmosphere that prevailed at Maine Road was a fragile commodity, a consequence of clever exploitation rather than a just reward for the virtues of team spirit and clubmanship to which all paid lip service. Success gained thus made men greedy, induced smugness and vanity, strained loyalties rather than strengthening them.

It was from this milieu that Matt Busby walked away without regret. The following season, 1936/7, Manchester City won the First Division championship. Within twelve months the club was relegated to the Second Division. The football world was amazed by City's rapid decline. Along the East Lancs Road Matt Busby was more convinced than ever that success gained by dubious means was no success at all. A mere player, Matt was in no position – yet – to right the world's wrongs. He would, however, later admit to some wistful reflection in the months after leaving City, during which his old club seemed to flourish while his new one hovered in the relegation zone: 'Liverpool deserved success because they treated everyone on the staff as human beings should be treated, with kindness, consideration and understanding,' he recalled. In contrast to many bigger clubs, 'Liverpool were always prepared to reward good service, even when they could so easily have evaded their obligations to players whose first XI days were ended.' As an example he cited Liverpool's treatment of Jimmy McDougal, a distinguished veteran who was reaching the end of his career when Matt arrived at Anfield. 'Jimmy, a tremendous worker on the field, had completed a little less than the four years' qualification period for his second benefit when the club decided to replace him with Jimmy McInnes, bought from Third Lanark.' Time spent in the reserves didn't count towards your benefit, but, as Busby explained, 'McDougal was re-signed on top wages although he had lost his place, and the following year was again signed at the maximum when he was not playing at all. When he told the club he had decided to retire from football his second benefit was paid to him. I well remember Liverpool's handling of McDougal. It made a big impression on me, and indeed on all the players, because even though it was nothing more than just reward for a loyal servant there were few clubs who would have acted similarly in pre-war days. Before the war generosity was a rare occurrence.'

The man who made the difference between generosity and the indifference common elsewhere was George Kay who'd been appointed Liverpool manager shortly before Matt Busby arrived at Anfield. Kay promoted the value of loyalty rewarded, being, in the McDougal case, the advocate who persuaded the directors to do the right thing. Busby remembered George Kay as, 'a very fine man and manager whom I grew to admire, indeed I always regarded him as one of the best I have ever met in this great game.'

Busby's reference to 'this great game' is a fascinating reminder of how enduring men's love was for a sport which was, in many respects, as Busby knew, far from great. Although he won no honours during his three seasons at Anfield Busby rediscovered football's beauty, which compensated for everything that was materially wrong with the sport.

The first task facing himself and George Kay when they arrived was to save Liverpool from relegation to the Second Division. Liverpool had won four First Division championships since gaining promotion in 1905, but the last of them had been in 1922/3 and since then the club had endured a more modest existence. By 1936 a weak regime and some ageing players had combined to leave them in the relegation zone with only a handful of games left to play. Kay and Busby made the difference and Liverpool survived. They had been a physical side, a style which Kay set out to change over the next couple of seasons using Busby's composed and authoritative presence to

72

set the tone. This role, in a side which never threatened to win anything, provided Busby with his most satisfying spell as a player. He had arrived as an expensive star but didn't act the part. A senior pro himself now, Matt espoused the values which had been absent in the Maine Road dressing-room. His influence was felt on and off the field.

During his time at Liverpool Matt Busby grew from prince to elder statesman. His natural ability as a footballer helped him to command respect, but other more personal qualities began to assert themselves. He was a kind, generous colleague, patient always with those who were younger or less gifted. He was also an attractive man, physically handsome and imposing with a captivating smile and a baritone Scottish accent which managed to sound, simultaneously, grave and gentle. The reserved young pro was now serene. Where reserve had once indicated shyness, serenity now suggested a strength which was all the more potent for not obtruding. As he approached his thirtieth year, Matt Busby's experiences fused with his natural physical attributes to create an extraordinary presence which left an impression on all who met him. To this natural aura Busby added his own effects. In David Miller's biography of Busby published in 1970, the author presents this remarkable image from Liverpool 1938:

'At about nine-thirty every morning a man boarded the tram just to the east side of the Mersey Tunnel. As often as not, already sitting there was someone noticeable for his tidy, dapper appearance; fawn overcoat, trilby, pipe, newspaper – a bank manager, perhaps, or the man from the Pru'. It was in fact Matthew Busby, professional footballer, on his way to Liverpool Football Club ground at Anfield.'

The man boarding the tram was Busby's Anfield colleague, Cliff Lloyd, who later became Secretary of the Professional Footballers' Association, which, a generation on, would achieve many of the original aims of Meredith's Players' Union. To Lloyd, himself an unusual professional footballer, Busby was an incredibly charismatic figure. The Crombie overcoat, trilby and pipe were to become Matt Busby's trademarks as he grew to eminence in professional football. It is, however, intriguing to reflect on the image he sought to cultivate during

73

his Liverpool years. In all other respects Matt was a man of modest taste, unconcerned with style in matters like the car he would drive, the house he would live in, the food he would eat, or indeed the social circles he would move in. Yet, in an era when his peers were more commonly attired in cloth caps and mufflers, Busby garbed himself in the uniform of the governing classes. Lest anyone should doubt it, Matt Busby, professional footballer, was no serf. This was confrontation without noise, a subtle yet conscious rejection of old assumptions about his caste.

Busby and Liverpool were good for each other. Not only did he enhance his reputation as a player but the challenge of transforming an ailing club forced him to put his ideas about leadership to the test. In the year when Neville Chamberlain returned from Munich with his piece of paper, Liverpool vindicated his theories by beginning to move impressively up the First Division table. Busby now felt certain that the qualities he believed in worked, and the pleasure he derived from playing was richer than ever. Always it was the game itself that redeemed all the indignities and frustrations of its attendant environment. On the pitch class asserted itself, courage was rewarded, weakness punished. The humblest man, even the most feckless, could conjure a moment of absolute beauty. As its drama unfolded, the game revealed its truths. Those strong in spirit invariably prevailed. This was as it should be, as it rarely was once the final whistle was blown, when the venal world once again encroached upon the spirit.

To the watching world professional football was glamorous. Men dreamed of running onto the beautifully manicured pitch in the colours of the team. They would do daring deeds, draw roars of acclaim from the packed stadium, be recognised, have their picture in the magazines and newspapers.

For the pro, especially one as well equipped as Matt Busby, the joy was rather different. The hours before a match were filled with fear and apprehension. Your stomach churned, the shivers of anxiety raised pimples on your flesh, doubt seeped into your soul. The heroes didn't look or feel like heroes in those grim, pensive moments before the dressing-room door opened and the noise of an expectant crowd hit you in the face.

74

These were the worse moments of the week. Except the weeks you lost. You lived for the better times when you got a result, the harder it came the more you savoured it. The joy was not running onto the pitch but walking off, drained but victorious, at the end. All fear banished, doubt dispelled, angry recrimination postponed. For a week at least. The professional wasn't chasing glory, he was running away from failure. The game that had at first been about mastering a toy was now about conquering fear. Once a way of introducing yourself to others, football, played by men for money, was now a means of discovering things about yourself. And the men around you. Respect was hard earned. You could deceive those watching, but not those with whom you had gone into battle. There were cheats, sunshine boys, who looked the part but never did the business when they were needed. There were quiet men, dependable and diligent, never noticed or given credit except by the other players who understood their value. Some men possessed raw physical courage, others were simply hard, impervious to danger and thus never knowing fear. But there was another quality, which Busby possessed, colloquially known as balls. Writing about one of Matt Busby's last performances for Liverpool, in its edition of 6 May 1939, the *Manchester Guardian*'s critic observed, 'Busby is the gentlest mannered and most philosophic of footballers.' In a side which, despite improvement, still found itself with its back to the wall on too many occasions, Busby never shirked responsibility. He wanted the ball, was never afraid, always coaxing by example. The quality most difficult to discern from beyond the arena was moral courage, the willingness to make mistakes for others, to carry their burden on the days they weakened. This Matt did, in the stylish, skilful, imaginative manner of the great Scottish players he'd admired as a boy. The contentment of the good days was sublime.

Contentment was the drug the professional craved . . . more than glory . . . more than money . . . more than anything. Contentment was to be spiritually fulfilled beyond the imaginings of the men who ruled you, who, however much they owned, would never know or share this treasured sacrament. For this feeling men from Meredith to Busby lived, devoted to the game, 'hearts', as Meredith explained, 'full of it', oblivious to football's ignominious treatment of them, its failure to respect or understand them. Between the Meredith and Busby eras only the maximum wage had changed. Four pounds became eight. Contempt remained constant.

The letter notifying Stanley Matthews of his selection for England began, 'Dear Matthews'. Tommy Lawton, England's centre-forward, was seen, by an FA official, to flourish the one pound, ten shilling's pittance he was paid for representing his country and heard to say, 'There's 70,000 here and this is all we're getting for turning out today.' For this observation Lawton was dropped for England's next two games. His indiscretion was committed before a wartime international. The reaction of England captain, Stan Cullis, was more typical: 'We were only being paid thirty shillings for a match; even the gatemen were getting more than we were, but there were two million of our fellows fighting for their lives, and ours, and I wasn't going to ask for more. I used to tell players how lucky we were to be doing what we did.' In the context of war this rationale was plausible, but the philosophy that professionals 'were lucky to be doing what [they] did' was prevalent whenever the subject of their working conditions was raised by players with the intelligence and guts to baulk at their serf-like existence. Lucky, professional footballers undoubtedly were, for they were healthy, gifted and comparatively well paid. The question was, with whom should they compare themselves? The gateman? The average working man? Or the master craftsman? At a time when the average working wage was £4 a week professional footballers earned double that. So when they reflected on the lot of the class they'd come from professionals could convince themselves that they were indeed lucky. They were doing something immensely satisfying and being better paid than the fellows they had gone to school with. But this argument was, as the more intelligent among them knew, fallacious.

The average workman or master craftsman didn't pack stadiums, didn't run the risk of career-ending injury every time he went to work, and could of course expect his working life to extend into old age. The master craftsman could change jobs and charge the going rate for his work. If he worked harder and produced finer products he would be better rewarded than his peers. The comparison with the *average* worker was absurd. Professional footballers were inordinately talented and to reach the top of their trade they were required to make great sacrifices, being unable to indulge in many of life's pleasures as others were.

The notion that an international footballer was lucky to be doing what he did was preposterous. That such a proposition could be credibly advanced by their more conservative colleagues to undermine the brave dressing-room spirits who questioned the system says much about the degree to which a sport conceived in a class-ridden society reflected the brutal inanities of its origins. Powerful though they seemed, football's rulers, the J. C. Cleggs and C. E. Sutcliffes of the Busby, Matthews, Lawton era, knew that tyrannical empires like theirs were fragile, vulnerable to the voice of reason because they were so preposterously unjust. Thus, the merest hint of dissent, such as a professional like Tommy Lawton even daring to raise the question of a thirty shilling international match fee, had to be swiftly and disproportionately punished, and had to be *seen* to be punished. 'Dear Matthews' was another ritual humiliation essential to remind the slave of his place in the order of things. To call this professional 'Mr Matthews', or 'Stanley', might be to encourage 'Matthews' to believe that he had rights, and was entitled to respect. From respect might come self-respect and from that God knows where things would end.

Collectively, professionals of the pre-war years were as lacking in self-respect as the men of Billy Meredith's time. Had they possessed respect for themselves they would not have sought to compare their work with the mass of working people but with the great entertainers of their time, in theatre, music-hall or film. Here was the true comparison, with people who weren't lucky, but very special. Like the great entertainers, professional footballers of the stature of Matthews, Lawton, Carter, Finney, Cullis, Busby and James rendered ordinary existence wondrous, romantic, *tolerable*. When presenting the FA Cup in 1909, Lord Charles Beresford, Commander-in-Chief

77

of the Channel Fleet, referred to the importance of the occasion in terms of morale to serving men and the community at large: 'Members of the service read the papers and know the men who have played this afternoon. *I do not think I have seen finer specimens of British humanity than those who played in this game*.' Unfortunately the men from the Football Association seemed not to have heard. For an hour or two each week the fans who flocked to the nation's football grounds experienced beauty, grace, courage and wit. Even on the bad days there was humour and a sense of community. There was always drama, an escape from the mundane.

Nobody was more sensitive to the slights and injustice visited upon the providers of football magic than Matt Busby. The man in the Crombie overcoat, with trilby hat and pipe, had his own way of declaring his independence. He knew the players couldn't win so he waved no banners, caused no fuss – there was no point in agitating. For him self-respect was a personal matter. Nobody doubted Matt Busby's sense of himself. There was more to his striking presence than bespoke tailoring.

The painter Harold Riley, for whom Busby later sat, himself a Manchester United junior when Busby arrived to manage the club after the war, offers this explanation of that presence: 'The fascinating thing about Matt from a painter's point of view is the source of his undoubted charisma. I did portraits of two popes and a couple of American presidents – and many other powerful people – so one acquires a certain awareness of a subject. What strikes me about Matt is, if you like, the paradoxical quality of his charisma. People who are charismatic are usually flamboyant. Now Matt is not a very flamboyant person. In fact charisma comes from variable things and Matt's comes from his dignity. The quality Matt possesses reminds me most of Pope Paul VI whose power also came from his great dignity. Pope Paul was very dignified, almost academic, whereas the present Pope has great charismatic flamboyance which is almost electric. In Matt's case it's necessary to distinguish between dignity and flamboyance. The thing about Matt that is really very important is the charismatic quality of him as an individual because it was the power that actually influenced people. And he still has that.

'There is a real humility there which in a sense comes from a very unassuming aspect of his character. He has always known what he is and that has given him enormous power as well. He is not an academic, or what he would consider an intellectual person. What he is is somebody with great feelings and powerful instincts and, I think, great personal and private standards. His standards are very high. He is a man of great principle. If people disappoint him, don't conform to those standards, he will just step away.'

Harold Riley's portrayal of Busby, offered with the benefit of hindsight, is poignant when set against the tawdry reality of pre-war English soccer. One can see why he commanded respect and how, guided by his powerful instinct, he stepped away from the politics of the dressing-room.

'He has always known what he is and that has given him enormous power.'

Riley's reference to Busby knowing *what* he is, and the enormous power derived from this, has particular relevance to the years between 1939, when Neville Chamberlain's declaration of war on Germany signalled the premature end of Matt's playing career, and 1945 when he took over as manager of Manchester United. What Busby understood – and this was the source of the enormous power Riley refers to – was the difference between people's perception of him and the real man. There was far more to him than the benign character he projected, the gentle-mannered philosopher of the *Guardian* profile who commanded respect and affection throughout the game. He had what is known today as a good image. This was in part due to his innate qualities but also, to a significant degree, to a shrewd assessment of how best to adorn what was natural while concealing his deepest convictions about the system of which, as a professional player, he was a humble servant.

At the outbreak of war Matt Busby, although no more than thirty, was a respected elder statesman among footballers. Had he chosen to he could have voiced his views about the nature of the game and urged reform upon its rulers. He chose instead to conform. Knowing *what* he was, he knew the price that would be extracted if he revealed *who* he really was; a man who was offended by much of what he had witnessed in professional

79

football, who believed that radical change was necessary, who was determined – if he got the chance – to do something about it. The dignified, principled man with very high personal standards described by Harold Riley might have been expected to rail against the tawdry reality of the pre-war game. But Matt Busby was wise, and interested in acquiring the power to change things. To that end he kept his peace.

Matt Busby appeared to pose no threat to the established order. On the contrary, those who ran football found him a reassuring figure, and when people questioned football's values its administrators could point to Busby and other equally well regarded contemporaries, like Stan Cullis, Joe Mercer and Cliff Britton, to sustain the argument that the game made men rather than demeaned them. The idea that Busby was the man he was, despite rather than because of his experiences as a professional would never have entered official minds. When preferment was in the offing it was to these model professionals that the masters turned. Stan Cullis was England's captain. The fact that he felt himself to be a 'lucky' man, and behaved accordingly, would not have hindered his promotion from the ranks. During the war years Matt Busby would also be chosen to captain his country, but that was not the summit of his ambitions.

When war was declared in September 1939 the Football League was suspended. The previous month, with war imminent, the professionals of Liverpool Football Club had volunteered en masse for the Territorial Army. Within weeks they were called up for full-time military service. For thirty-year-old Matt Busby the timing was unfortunate. A war of any significant duration would almost certainly terminate his career as a top-class player. Liverpool had finished eleventh in the First Division in 1938/39, their highest placing since Kay and Busby had arrived at Anfield. Both believed that the side would win honours in the years ahead, a claim that is lent some substance by the fact that Liverpool, led by Kay, won the First Division championship when hostilities ceased in 1946/47.

War Office policy was that football should continue, but on an ad hoc basis, with professionals free to guest for whichever League club was nearest to their Force's base. It was further decided that when on duty professional sportsmen could best serve the war effort by acting as Physical Education instructors. Their experience and distinction would help keep the troops fit and in good heart.

Matt Busby's reputation preceded him into the Forces. Stanley Rous, later to become Sir Stanley and the most powerful legislator in the game, had been a first class referee. He was asked by the War Office to recommend 'suitable sports players' to join the Army and RAF Physical Training Staffs. Rous, who had refereed the 1934 Cup Final in which Busby played, now added Matt's name to the list of those considered officer material which he submitted to the authorities. After his initial training he was sent to Aldershot where he became an NCO with the title Company Sergeant-Major Instructor Busby. Matt continued playing throughout his spell in the Army as a guest for Reading, Aldershot, and Hibernian in Scotland. He won seven more international caps, the last of them when his country endured a crushing 6–1 defeat by England at Hampden Park in 1945.

More significantly, in terms of his future, Sergeant-Major Busby vindicated Stanley Rous's estimation of his leadership potential. When the Allies invaded Italy Busby was given command of the British Army team sent to entertain the troops behind the lines. His squad included some of the finest players in Britain, drawn from the most distinguished clubs in the game. As Officer-in-Charge of the team he was effectively its player-manager. The experience of managing these players, among them Joe Mercer, Frank Swift, Tommy Lawton and Cliff Britton, proved invaluable. Matt had been used to having influence at Liverpool, now he learned about power. He was responsible for training, tactics and selection of the team. Arthur Rowe, later to be one of the most respected post-war managers with Spurs, was Busby's second-in-command.

Wielding authority in these circumstances was more complex than at club level in peacetime. The imposition of discipline had to be tactful; this was war. Men (and women) tended to live for the day, easing the anxieties of the time by breaching the norms of behaviour that would apply in other circumstances. Busby's leadership was further complicated by the fact that the men he was responsible for were stars in their own right, their task now to play mere exhibition games, in which the normal imperatives of fitness and discipline were not as obviously important.

He wisely assessed the nature of his job and ruled with a light touch, fostering a co-operative rather than authoritarian régime. Tasks were delegated to each of his famous players. There were to be no gulfs between manager and players in this travelling football club. Joe Mercer was 'promoted' to 'messing officer' or scrounger-in-chief with responsibility for putting food on the table. Tommy Lawton and Frank Swift were jointly in charge of all baggage. Cliff Britton got the transport department. All felt committed to the success of the adventure. They were a happy crew.

Busby and his men lived much more closely than normal. Many hours were spent off-duty, hours of conversation and reminiscence, much of it light-hearted, some more reflective and serious. It was during these sessions that Busby discovered that the ills he had identified in football were widespread, common to the experience of players with the best of Britain's clubs. The Manchester City of his time had been the rule rather than the exception.

Listening to the great professionals gathered round him late at night behind the front line, Busby began to develop his convictions about his craft. However great the player, however renowned the club, the problems seemed to be the same. Pettiness, humiliation, greed and injustice, bullying and cheating, the gulf between master and slave ran deep and wide. Each anecdote confirmed this sorry reality.

The stories invariably featured managers who were either yes-men or bullies, occasionally both. Directors who blustered and bungled, who were snobs affecting disdain also figured, as well as footballers who were bitter, resentful and greedy. Before the war ended many of the ideas Busby had nurtured for years had taken shape, one more insistently than all the others; that a football club could not function without management that was firm yet fair. Directors who thought they could pick the team and use the manager as an errand-boy would have to be put in their place. Players who thought the game was awash with money, who were feckless, irresponsible or bullies would be subject to discipline, put very firmly in *their* place.

Power on a day-to-day basis must devolve to the man whose job it was to run the club, who was, after all, answerable to players, directors and supporters – the manager. All were dependent on each other. A football club should be like a family with a manager at its head. Sergeant-Major Matt Busby had redefined the role of the modern manager. He now had to find a football club that would let him have his way.

5

The Job

'Mr Busby has ideas and a rare
honesty of purpose.'

James Gibson, Chairman of
Manchester United

Manchester
15th December 1944

Dear Matt,

No doubt you will be surprised to get this letter from
your old pal Louis. Well Matt I have been trying for the
past month to find you and not having your Reg. address I
could not trust a letter going to Liverpool, as what I have
to say is so important. I don't know if you have considered
about what you are going to do when war is over, but I
have a great job for you if you are willing to take it on. Will
you get into touch with me at the above address and when
you do I can explain things to you better, when I know
there will be no danger of interception. Now Matt I hope
this is plain to you. You see I have not forgotten my old
friend either in my prayers or in your future welfare. I hope
your good wife and family are all well and please God you
will soon be home to join their happy circle.

Wishing you a very Happy Xmas and a lucky New Year.
With all God's Blessings in you and yours

Your Old Pal
Louis Rocca

Louis Rocca's letter was typical of him: a touch conspiratorial, a
dash of piety, mention of the 'good wife and family', signing off
'Your Old Pal'. Louis was everyone's old pal. He was a fixer
who'd served Manchester United for nearly fifty years when he
wrote to Matt Busby in late 1944. Louis had joined the club as a

tea-boy in the 1890s when United was still known as Newton Heath. He would occasionally claim that it was he who suggested the name Manchester United when the club decided to abandon the original Newton Heath in 1902. He was nineteen at the time. He must have been an influential office-boy.

When Louis wrote to Busby he held the titles assistant-manager and chief scout. The great job he referred to was manager of Manchester United. The club hadn't had a proper manager since Scott Duncan resigned in 1937. Club secretary Walter Crickmer had filled in as manager since Duncan's departure.

United had been Manchester's second club for almost twenty years, and during that time had survived some traumatic experiences, most of them to do with finance. J. H. Davis, who had saved the club in the early 1900s and financed the ambitions of Ernest Mangnall and Billy Meredith, died in October 1927. At a board meeting on 25 October the directors referred with 'reverence to the passing of the President, Mr. J. H. Davis, and deeply deplored his loss to the club'. The minutes of that meeting conclude, 'it was unanimously resolved that the deepest sympathy and condolences be conveyed to Mrs Davis and family in their sad bereavement and that she may be comforted by Divine Consolation in her very trying ordeal'.

The death of this great benefactor heralded the most desperate period in United's history. The club was in the First Division and, ironically, had felt economically secure enough just before Davis died to decide to clear the mortgage debt on the Old Trafford ground. By 1927 United had reduced a debt of £38,000 to £15,000. Always ambitious in Davis's time, the diminishing debt encouraged the ultimate aspiration to own the magnificent stadium at Old Trafford.

Three years later survival was back on the agenda. There were a number of contributory factors to this change of fortune. The depression of the late Twenties had grievously hurt the city and football had become a luxury fewer people could afford. More of them chose to spend their money watching City, who were riding high while United were struggling at the bottom of the first Division. In these trying times J. H. Davis's money and entrepreneurial flair were badly missed.

In the 1930/31 season these factors combined with a disastrous spell on the field to threaten United's existence as a Football League club. By mid-October 1930 they were bottom of the First Division. They had lost all eleven of their opening League fixtures, some spectacularly. After a 5–1 defeat by West Ham the Supporters' Club called a public meeting for Friday, 17 October, the eve of one of the season's most attractive home fixtures against the FA Cup holders, Arsenal. Over three thousand angry Mancunians packed Hulme Town Hall. United had stood on the brink of relegation every season since returning to the First Division in 1925, and the fans were ready to take the Board to task. They accused it of lacking ambition and, as a result, of spending no money on quality players. The Meredith–Roberts–Turnbull era had given United fans a penchant for stars. Now City was *the* club in Manchester, United's lack of enterprise having just been highlighted by their neighbour's signing of a whole forward line for big money.

To noisy acclaim the Hulme Town Hall gathering approved two motions proposed by Supporters' Club secretary, Mr Greenhough: 1) there was no confidence in the Board of Directors; 2) the following day's game against Arsenal would be boycotted. Among those who spoke against the second motion was Charlie Roberts, a hero of better days, who said the players had his 'deepest sympathy'.

It is impossible to gauge how successful the call for a boycott was. Newspapers speculated that the visit of Arsenal might attract a crowd of 50,000. However, it rained heavily in Manchester on the day and the attendance, estimated between 25,000 and 30,000 was probably only marginally affected by the anger expressed the previous night. United lost 2–1 to the Cup holders. Seven days later they lost 4–1 at Portsmouth.

With relegation inevitable, attendances slumped dramatically through the winter months. Only once in those darks days which preceded the drop to Division Two did the Old Trafford crowd exceed 10,000 and that was against Manchester City. On 4 May 1931 Manchester United drew 4–4 with Middlesborough at Old Trafford. Both clubs were going down. Both had gained just 22 points that season, the lowest total ever recorded in the

First Division. United had won seven games and conceded an astonishing 115 goals.

The season's final fixture, against Middlesborough, drew a mere 3,900 spectators to the magnificent ground Mangnall and Davis had conceived and built in the glorious early years of the century. There was, according to newspaper reports of May 1931, an uncanny atmosphere in Old Trafford that day. The terraces stood empty, the shouts of derision echoing through the empty grandstand. On this desperate afternoon those belonging to the club who were present to witness its darkest hour felt a tinge of envy for Herbert Bamlett, the hapless manager United had dismissed two months before.

Prominent among the mourners were Louis Rocca and Walter Crickmer, who was now the secretary-manager. Things would deteriorate rapidly through the coming months. The ultimate calamity of insolvency was a real threat, for the balance sheet for 1931 showed debt spiralling beyond control. The mortgage on the ground stood at £17,849.18s.8d. Sundry creditors were owed £11,222. The bank overdraft was £2,105 and cash in hand was only £12.12s.9d. There was no guardian angel to underwrite these debts. But United's plight attracted little sympathy. In the wider economy businesses were daily going to the wall.

Survival depended upon the contrasting talents of Rocca and Crickmer. Louis promised cheap players and undertook to spread his emollient charm around the city in search of a wealthy saviour. The sterner task of soothing creditors fell to Crickmer, who looked what he was, respectable, honest and competent. He begged the Brewery Company who held the mortgage on Old Trafford to allow the interest payments to lapse for a while. Permission to pay certain road charges in instalments was sought from Stretford Urban District Council. Both requests were granted, reluctantly. The Inland Revenue also settled for promises. Billy Behan, later to become United's renowned Irish scout, was a reserve goalkeeper at Old Trafford during this destitute period. 'We often sat in the dressing-room until half-one or two o'clock on a Friday waiting for our wages,' Behan remembers, 'but they always came.' In fact that was not the case. On Friday 18 December Walter Crickmer was politely but firmly turned away from the National Provincial Bank in Spring Gardens, Manchester. Crickmer returned empty-handed to the waiting players at Old Trafford. The game was up or so it seemed, until Louis Rocca's streetwise instinct led him to Mr J. W. Gibson, a partner in the Manchester clothing firm of Biggs, Jones, Gibson Ltd. Louis had heard a whisper that Jimmy Gibson, a man with various business interests, was an enthusiast who just might be persuaded to get involved if the worst came to the worst. That weekend Louis turned the trick.

Gibson immediately placed £2,000 at the club's disposal, enough to pay the wages for three weeks. Mr Gibson was a realist. He made it clear to the press that there would be limits to his generosity. If the public responded to the crisis by turning up to support the team, he pledged a more substantial sum of money would be made available to employ a new manager and buy good players. If, however, his initial gesture failed to touch the public's heart Gibson indicated that he would withdraw. Money was so tight that a decision was taken not to re-engage the band who entertained the crowds at Old Trafford. But as the band-master offered to reduce his fee to £2.2s.0d. per match the directors changed their minds.

On Christmas Day the people of Manchester played their part in salvaging their impoverished second football club: 33,312 spectators watched the team beat Wolves 3–2 in a Second Division game. Some measure of the depth of emotion which attended this occasion, engulfing all present, but particularly the players, can be gained by reflecting on the scoreline of the following day's return fixture at Molineux; Wolves won 7–0. Christmas Day had been enough to convince James Gibson; public and players had given their answer; glimpsing magic through the gloom, the agnostic benefactor was converted to the cause.

At a press conference the next day Gibson spoke enthusiastically about the revived club. He promised that old glory would be restored. Among those he publicly wished to thank was one C. E. Sutcliffe, Meredith's old adversary who, as Vice-President of the Football League, had approved the rescue package. Gibson thanked with equal sincerity the sender of 'a postal order for one shilling from a working man who said he was never able to get to matches on Saturdays but hoped that his mite would help to keep the old Club together'. Gibson closed his press conference with a reference to the ancient tenets promulgated in another context by King James I: 'A football interest,' Gibson proposed, 'was a very important factor in maintaining contented and healthy-minded workpeople.'

These dramatic events were watched from across the city by young Matt Busby who had recently survived traumas of his own and was now an established first team player at Maine Road. The rivalry between the two clubs had always been friendly. On 20 January 1932, City held their Annual Hot-pot and Social at the Stock Exchange Restaurant. In his afterdinner speech, City's chairman, Albert Hughes, urged his guests to do all they could to support United's fight for survival.

Louis Rocca had rendered United a great service. In the club's mythology Rocca is the football scout of infinite wisdom. The truth is that Louis knew more about people and the city of his birth than he did about the game. He wasn't so much a judge of a player as the man who knew a man who'd heard about a talented youngster. His resourcefulness proved to be one of Manchester United's greatest assets in the years between the Gibson rescue and 1944 when he wrote his carefully couched letter to Matt Busby.

The club's fortunes fluctuated wildly in the pre-war era. In 1934 United travelled to Millwall for the final Second Division game, needing a win to avoid relegation to the Third Division North. A new manager, Scott Duncan, had been appointed in 1932 but money remained a problem and on 5 May 1934, a fortnight after Matt Busby had won his FA Cup winner's medal with City, Millwall were favourites to gain a victory in a game that would ensure their own survival in the Second Division. Thirty-five thousand people packed The Den. Against the odds United silenced the raucous Docklands crowd by scoring two goals without reply, thus avoiding the humiliation of Division Three North. Later that Saturday night more than 3,000 jubilant United fans turned up at Central Station to welcome the team home.

In 1936 United won promotion back to the First Division only to be relegated again twelve months later. In 1937 Scott Duncan resigned. The club had decided on some policy changes which left Duncan feeling his position was untenable, and he left to manage non-league Ipswich Town. The main plank of United's new policy was to devote more money to ground improvements and concentrate on a youth policy through the newly created Manchester United Junior Athletic Club (MUJAC).

Although later credited to Matt Busby, the philosophy of producing home-bred youngsters was introduced by James Gibson in 1931. At a Board meeting that year Gibson spoke of 'the advisability of running a colts or nursery team from next season'. The principle laid down was that the job of cultivating young players 'must be thoroughly done to be effective, so that a common idea and technique shall unite the junior with the senior members of the playing staff'. The philosophy and indeed the language was identical to that espoused by Busby and Jimmy Murphy a decade later.

Walter Crickmer replaced Duncan with his old title of Secretary-Manager. Louis Rocca bearing the title Chief-Scout was in fact what might in these days be called Special Adviser to the Chairman, and anyone else who needed guidance on matters as diverse as the cost of footballs, the latest prodigy he'd heard of in Manchester schoolboy football, or how much to 'bung' in under-the-counter payments where they were necessary to seduce new signings. Rocca was responsible for the appointment of Tom Curry and Bill Inglis as trainers.

Three of the greatest players in Manchester United's history were acquired during this period when strictly speaking there wasn't a footballing brain on the administrative side of the club. Rocca is credited in United's history books with the signing of Johnny Carey, captain of the first great Busby team. An analysis of the Carey deal sheds some light on Rocca's *modus operandi*. He had heard of a player called Benny Gaughan who was playing with the Dublin club Bohemians. Together with Scott Duncan, then still in charge, Rocca travelled to Dublin in November 1936. Billy Behan who had retired to his native city acted, informally, as his old pal's guide in Dublin. They watched Gaughan and decided to sign him. They were told that the deal would cost £200. Not having cash they were stymied, because, as this would be an under-the-counter payment, they couldn't sign a cheque. It was agreed that they would return the following week with the money. Meanwhile, Glasgow Celtic snatched the prize from Bohemians for £300. Not knowing what had happened, Louis Rocca arrived back in Dublin, cash in hand. Billy Behan recalls, 'Louis was nearly crying. "Look," I told him, "there's a much better player than Gaughan in the country. Wait until Sunday and I'll take you to see him." ' Johnny Carey played brilliantly for St James's Gate on that Saturday and Rocca paid the £200 for his signature.

Louis Rocca's faith in Billy Behan was, arguably, as important as any footballing knowledge in the acquisition of Carey who was to become one of United's greatest players.

Jack Rowley was signed in equally unscientific circumstances. Jimmy Gibson liked to spend his weekends in the bracing air of Bournemouth. On a visit to the south coast in 1937 Gibson attended the local League club's fixture where he spotted Rowley and promptly did a deal which took the centre-forward to Old Trafford for £3,500.

Stan Pearson was signed from local junior soccer following a tip-off to Rocca, and later in 1938 a young wing-half called Chilton arrived from the north-east. That year United, managed by Walter Crickmer, regained First Division status.

James Gibson was not typical of the Boardroom class. He was an old-fashioned paternalist, a patron rather than a parasite, concerned not simply with success measured by cups, medals and glory, but with the greater good of the community to which he belonged. At the AGM of 1939 he expressed the following ambition when reporting another successful MUJAC season: 'It is from these unusually comprehensive nurseries that the Club hopes an all-Manchester team at some distant period might be produced.'

Between them Gibson, Rocca and Crickmer had laid extraordinary foundations for the kind of professional football club hitherto unknown, a club with a noble philosophy, the kind of institution Matt Busby had quietly aspired to belong to since he'd entered the professional game.

At United's last AGM before the war James Gibson spoke

proudly of the season just ended. The first team had finished fourteenth in the First Division. But, he argued, the club's promise for the future lay in the performances of the reserves and juniors. The reserves had won the Central League for the first time in eighteen years; the 'A' team, average age seventeen, had won the open-age Manchester League, and the MUJACs their division of the Chorlton League. 'We have,' Gibson proclaimed, 'no intention of buying any more mediocrities. In years to come we will have a Manchester United composed of Manchester players.'

A sad note was struck when the meeting was informed of the death of Charlie Roberts, 'the greatest captain Manchester United ever possessed'. A message of condolence was conveyed to Roberts's widow. Thirty years after he, Meredith and Bloomfield had been pilloried for seeking a just and decent world for professional players, Roberts was offered a valedictory morsel in a *Manchester Guardian* obituary which alluded to his 'great service to the game in the widest sphere'. Recalling his contribution to the formation of the Players' Union the *Guardian* concluded: 'Today the Union flourishes. It is not an unworthy memorial to a great player and a great sportsman.' The reality of the Players' Union of 1939 was that it was a mouse which seldom shouted, much less roared. Far from flourishing, the Union was neither a memorial to Roberts nor a vehicle for reform. Except as imagined in the noble thoughts of James Gibson and Matt Busby, professional soccer in 1939 was what it had always been, more a mirror on an indecent society than a memorial for decent men.

Matt Busby was excited by Louis Rocca's letter. He knew that United were looking for a manager and this was the job he'd secretly set his heart on. He was also aware of Rocca's influence at Old Trafford, particularly with Jimmy Gibson. Liverpool had already offered him a coaching job, as had Reading. Ayr United in Scotland promised the job of team manager. But Manchester United was the perfect opportunity provided the terms were right. Money wasn't going to be the issue, authority was what mattered. The ideas Busby had about the football manager's role were radical. He wanted to be Boss not office-boy. Being in charge was, he knew, different from being responsible. Responsibility without power held no attraction for him.

United was a big club in all but achievement. Their last major trophy, the First Division Championship, had been won in 1911. Expectations wouldn't be as great as at other equally large clubs, but Matt knew he would have time, and he knew United had some good players. The club had been pleased to finish fourteenth in 1939. Matt could do better than that.

The Rocca–Busby connection went back a long way. Louis Rocca was a Catholic, a Manchester Catholic who had met and admired Matt Busby, the Manchester City player.

The young Catholic footballer, stylish and dignified, had done well by his faith in a city bearing a residue of vicious anti-Catholic prejudice. A long time had passed since the *Manchester Guardian* had editorialised on newly arrived Irish Catholics as follows: 'The extensive immigration of poor Irish has inflicted a deadly blow upon the health and comfort of the working class. They are a most serious evil with which our labouring classes have to contend.' Louis Rocca and Paddy McGrath, Catholic friends of Matt, grew up contending with the legacy of hatred formed by diatribes such as this. It was tough being a Collyhurst Catholic in the Twenties. Catholicism in Collyhurst went back to the Reformation, after which it is claimed the first Catholic church bells rang in the local church. McGrath and Rocca could remember newspaper ads for jobs declaring, No Catholics or Jews need apply. This prejudice spilled over into sport. Paddy McGrath went to school with Charlie Stiles, Nobby's dad, at St Pats in Collyhurst: 'Charlie was a great footballer, but he'd no chance of playing for Manchester Boys. Catholics were never picked. Charlie played for North Manchester. That was it. Even the referees were biased against Catholic school teams. They used to have a cup called the Daily Dispatch Shield and the decisions went against us every time. Our teacher Mr McIvor finally stopped us entering the competition 'cause you wouldn't get a fair crack of the whip,' McGrath recalls.

To men like Rocca and McGrath, Matt Busby was more than a football idol. Busby was the most prominent Catholic in Manchester public life, a symbol of the faith to which he belonged, a Catholic admired and respected, around whom his co-religionists could proudly rally. Thus, Matt and Louis Rocca became acquainted, socialised and contributed wherever they could to the Catholic cause.

When he first arrived at Maine Road young Matt Busby was, according to McGrath, victim of a bigoted aside by a senior professional. 'There was a fella called Bell whose father was a Presbyterian minister, I think he was a Mason, who had a go at Matt early on. He was very hurt. I think he thought he'd left all that behind in Scotland.'

Manchester *was* different. There were more minorities than in most other English cities, all in their own way victims of prejudice. A census of Manchester and Salford towns in 1851 showed that of the 400,000 inhabitants 220,000 had been born elsewhere. The scope for serious bigotry was, therefore, somewhat limited. The outsiders, first or second generation Catholics, Jews, and Italians shared common ground, more acreage than the bigots. Manchester was *their* city although in the 20s and 30s this was yet to be established.

Matt Busby was drawn back to this cosmopolitan atmosphere. Manchester had the feel of a place where things weren't yet decided, where identity could be determined by the kind of person you were – and the things you did – rather than the tribe you belonged to; Manchester was still working out its identity. Football had played a significant role in the creation of the city's image of itself. Billy Meredith's flamboyance and his romantic rebellion against conservatism had found an echo in Manchester's soul. The outsider triumphant nourished this community which was, more than most, composed of drifters who had followed their star.

'The character of Manchester and Salford owes a great deal to the Irish/Jewish/Italian influences,' Harold Riley explains. 'Marx and Engels were Jews who lived and worked in Manchester and Salford. Engels owned Winterbothams Mill in Salford which was one of the most profitable businesses in the area. Marx worked in Manchester for a long time and Engels financed him. At the same time the Irish arrived in Manchester. They came up on the Ship Canal, they were called navigators, hence the origin of the word "navvy". But the Irish presence goes back a long way. The first Irish were brought there by the De Traffords. They were a Catholic family, and persecuted for it at the time of the Reformation, but they were the biggest land-owners in the area and owned the ground where United play, Old Trafford. The De Traffords brought the educated Irish as doctors, lawyers, solicitors and priests and they built a foundation in the community for the workers who came at the time of the Industrial Revolution.'

So for Catholics, whether Irish, Scots or Italian, Manchester was fertile ground for the planting of new roots. For the Busbys, Roccas and McGraths as for the Jews, there was a sense of place, of belonging. 'The Irish, Jewish and Italian communities formed an interesting triangle in the city,' Riley says.

Interesting and comforting, each minority had important shared values and characteristics. Family mattered. Loyalty to your own was a guiding principle. Characters, rogues with charm and humour, were part of every Jewish/Irish/Italian family's folklore. There was a Jimmy Greer in most outsiders' families, and a tolerance for human frailty, for the generous, the extravagant, the big-spender who was just as often 'skint'. Desperation was understood, as was forgiveness. These were warm, sensuous people, earthy in a most un-English way.

The Protestant ethos of men like Sir Harry Platt, the founder of the great engineering works in the nineteenth century, was present too, its values espoused by the Scottish and Welsh working-classes who worked alongside the Catholics in factory and mill. But Italian charm and Irish laughter mellowed all but the fiercest adherents to Protestantism. The blood of Manchester was mixed in delightful proportion. It seemed to Matt Busby the most human of places when he contemplated going back in 1945.

That humanity was reflected at all levels in the city's cultural life. The pubs filled up in the evening and nightclubs and dancehalls were full and merry. The laughter was good-natured, often self-deprecating. Inhibitions were cast away in the seductive gloom of a Manchester night, as people whose souls had been touched by hardship reached with lusty relish for fruit scarce or forbidden on other nights when money was short or the guilt of an Irish, Jewish, Italian psyche

95

prevailed, conscience winning the battle with the spirit. Manchester wasn't Paris or New York, but it wasn't Birmingham, Sheffield or London either. There was a hint of Rome or Dublin, without the decadence of Protestantism purging *its* angst. The gloom of this city was lit by gaiety. Manchester was a small town, everything was within feeling or touching distance. You could play or not. You could simply console yourself that raw and generous life was in town if you wanted.

Manchester's culture was further enriched by its thriving theatrical tradition. Harold Riley remembers: 'When we were at school we had phenomenal theatrical contests. It was from this that people like Albert Finney and Sheelagh Delaney, Jimmy Jewel, and Ben Kingsley emerged. The actors Robert Powell and Bernard Hill, Dame Wendy Hiller and the playwrights Trevor Griffiths and Robert Bolt all hailed from this unusual provincial city. Miss Horniman's famous theatre was in Manchester and she would bring stars like Dame Sybil Thorndyke and Lewis Cassell from the United States. Beckett put on his first nights here, it was tradition that attracted him.'

Others were attracted by the dog tracks, the racecourse and the gambling clubs, legal and illegal. You could sample most of life's pleasures, high-life and low, within a square-mile or two of the city's heart. Sport and culture dissolved all differences: Matt Busby, Sir John Barbirolli, Beckett, Dame Sybil Thorndyke and in Salford Lowry the painter making his matchstick men and women. Harold Riley, a Fellow of the Royal Academy, illustrates how cohesive and different from London this town was. The gap between art and sport was narrower, between people of all kinds and classes. Sport was very often the binding force as Riley explains: 'I was born in Salford and have lived here practically all my life. My father and brother were City supporters. I was always a United fan because of Stan Pearson. The Pearson family lived on the same road as we did and Stan was a great idol. His brother Albert, the younger brother, was a very fine footballer and he used to play with us.'

Riley was born on 31 December 1934. 'I went to the local grammar school and from there to a state school which is part of the University of London. I won a painting scholarship which allowed me a year in Rome and another year in Florence. Then I had a British Council scholarship which enabled me to live wherever I wanted for a year. I chose Castille. Not many people wanted to go to Spain in the Fifties. After two years National Service I came back to Salford in the early Fifties. The purpose of coming back was to continue the project of L. S. Lowry. He started to paint Salford at the beginning of the century, to record the place, which is the work I continue.'

Riley was a gifted young footballer who played for Salford Boys. 'I always went to Old Trafford when I could.' Once he persuaded Lowry to go with him. 'He was a life-long City supporter,' Riley smiles, 'who had vowed he would never go on United's ground. We went one Saturday. I took him to the place I always stood, not the Stretford End, the other end where the old scoreboard used to be. I stood there for years with a few cronies. Lowry amazed me by describing very clearly and lucidly – he even made sketches for me – how he remembered all of the Meredith era. He told me in absolute detail of a game between Manchester City and Brighton Towers, who were a first division team at that stage, and how Billy Meredith mesmerized everyone present.'

Through the Arts, theatre and sport, Manchester people got to know each other. There was nothing contrived, as at other times in other places there would be, about the attendance at Old Trafford of the painters Riley and Lowry. This was not the Dickie Attenborough-at-Chelsea syndrome. It seemed as natural for the painters to be on the terraces at Old Trafford alongside clerks and factory workers as for the self-made businessman to attend Miss Horniman's Theatre or Beckett's first night. The communal intimacy was real and entertainment, the Arts and sport were the points of contact. One night Barbirolli would perform with the Hallé orchestra, the next Frank Sinatra would play the same venue. The audiences would not be identical but there would be a surprising number of the same faces and many of them would not be unknown at the racecourse or at Old Trafford or Maine Road.

Ideas about respectability were not formed as rigidly in Manchester as elsewhere. Almost everyone had a past of kinds, old money was rare. There was no aristocracy, except of those who made things or sold them or otherwise excelled, even if it was only at the art of living. The Prince of Punters, Alex Bird was a fabled Mancunian. He was born in the converted Travellers' Rest pub in Newton Heath where his coal merchant father was a part-time street bookmaker. His legendary tilts at the betting ring made him one of the few who have ever become wealthy through professional gambling. As a result of successful gambles – 'investments' he liked to call them – Bird acquired a series of Rolls Royces, his own aeroplane, a string of racehorses and a sixteenth-century moated manor house set in twenty-five acres of lush Cheshire land.

The great Blondini was a Gorton lad of Irish descent, Mike Costello. He achieved worldwide fame when he was buried in a coffin for seventy-eight days at Belle Vue for a £500 wager. Another favourite Blondini stunt was to be in an ordinary coffin blown apart by dynamite.

Alcock and Brown, the men who made the first Atlantic crossing by air in 1919 were Manchester men, Brown from Chorlton-cum-Hardy, Alcock from Ladybarn. Both were pupils of Manchester Central High School. They were knighted after their historic flight.

This uniquely human town that was so short on snobbery and bitterness was the place Matt Busby wanted to live in. There was another side to his character, a private personality curiously at odds with the gentlemanly mien of public perception. He was no playboy, but he loved characters whose spirits were freer than his own. Jimmy Greer would have loved Manchester, its looseness, its *joie de vivre*, its tolerance. Matt didn't play but he liked to spectate, to be in the company of larger-than-life characters in his leisure time. He also liked a bet on dogs and horses, a serious bet which meant one that hurt a little if you lost. From his playing days he frequented the Belle Vue and White City greyhound tracks and never missed the chance to go racing. He drank little, the odd beer to be sociable. In good company he was good company, occasionally at parties he would give a fine rendition of Harry Lauder's 'I Belong to Glasgow'. One of the happy enduring memories of his youth was of going to the Glasgow Empire with Jimmy Greer to see the great music hall acts of the day. Jean had matured into a vivacious woman. She loved to go to the shows and her easy warm personality made her the perfect companion for Matt who, when not in the company of intimates, was uneasy with the banality of cocktail-party chatter. Jean loved Manchester. She knew more than most about being an outsider. Manchester's comforting, cosmopolitan embrace was as soothing for her as for her eminent husband.

Busby's public persona won him admiration and respect. The private man attracted affection. In the company of football people, rogues and colourful self-made men, the kind of company he liked to keep, he was affable and generous. He didn't want to be the life and soul of the party, yet he loved the banter, the light undemanding hail-fellow-well-metship of dog-track, pub or party.

The Catholic Sportsmen Club met in such an atmosphere. The Club met several times a year at social functions put on to raise money for charity. The patrons were the better off Catholics in Manchester. The Sportsmen Club was a way of keeping in touch – with each other and their roots – and of raising money for the less well off members of their tribe, many of whom were new immigrants to the city. Louis Rocca was a prominent member of the Club to whose activities Matt had always contributed by his presence. It was Rocca who arranged for Matt to see James Gibson about the United job. The meeting, initiated by Busby, took place when he was on leave from his Army duties in early February 1945.

Busby and Gibson met at Cornbrook Cold Storage, one of the businessman's companies about a mile from Old Trafford. They found much common ground. Busby impressed Gibson. Reporting to his Board of Directors on 15 February, Gibson spoke of 'Mr Busby's ideas and honesty of purpose'. This dry, minuted reference to their first meeting hardly conveys the intensity of the discussion which took place. Gibson's vision of what a football cllub should be was not in conflict with Busby's own ideas. The question they focused on was how best their shared vision could be achieved. For Busby the time for deference had passed. Always respectful of authority, or at least capable of projecting respect, Sergeant-Major Busby now demanded that the post of manager of Manchester United should carry with it power commensurate to the responsibility he would bear. As manager he insisted on managing. He would appoint his own staff and exercise absolute control over all matters that affected the playing side of the game. What Busby thought was, as he remembers, 'unheard of at the time'. The 'honesty of purpose' alluded to in Gibson's account of their meeting was diplomatic language for the degree of uncompromising conviction with which Busby outlined his views on the role of the manager. The ideas were radical, revolutionary even, yet they were presented in a reasoned low-key manner which was impressive. Offered a three-year contract, Busby explained that the kind of club he and Gibson aspired to would take time to build, and a five-year agreement would therefore be more appropriate.

Any reservations Gibson may have had about the demands being made of him were balanced by Busby's assurance that he would not be extravagant with the club's money; on the contrary, he declared, financial prudence would be of the essence, a fundamental value, of the club he proposed to lead. From Billy Meredith's time, through the years when Busby himself had arrived at Maine Road only to be discouraged by City's decision to purchase a complete forward-line in one expensive raid on the transfer-market, Manchester's football clubs had traditionally sought to buy success. That was not the route Busby would choose, he assured James Gibson. Success would require prudence, patience and hard work.

On 19 February 1945, Company Sergeant-Major Instructor Matt Busby was publicly confirmed as Manchester United's new manager. The appointment, for five years, would date from one month after his demobilisation. His salary would be £750 per annum. And he *would* be manager in more than name only.

6

Confident Start

> 'Bullying could only bring instant
> obedience, never lasting results.'

Matt Busby

Matt Busby rarely acted on impulse, yet when he asked Jimmy
Murphy to join him at Old Trafford he cast aside his normal
caution. An Allied victory was certain when Busby and Murphy
met in Bari in south-east Italy. Sergeant Murphy was in charge
of a service sports recreation centre for troops who'd defeated
Rommel's Afrika Korps in the Western Desert. One afternoon
Matt wandered down to the sports centre. In a far corner of the
soccer pitch he saw a group of young soldiers gathered round a
figure he recognised.

Busby strolled over to the group and stood on the fringe, as
unobtrusively as he could. At this stage of the game few pro
footballers took their Army duties too seriously – the war was
over, it was time to relax – and most NCOs in Sergeant
Murphy's position would have been larking about. Murphy,
however, was preaching football to his men with all the passion
of an evangelist. Jimmy saw Matt but he didn't pause; duty first,
old acquaintance afterwards.

Busby was a renowned figure by the time he encountered
Jimmy Murphy on this sweltering late summer Italian afternoon. Matt was captain of Scotland, having won seven caps in
wartime internationals. Although he never betrayed his
feelings, Busby believed, as did most other observers, that
anti-Catholic bigotry had denied him his rightful place on
Scottish teams before the war. He wouldn't have been the first
Scottish Catholic to be discriminated against in this manner.
The great Hughie Gallacher from Bellshill had been a victim of
the Scottish FA's unstated conviction that 'Tims' should only be

honoured as a last resort. Scotland's wartime record against England was appalling and included a record 8–0 thrashing at Maine Road in October 1943. In such circumstances Matt Busby's claims could no longer be ignored.

The news that Busby was to take over as Manchester United's manager had reached Jimmy Murphy. Like everyone else in football, Murphy sensed that the man standing listening to him on this sports field in Bari was going places. But Jimmy was more interested in the job of the moment than pausing to introduce this distinguished observer, even though to do so would have been good politics, boosting his own standing in front of his men, by being familiar with the famous Matt Busby. He talked zealously on. Busby was impressed by his passion, and by his devotion to duty. These men weren't footballers, there was no profit to be gained from evangelising to them. Most would have thought it a waste of an afternoon but not a born teacher, someone with a vocation and an untarnished love of the game.

When Jimmy was finished, Matt offered him a job at Old Trafford. It wouldn't be easy, Busby explained. Old Trafford had been bombed in 1941 and there was no prospect of playing games there in the foreseeable future. United were heavily in debt. Money would not be available to buy players. They would have to work with what they found and develop young players themselves. That would be Jimmy's task. Impressed by Busby's quiet assurance, Murphy accepted without hesitation.

Jimmy was thirty-five. He'd been a first class player with West Brom, winning twenty-two Welsh caps. During the summer of '39 he'd been transferred to Swindon Town for whom as it turned out he never kicked a ball. Busby and he were acquainted only through playing against each other. 'Tapper' Murphy as he was called because of his fierce tackling, had been a wing-half. With West Brom and Wales he'd been on losing sides more often than not. Yet he was always the last man beaten. He'd hound opponents while railing against colleagues who wanted to pack it in. Jimmy was honest and hungry.

Character was then, as now, a much parroted buzzword in professional soccer. Few understood what it meant, but Matt Busby did. Of course battling to the final whistle showed character. But that was only part of the story. Character could be assessed in other ways: how you trained; how you behaved towards kids in the dressing-room; how you lived away from the game; whether the ruthless business of professional soccer had drained you of generosity, corroding your spirit with cynicism. In Jimmy Murphy Busby saw a man untainted by the hazards of his occupation. The Welshman was decent, honest and, unlike Busby, openly, uninhibitedly emotional.

When he chose Jimmy Murphy Matt followed his instincts. His experience with George Kay at Liverpool also pointed him in Jimmy's direction. Busby's admiration for Kay was not diminished by his former boss's apparent failure to contain his emotions. 'George was a real grafter throughout his managerial career,' Busby reflected in his autobiography. 'He was often misunderstood because he could never control his feelings during a match. George was a familiar figure on the trainer's bench: shouting, beseeching, wringing his hands, holding his head in apparent anguish, and making an excellent attempt to head and kick every ball in the match. Perhaps he took his football too seriously, but a fanatical enthusiasm for his job – *which could never be condemned* – was entirely responsible for those odd mannerisms.'

Kay's fanatical enthusiasm had proved compatible with Busby's eloquent control. In Murphy Busby saw the image of his old mentor. Time would show that Jimmy was an inspired choice.

Murphy's background was uncannily similar to Busby's. Murphy was a Catholic from the Rhondda mining village of Pentre. His father was an Irishman from Kilkenny who had emigrated to find work down the coalmines in the early 1900s. Jimmy's mother was a widow with six children from her first marriage when she met and married his father. Florence was Welsh Chapel, William an Irish Catholic. Jimmy, their only child, grew up a Catholic in a happy home where all his step-brothers and sisters were Protestants.

Like Nellie Busby Jimmy's mother wanted her son to be a teacher. Football interfered with this ambition. Jimmy was a good scholar and, in his early teens, a promising musician who played the organ in Treorchy Parish Church. But he was also an outstanding footballer, representing Wales in schoolboy internationals before West Brom arrived in Pentre to offer a career in the professional game.

Despite his success as a player Jimmy Murphy remained a plain man without conceit or affectation. When the business was done he was a cheerful companion. He liked a pint of ale. He liked to drink it in the tap-room. He smoked Sweet Afton. Jimmy was a committed Catholic who took the Sacraments of Confession and Holy Communion every week. His language would make a sailor blush.

The deal as Busby outlined it was that Jimmy would run United's reserve team, and coach the youngsters on Tuesday and Thursday nights at the club's training ground, The Cliff in Lower Broughton. Busby would take care of the first team on Saturdays and both would share the day-to-day training. Busby had no revolutionary ideas about physical conditioning. Keeping fit was a simple business; for the first hour of a normal morning players would lap the pitch, gradually increasing the pace from a jog to three-quarter speed for a couple of laps, ending with, perhaps, three or four flat out gallops. This work would be broken with a lap of walking or slow jogging during which players chatted among themselves.

Occasionally the lads would put on spikes for a sprinting session. On Fridays a few laps and a few sprints would suffice. When heavier work was required it would consist of long road runs or a forty-five-minute session running up and down the mounds of wild slag that surrounded the Cliff which bordered Manchester Racecourse. Later, when Old Trafford was restored in 1949, the severest morning's work would entail running up and down the terraces.

Where Busby did depart from conventional wisdom was about the availability of the ball during the week. On the business of keeping fit he believed that the right types – the kinds of players he proposed having at United – would look after themselves. As far as the ball was concerned footballers couldn't have too much of it. A popular cliché of the time in professional football was that if they didn't see the ball during the week players would be 'hungry' for it on Saturday. This,

Busby knew, was quack psychology. Every morning's training at his club would be climaxed by a game. He and Jimmy would play on opposite sides. They would inject a bit of needle to make sure the contest was keen.

The notion of a manager in a tracksuit was barely conceivable to the professional players who began to drift back to United after demobilisation. For Busby his presence on the training ground was the essence of the new philosophy he intended to bring to professional football. The club was a family, *his* family, there would be no secrets, no gaps in communication, no misunderstandings. His office door was always open, he told the players during his first meeting with them. Not just for football problems, for anything, however personal and seemingly remote from the game.

His early experiences in Manchester had taught Matt that nothing which affected a player's life was irrelevant to his performance on Saturday. Jean had had a series of miscarriages before Sheena their first child was born which had troubled Matt to the point where his game suffered. Nobody had given a damn. His troubles were personal and therefore deemed to be his own business. He knew different. If a player's performance suffered it was football business. You were expected to dedicate your whole life to football not just the time you spent at the ground. The club had a duty, if for no better reason than self-interest, to care about your person as well as your body. Jimmy McMullen had cared for him, which really amounted to doing City's business for them. When Sheena was born at home she'd been a 'blue-baby'. Only the kindness and nursing knowledge of City goalkeeper Len Langford's wife, a neighbour, had saved the child's life. Peter Hodge, City's manager, probably never even knew Jean was pregnant.

Matt Busby wanted to know everything. If a player had a gambling debt, that was Manchester United's problem. If someone drank too much, or was enduring family or domestic troubles of any kind Matt wanted to know. The training ground was the place to find out about his people. Manchester United's professional footballers *were* people. This was one of Busby's fundamental principles. Every experience of his life, good and bad, now converged to form a philosophy whose aim was

105

transform the nature of a professional football club. Human beings had weaknesses, inhibitions and individual traits. All must be accommodated provided the basic character was sound. Matt Busby's reference points ranged from Jimmy Greer, to the loss of his father, his victimisation as a result of casual callousness at Maine Road, the contrasting career-saving kindnesses of Jimmy McMullen, Len Langford, and Phil McCloy. He knew what it was like to be vulnerable, to have your family life traumatised by death or alcoholism and to have the spirit knocked out of you by incidental cruelties. A bruised person was a diminished footballer.

In the winter of 1945, for the first time in his life, Matt Busby was in a position to enforce his will. Busby's understanding of the critical link between the private individual and the public performer, between person and professional, would serve to distinguish his teams from those managed by others, like Stan Cullis and Cliff Britton, who had played in the pre-war era. Cullis and Britton had identified many of the same ills that Busby had: the fecklessness; the conceits of the best players which inevitably led to resentments and poor team spirit; the lack of discipline, organisation and, frequently, basic fitness. As Cullis and Britton understood it, the cure for professional football's endemic ills was discipline, rigorously imposed. Freedoms would be abused if granted. Rules were laid down. Britton, for example, would not tolerate drinking under any circumstances. Everton players returning from a match in London would have to make do with soft drinks. Busby, in contrast, would have a couple of crates of beer in the home team dressing-room immediately after the game.

Stan Cullis terrified his Wolves players, to considerable effect the records show. His anger was legendary, his loud denunciations reverberating down many a football corridor, the echo of recrimination often reaching the opposition dressing-room, where it afforded some comfort and amusement. The Wolves training ground was not a place to betray weakness. Men worked as they would play: vigorously, relentlessly, the régime designed to make Saturday afternoon a relatively tolerable experience.

The destiny of professional football was, like any other

business, shaped by the formative experiences of those who inherited power and responsibility. The new men would not repeat the mistakes of the old men.

Busby and Cullis, who were to become the most influential football managers in the fifteen years after the war, had experienced contrasting fortunes as players. Cullis grew up in Ellesmere Port, an ordinary schoolboy and youth player, who failed even to be selected for Cheshire Boys. Hard work got him to Wolves, where the renowned disciplinarian Major Frank Buckley was manager. Cullis blossomed under his authoritarian regime. He thrived as a result of discipline and application, the former imposed by the fearsome Major, the latter a consequence of Stan's own desperate desire to make his way in the game. He was a centre-half, a destructive rather than creative force, who by his early twenties was England centre-half and captain. Discipline worked for Cullis. He fulfilled himself as a footballer to a greater extent than Busby did, although both careers were foreshortened by the war. When he took over as Wolves manager, Cullis applied the Buckley philosophy which had served his career so well.

Matt Busby had not really fulfilled himself in League football. One FA Cup medal and a solitary peacetime game for Scotland were scant rewards for his talent. The years at City had been, as often as not, frustrating. Liverpool provided a relatively obscure stage for a player of his potential. If Cullis, the redoubtable striver, was the quintessential Englishman, Busby, reared on the spellbinding wit and imagination of Alex James and Hughie Gallacher, was a Scot to the core. A creative player himself, Matt, while acknowledging that discipline and application were fundamental virtues, knew that there was more to football than efficiency. Beauty, the exquisite touch, the impudent verve of the Wee Wembley Wizards, icons of the Scottish tradition, this was what Matt Busby loved and what he sought as a manager. Brilliance was not, he believed, a by-product of obedience.

'Bullying,' he observed, 'could only bring instant obedience and never lasting results.' Obedience off the field would yield mere comformity when the stadium was packed. In essence the Buckley/Cullis philosophy proposed that players couldn't be trusted. Busby's deepest conviction about the game on the field was that it belonged to players. They *had* to be trusted.

When Sergeant-Major Matt Busby was demobbed in October 1945, he and Jean, and their children Sheena and Sandy, moved to a semi-detached club-owned house in Chorlton, a couple of miles from Old Trafford. Old Trafford was then a bomb-damaged ruin, so Manchester United FC was administered from a small office in James Gibson's Cornbrook Cold Storage depot. Busby shared this room with Walter Crickmer, a young assistant Les Olive, and a typist borrowed from Gibson's business. To reach the Cliff for training on Tuesday and Thursday evenings Busby took two bus rides, one to Victoria Bus Station in Manchester, the second from there to the training ground at Lower Broughton in the heart of Salford. This journey took an hour.

When Busby took over at Manchester in October 1945, United were in sixteenth position in the Northern League and most of the players were still in the Forces. The first team he fielded, against Bolton Wanderers at Maine Road, was: Crompton, Walton, Roach, Warner, Whalley, Cockburn, Worrall, Carey, Smith, Rowley and Wrigglesworth.

This was a makeshift side, deprived of the services of most of the better players on United's books who had yet to return from wartime duties. The Bolton match was Johnny Carey's first for two years. Missing from this first Busby team were players who would subsequently distinguish themselves in United's colours such as Pearson, Mitten, Morris, Chilton, and Aston. One by one they would drift back from the Forces, but it would be the beginning of the following season, in which the Football League proper would resume, before Busby could field the team he wanted. Meanwhile he assessed his situation and improvised with team selection to such good effect that United finished his first season in fourth position in the League North table.

When, during this transitional period, Matt reflected on the challenge he faced he realised that the good news outweighed the bad. Having no home ground to play on was, he felt, the most serious disadvantage to be overcome. United's empty bank account was of lesser concern to him. Peace had fostered optimism in the country at large, a fact that was reflected in football by a rapidly inflating transfer-market. Matt had virtually no money to spend but he wasn't too bothered by that. He knew that you couldn't buy success. He knew that Charlie Mitten, Chilton, Stan Pearson and Johnny Morris were quality players around whom he could build a side, and that there was much more satisfaction working to improve players than attempting the short-cut of paying large sums of money for footballers moulded by others. Busby believed in himself.

During the first season in charge his confidence in his own judgement received a couple of spectacular boosts. Henry Cockburn and Johnny Carey were inside-forwards when Busby arrived. Cockburn, a twenty-two-year-old Manchester lad recruited by Louis Rocca from an outstanding local junior club, Goslings; Carey, the Irishman, signed pre-war also by Rocca. Cockburn and Carey could play but, as inside-forward, neither made much impact.

Cockburn had joined United in 1944. He'd come with a big local reputation. 'We played Tranmere Rovers at Maine Road in one of Matt's first matches,' Henry recalls, 'I don't think he liked what he saw of me as an inside-forward. The next Tuesday he said he was going to try me at wing-half. That was it. I did well facing the ball.' Henry Cockburn did more than well. Within weeks he was being talked of as a future England player, which he became the following September. Cockburn stood less than five feet five inches in height, but Busby didn't care about that because the little fellow could tackle, was superb in the air and, above all, could play football.

Manchester City had taken two years to discover how best to use Matt. The imaginative redeployment of Henry Cockburn was achieved within a fortnight. Busby wanted his team to play football from the back, so moving forwards to defensive positions served his abiding philosophy about how the game should be played. He knew from his own playing days that forwards could adapt to become good defenders. He had done so himself. Defending was about brain more than brawn, about reading the game rather than lunging tackles. Good players were good players. They could all read the game. Good players had sound instincts. Most of the really important aspects of defensive play were matters of judgement; what position to take, *when* to tackle, when not; anticipation solved most of the problems, muscle very few. The basic principles of football applied throughout the field. Busby was convinced the bonus of converting forwards to defenders was twofold; forwards were usually more mobile than the typical defender of the immediate post-war age who – the best excepted – tended to be employed for purely destructive reasons. Football, as conceived by Busby, was about creation first; destruction was a necessary second principle.

The successful conversion of Henry Cockburn from ordinary inside-forward to international class wing-half was worth around £12,000 to United. This was a huge sum of money at the time, but Busby was pleased beyond monetary measure. His conviction that knowledge of the game and imagination were the most priceless assets a football club could possess was substantially reinforced.

Johnny Carey's problem took longer to solve. Carey was approaching his twenty-seventh birthday. He'd been at United almost ten years, six of them, of course, wiped out by the war. Carey's persona was infinitely more impressive than his early performances for Busby. The man was cool, well-mannered and intelligent, he dressed impeccably and read the more serious newspapers, he trained hard. A devout Catholic, Carey didn't swear or drink: Johnny was what people thought of as a model pro. He was a leader, a natural leader, similar in many respects to the younger Matt. Busby respected Carey and made him captain of the side.

The problem was that this fine character was no more than a journeyman inside-left. Charlie Mitten who played outside Carey remembers, 'Johnny was a bloody terrible inside-left, he was a bad player, slow and cumbersome. He wasn't up to it in the First Division.' Nor was this paragon of outsiders' perception too popular in the dressing-room. Johnny was not one of the lads. He was quiet and distant. When more exuberant spirits like Mitten – with whose mum he'd lodged for two years after he arrived in England – Cockburn or Johnny Aston started messing, Carey's manner would indicate disapproval. He had short arms and long pockets; he was careful with his money, a fault according to the dressing-room code. One man's Right Type is another man's pain in the arse.

110

Busby knew the score. He wanted Carey's poise to be the hallmark of his team. Carey's character was a plus in his manager's book, a desirable counterpoint to the inevitable raucousness of dressing-room life.

Carey's character should be seen in broader perspective than that afforded by his dressing-room peers. In 1939 when war was declared he could have chosen, as most Irishmen did, to return to the safety of Dublin. Instead Johnny volunteered to fight against Hitler for the country in which, as he pointed out, 'I earn my living.' Character judgements made on the basis of dressing-room consensus can only be trusted up to a point. On all bar match days the atmosphere is a mixture of barrack-room and school playground. There is little tolerance for individuality of a certain kind; for the fellow who doesn't join in, who fails to conform to the group ethos, which is more often than not based on values more appropriate to adolescence. Thus, Henry Cockburn today remembers Carey's carefulness with money, 'he were tight were Johnny', rather than his war service. Johnny Giles, who arrived at Old Trafford over a decade after Carey left, recounts an anecdote about Busby's captain current in his time: 'They say he was mean all right. He and Jack Crompton. They used to sit at the front of the bus on the way into town after training in case the bus-conductor reached them first and they'd have to pay for the other lads at the back.' By such criteria men were judged 'good lads' or not.

Care must also be taken when assessing Carey's ability as an inside-forward. He undoubtedly needed more time around the ball than was available in the First Division. But he was technically good, with excellent control, and a fine passer of the ball. In United's last home game before Old Trafford was bombed in 1941, Carey, on leave from the Army, scored a hat-trick against Bury in League North.

Nevertheless, in the team Busby was constructing there was no place for mere competence. What to do with Carey continued to torment Busby for several months. His captain's fallibility also led Matt into serious conflict with his Board of Directors. During one home game at Maine Road a board member, Mr Harold Hardman, loudly and pointedly questioned the manager's perseverance with the Irishman. 'How he can keep picking him God only knows,' Hardman remarked within earshot of Busby.

Busby, incensed, confronted Hardman in the gents toilet at half-time: 'Never dare say anything like that to me again in front of people,' Busby warned him. Not content with this rebuke, Busby placed an item, 'Interference by Directors', on the agenda for the next board meeting. It was, Busby felt, particularly important to confront Hardman. A small, wiry Manchester solicitor, Hardman had played with distinction as an amateur. He had won an Olympic Gold Medal for Great Britain in 1908 and was at one time on Everton's books. If Busby's position was to be undermined, Hardman was best placed to do the job. On the other hand, if Hardman could be faced down, other, less well informed directors, would take note. James Gibson ensured that Busby's arguments were listened to at the ensuing board meeting. A crucial principle had been established.

As soon as an opportunity presented itself Busby dropped Carey back to right-half. The move was successful. The old solution proved even more effective when chance allowed Busby to push his captain into the right-fullback position towards the end of the '45/'46 season. 'The further back Johnny moved the better he became,' Henry Cockburn confirms. 'He was still slow, there was an outside-left at Huddersfield, Metcalfe, who used to do him, but he was good.'

Charlie Mitten adds, 'Johnny made himself a player by his own efforts.' Johnny Carey is remembered as one of the game's greatest players. He played in nine different positions for Manchester United and captained the Rest of Europe against Great Britain in 1948. He became the leader Busby was looking for. Perhaps more than any other player, Carey confirmed Busby's belief that the qualities of character and intelligence, sensitively nurtured in the right environment, were indispensable to a football club. Ability on its own would never be enough. There were other less tangible personal qualities, other, that is, than power, pace and skill, from which the character of a player, a team and ultimately a football club could, indeed must, be wrought. The lessons applied to crack the Carey problem were those of Busby's playing days.

When he took stock of his first season's work Matt Busby had cause for satisfaction. Two other positional adjustments had further shaped the team which would embark on the 1946/47 season, the first full post-war League campaign. Chilton was moved from wing-half to centre-half and Johnny Aston from inside-forward to left-back. Jimmy Delaney was signed from Celtic for a bargain-basement fee of £4,000 to add width and pace to United's right flank. The signing of Delaney was a gamble. Bald-headed, an awkward mover, the Scot didn't look the part and bore the nickname 'Brittle-bones' because of his proneness to injury. But time proved the sceptics wrong, and many years and many great players later Busby could claim that Jimmy Delaney was his most inspired acquisition in a transfer-market he never really trusted.

On a broader front Busby felt the club was assuming the identity he desired. Wherever he looked there were good people: Jimmy Murphy was his own choice; others he felt fortunate to have inherited. Louis Rocca, for example would tackle any problem and solve most. If footballs were scarce, Louis knew a man who'd give them a deal. The cost of training gear was a worry? Leave it to Louis. And he was good at his designated job as well. Louis, chief-scout, always knew where the latest schoolboy prodigy was playing. His contacts were spread far and wide, from Ireland – North and South – to Scotland, Wales and all corners of England, the South excepted.

Tom Curry and Bill Inglis were Rocca protégés hired as trainers in 1934. Tom's title was First Team Trainer, Bill looked after the reserves. Once more the titles are inadequate to define the contributions made by Curry and Inglis. Together they ran the United dressing-rooms at the Cliff and Maine Road. A football club's soul is located in the dressing-room. The spirit emanating from this room will touch everyone, colour every aspect of club life. A dressing-room changes day-to-day, hour to hour, the mood swinging from carefree to sombre depending on all kinds of things other than results. Jealousy and resentment are harboured here, alongside pride, fulfilment and hope. Fear is also present, despair as well. Emotion is high in this unique workshop-cum-playground. Every man will have his day – good and bad – the wounds are bare for all to see, the glittering jewel of victory or preferment visible also, incongruously adjacent, reminding the losers of the fine line between success and failure.

The nature of a dressing-room is determined by the senior players and the men like Curry and Inglis for whom it is a home. 'Tosher' Curry looked and dressed like a fairly prosperous suburban shopkeeper. He and Bill wore white coats over their street clothes. They did everything but the job of training the team, implicit in their titles. They bandaged wounds, rubbed liniment on aching limbs, laid out the kit for training, and on match days Tosher and Bill also filled the baths, made the tea and acted as foremen overseeing the various tasks – from cleaning the boots to scrubbing the baths – allocated to the youngsters on the ground staff. Tosher and Bill catered for every dressing-room need, knowing more, in many ways, about the men they looked after than 'The Boss' or Jimmy.

Curry was quick-witted, his wry, earthy Mancunian sense of humour enabling him to give as good as he got in the banter stakes. He was a droll character who wouldn't stand for any nonsense, yet treated men like men. Tosher smoked a pipe and had an old-fashioned pipeman's unfussed approach to life. About 10.45 each morning he would emerge from the dressing-room to check on the lads lapping the pitch. As Tosher stood on the sidelines, arms behind his back, the pace of the runners would quicken, the talking about the night before would cease, an air of purpose would descend on proceedings. He was kidding them, they him. But only to a point. His authority was real, the players' response an acknowledgement of the respect, born of affection, they felt for him.

Bill Inglis was gentle. A larger man than Tosher, quietly spoken, a glint of mischief lightening his doleful features; Bill radiated kindness. Where Curry would engage in banter, Bill would smile knowingly to himself and get on with his work.

'Tosher and Bill weren't great academic trainers,' Charlie Mitten explains, 'but they were great fellas. We were like boys with their fathers, they were great *men*, that was what mattered.'

Arthur Powell was the third character in United's dressing-room. Arthur was the youth trainer with particular responsibilities for overseeing the domestic duties of the ground-staff boys. Arthur was the rebel. He wouldn't wear his white coat like Tosher and Big Bill. He was cranky or affected to be, feigning irritation at all around him, particularly his white-coated seniors. New arrivals feared Arthur's stern countenance, and his squat bull-dog appearance at the boot-room door would cast a shadow over all therein. Old hands knew better; Arthur was a pet behind the brusque façade. Bill would make teasing fun of him 'That bathroom's a mess today; what's happening with those young fellows, I don't know,' Bill would muse, shaking his gentle head. Arthur would bristle and waddle off to take a worried look at his neglected patch of territory, which would be perfectly clean, of course.

'Buggers,' Arthur called them. In the quiet of the afternoons he would be in charge some days. The lads had to stay until five o'clock on the nail. Now it was Arthur's turn to tease. No, they couldn't bloody well go if they got the work done by four-thirty. 'Buggers,' he'd mutter to himself. Some afternoons he *would* relent: 'Off you go, go on out of it, before I change my mind.'

Other days Arthur would sit mellow in the dressing-room reminding the young lads that he'd got to stay as well. Sometimes he'd reminisce about his wartime adventures on navy minesweepers. His football career had been destroyed by that bloody war he'd tell them. 'Could have had an England cap' was one of his favourite themes. 'Lost it for you buggers,' he would moan mock-sourly. The older players told a different story, at least a variation which got Arthur going. He'd never played football and had only been in the Merchant Navy. Bill would pluck the larded game: 'Has he been telling fairy tales to you young lads again?' Arthur would storm off. And now he meant it!

The atmosphere in United's dressing-room was not devoid of coarseness, there were the usual rows, the inevitable personality clashes, but the prevailing spirit reflected the characters of the three men who presided over all.

The fact that United's dressing-room had no history meant that Busby and his staff could influence the mood from the beginning. The average age of the first team squad was twenty-

115

six, but, as Mitten pointed out: 'We were all greenhorns just coming out of the Forces, we were glad to have come through the war, to be alive. This helped us get along together, we realised how lucky we were to be playing football at all.'

An objective analysis of the club soon to enter the history books as Matt Busby United must allow that he began his managerial career in remarkably fortunate circumstances. Almost all the assets he possessed in the summer of 1946 were the product of work completed before he took the position of team manager. Busby had hired Jimmy Murphy and spent £4,000 on Jimmy Delaney. The positional changes he made, those concerning Carey and Cockburn in particular, were inspired. But others, notably Louis Rocca, Walter Crickmer and Jimmy Gibson had laid the foundations with painstaking care over a period of more than a decade. Busby's wisdom was to leave well alone. His presence itself was an asset. He was respected throughout the game, especially in Manchester. His philosophy about what was desirable in professional football was compatible with that outlined in Manchester United's last pre-war AGM by Jimmy Gibson.

Gibson had spoken with pride about the MUJACs, declaring that United had 'no intention of buying any more mediocrities'. His stated aspiration of, 'a Manchester United composed of Manchester players', would prove a touch idealistic in the world of professional football. Nevertheless, this ideal was closely related to Busby's convictions about the club as family, producing from within its own distinct environment a different kind of professional to the ones he had grown up among. Gibson and Busby were both radicals, offended equally by the seamy expediency then endemic to the professional game. Without one the other could easily have failed. Gibson needed a professional to realise his dream, Matt Busby, needing a patron, was bequeathed a legacy considerably richer than he might reasonably have expected.

7

Matt Busby United

'On our day we never thought
anyone could beat us.'

Charlie Mitten

Pre-season training began at The Firs in Fallowfield in mid-
July. The summer of 1946 was hot. Clement Attlee was Prime
Minister of a Labour government which was going to build a
just society. Although ration-books were still around, people
felt a new age was beginning. Old values had, with Winston
Churchill, been rejected. This sense of a different order was
reflected in the Manchester United camp at Fallowfield. The
Busby regime was different, better, than any of the players had
known before.

Manchester United had been a pre-war music-hall joke. The
yo-yo, team, up and down between Division One and Two. No
manager, no wages on one still remembered occasion. By his
very presence the great Matt Busby dramatically altered the
club's sense of its identity. His benign, track-suited presence
created a buzz on the training ground. Morale was high before a
ball was kicked in earnest. The players were back on full-time
training, all except the remarkable Henry Cockburn, who was
still working as a textile engineer's fitter, and Joe Walton, a
promising young right-back who was a plumber by trade.

If Attlee's was a humane, people's government, Busby's
United was its footballing equivalent, a players' club where all
were equal, pulling together in the cause of enlightenment.

Charlie Mitten recalls the liberating effect Busby and
Murphy had on their first United team: 'They were man-
management men. They understood their players and left them
alone. We were good players; Stan Pearson, Chilton, Jack
Rowley, Jimmy Delaney, Little Henry, Carey when he moved

117

to full-back. There wasn't a lot they could teach us, they weren't coaches in the technical sense. They made you feel good.'

Henry Cockburn confirms Mitten's account, with a fascinating caveat: 'Matt always used to say "keep the ball flowing". When I finished playing and went on coaching courses they had invented one-touch and two-touch games as part of the coaching system. It was only then I realised, hell, Matt had us playing like that, unknowingly.'

When one looks back to the Manchester United training ground of 1946 from the bleak world of the 1990s when the dogma of coaching has all but rid the British game of the beauty Busby conspired with his players to create, one sees a brutal irony in the transformation that has taken place between then and now. Busby had lamented the absence of teaching and guidance in his own playing days. So he put his track-suit on and worked with his players. He was the first coach. The wisdom he imparted was, as Cockburn illustrates, absorbed 'unknowingly'. Was there, therefore, nothing to it?

Out in Fallowfield Busby preached a simple gospel. His revolution was founded on basic, easily understood principles. In their five weeks of pre-season training United's players saw more of the ball than in any other five-month period of their careers. Practice matches, three or four a week, were the medium Busby used to convey his message. Just as the absence of history helped foster a new spirit in the dressing-room, it facilitated the propagation of a new footballing philosophy on the training ground. The fact that the pupils were not youngsters but mature pros was another bonus. Matt Busby's credibility as a teacher was further enhanced by the fact that, as Henry Cockburn reminds us, 'he was the best bloody player in the club'.

In the practice games Busby played on one side, Jimmy Murphy on the other. There were no convoluted tactical schemes. The message was precise: 'The ball is made round to go round.' Passing was the key to all doors. 'Give it to a red-shirt.' Time after time this simple imperative echoed across the sun-drenched playing fields. 'Keep it simple,' they told the players, 'keep it moving.' The instruction was easy to comply with. And that was its most profound virtue.

Fear was the enemy. This enemy manifested itself as intimidation in the dressing-room, as confusion on the football field. Confidence had to be imbued on and off the field. Being confident was feeling you belonged, being confident was feeling you were capable of fulfilling expectations. As far as football went, Busby's expectations were within any professional's compass. All were psychologically reassured by their first encounter with the 'Great Matt Busby'.

Confidence was, he knew, a fragile yet precious commodity in football. Most players' performances in any game were determined in the opening fifteen minutes. If you went onto the pitch unsure of what lay in front of you the risks were all the greater. Fear came in many forms: fear of the opposition, induced, perhaps by an over-anxious manager; fear of being unable to live up to the grandiose rhetoric of your manager's team talk; fear of the unknown, which frequently had as much to do with confusion in your own ranks as anything the opposition was likely to fling your way.

The confidence Busby and Murphy bestowed upon their players was the certainty that they could accomplish the tasks they were given. Busby's belief was that games couldn't be won on the training ground or in the dressing-room, but they could be lost in both places. Football was a player's game, and any man good enough to be a pro required nothing more than confidence to fulfil the gifts he'd been born with. Providing confidence was his job. Manage the man and the magic would take care of itself.

Charlie Mitten believes that neither Busby nor Murphy knew the game in a technical sense: 'In terms of knowledge . . . zero. Both of them. Jimmy had guts and he imparted that to the players. Jimmy has yet to tell me something about football I didn't already know. Matt was the boss, he understood players and geed them up.'

Wherever football academies have met and the subject of Busby and United has cropped up, the question of whether his philosophy was wise or merely simplistic has surfaced. As football changed from a player's game to a coach's the view prevailed – most vehemently among a group of players within his own club – that his message was a joke or alternatively, that if the speaker had the players Busby had, *he* would be happy to let them just 'go out and play'. Thus, the phrase man-management became a synonym for knowing damn all, or, as Charlie Mitten succinctly puts it, 'zero'.

Mitten's claim that there 'wasn't a lot they could teach us because we were good players', prompts one to examine that assertion in the context of the summer of '46. Charlie himself had been at the club since 1936. Born in India, the son of a soldier, Mitten was reared in Manchester. When war broke out he went to volunteer for the RAF – 'Being a bloody stupid lad I wanted to be a rear-gunner, wanted to fire guns and kill Germans.' He was sent to Blackpool for training. 'One night I was in the Winter Gardens – war-time in Blackpool was great, the best pubs and social life in the country – when I met Stan Matthews who was a Sergeant in the RAF.

'He said, "What are you doing here." I said, I'm on an air-gunner course. He said, "Are you bloody mad, they'll be sweeping you out of the gun-turrets in bits." ' Matthews told him that the RAF were looking for footballers to be PT instructors and promised to have a word with the Squadron Leader. ' "I hear you've changed your mind Mitten." . . . "Yes sir, I've decided I'd like to live a bit longer." . . . "Nothing wrong with that Mitten, what can you do?" '

Charlie travelled around Britain's aerodromes organising fitness courses for the men. Among those he served under was Walter Winterbottom, a former United reserve player who went on to manage England, and become the high priest of coaching, after the war. Charlie ended up serving in the Azores and guesting for Tranmere Rovers and Chelsea. He recalls playing at Stamford Bridge one day during a buzz-bomb raid: 'It was amazing. We were playing away and all of a sudden it went deadly quiet. We could hear the buzz-bomb, it came straight across the ground and we all stopped, held our breaths and prayed that it would keep going.'

When he was demobbed in 1945 Mitten returned to United to sign professional forms. Before Busby arrived, the man, who in hindsight believed that there was little he could be taught, had played no League football. In the summer of '46 Charlie's experience amounted to a season in the League North. He was twenty-five when he made his Football League début proper against Grimsby in August 1946. Matt Busby had been teaching him, full-time, for five weeks.

The notion that Busby inherited a ready-made team doesn't bear scrutiny. Carey, the captain, was still learning the full-back position. Jack Crompton, the goalkeeper, was another débutant against Grimsby having been signed from local amateur football during the war. Cockburn was still a part-timer, if a very special one. But Henry was a product of Busby's imagination. The Grimsby game was also his first taste of the real thing.

Chilton had been converted from wing-half to centre-half by Busby. Chilton was two weeks short of his twenty-eighth birthday when he played his second match in the First Division. He had made his début for United on 2 September 1939, the day before war was declared. There can be no doubt that this dour Geordie had much to learn from Busby and Murphy. In one of the pre-season practice games Busby had played centre-forward in the reserves and from there coached Chilton in the art of central defending. This kind of tutorial was to be Matt's and Jimmy's *modus operandi* in the years to come. No jargon, no confusion, no loud proclamation – at least not from Busby – rather the quiet word offering practical advice, leaving the rest up to the player who, if he had a footballing brain, which, in Busby's and Murphy's opinion, all good players instinctively had, would work the rest out himself.

Even the more distinguished of those who lined out for the opening games of the '46/'47 season were by no means the finished product. Stan Pearson had played one season of First Division football in a struggling United team before the war. Jack Rowley's experience was similar. Jimmy Delaney was a thirty-two-year-old Celtic cast-off. Johnny Hanlon, who played centre-forward in the opening games, had been a brilliantly promising junior. He too was making his First Division début. Sadly, Hanlon had been knocked around during the war and would be forced to retire within a couple of seasons.

Manchester United's circumstances must be seen in perspective. The war had in one way or another wreaked havoc with most football clubs' plans. Established senior players, like Busby and Murphy themselves, were too old to resume their careers. Many promising youngsters never had the opportunity to learn the game and develop their talent. Uncertainty was rife as the first full post-war season opened in August '46. This is what encouraged those clubs who could afford to – and some who couldn't – to plunge into the transfer-market. This option did not exist for United. Busby was better off than some, worse off than others. What is undeniable is that he didn't 'have the players' his detractors would subsequently claim he had.

Only two of the team that made a sensational start to the '46/ '47 season cost transfer-fees: Delaney for £4,000 and Jack Rowley who'd cost £3,500 from Third Division Bournemouth in 1937. The rest were, as Mitten paradoxically admitted, 'greenhorns', certainly in terms of challenging for the Championship.

Although Liverpool managed by George Kay eventually won the Championship, it was Manchester United who captured the public's imagination. Almost two million people paid to watch football at Maine Road that season. Manchester City who won promotion from the Second Division drew their share of Manchester's football-hungry population, but well over one million came to worship Busby's team, playing football as it had never been played before. The crowds flocked in droves to see United wherever they played, home and away they attracted the highest aggregate attendances in the First Division. During a season that exceeded by far Busby's expectations he made two significant changes to the side. Johnny Morris and Johnny Aston were both local graduates of the MUJACs. Morris returned from the war in November 1946 to make his début, aged twenty-two, in a 0–0 draw at Villa Park, and twenty-five-year-old Johnny Aston played his first game as an inside-forward against Chelsea in September. The following February Busby created another international defender when he switched Aston to left full-back, a position in which he was to gain seventeen England caps.

Earlier that season, in September 1946, Henry Cockburn won his first cap for England against Ireland in Belfast. The Irish defied a Football Association edict by including four players from the South, among them Johnny Carey. The presence of his two recently converted pupils in the company they kept on this occasion bears remarkable testimony to Busby's vocation for teaching. Henry was still working part-time as an engineer's fitter in the mill. Among his England team-mates in Belfast were some of the greatest players ever to grace the English game: Frank Swift, George Hardwick, Billy Wright, Neil Franklin, Stan Matthews, Raich Carter, Tommy Lawton and Wilf Mannion. Tom Finney was a reserve. These were incidently, the kind of players Busby *didn't* have at his disposal when he set out to create his first great side.

Two days before the international, Henry Rose filed the following revealing report for the *Daily Express*:

> Football-golfers among the England team who play Ireland here at Windsor Park on Saturday had a knock at the picturesque Newcastle (Co. Down) links adjoining the Slieve Donard Hotel where they are staying 27 miles from Belfast.
>
> The club accommodated their distinguished visitors with clubs, shoes and other paraphernalia and gave them the courtesy of the links. But when they finished their game they were not allowed to enter the clubhouse because of a rule of the club which prohibits any professionals from the privilege. Captain Burrell, the secretary of the golf club told me: 'This is a private club and it has always been a rule not to allow the use of the clubhouse to professionals. We do not even allow our own professional to come into the clubhouse. It is nothing unusual, being a private club we are entitled to make any rules we see fit.'

Explaining the distinction he was trying to draw, Burrell told Rose: 'We have had Mr Winterbottom in and also the FA people in charge of the party. We shall be glad to have you join us as well.' Rose does not record whether or not he accepted this invitation. He does, however, note sardonically, 'For Mr Burrell's information, ex-Wing-Commander Walter Winterbottom is a *paid* team manager of England.' A couple of days later England beat Ireland 7–2. Expressing himself 'lost for words', Raymond Glenndenning observed that 'the English team played football such as one dreams about but rarely sees'. According to Glenndenning, 'Cockburn was the find of the day.'

Busby's reputation was growing. Frank Butler of the *News of the World* spoke for most, commentators and fans, when he described what he called 'Matt Busby United' as 'the finest footballing team in the country'. Busby did not court publicity of this kind. It was, perhaps, inevitable that journalists seeking to explain United's spectacular football would seek to do so in terms of the manager's imposing personality. He was always accessible to the press. Up to a point. He understood the value of good public relations and used his unique charm to woo the sportswriters. He promoted the club's values and acknowledged outstanding contributions made by his players. Again the objective was to build confidence. But for most journalists he remained the story.

'Matt Ends a Great First Season,' Tom Jackson proclaimed in the *Manchester Evening News* in June 1947. Recounting how Busby had first arrived in the city 'clutching a suitcase containing little more than a pair of football boots and a generous slice of his mother's home-made cake', Jackson went on to describe the 'Busby Method':

'He never browbeats a player for some blatant mistake on the field. He takes him to a quiet corner, gives him a fatherly chat and a pat of encouragement. The player is refreshed and unembarrassed at being shown the right way.'

Alongside this tribute to Busby's first season's work Tom Jackson ran a story which tempered somewhat the United manager's pre-season contentment. Henry Cockburn and Joe Walton, another gifted young United player, had both asked for transfers after failing to agree terms with Busby. This news created a sensation in the Manchester papers which led with the story in banner headlines. 'Cockburn, left-half and Walton, right full-back are two of the most brilliant young players in their positions in the game,' wrote Henry Rose, the doyen of Northern sportswriters. The dispute was over money, as Rose explained: 'The players have asked to be placed on the transfer list because they are dissatisfied with the wage offered them for next season.' As they told Rose: 'We have told Mr Busby that we are prepared to give up our jobs and become full-time professionals. We were told we would not be given the maximum wage of £12 and £10 in the summer and we think we are entitled to full pay. We feel we have been given a raw deal. Neither of us cost the club a penny. We have given our best in every match we've played and think that this refusal to give us top wage is poor return for our efforts.'

Busby replied via Jackson's *Evening News* column the same night: 'We have offered them reasonable terms,' Busby pleaded, 'but they have asked for maximum rates for next season as full-time men. There are certain regulations about wages to players which have to be recognised and I can state quite categorically that Cockburn and Walton have been offered maximum rates according to these.'

The regulations Busby was invoking concerned the Ministry of Labour National Service Act which decreed that men like Cockburn and Walton who had been exempted from service in the Forces would have to have their cases reviewed before being permitted to turn full-time professionals. A separate Football League rule insisted that they would have to play six games as full-time pros before being placed on the maximum wage.

Most football managers would have come to some arrangement to circumvent these regulations which seemed to be, in Cockburn's case in particular, a matter of semantics. Henry Cockburn was after all an England international and one of Busby's great discoveries. But Busby was not an under-the-counter man. The regulations existed and must be obeyed.

'He would always refer back to the League's regulations,' Henry recalls. 'It was the League's decision and it had to be obeyed. He never gave anything under-the-counter.' Cockburn was eventually satisfied by a promise that he would get what was fairly due to him by League regulations when it was possible. Walton proved a trifle more recalcitrant and was transferred to Preston a few months later. Busby had, however, laid down a marker for future reference. In his family, underhand dealings, common currency elsewhere in professional football, were not on.

This policy was a consequence of both his personal philosophy and practical considerations related to football and the needs of Manchester United. Although he kept his politics well concealed from public view, Matt was a Labour man, as indeed were most Manchester Catholics. He believed in equality of opportunity and reward. His natural prudence ensured that what he described to me as 'strong' political views remained a private matter. More practically he felt that illegal payments in football created the very distractions within a club that he was determined to erase. Underhand payments invariably went to the strong at the expense of those who were young and weak. Word of such reward inevitably leaked out causing resentment. He'd seen it as a player and wasn't going to sponsor illegality as a manager. Authority which lent itself to this kind of practice conceded the moral high ground. Authority must be fair – and seen to be.

For those reasons the rules must be observed. Another compelling reason for not being carried away by the success of the first full season was United's financial position. Success on the field had not provided an instant cure for debt – the club made a profit of £10,215.15s.1d. in 1946; in 1947 this rose to £13,393.2s.1d. Alas, United had still to return to Old Trafford. Lengthy negotiations with the War Damage Commission had thus far yielded a sum of £17,478 in compensation for the damage Hitler's bombs had caused to Britain's finest football stadium. The club's persistent attempts to put pressure on the government met with little success, despite the support of Mr Ellis Smith MP who, although the member for Stoke-on-Trent, was a lifelong United supporter. When United sought through Smith's intervention to erect a stand at Old Trafford built of 'a light alloy' the Minister of Works refused permission. Walter Crickmer despaired. He wrote to Ellis Smith: 'While we are pleased for any small mercies received these days, I think the big song made is out of all proportion to the very trivial licence we are going to be granted.' This was a reference to the £17,478 the club had been empowered to spend under War Damage Commission licence.

This would be hopelessly insufficient, Crickmer pointed out, continuing: 'It certainly seems to have misled everybody who appears to have got the impression that we are coming back to Old Trafford to a completely re-instated ground which as you know is far removed from the truth. It is no use, Ellis, I cannot see First League Football being staged here without a stand, although driven into a corner we may have to put up with anything. If so, I dread the consequences, one would have thought in our present glory our friends at Court might have arranged to stretch a point and allow us to do something really substantial if only as a compliment to this great industrial centre, whose people have certainly made a magnificent effort in the export drive.'

It was against this desperate background that Matt Busby worked with the most admired team in the country. His seeming meanness with Henry Cockburn was simple care with money, shortage of which remained a continuing burden on his club. Busby's attitude to money would continue to be in conservative contrast to his radical approach to football on the field. It was not in any case part of his nature to be profligate with other people's money. And although he regarded Manchester United as *his* club, he saw his powers extending only to matters that affected performances on the field. Insistent on his own authority where he felt it might be usurped, he was not inclined to intrude onto administrative ground which was properly the responsibility of others, be they Walter Crickmer, James Gibson or indeed the Football League and the Association whose business it was to make the rules with which he and his players would have to comply, like it or not. The subject of money was to arise with more dramatic effect before very long.

At the beginning of the '47/'48 season Busby filled an important gap in the club's coaching staff by appointing Bert Whalley to assist Jimmy Murphy with the youths and reserves. Whalley had been on the club's books as a player since 1934, making only thirty-three Football League appearances in a career blighted by the war. He was a diligent wing-half, no more, but very popular, his pleasant disposition and sense of humour belying his deeply held religious convictions. He was a Methodist Lay Preacher, but not of the fire and brimstone variety. In fact he was in no way sanctimonious, being as willing to laugh at the jokes of which he was the occasional butt as the dressing-room characters who cracked them. This appointment serves to nail another myth about Matt Busby's United: that it was a Catholic club in the sense that preferment could be

127

determined by the God one worshipped. Character rather than religion was always the criterion, although there is much evidence to indicate that, fond though he was of roguish types in social circumstances, when it came to the business Busby sought to surround himself with decent, dependable men. This he probably did associate with religious conviction, but not necessarily Catholic convictions.

Although unyielding in financial dealings with his players, Matt Busby never passed an opportunity to indulge them in other ways. The first team made regular trips to Blackpool where they stayed at the Norbreck Hydro, the resort's best hotel. There would be trips to the great shows at the club's expense and in general Busby was anxious to raise his professionals' status in any legal way he could. When the star of the show announced the presence of the Manchester United team the house would rise to acclaim them. The happiest day of the normal week was Monday when *all* the club's professionals were treated to a day out at Davyhulme Golf Club which, unlike Newcastle, Co. Down, was proud to have the city's renowned professionals in the clubhouse or anywhere they wished to go. After training the players went to Davyhulme for lunch, followed by a round of golf or, for those who preferred, games of cards and billiards. An evening meal of mixed grill would follow. Busby himself always attended. He loved his golf and the company of footballers away from the formality of the club. His men were in such circumstances treated like kings rather than slaves. That applied to all his players down to the most unlikely future star, whose name Matt would know and make a point of mentioning lest anyone should think that a fellow's limitations as a footballer extended beyond the game to life itself. Off-duty stars received no more consideration than the humblest pro.

At Davyhulme Busby observed his players as human beings. And allowed more than a glimpse of himself. 'We knew he liked a bet on the horses,' Charlie Mitten confides with a smile, 'we could hear him phoning his bet through.' Mitten was an inveterate gambler himself. He usually had a greyhound and if not, a tip for one. Matt was always interested in the dog – or the tip. Johnny Aston and Henry Cockburn were, along with

Charlie, the rogues, taking the piss out of someone or other, usually the drier members of the fraternity like Carey, Jack Rowley, Chilton, or Jack Crompton. Better types were usually fair game for the Lads. Jimmy Delaney was, like Stan Pearson, amiable, willing to share the joke if not the inspiration of it. Of all of this Busby was tolerant; he enjoyed a laugh although he didn't swear himself, nor outwardly baulk at the use of bad language. Only the most insensitive, however, missed the point at which order had been breached.

On Saturdays Matt was remarkably tolerant of Mitten's habit of waiting until the result of the 2.30 race was known. On Mondays at Davyhulme the same easy sense of his own authority steered him through circumstances few managers would have been able – or indeed would have wished – to negotiate. From this camaraderie with its backdrop of benign paternalism one player stood apart; Johnny Morris was an independent spirit. A brilliant footballer, with excellent technique, a maker and scorer of goals, Morris, at twenty-three the youngest of them all, was popular with the other players. Henry Cockburn used to kid Johnny that he was 'a Commie', for Morris had opinions about the game and, in the manner of Billy Meredith, a player's place in the order of things. Paternalism was, he felt, condescension in disguise. Busby's acute antennae picked up the signals. Their relationship was never better than tolerable, despite Morris's superb contribution to the team.

Manchester United picked up where they'd left off in the season '47/'48. Johnny Aston had established himself at left-back. Morris, as well as being a regular goalscorer, added a delightfully impudent dimension to the team. Stan Pearson's confidence grew, and he became the man who controlled the rhythm of games. Jack Rowley scored twice in the opening away fixture at Middlesborough and four times a fortnight later in a 6–2 win at Charlton. Busby had, unusually for him, predicted that United would win the Championship before the season began. Boastful declarations were not his style. In the next few months he learned a lesson he would not forget; let your team do the talking. After losing 2–1 away to Arsenal – the eventual champions – in their fifth League game, United

129

suffered an indifferent spell during September and October which virtually placed the title out of reach.

The loyal Manchester crowds did not desert the team that always promised the exotic. On 8 January 1948, 81,692, the second biggest attendance in Football League history watched a 'classic exhibition' of football when Arsenal visited Maine Road. The result, a 1–1 draw, left one correspondent commenting the next day: 'I left the game disappointed. Unbiased, as I was, I wanted this wonderful attacking machine of Matt Busby's to score a winning goal. But they couldn't.' He and others rooting for Matt Busby's United didn't have long to wait for their desires to be fulfilled.

United drew Aston Villa away in the third round of the FA Cup. They were a goal down after ten seconds without a United player touching the ball. Jack Rowley equalised in the sixth minute, then Morris scored twice, Pearson and Delaney gave them a 5–1 half-time lead. A couple of minutes into the second half Edwards scored for Villa direct from a corner. Nine minutes from time Villa scored from the penalty-spot to make it 5–4.

'On our day we never thought anyone could beat us,' Charlie Mitten admits. At half-time they believed that this was their day. As Villa pressed for an equaliser, roared on by 60,000 fans, it seemed Busby's team had once again stepped the wrong side of the line between confidence and complacency. Desperation evaporated a minute from the end when Mitten broke through on the left to give Stan Pearson an opportunity to score United's sixth goal.

United drew League champions Liverpool at home in the next round, but as City also came out of the hat first Maine Road was unavailable. Busby cheekily chose to play the tie at Goodison Park where, within roaring distance of Anfield, Liverpool were easily beaten 3–0. In similar circumstances, City again having first call on Maine Road, United chose Leeds Road, Huddersfield, to entertain Charlton in the fifth round. The London team were comfortably seen off 2–0. Preston were United's quarter-final opponents and United won 4–1 before a full house at Maine Road.

United were now favourites to win the FA Cup. They had

reached the semi-final in style, scoring fifteen goals, conceding just five. Arsenal were clawing their way to the Championship, but it was to Busby's daring side that a country wearying of post-war austerity looked for verve and a dash of brilliance on an otherwise bleak horizon. United had broken all attendance records on the way to the semi-final where Derby County were to be their opponents: before the Liverpool tie crowds had formed six-deep outside Goodison Park; black marketeers had enjoyed a field-day before the Preston game selling two-shilling tickets for ten shillings, and even as hundreds fought desperately to buy at this inflated price, one enterprising tout conducted an auction during which the price for a two-shilling ticket rose to a £1 note.

As Busby prepared his team for the semi-final word reached the players that their opponents had been promised a bonus of £100 a man for victory. In 1948 the maximum wage had risen to £14. One hundred pounds seemed an unearthly reward. The United players held a meeting during which Johnny Carey was urged to approach Busby to see if the club would be prepared to match Derby's offer. Johnny Morris was the most militant advocate of rebellion, although most of the others felt sympathetic to the argument that everybody seemed to be doing well out of United's success except the men who did most to achieve it. Carey reluctantly delivered the message to Busby whose response was a rare display of real anger.

Everything Matt Busby had done at Manchester United had been aimed at fostering an ethos different to that which prevailed elsewhere in professional soccer. Men were treated fairly in all matters, generously to the very limits the laws governing football permitted. The golf at Davyhulme, Blackpool at the best hotel, the best shows. He'd arranged for United's players – *all of them* – to have free passes for the leading cinemas in Manchester. They wore smart new blazers with the club's crest, and neat grey flannels. They had moved forward in many ways from the cloth-cap and muffler era he'd played through. His players were respected, in order that they would respect themselves. He'd fought with the Board to get the money for golf, Blackpool and shows. Only the best for our players had been a core value for him – one not readily accepted by all upstairs. His anger was genuine, the more deeply felt because this demand for dirty money was conceived at the moment when the glorious fulfilment of a Wembley Cup Final was within reach. You couldn't buy pride or loyalty, he told Carey, who shared his convictions. If you could there was no point in being in the game. Football would be just another business. The idea was repugnant to Matt Busby. Those who promoted this idea were failing him; he felt he had failed in some important sense to create the kind of club he wanted.

Derby County were a money club. Big spenders who'd paid £21,000 for Billy Steel and Raich Carter, their two great inside-forwards. In the semi-final at Hillsborough Steel and Carter's counterparts in Matt Busby's team were Stan Pearson and Johnny Morris. These two local players cost United a total of £20 – two £10 signing-on fees. For Busby this was a source of pride. For Johnny Morris a cause for disenchantment. Neither man was wrong.

Busby refused to compromise. United beat Derby, Stan Pearson's hat-trick ensuring their passage to the Final. The words he uttered afterwards underline Busby's ability to inspire his players by means other than tactics and money. 'All this time I was thinking of Matt Busby's words: "The greatest thrill in soccer is playing at Wembley on Cup Final day" – now I'm going there.'

Three men dominated the build-up to the 1948 Cup Final: Matt Busby, Stanley Matthews and Johnny Carey. Matthews was thirty-three, a legend, yet still to win a Cup or Championship medal. Gordon Richards, the greatest jockey of those years, had never won a Derby. Every spring and summer the nation would wonder if this was to be Matthews's Year or Richards's Year. Ironically 1953 would see both these great British sportsmen crown their careers with the most coveted prizes their sports could offer.

Carey had been voted Footballer of the Year. The Irishman was seen to embody the values – on and off the field – of Busby himself: élan in battle, dignified, modest acknowledgement of the acclaim which greeted victory. Carey was the sportswriters' choice and the people's. Had the ballot been confined to United's dressing-room Little Henry, Stan Pearson or Johnny Morris would have been the main contenders.

Busby's charismatic presence stood silhouetted above all as the two teams took the field for this all-Lancashire Cup Final. Immaculately dressed, striped tie, white shirt and trilby, he strode elegantly across the perfect green turf looking more regal than His Majesty King George VI who presided over this great occasion. He was proud. Not for himself, but for the things he believed in and the people he loved and belonged to. The values which he believed had created this moment went beyond football as it was, extending, really, to life as it should be lived. His football club reflected what had touched him most in his life: the camaraderie of the coalface in Old Orbiston; in Carey the shining symbol of Catholic behaviour, as Nellie Busby, sitting now close to the Royal Box at Wembley, had preached it in her home; behaviour overcoming bigotry, a means by which the despised, whether Catholics or *professionals*, would triumph in the end; in his team, the daring and brilliance of Alex James and Hughie Gallacher with which Matt had fallen in love after his father was killed in the First War; most of all he was moved now not by the glamour of this grand occasion but the simple thought, family: Tom Curry and Bill Inglis, the youngest player on United's books, and the ladies from the office who made the tea. And all his pals, the bookies and showmen, the gamblers, Jimmy Greer and the Glasgow Empire, Jean, Sandy and Sheena, Phil McCloy, Jimmy McMullen, Len Langford and his wife who'd saved the 'blue-baby'. Kindness shown by your own to your own.

He had sent his team out with the usual instructions: 'Give it to a red-shirt. Keep it tight in the first fifteen minutes. Enjoy the occasion.' Charlie Mitten was delegated to drop deeper to assist Johnny Aston in containing Matthews. Busby was confident. Wembley was the perfect stage for the football he had inspired his team to play. The lush turf would facilitate the passing game and punish most those who had to chase the ball.

The afternoon was compelling, rendered so because the unexpected happened. Blackpool went ahead fifteen minutes into the game when Shinwell scored from the penalty-spot after Chilton had fouled Mortensen. Rowley equalised after a furious bout of United pressure. Five minutes later Mortensen gave Blackpool the lead which they held until half-time.

133

Busby's composure during the interval was striking. He and Carey insisted 'keep playing'. After sixty-nine minutes of thrust and counter-thrust Blackpool were still in front. Johnny Morris, sharp-witted as ever, saved United just when Manchester hearts were sinking low. The little rebel's quick free kick allowed Jack Rowley a couple of yards of space and the scores were level. Stan Pearson got the decisive goal eleven minutes from the end. Johnny Anderson distorted the afternoon's events with a chance thirty-five yard punt which made it 4–2. Busby had included Anderson at the expense of the veteran Jack Warner whose legs he felt would not last the ninety minutes on the strength-sapping Wembley sod.

Triumph over adversity was an appropriate parable of Matt Busby's life, of the city he loved and the club whose name would now be engraved on the FA Cup almost forty years after Billy Meredith first placed it there.

W. Capel Kirby writing in the *Empire News* commented: 'There may have been better Cup Finals, but certainly not within my memory over a period of 25 years. Neither can I remember any team winning the Cup after twice being in arrears. For this alone Manchester United fully merited their success. Never at any time did they depart from the pure, subtle principles outlined by their manager, Matt Busby.'

In Manchester people left their wireless sets to flock jubilantly onto the streets. Further north in the Northumbrian mining village of Ashington a ten-year-old boy vividly remembers that afternoon: 'We played for East Northumberland Boys in the morning,' Bobby Charlton recalls, 'and we were invited to go to one of the lads' houses to listen to the Cup Final on the radio. We had no television in those days. After a while we went out onto the street to play football – we couldn't get enough in one day – and every so often we would come in to ask the score. I remember United equalising. The next we heard they'd won. They said it was the greatest Cup Final of all time. I think it was from that day that I wanted to be a footballer and join Manchester United.'

One hundred thousand Mancunians turned out to welcome the heroes home the following day. One eleven-year-old boy ran perilously close to the open-topped bus bearing the team and the gleaming silver trophy. Shay Brennan never knew a moment so dazzlingly exquisite.

Before their triumphant procession through the city to the Town Hall in Albert Square, the team stopped at the home of James Gibson who'd been too ill to watch any of their games that year. 'You have fulfilled my greatest ambition,' he told them. Only two of the side had cost transfer-fees, seven were local lads; a Manchester United composed of Manchester players, the team he'd promised in 1939.

8

Reality

'Matt was very strong on his
principles.'

Paddy McGrath

With success came problems. They were various; who should
get the credit; who was hogging the glory; and what about the
spoils of victory which can be spent in the shops, money. Matt
Busby's Manchester in 1948 was no different in this respect
from the years when Billy Meredith cast the city in the mellow
light of glory. Busby and his players went off to Ireland during
the summer on a tour whose declared objective was to honour
Johnny Carey before his own people. Two games were played
in Dublin, one in Belfast. For the players this was a holiday, for
Busby Ireland had particular meaning as the country from
which his forebears had travelled to Scotland in search of work.
He loved the South of Ireland and would return many times in
the years ahead, often, at low points in his life, taking a motor
car in Dublin and travelling alone through the countryside.
Before the television age he could travel unrecognised, have a
few drinks, which he now enjoyed, and go racing at Leopards-
town or the Phoenix Park, mixing with the trainers, jockeys and
bookies. Paddy Prendergast, the great flat-race trainer of the
time was the kind of rakish character Matt was especially fond
of. The horses or dog-racing at Shelbourne Park, easy,
gregarious company and a few jars, perhaps a game of golf,
enjoying these simple pleasures he could shed the mask of
dignity, at least the cultivated layer which marked the football
man. Billy Behan, United's Irish scout, a part-time bookmaker,
was his guide on these occasions.

The post-Wembley holiday was pleasant. The games, against
a Shelbourne Select XI and Bohemians, the grand old Dublin

amateur club, were comfortable, a chance to show off. The food was a real treat, eggs and steak, rare commodities in Britain. A trip like this saw Busby at his best. Men were men and treated accordingly. Rules about drinking were waived. The odd peccadillo – if discreetly embarked upon – was permissible.

Knowing their penchant for a bet the hall-porter at the Royal Hotel in Bray, a few miles outside Dublin, approached Charlie Mitten, the most obvious and fearless punter, with some information: the porter knew about a dog that would win at Shelbourne Park. He and the trainer were anxious to make sure of victory. Substantial sums stood to be won. Was it true that the great United team took, er, 'special stuff' for big games? Charlie, not wishing to disabuse his new friend and therefore be excluded from the coup, hinted that yes, of course, there were special embrocations and 'other things' that boosted performances. He'd have a word with their medical men.

Ted Dalton, United's physio and Tom Curry were joined in the conspiracy. Various potions were produced, all of which looked effective, none of which would make the slightest difference to the dog's performance. By the appointed evening Charlie had convinced the porter, who in turn persuaded the trainer to deliver the greyhound to the Royal Hotel where the magical substance – undetectable the trainer was assured – would be administered in secret in Dalton's room.

Whatever it was it *smelt* convincing and dog, trainer, porter and players piled into taxis for Shelbourne. Busby and Jimmy Murphy were enthusiastic co-conspirators. At the track they were all 'on'. The dog won. Despite the magic potion.

This harmless escapade provided some temporary easing of the tensions growing between Busby and his players. Resentment simmered beneath the surface. The Cup victory had rewarded everyone except the players who'd fought so heroically. Busby himself was the most renowned football man in Britain. He was honoured to be appointed manager of the Great Britain Olympic team for the 1948 games. In Manchester a legend was growing around him. Johnny Carey, Footballer of the Year, was similarly fêted. A newspaper campaign had begun to nominate him for the captaincy of the Rest of Europe

137

team due to play Great Britain in the autumn. Matt Busby United were wanted for foreign tours, offers were on the table from Argentina, the United States and most countries in Europe. Yet for the men who'd done the business the financial rewards, for breaking attendance records, finishing second in the Championship and winning the FA Cup, were paltry. The maximum wage was £12 a week, £10 in the summer. For winning the FA Cup United's players received the statutory £20 bonus. Blackpool's players had been rumoured to be on £100 a man. Two years previously Derby County, winners in 1946, had given their heroes a gold watch as a present for winning. Bending the rules was common practice within the game. Everybody knew it.

Back in Manchester for pre-season training Busby's players held a meeting among themselves. Summer had hardened their mood. Carey was again asked to approach Busby to see if something extra could be done. He refused. Even the dressing-room moderates felt aggrieved this time, and men like Chilton, Jack Rowley and Jimmy Delaney, who would normally have remained neutral, spoke up in support of Morris, Mitten, Cockburn and Aston, the awkward squad.

Their circumstances must be remembered. Most of them were getting on, the dismal age of thirty was not too far away. They had achieved things they might never achieve again. Now was the time to make a stand. 'We were living in club-houses,' Mitten explains. 'Nice houses, at a normal rent of 30 bob a week. But this was from £12 – £10 in summer. We knew what others were getting, guys we were playing against . . . and beating.' And of course the thought was never far from men's minds – especially those who could see the end in sight – that the day would come when the club demanded *their* house back. For the United players these considerations were all the more pressing because they had already lost good earning years serving their country in uniform. They'd paid the price for that victory, now it seemed fate was cheating them again. Even the fucking glory wasn't fairly spread. To the papers and the fans Matt Busby and Johnny Carey had won the Cup. The lads had been mere extras. They were not in a philosophical mood. Carey was shouted down. The players insisted on seeing 'The Boss'.

138

'The Boss' referred them to the Football League rules. He had done everything he could. Morris was not the only rebel this time. Chilton spoke up, so did Charlie Mitten. The mood of the room was behind them. Busby sensed the scale of the revolt. He reminded the players of the club's generosity . . . Blackpool, golf at Davyhulme, the National Savings certificates they were given at Christmas, the trips to Belle Vue to see the big fights, the outings he'd instituted to Colwyn Bay and Blackpool in the summer for them and all the other members of the staff. The club would do anything it could. Within the rules. Other clubs could do what they wanted, *this* was Manchester United he replied when the going rates elsewhere were alluded to.

His response was firm and unequivocal. The sullen silence was broken, nobody remembers now by whom. Perhaps a compromise could be reached. Instead of money or a gold watch, a set of golf clubs would be given to each player – legally – as part of training equipment. Here was an opportunity for Busby to quell the revolt. He declined to take it. The players insisted that they would like to put their case to the board. If the rules were Busby's concern the players wanted to speak to the men who made them. The following day Harold Hardman, acting for James Gibson who was ill, came to the dressing-room where he reiterated the club's position. Extra payments or gifts were against the regulations and Manchester United wouldn't break the rules. No, not even a set of golf clubs as a gesture of appreciation.

Fifty-two thousand people turned up to watch United play Derby County at Maine Road in the opening League game of the '48/'49 season. The public were not aware of the bitterness behind the scenes. United lost 2–1, the result of a desultory performance which reflected the dressing-room atmosphere. Two days before this vital first game of the season the players had upped the ante by threatening to strike if no concession was made to them. Busby, dejected by now, had dropped a hint that 'something' might be done if an acceptable way around the rules could be found. The loss, to Derby of all teams, big spenders and rule-breakers, left a sour taste in Busby's mouth. Of United's performance Johnny Aston would later say, 'We

139

were spectators for most of the game.' In truth, the row, protracted as it had been, had drained everyone's emotions.

This was a critical phase in Matt Busby's football life. His character and that of the institution he was trying to shape now faced a challenge as old – and definitive – as professional football itself. Busby was in a trap from which no decent professional football man could escape with honour. He was where Billy Meredith, Charlie Roberts, Herbert Bloomfield and indeed Manchester United had been before him – where all professionals ultimately arrived, the point of Original Sin. He had only two options: he could comply with the regulations governing professional football or obey the laws of natural justice. There was no middle ground between the bigoted, expedient Football League rule book – the Slaves Charter – by which Busby now felt himself bound, and the values of fairness, decency and equality he sought to foster in his football club, his family. If he enforced football law he was denying his players what was rightfully theirs. If he pursued the course of natural justice he would tarnish himself and risk Manchester United's reputation.

It would be false to suggest that he saw the issues as clearly as they are outlined above. Or that he felt any great conflict between his duty and justice for his players. He was a football manager acting in the greater good. The private man, who might have seen the broader picture, the player as slave, as others, like Meredith, Carter, Mannion and later Blanchflower and Jimmy Hill did, had been formed by the times he'd lived through. He accepted authority. He may not have liked its values but he understood its power.

There is a conventional view of Busby presented in all the literature about him and Manchester United. In this he is the 'purist philosopher', the 'idealist', the paternal 'father of football', wise, benign, a man of great dignity and tolerance.

This depiction of Busby is not without foundation, rather it is incomplete. Many who have been close to him, many who have admired him and fallen under his charismatic spell, speak of another tougher character capable of the kind of ruthlessness with which he would soon deal with Johnny Morris, later with Charlie Mitten and others who threatened his family.

'Matt was very strong on his principles,' his close friend Paddy McGrath confides, adding for emphasis 'very'. Charlie Mitten describes him as 'watertight when it came to money. He'd give you tickets alright, but when it came to money you got what you were entitled to, not a penny more.' The streak of ruthlessness would manifest itself from time to time over the next twenty years, occasionally to deal with great players and friends, most notably Denis Law when he fought for money.

Within this large character there were many different, sometimes irreconcilable traits. He kept journalists and biographers at arm's length. Busby is a private man, charm the barricade he erects to ward off intruders.

In the summer of 1948 he was still a rookie manager learning about power – how to use it as opposed to subverting it in order to acquire it. He was in the process of establishing the values which would prevail in his club. The threatened strike and protracted hassle over Cup Final bonuses was a formative experience. He tried charm, he offered the perks of Blackpool and other treats, in the end he was brutally singleminded.

He didn't see the issue as being one of human rights because he was not a dreamer like Meredith or an agitator like Morris, he was certainly no purist philosopher nor, when it came to the conditions of employment footballers were bound by, was he a starry-eyed idealist.

It is important to distinguish between the football man whose radical vision revolutionised the game on the field and the person born in Old Orbiston in another age. The person was as Harold Riley describes him, modest, someone of great humility, knowing exactly what he was. Matt Busby had no interest in power as such, nor was he engaged by abstract notions about justice and equality. He was not in fact a philosopher seeking to change the world. He was, though, deeply committed to changing that part of the world around him. The part he could control. The power he was interested in was the power of football manager vested in him. This wasn't power for its own sake. It was power used for a purpose, to create the game of football on the field the way he imagined it in his mind. If he had to be ruthless so be it. On the other hand if he had to be obedient that was all right as well.

141

Matt had always got what he wanted by negotiating with authority rather than by confronting the bosses. This was the Catholic doing secret deals with the Almighty, sinning and being forgiven, with a pragmatism that was offensive to the more rigorous, righteous Protestant mind. Morality was not an absolute, no more than justice or equality.

The lesson of his home was similarly compelling. He appeared to conform to Nellie's wishes but in the end he got his way and didn't end up in America. Subtle and patient, no confrontation necessary.

Confrontation and agitation were, like lofty rhetoric about freedom and solidarity, anathema to Mattha Busby who remembered the General Strike of 1926, its heady promises evaporating to leave the miners isolated and humiliated. This was power, naked and brutal and he had no intention of being a victim. Everything he'd seen in professional football confirmed the formative experiences of his young life: authority was to be respected: you ignored that imperative at your peril; to do so was idle. Thus as Riley correctly points out, Busby always knew exactly what he was and where he stood in the order of things.

The public man of great renown in 1948 was a politician who had bargained for power in a cruel business, professional football, not for fame or wealth but for the game itself, its magic which had nourished him first in grief, when Alex Busby had failed to return from the war, and which had continued to be the most delightful, beautiful, innocent pleasure in his life – Jean, Sheena and Sandy apart. Through the grime and filth of the coalface, through the wicked sectarianism of Bellshill, through the callous early years at Maine Road and the wasted futile years of fighting Hitler, through life itself and people, above all material considerations, there existed one thing which never disappointed or failed Matt: football, played gloriously as James and Gallacher had played it, as he himself had tried to do.

Busby was a politician with a purpose, an ideal. There was room in him for both characters. They were in essence the same. The football man. The private man was genial, capable of great tolerance and sympathy. But family apart, Jean above all, private life was, as it is for most great public achievers, a cursory

142

affair, consuming little of import to him, a trivial pursuit and indulgence of the genes inherited from Jimmy Greer.

When Matt Busby went to work there was always in his heart a sliver of ice called experience. He would be as good as it was possible to be. 'He was always firm in his principles,' Paddy McGrath suggests. The reality was that the precepts he now had to enforce were not *his* but those which governed professional football. The deal he brokered was on the bosses' terms not his. Alas, doing the best he could, for what he cared the most about, Busby, unlike Meredith and other great football men before 1948 and since, contrived not to see the professional game as it was but as he wished it to be.

Johnny Morris was a Meredith man. He saw the venality and the absurdity of observing laws which were meaningless to those who made them when it suited their own ends.

The Manchester United FA Cup heroes got their golf clubs in the end. A wealthy businessman friend of Busby's presented the clubs as a gift. This was an unsatisfactory compromise, charity instead of due reward. Busby himself had received due reward, a bonus of £1,750 for the Wembley victory. In October 1947 his original salary of £750 had been substantially increased to £1,750. So for the players a bonus of £20, or one and a half weeks' wages; for 'The Boss' a year's salary.

United recovered from their first game defeat to establish themselves among the leaders during the first three months of the '48/'49 season. There were disappointments; a 4–3 defeat at home to Blackpool and a vital 3–2 loss to Wolves at Molineux. Morris was as usual a serious contributor, scoring six goals and generally providing for others, but his uneasy relationship with Busby endured. On Tuesday mornings in the practice matches he never missed an opportunity to dig hard at Busby or Jimmy Murphy. They wanted it serious they could fucking have it serious. As well as being a goalscorer and dribbler Morris was a tough little bugger able to put himself about. 'I never met anyone harder,' Jimmy Murphy would say and he would know. One morning Johnny used his skill to taunt 'The Boss'. United had conceded a goal the previous Saturday to a free-kick just outside the box. A remedy was sought in training, a five-man wall to protect the goal. After much experimentation the composition and placement of the wall was agreed to every-one's satisfaction, Busby's in particular. But Morris demurred. There was still a possibility of scoring, he insisted. Irritated, yet again, 'The Boss' invited Johnny to try to prove his point. The odds were stacked against Morris. It is notoriously difficult, virtually impossible, to score 'cold' like this when everyone knows what's coming. Surprise and disguise are the weapons you need to score from free-kicks like this in match situations. Against your mates on the training ground, forget it. Busby was on a winner until the ball dipped wickedly over the wall into the back of the net. The laughter was not suppressed. Authority was not amused.

Morris was injured shortly afterwards, missing a couple of games. Ronnie Burke took his place and did well, scoring a couple of goals which ensured revenge in the return fixture with Derby County at the Baseball Ground, and one each in the vital Christmas victories over Liverpool and Arsenal.

When Morris was fit Busby didn't put him straight back in the side. The brooding rebel now had a cause. The row took place in front of the other players at the Cliff. Morris wasn't putting it in in training. Busby pulled him. What's the point in training for reserve games Morris responded when Busby confronted him. With that he made towards the dressing-room. Authority couldn't allow this challenge to pass. 'If you walk off this pitch you'll never kick a ball for this club again.' Busby's words echoed around the quiet ground. Morris cast a dismissive look over his shoulder and continued on his way.

After training, Busby went to his office and called the Press Association with the sensational news that Johnny Morris, Wembley hero, was available for transfer. Morris first learned of his fate when the journalists contacted him.

This was a watershed in Busby's managerial career, the moment when he – and those who belonged to his family – discovered the boundaries of tolerance, the point beyond which even the most gifted dare not tread. Johnny Morris was expendable – despite being the most valuable player in the club. Aged twenty-four he was younger than the others by a considerable distance. Some of the others in the Cup-winning team were approaching, if not at, the veteran stage. Morris and

Henry Cockburn were ones for the future. In eighty-three games Morris had scored a remarkable thirty-two goals – and made more again. He was Busby's type of player. But not his type of man.

Busby could never fathom Johnny Morris, he subsequently confided to an early biographer: 'I've tried every angle. I've bullied, I've used flattery. I've tried every way, but I just can't get through.'

One could argue that far from being unable to fathom Morris, Busby understood him perfectly. Morris was a talented man, intelligent, of independent disposition, who possessed convictions about his rights and the true nature of professional football which were correct and not amenable to 'flattery' or 'bullying', to paternalism or authoritarianism. Johnny Morris might be most fairly described as an uncomfortable reminder of the nature of the deal Busby had entered into with authority. It could be said that rebellion was the only honourable response to slavery, but, that was not the way Matt Busby saw things. Dissent was a threat to his club. Matt had heard rumours of illegal approaches to Morris and Busby had learned of secret negotiations in which all kinds of bribes were dangled in front of Morris. There was intense speculation about where Morris would go and for how much. Derby County were favourites to sign him. 'Matt was told that Derby had offered Johnny a tobacconist's shop to sign,' Paddy McGrath reveals. 'Matt had him in and warned him that he didn't want Johnny coming to the club about these offers. "Don't upset my players," Matt told him. "I don't want Jack Rowley and Charlie Mitten and the other lads unsettled by this kind of talk." Matt told him he wouldn't inform the League about what he'd found out provided Johnny kept his mouth shut.' If he fuelled discontent at United, Morris was warned, 'I'll have you before the League.'

In March 1949 Johnny Morris signed for Derby County for a world record fee of £24,000. United were due to play Wolves in the FA Cup semi-final a few days later. The game with Wolves ended in a 1–1 draw, Wolves winning the replay 1–0. There is little doubt that Johnny Morris would have made the difference between Wembley and defeat. Busby had willingly paid a high price for the principles upon which he was determined to build Manchester United.

Johnny Morris played 336 more League and Cup games for Derby and Leicester City, scoring seventy-seven goals. His replacement, Johnny Downie, was a twenty-three-year-old Scot from Lanark bought for £16,500 from Bradford Park Avenue. This was Busby's most expensive signing at the time but Downie enjoyed four good seasons at United and played a prominent part in the Championship-winning season of 1951/52.

Rigorous about illegal payments, Busby was scrupulously fair about money players were entitled to. When Johnny Aston roomed with Tom Finney on an England trip he learned that Preston counted time spent on the club's books as an amateur before the war in calculating when five-year benefit payments were due. Thus, Aston discovered that although he had been a pro for only four post-war years he was now entitled to his benefit under Football League regulations. Back at United Aston went to see Busby, who told him he was wrong. Aston explained about Finney and Preston, so Busby checked with club secretary Walter Crickmer and discovered that Johnny was correct and promptly back-dated benefits due to eight first team players.

Manchester United finished second in the Championship for the third year running in 1949 and their semi-final exit to Wolves in the FA Cup heightened Busby's frustration. For all their style they were just short of Championship quality and this team was not getting any younger. History proves that what would be remembered as the ' '48 Team' had in fact reached its glorious peak that day at Wembley. Now they seemed to be wearying and no obvious solution was to hand.

By 1949 Busby knew they would not improve. The conventional wisdom suggests that he was sanguine about this, secure in the knowledge that the youth policy was working, with a number of extremely gifted young players on stream waiting to burst into the first team. This is far from the truth. Indeed as the expensive acquisition of Johnny Downie in 1949 indicates, the first four years of the Busby/Murphy regime yielded nothing in the way of home-bred players. After winning the Central

146

League in 1948 Jimmy Murphy had confessed to Busby that not a single player in the reserve side was good enough for the first team. So behind the frustration of the near misses in FA Cup and Championship in '48/'49 lay the worry about the future.

Louis Rocca, who had been there from the Newton Heath days was also slowing down. He had served United magnificently in many roles, chiefly that of contact-man, and in essence the '48 Team was his final legacy to the club. The following year, 1950, Rocca died, his legend, if not the nature of his contribution, secure. Matt's first great team had been built with men Rocca had found, the fruit of native cunning rather than football wisdom.

Seeking someone to replace Rocca, Busby turned to Joe Armstrong, a fifty-four-year-old GPO engineer who had been scouting for Manchester City. As in Rocca's case, a myth which spoke of his unique eye for talent would envelop Joe Armstrong. As with Rocca, the reality of the great scout – which both men undoubtedly were – is in Joe Armstrong's case more intriguing than the mythology. Joe was a more conventional character than Louis. But he possessed the same emollient skills, coming from the same Manchester Catholic background as his predecessor. A tiny man, his thatch of grey hair crowning a mischievous laughter-lined face, Joe was a charmer. He was a delightful man with a shrewd mind and an instinctive grasp of the human condition, a man of his caste and his city. Whatever Joe knew about football he knew more about people, working-class folk, men and especially mothers. The appointment of Joe Armstrong was as vital as any Matt Busby made in his managerial career.

Once more an understanding of people proved to be of as much importance as knowing the game. As a consequence of the dearth of good young players at United Busby resolved in the summer of '49 to intensify the search for gifted schoolboys. The club had made a handsome £50,000 profit that year but the money would not be invested in instant solutions to the problems Busby knew awaited him. He was encouraged to take the longer view by the three-year contract United awarded him in March 1949. His salary of £3,250 was enormous at that time, five times the maximum his players could earn, four times his original salary. Nevertheless few managers, if any, finding themselves in Busby's circumstances would have had the courage to eschew the transfer-market option.

Joe Armstrong's instructions were to get the best, which meant keeping a close eye on representative schoolboy football at international and Schools' Trophy level. Talk of scouring the parks and making divine judgements based on a mystical gift for spotting talent – the stuff of scouting mythology and the Rocca and Armstrong legends – is nonsense. Everybody knew who the most gifted youngsters were and where they were. Of course judgement had to be exercised but that took place later in the process when youngsters had arrived at the club to be tested by Jimmy Murphy and Bert Whalley. *They* were the football men, Joe was the procurer. Charm was Joe's great weapon. Mothers were the target. Other clubs offered money, Joe provided reassurance. Women liked him. He was kindly yet flirtatious in a comforting way. He was the type of man you'd feel would look after your lad as a lad as well as a footballer. Mothers didn't understand professional football and were apt to be apprehensive about big city life with all its temptations. Joe understood their fears only too well. That was always his opening pitch. The box of chocolates and the bunch of flowers invariably followed, not on the first visit to the house, and not in an obvious way, but when the time was right for the intimacy implicit in the gift. The more cynical families might rebuff the flowers and chocolates routine, but this was OK. Manchester United didn't want a certain type, they wanted the Right Type.

As Billy Behan emphasises: 'They would always ask about the family, what was the father like, what sort of people were they. It didn't matter how good the boy was if the other things were wrong.'

If the family was religious Joe would add a Miraculous Medal he'd brought specially from Rome to the other gifts he bore. The medal would be for real, as were the other kindnesses.

Fathers were handled differently, more man to man over a pint of ale in the taproom if that suited. Men, knowing more about football, were impressed by United's style, even more by Matt Busby's renowned character and most of all by United's policy of giving youth a chance.

148

The Armstrong approach worked in many ways, not the least of them being that the greedy, cynical and insensitive would be weeded out at the wooing stage.

All of this remained a hypothesis before Joe hit the road in the summer of '49. Of the great team that would emerge from this unique system only four youngsters were on United's books when, on 24 August, the club returned to Old Trafford for their opening home game of the season against Bolton. United won 3–0, Charlie Mitten striking the first goal scored at the ground for eight years. Among the 41,000 watching were four young men, Roger Byrne, Jack Blanchflower, Mark Jones and Jeff Whitefoot.

The '49/'50 season was a disappointment in the end. Manchester United finished fourth in the First Division and lost 2–0 away to Chelsea in the sixth round of the FA Cup. This was disappointing only by the standards Matt Busby had set and the expectations of United's supporters and those in the game in general. Busby was particularly troubled by the side's poor finish to the season. After beating Middlesborough 3–2 at Ayresome Park on 11 March United went eight games without a win before ending the season at Old Trafford as they'd begun with a 3–0 victory over Fulham. During that bleak series of games they lost at home to Birmingham, Blackpool and champions-elect Portsmouth.

His established players had all performed well, but not well enough. Charlie Mitten had been the outstanding player of the season. Ever present, Charlie scored sixteen League goals from outside-left, four of them coming in a 7–0 rout of Aston Villa at Old Trafford early in March. He didn't score again that season, a lean spell which coincided with Stan Pearson's. But for a winger sixteen goals was a splendid year's work.

The most obvious weakness in Busby's side was goalkeeper Jack Crompton. Aware of this Busby had signed an eighteen-year-old from Darlington for a modest £6,000. Ray Wood was for the future. In the summer of 1950 Reg Allen was purchased from QPR.

An uncomfortable degree of uncertainty about United's prospects in the new decade notwithstanding, Matt Busby had much to be contented with in his fortieth year. He was among

149

the most respected men ever of his caste, but in more practical terms he wielded more influence within his club than any professional ever had. To all he was 'The Boss', and in general this title was a reflection of the respect he commanded. Respect rather than fear characterised the relationship between him and his players. They thought him shrewd and tough. On money he was unyielding, in other matters he was sympathetic. This was especially appreciated in matters directly related to football. He was patient if you were having a bad time, forgiving if you made a mistake which cost a game. He never demanded the impossible, there was no ranting and raving. United's dressing-room was a refuge unlike many others which resembled nut-houses with all the violent mood-swings of a psychiatric ward. For United the enemy was outside which made a change from other clubs where he was known as the manager.

Busby's relationship with his Board was excellent, the real source of his unprecedented influence as manager. The radical change he had sought to achieve in the manager's status was realised, and when James Gibson was terminally ill, Busby was an assiduous visitor to his chairman. They had had their early troubles, but these were now long forgotten. The decisive confrontation had taken place soon after Busby arrived when the club's office was still on Gibson's business premises at Cornbrook Cold Storage. The possibilities for a meddling director were too tempting, and Gibson succumbed once too often to suggest that United needed to buy a player he fancied. He had after all secured Jack Rowley. Busby's account of this affair does not quite ring true. In the books Matt claims to have rebuffed James Gibson by telling him in no uncertain terms that *he* was the manager and that he'd survived before joining Manchester United and if necessary would survive without the club. The chairman is said to have left the room angrily. Fifteen tense minutes later he returned to apologise and assure Matt that there would be no more interference.

Today Matt smiles and shrugs his shoulders when asked about this scene from another life. It was not his style. But there is no doubt that, like Harold Hardman, James Gibson got the signals right even if they weren't conveyed so bluntly. Matt was far too subtle a man to issue ultimatums of that kind.

In 1950 Gibson was his greatest admirer and protector. Busby had delivered his dream precisely as ordered. Now this fine man, who had in his own way done as much as Busby to restore old glories to United, was chiefly concerned that in his absence nobody else was creating problems for 'The Boss'. When Gibson asked, 'Is anyone interfering, Mr Busby?' he had his putative successor, Harold Hardman, foremost in his mind. Busby assured him that he was OK.

Life outside football fulfilled the part of Busby not consumed by the game. His salary was huge by contemporary standards. Yet he remained a man of modest tastes. He liked to drive a top-of-the-range car and dressed immaculately as always with some distinctive style. He was in this personal regard image-conscious – not for vanity, but rather as a reminder that he was no slave.

His most profound pleasure was in his family – his real family – Jean, Sheena and Sandy. They were very close. The man who came home was unaffected by his public life. On Fridays, at lunchtime, Matt would stop at the fish and chip shop for the family meal. The Busbys lived in the same modest semi in Chorlton. To their neighbours they were lovely people, this feeling was reciprocated.

Social life took place at weekends. Jean and Matt liked to go out for dinner, usually with a couple of friends – Paddy McGrath and wife Jean, Johnny Foy, a bookmaker and, like McGrath, a Manchester-Irish Catholic, or Eric Richardson who was in the carpet trade. They went to restaurants in the pretty Cheshire villages a fifteen minute drive from town. Steak Houses were beginning to open up although they were still beyond the reach of the population at large.

Jock Dodds, a famous, recently retired Scottish international introduced Matt to Paddy McGrath and their life-long friendship began in Blackpool immediately after the war. 'Matt had just taken over United,' Paddy explains. 'Jock introduced us in the Savoy restaurant in Blackpool.' Dodds and McGrath were dining when Busby walked in. 'There's Matt, he's a good lad,' Dodds told McGrath, whom he knew to be a great United fan. 'Would you like to meet him?' Busby and McGrath hit it off straight away. They had much in common.

McGrath, a Collyhurst lad with an Irish Catholic back-ground, moved to Blackpool in 1939. He'd once earned a living as a prizefighter in the fairground boxing booth. He worked on distribution for the *Daily Mirror*, then when war broke out used his experience as a pro boxer to get the relatively cushy number of PTI with the RAF. Based in Blackpool, Paddy embarked on what he describes as 'a varied career'. Fighting Germans was the least of Blackpool's concerns between '39 and '45.

Paddy mixed his duties for the *Daily Mirror* and the RAF with some commercial activity of his own. 'I started an ice-cream business. Then I sold it and went into candy floss and rock. Blackpool was at its peak during the war. Those were great years, you've no idea what the war was like here. Apart from the fellas in Burma and elsewhere who were suffering, if you were home on leave every pub was like New Year's Eve because everyone thought I'm not stopping in. There was no television, only a few wirelesses and there were so many girls whose husbands were away. It's only natural. It's physical. And a lot of girls who wanted to remain faithful nobody would take them out. After two or three dates they would be dropped. So a lot of women had to go crooked.

'There was so much life. There wasn't a bomb in Blackpool all through the war. All the scum, all the prostitutes, all the villains came to Blackpool. There were 80,000 airmen there. You could double that with Yanks. There was a lot of anti-American feeling of course because they had more of every-thing. I often said to English people, "How can you get on with the Irish or anybody else when you can't get on with your allies?" They used to say about the Yanks, over-paid, over-sexed and over-here. The girls were very loose, they loved them.'

Everything was in short supply – well most things – so this vast playground needed servicing. Paddy played his part. He didn't belong to the twilight world of the Blackpool night, but he knew the boys who ran the place. A big, handsome, Irish rogue, he clung to the Busby-style notion of respectability. He remained a Catholic boy, conscious of his roots and faith yet possessing the subtlety of mind to reconcile worldliness with the religious convictions he espoused.

The young McGrath was a bit of a scrapper. 'We were at Belle Vue at the boxing one night with our wives,' Paddy recalls. 'There was a disputed decision and I was on my feet screaming at the ref. A few Scottish tearaways, Prods, spotted me and Matt. They started having a go at Matt, "You papish bastard Busby", that sort of thing. I was going to have 'em – they wouldn't have done it in Blackpool 'cause they'd have known the score with me – anyway Matt got hold of me and calmed me down. I always listened to him. He had that thing, that air of authority. He woudn't shout but you took notice.'

Matt and Paddy on the town, two handsome guys, smartly dressed, cut a dash. And they did venture out to play. Prudent Matt was, a prude he was not. Matt enjoyed the company of self-made men, the better if they were amusing, a touch extravagant by nature, untainted by pretention. Wherever they went on these outings he was greeted reverently. Restaurants would hush as he walked in, handsome, large, impressive.

The Irish writer John McGahern recalls seeing Matt in the old Russell Hotel in Dublin at this time. The Russell was small but grand, nestling on the corner of St Stephen's Green, the city's most fashionable Georgian square. Here the young Charles Haughey and other dashing blades cavorted in the post-war years. McGahern knew nothing of football and Manchester United. 'This incredibly imposing man walked in off the street. He was an extraordinary presence, like a great politician or theatrical figure. Who is that we all wondered.' Forty years later the writer's memory of Mattha from Old Orbiston remains vivid.

On Sundays Matt would take Jean to Manchester's Opera House, where Tommy Appleby, the manager, was another pal, and the Busbys would sit in the best seats as his guests. Afterwards, backstage, they would meet the stars. Jean enjoyed this more than Matt. She, more extrovert than he, was fascinated by the glamour of such evenings.

When business took Matt and the team away Jean would often take the players' wives for a night on the town. She was as much a woman's woman as Matt was essentially a man's man. She gossiped and laughed, enquired about families, kids at school, teenage traumas and other ordinary preoccupations.

153

For Jean as much as Matt Manchester United was infinitely more than a football club chasing medals and glory. It was family. The most rewarding moments were not those of public acclaim – pleasing though that was – but the more intimate, personal times, when troubles were shared as often as triumphs, lives intermingling, a sense of togetherness and community offering the kind of emotional security, the feeling of *belonging*, which had not always been there in her life or Matt's.

Gambling was Matt's one vice. He was a keen dog man and would visit the tracks with Eric Richardson whenever the mood took him. This indulgence he could well afford although he gambled, like all the inveterates, until it hurt. Apart from that there was little pain in a private life that promised much the year he was forty.

9

Unlikely Champions

'I admit we do not appear to be as
good as we were – but we are not as
bad either.'

Matt Busby

In the summer of 1950 Manchester United went to the United
States to play a series of games there and across the border in
Canada. It was the trip of a lifetime. They travelled tourist-class
on the *Queen Mary* from Southampton. The tour was a great
public relations success. Football was enjoying one of its
periodic booms in North America and the 'Great Manchester
United' were fêted everywhere they went. The fun began on the
Queen Mary on the Atlantic crossing. The smart, handsome
footballers caused a frisson of excitement – especially among
the ladies – in the bars, restaurant and the ballroom of the
Queen Mary. The ship afforded them undreamed of luxuries
which could be savoured without dread of the forbidding
routine of daily life on the training ground. They cut a dash
enjoying the fun, the dancing and romancing, knowing they
wouldn't have to pay for it the next morning.

Soon after they docked in New York, though, the glamour
began to pale. Results were poor, the travelling, mostly by
train, soon wore them out. In a ghosted column he was filing for
the *Manchester Chronicle*, captain Johnny Carey wrote of the
wonder of it all. His report was headlined:

JOHNNY CAREY WRITES A LETTER FROM HOLLYWOOD
We've all had an experience we shall never forget: A visit
to the M.G.M. film studios in Hollywood and talks with the
stars.

How wonderful this was to us, accustomed as we are to
having the spot-light focused on ourselves so frequently!

155

We made our way through the huge gates and directly into the restaurant, where we were accommodated at two long tables laid ready for us.

The restaurant was just like any other restaurant – except that our fellow-diners were celebrated people. We hardly ate anything, so engrossed were we all in spotting the stars.

We saw Arlene Dahl and Evelyn Keyes having lunch together, and in the corner was George Murphy, well known to film lovers for his musicals.

Clark Gable came striding in and hung his Stetson on top of my cap!

Ladies, may I tell you that he looks as handsome off the screen as on it: and I don't say that because he was courteous enough to come over to our tables and bid us welcome to M.G.M. and hope we would have a good time in Hollywood.

Reality was less enchanting. The players were allowed five dollars a day spending money. But, because North American hotels didn't include meals in their tariff this money was literally eaten away. This consumer's paradise was no place to be without money. The atmosphere of uninhibited materialism exacerbated the mood of disenchantment among the heroes with empty pockets. The arduous trips across this vast continent added to their annoyance. They were playing to big crowds, everyone was very nice, but they were having to scrimp and save to eat.

When 'The Boss' was approached he was unsympathetic. Weren't they lucky to be here at all? Rules were rules.

One evening in New York, where United were staying at the Times Square Hotel, Charlie Mitten received a phone call from Neil Franklin, Stoke City's England centre-half. Franklin had been approached by an agent for Sante Fe FC in Bogotá, Colombia. The Colombians were offering unbelievable money if players were prepared to go to Bogotá.

'How much?' Charlie asked.

The first newspaper accounts suggested the offer was £2,500 a year and £40 a week.

Mitten claims it was more: 'Neil said they were offering five grand to sign on and guaranteeing another five grand a year, £40 a week, plus £35 for a win and £17 for a draw. We were on about

£750 per year including bonuses. So I said, sounds alright to me. We had finished the tour so I went to Matt and said I'm going now. Good luck, Boss. He said, "Oh no you're not, you've got a contract." '

'I reminded him that my contract had expired. You didn't sign me on a new contract so I'm a free agent, I told him.'

This was true. Players' contracts were a formality in the English game. Technically a player was free once his contract expired, but in reality the only option to renewing his contract was to find employment outside the game. The club could decide not to re-engage the player, who was bound as surely as any serf. In the event of dispute the club could retain a player's registration – his licence to work – indefinitely in return for a nominal wage on the lowest scale of a few hundred pounds a year. The agreement which governed a professional's working life could hardly be described as a contract.

Matt Busby's first reaction to the devastating news of Mitten's defection reflects the smug disregard for professionals' rights prevalent at the time. The Slaves Charter applied worldwide wherever the game's international governing body FIFA's writ ran. What Busby didn't initially grasp was that Colombia was not a member of FIFA and therefore Mitten was free to go. Charlie would not be joining the line of United players trooping into Walter Crickmer's office to sign on again when pre-season training began the following month.

Matt was shattered. This was a crippling blow. Charlie Mitten was one of United's best players. He had played 113 consecutive games for United, scored sixty-one goals in 161 appearances at outside-left, and was reckoned to be the best uncapped winger in England. At twenty-nine Charlie was at his peak, he was irreplaceable. Worse, unlike Johnny Morris, Matt liked the stocky, effervescent little character who was now blithely saying goodbye. Charlie was good for morale on grey mornings on the training ground when the banter, for which he had a gift, kept spirits high. You could measure Charlie's contribution on Saturday afternoon in terms of the goals he scored and created, but his personality was an intangible asset to the family, beyond price.

The news caused a sensation when it broke. Neil Franklin

was England's centre-half. As well as Charlie and Franklin, George Mountfield, also from Stoke, and Everton's Billy Higgins had accepted contracts with Sante Fe. And there were rumours that others might join them. Busby's anger grew when he learned that Henry Cockburn and Johnny Aston had also been approached. When he challenged Charlie's two pals they admitted that an offer had been made. The return journey on the *Queen Mary* was sombre.

Meanwhile, Charlie was in Bogotá. 'I went down and had a look and it was a nice place. I had a training session, played a match which was a sort of trial, signed-on and got the readies. It was fabulous. We had a marvellous house, a maid and a chauffeur.'

A few weeks previously Johnny Carey had dismissed the Colombian gold in a piece filed for the *Evening Chronicle*. Under the headline £3,500 A YEAR DOES NOT TEMPT US Carey wrote disdainfully: 'The Millionairos Club of Colombia are looking for players to go there. I've had a phone call at my hotel saying that a representative of theirs will be contacting me and some of the other United players. The salary he is said to be offering is £3,500 per year.

'We have not seen him yet and you can take it from me, that none of the United players would consider such a proposition because it would mean "finis" as regards our future in Britain.'

Charlie Mitten had demonstrated how misguided this analysis was. As the United party headed for Southampton there seemed every prospect that Cockburn and Aston would follow their mate. They were considering the proposition. The offer, like Carey's apparently smug disregard for it, must be seen in the context of the times. The signing-on fee plus the first year's salary was equivalent to a lifetime's earnings in Britain. The term professional meant you played the game for money. So why accept £750 a year when you could earn ten times as much elsewhere. The maid and chauffeur were mere symbols of respect for the craft you had mastered. Carey's attitude testified to the extraordinary psychological confidence trick the Masters had played on their Slaves. To even contemplate liberty was dishonourable. You belonged with your club in the English game. This was *natural*. The idea that, like other professionals,

158

be they carpenters, entertainers or the very businessman who was reminding you of your *duty*, you should work for the best money available was treacherous, and treachery would not be forgiven.

An astonishing example of the values which copperfastened this system is revealed by Tom Finney, one of the greatest English players of all time. Finney spent his whole career at Preston North End. In 1952 after England had drawn 1–1 with Italy in Florence, Finney was approached by the president of the Sicilian club, Palermo. He was offered £10,000 to sign for the Italian club, wages of £130 per month, huge bonuses, a villa on the Mediterranean and a car. Preston were paying him £14 a week, £12 in the summer, £2 for a win and £1 for a draw.

Finney was tempted by Palermo's offer. When he got back to Preston he sought an interview with Nat Buck, the local builder who was club Chairman at the time. Buck was incensed at Finney's nerve. Alluding to his great player's local renown, the chairman said without blinking, 'What's 10,000 quid to thee Tom? Nay lad, tha'll play for us or tha'll play for nobody!'

The great players were treated like dirt. The Football Association rule on travelling to and from international matches at this time offers another damning illustration of the status of the game's greatest players. When playing for their country, players were obliged to travel in the same class on trains as they did when playing for their clubs. Only Arsenal travelled first class. Thus, after helping England beat Scotland at Hampden Park one year, Wilf Mannion of Middlesborough had to stand in the corridor throughout his wearying journey home.

It is, in retrospect, tempting to scorn men like Carey, Finney and Stan Matthews for conforming to the whims of the merchant class who governed the national game. But they were, like Matt Busby, men of their time, with the mores of a class-ridden culture ingrained in their souls.

When rumours of the Colombian approaches first surfaced early on the North American tour Matt Busby had been unconcerned. Henry Rose filed a report from Toronto for the *Daily Express* which was as emphatic as it was to prove inaccurate: 'The touring Manchester United lost their first match here last night by 4–2 to an FA XI, but they are not losing Mitten and Cockburn to gold-paved Bogotá. Nimble-footed Charlie and midget Henry turned down feelers by Franklin's club. "Please yourself," they were told by Matt Busby. Both are glad to be soon going home and prefer to stay there.'

Busby had certainly not told his players to please themselves, for he knew that the loss of Mitten, Cockburn and Aston would destroy his team. That was the prospect as the *Queen Mary* arrived in Southampton.

Johnny Aston was the first to relent and declare his loyalty to United. Cockburn told Alf Clarke that he was giving the Bogotá offer 'serious consideration'. Finally Busby persuaded Henry, but it was a close shave. Using the press adroitly to affect indifference, Busby kept his nerve in public while privately deploying the force of his unique personality to the full. The problem of replacing Mitten remained. Newspaper speculation linked United with Wolves's international winger Johnny Hancocks, whose fee, an estimated £20,000, would consume a substantial proportion of the £35,000 profit the club made in 1950. Busby's distaste for the transfer-market, allied to his belief in his own power to improvise and motivate sent him instead to Bolton where he bought Harry McShane, a thirty-year-old veteran journeyman, for a song. Harry, father of actor Ian McShane, had grown up a stone's throw from the Busbys' cottage in Old Orbiston, and Matt and Harry were well acquainted from twenty years before when, every summer, Matt returned to spend his three-month summer holiday among his own.

'When I was a boy,' Harry remembers, 'Matt used to come around to the pitch at Orbiston and play with us. He was always a gentle, decent kind of man, a lovely fella.'

When Jock Dodds helped lure Charlie Mitten away from Old Trafford Busby was angry. But he had not lived in an ivory tower and was well versed in the ways of the world. Yet, for all his bonhomie once the business was done, for all his fondness for characters like Dodds and McGrath, he was unforgiving when impropriety tarnished his own patch. This points to the difference between Busby the man and Busby the manager.

One doubts whether Johnny Carey, for example, would fit in the 'good lad' category. In the lexicon of pro football, then as now, 'good lads' are game for a laugh, a drink or a gamble and tolerant rather than idealistic about life. Johnny Morris was a 'good lad', Charlie Mitten also. Matt Busby was good in those terms, but only up to a point. When it came to running his football club he was against 'goodladmanship' if it ran counter to the laws of the Football Association. Thus, as McGarth vouches, he remained 'firm on his principles'. He also minded his behaviour.

Twelve months after leaving England, Charlie Mitten was forced to return when Colombia joined FIFA and became bound by Football Association law. Charlie went to see Busby hoping for a pardon. 'I was a better player, I told him, I'd learned a lot about the game in South America. I'd played for Millionairos with Alfredo Di Stefano and some of the best foreign players.'

Busby was unimpressed. United still hadn't replaced him but he had to go. He was fined £250 and suspended for six months, before being transferred to Fulham for £20,000. During his suspension Busby refused to let him train at Old Trafford. No contamination could be allowed although he was still fond of 'Cheeky' Charlie. Mitten played for a pub team on Sunday mornings to keep fit.

The Bogotá Affair opened Matt's eyes, made him realise how vulnerable his family and the English game in general was to a world beyond its narrow boundaries. Money talked, and the noise would only grow louder and more insistent.

Mitten's defection was reflected in the following season's performance. The statistics of season '50/'51 don't reveal the extent of the disruption caused. United finished second in the First Division, ostensibly an improvement on the previous year, but lost 1–0 to Birmingham in the sixth round of the FA Cup. United's high league placing behind champions Portsmouth was due to a powerful finish to the season in which eight victories in the last ten games enabled them to leapfrog past clubs who had been in serious contention when it mattered. The absence of Mitten threw the whole side out of kilter. Astute shuffling of his resources had always served Busby in the past, and in the '50/'51 season he did his best to conjure his way out of trouble once more. Billy McGlen, a defender, was given the number 11 shirt for the first seven games. That failed. Next it was Harry McShane's turn. Harry lasted until Christmas. United had a shocking holiday series, losing three games in succession, two of them at Old Trafford to Bolton and, 3–5, to Sunderland.

People began muttering about new players. Even Busby himself was the target of some speculation. In January he was forced to go public to deny a rumour that he was in danger of losing his job. 'I'M NOT GETTING THE SACK' the headline screeched from the front page of a popular sports magazine, *All Football*. Busby, most uncharacteristically, lent credence to the stories by the vehemence of his response.

> Let me scotch first those rumours which I am told go the rounds – I am not resigning. I am not being sacked and there is neither trouble or panic in our camp. These rumours seem to have started because we are not the glamour team we used to be. Maybe we are not. You cannot stay on top all the time and we had a longer run than usual. A set of players hit such a wonderful peak only once in a lifetime. Now I admit we do not appear to be as good as we were – but we are not as bad either. We are in the top half of the First Division and there are many worse teams in the land. We had a big shock when Charlie Mitten went to Bogotá. We were not prepared for that. Who was?
>
> Some of my critics say I should have gone out and spent some of our £50,000 profit. Well you can call me a canny Scotsman if you like, but I don't believe you can buy success.

Busby's remedy was to try some more alterations to the side. He preferred the men he knew to outsiders not versed in his way of playing the game. There was also a serious question mark against the ability of many players who would have cost large transfer-fees. He believed that this was a non-vintage era in English football. The game was still suffering the after-effects of the war, for during the six years between 1939 and 1945 no new players had been properly blooded in the professional game. Good news was coming from Jimmy Murphy and Bert

Whalley: the kids were better than they'd been. So, instead of buying, Matt held his nerve. Jack Rowley moved to outside-left for the final Christmas game and stayed there for the rest of the season. Johnny Aston was pushed up to centre-forward, being replaced by Billy McGlen at full-back. Harry McShane switched from left to outside-right and a youngster, Don Gibson, made his début at right-half. Thus, the crisis was beaten off, time was borrowed. That at least was the intention.

The youngsters who were the source of all Busby's hopes in the summer of 1951 included Roger Byrne, who at twenty-two hardly fitted the category of kid. Roger, a left-winger, had been signed in 1949 from local soccer where he played for Ryder Brow Boys Club. Jeff Whitefoot was a wing-half, a beautiful striker of the ball who had already played for the first team, the youngest ever to do so, at sixteen years of age. Jackie Blanchflower and Mark Jones were two more of whom great things were expected. The most exciting of all the youngsters was seventeen-year-old Cliff Birkett, a winger from Newton-le-Willows, who was certain to be a future star. Busby reassured his directors that the future would be as exciting as the past.

James Gibson had signed his last minutes as chairman on 20 June 1950. He was to die on 11 September 1951. Mr Gibson's dying wish, conveyed by Mrs Anne Gibson to their son Alan who would succeed him on the board, was that the young man should support Mr Busby at board meetings. James Gibson's role in the rebirth of Manchester United, the values and disciplines he brought to the task of administering the club, have too often been overlooked. He was a fine man, far from typical of the boardroom breed. The football on the field bore witness to him as well as 'The Boss' in the dressing-room.

A poignant entry in the United minutes of that period, its presence due as much to Busby as to Gibson, records that United made an ex-gratia payment to Billy Meredith to enable the great old man to clear the mortgage on his home.

Matt Busby had little reason for real optimism as United faced into the '51/'52 season. The memory of January was fresh in his mind. In his seventh season he'd delivered one trophy and, so far, the promise of his early days had not entirely been fulfilled. United were always to be respected but, in a less than enthralling First Division, they were no longer feared. The club made a profit of £22,677 in 1951, and that summer Busby spent £25,000 to buy Johnny Berry from Birmingham. Berry was twenty-five, fast, brave and direct, a right-winger with guts and an eye for goals. At the end of the '49/'50 season Berry had scored one of the best goals ever seen at Old Trafford to defeat United.

Busby's best hope was that United would not lose ground. Remarkably they won the Championship. The '52 Championship is hardly what Matt Busby is remembered for, but this achievement bears unique testimony to his football wisdom, and his powers of man-management. The themes never changed, the simple gospel of simple football preached to men who had been listening to it for seven years. The backbone of the Championship team was formed by the heroes of '48. Carey moved to right-half in mid-December, just short of his thirty-third birthday, now to scale new heights as a player and a leader. Johnny Aston missed the first half of the season through illness. In January he returned at centre-forward to play his part, vastly different from his role in '48. Ernie Bond, a young man signed from non-league football, played outside-left early on before Jack Rowley replaced him. Thirty-two years of age, Rowley was the magnificent inspiration of United's challenge for a title it had seemed they'd never win. Jack scored hat-tricks in the first two games of the season, another against Stoke City in September and finished with three goals against Arsenal, who were beaten in style 6–1 on 26 April 1952. The Championship trophy was back at Old Trafford for the first time since 1911. Jack Rowley's thirty goals did most to secure the triumph. For Rowley, Carey, Chilton, Cockburn, Stan Pearson and Johnny Aston, who'd been with 'The Boss' from the start, this was a glorious, unexpected last hurrah.

For Roger Byrne, who'd made his début at Liverpool in November, the old heroes' valedictory season was a beginning. He'd played left-back on his début but finished the season scoring seven vital goals in seven games at outside-left. For Matt Busby the Championship was a relief, some time bought, proof that people mattered as he'd always thought they did, that, properly prepared, they were capable of anything.

10

An End – A Beginning

'Matt Busby was like a god. You'd
be conscious of him sitting in the
stand, you wanted to show him how
good you were.'

Bobby Charlton

Matt Busby's most profound achievement in his first seven
seasons at Manchester United was the creation of the kind of
football club he would have wished, as a player, to play for. He
had been firm in his resolve to acquire the power he believed
was necessary to do the job. He had used that power wisely. In
so far as was possible, given professional football's iniquitous
governing ethos, the club he had built reflected his values. This
applied both to the football played and to the atmosphere in the
dressing-room and on the training ground. The United captaincy was important to Busby. His skippers were no mere
coin-tossers. In this respect Manchester United were about to
make a significant change. At thirty-three Johnny Carey had
decided to accept an offer to manage Blackburn Rovers,
declining the coaching job Matt Busby offered him at Old
Trafford.

Carey had served Manchester United magnificently. In his
time at the club, stretching back to 1937, he had played in nine
different positions. More importantly, he provided leadership
which was (the narrower, rather grudging dressing-room perspective notwithstanding) symbolic of the ethos Matt Busby
had sought to inculcate into his football club from the beginning. Carey was loyal and decent, his behaviour always impec-
cable. He played the game graciously.

Johnny Carey was neither militant nor one of the lads. But
that was not what was required of him. Like Busby, he came

to stand for something by which Manchester United wished to be known: something that was noble rather than feckless, dignified rather than coarse.

Before he departed Carey was invited to the boardroom at Old Trafford for a small celebration with the directors. This was the first time he had ever been invited upstairs.

Roger Byrne replaced Carey as captain. He was a very different type. Byrne was a tough, cool customer. He was his own man, intelligent, with a view of the world which didn't conform to dressing-room values, or anyone else's for that matter. He respected 'The Boss' but he wasn't a Boss's man. He had a temper. When roused, Byrne was defiant. Nevertheless, Busby valued him highly as a player and a potential leader. But there would be only one 'Boss' at Old Trafford.

Any assessment of Busby's first phase in management must extend beyond trophies won. His club would be about the character of the people in it: men like Byrne, Bert Whalley, Tom Curry, Bill Inglis, Jimmy Murphy and Arthur Powell. Here gifted young footballers experienced the professional game for the first time. Here, as Busby through his own experience knew only too well, dreams dissolved to become a reality.

Apart from Busby, Jimmy Murphy was the most influential of these characters. Jimmy Murphy lived in Whalley Range. Every morning he was up first to make a coal fire in the kitchen, and cook breakfast. His wife would get up after her morning cup of tea to get their six kids ready for school. Except for Sundays this was all the family saw of Jimmy. He worked long hours. He'd been doing this for seven years.

Jimmy travelled to work by train – he never drove a car. Whalley Range to London Road (now Piccadilly) then to the railway station that ran alongside Old Trafford. He was an anonymous commuter, always smartly dressed in a suit, striped tie, white shirt, in winter a dark overcoat. He was medium height. He'd be hard to place on the train. A small businessman perhaps, under pressure to keep things going. He bore an air of restrained anxiety about him. Jimmy couldn't wait to get to work.

By the early Fifties a man of lesser passion would have been demoralised. He worked a seventy or eighty hour week with little to show for the time invested. The first team's success had had little to do with the reserve and youth policies. The old boys had done it. Roger Byrne, the best of the newcomers, had bypassed the system. Roger was a grammar-school boy who'd done his National Service before signing for United as a young man. When Matt needed a player he'd invariably had to forsake his principles and go out and buy. Johnny Berry . . . Harry McShane . . . Johnny Downie . . . Reg Allen.

Jimmy's reserves had been disappointing. Brian Birch, an inside-forward he'd fancied had not made it. Billy Redman was in and out of the side. Don Gibson was another fringe player. Tom McNulty had done well at full-back. That was about it. Jimmy hadn't set the world on fire. But he'd tried.

And now he was optimistic again, about Cliff Birkett, Jeff Whitefoot, Mark Jones and Jackie Blanchflower. There was another lad, John Doherty, an inside-forward, a certainty.

So he kept going, working in the bowels of the club away from the glittering surface. He was feared was Jimmy. The older players didn't like him. He was aggressive. He swore at them. They usually encountered him when they'd been dropped to the reserves. For him it was life and death in the Central League, for them humiliation, beneath them, a bleeding chore. It was bad enough being out of the side without having this fucker screaming at you.

The first thing Jimmy would do on Saturday afternoon was rip up the opposition team-sheet. There would be well known names on it. 'Forget them, they can't play. They're useless, *names*,' he'd spit, kicking the ball of paper into the corner of the room.

'He was a man you could take an instant dislike to,' Harry McShane remembers. 'He was a very aggressive character, always het up, a typical Welshman. He didn't encourage you at all. He told you. You could hear him shouting in the other dressing-room, "get bloody stuck in" that was his favourite expression.'

He never tried to tell the older lads like Harry how to play, but made sure that the reserves was no sinecure. 'To be fair to

167

Jimmy, he never asked the young lads to kick people, he only harnessed the kickers to do that,' Harry explains. Jimmy's dedication was unbelievable to McShane who'd been around and knew the going rate elsewhere.

'We were training at the ground one morning and I was running round the track with John Doherty who I was pretty close to. We'd played Blackpool away in a Central League match on the Saturday. We won 9–1. John scored 3 or 4 and made the rest. He was a brilliant young player. There was no doubt he was going to make it. Jimmy appeared at the end of the tunnel. John said, "I wonder what he's doing out." I said, "What the hell are you worried about we won 9–1." So anyway we could see that he was going to collar us. He called John over and told him to be back at 2 o'clock.

'The next day when I saw John I asked him what was up. He said, "When we were playing Blackpool I knocked a ball up the left for the winger when I should have switched the play to the right." So I said that was only once and he said "Never mind, this is what you have to do *all the time*." '

They spent an hour recreating the situation, with Murphy explaining the importance of changing the play. The quest for perfection never ceased. Beating Blackpool 9–1 was not the object. Jimmy had his own standards. To young fellows he seemed a very hard man to please and an hour was a relatively short stint on the training ground. Some afternoons Jimmy would be out until five o'clock drilling home some basic element of the game. 'The basics', you had to get the basics right. Jimmy wasn't a coach with a text-book full of complicated stratagems, he was a teacher with a simple set of precepts. They were the ones football was founded on: passing, changing the focus of attack, marking your man when you had to, losing him when the ball was with a red shirt.

Getting the ball. Tackling. Winning it. Make it bloody hard for them when you've got it. Make it bloody harder for them when they've got it. Guts and desire were the things Jimmy sought. Hunger. He loved talent, but he took it for granted that 'his lads' had talent. Otherwise they wouldn't 'be 'ere'. He loved the great players: Carey, Cockburn, Rowley, Pearson. He loved them for their talent but he loved them more for their spirit. They were hard men, the great players, hungry bastards once the whistle blew. They'd slaughter you; psychologically they were deadly. Talent was a weapon, not an end in itself but a means, and fulfilling your talent depended on guts, heart, being tougher on yourself than others. That was his lesson: be hard. On yourself.

Jimmy worked from nine in the morning until late at night; first with the full-time pros until lunchtime, then the afternoons of remedial teaching. At six o'clock on Tuesdays and Thursdays he'd be at the Cliff with the youths, part-time pros and amateurs. There was no going through the motions at nights. These youngsters were the future, Jimmy was as hard on them as the older pros. He liked to get to the pub for a couple of pints of ale before closing time. He smoked like a chimney. It would be eleven-thirty when he got home to a silent house, the embers dying on his morning fire.

On Sundays after Mass he'd be at the ground with Matt, Bert Whalley, and Ted Dalton who'd be treating the injured. They'd have a whisky about twelve o'clock, then Jimmy would go off to the Quadrant, the pub, tucked away behind the Lancashire cricket ground, used by United's players, then home at half-past two for lunch with the family. Football was his life, from day to day, hour to hour, minute to minute. His heart, like Billy Meredith's, was 'always full of it'. The man in the pub on Sunday lunchtimes was not aggressive. He would laugh and joke, there was a real warmth about him but whenever the subject switched from football he would switch it back. Jimmy Murphy's idea of a discussion was a debate about the respective merits of Stan Matthews and Tom Finney. He was himself a Finney man, so was Matt and most pros. Finney was harder.

On Monday mornings for seven years Jimmy set off from Whalley Range to engage in the thankless task of turning talent into professionalism. Most brilliant kids didn't have it. By the time Jimmy found out he'd spent a lot of passion.

Jackie Blanchflower was one of the first of the new kids to arrive in Manchester. He was from East Belfast, a Protestant working-class ghetto, his father an iron-turner in the shipyards. His brother, Danny, seven years older, was already a pro with Barnsley. Jackie was medium height, sturdy, with jet-black hair

169

and a pleasant round face. Like his brother Danny, he was intelligent and articulate. The football came from their mother's side. She worked in the ropeworks and played for a ladies' team in Belfast. Their father was away fighting during the war.

He arrived in Manchester's Victoria Station at seven-thirty one morning in March 1949, having travelled over on the ferry from Belfast to Heysham. He remembers it was a dismal day. Not horrible or rotten, dismal. Matt Busby met him at Victoria, and they went to the Busby house in Chorlton for breakfast. Being only sixteen, Jackie had to have a legal guardian to leave Ireland. Busby had signed the papers.

Jean made him breakfast, and afterwards he went with Matt to Old Trafford. The ground was a mess, and had yet to be re-opened for League football. The pitch itself hadn't been used since 1941. It was just a field full of weeds. They were building a little covered stand on the popular side of the ground, and there was a Nissan hut where the dressing-rooms are today. Jackie remembers the contrast between the glamour he'd imagined, the glorious sense of the '48 Cup win he'd listened to on the wireless, and the bleak ruin he walked through that morning. At lunchtime he met Louis Rocca, an old man sitting having his lunch in the Nissan hut. Louis didn't like skins on his tomatoes, so he was peeling them off when Jackie was introduced to him.

Rocca took Jackie to see his digs at Mrs Browne's. He was lonely. The next day he moved into the digs and reported for work as an apprentice plumber. For the time being his football would be restricted to Tuesday and Thursday nights at the Cliff. If he did well he'd sign pro on his seventeenth birthday.

When he went training the talent scared him. He was a wing-half, skilful, well balanced, a neat passer of the ball. He was a natural. But some of the other young players seemed un-naturally gifted. He started playing in the 'A' team. Bill Foulkes played right-back, Roger Byrne left-back, Jeff Whitefoot, Mark Jones and Jackie were the half-back line. Cliff Birkett was outside-right. Brian Birch was inside-left. It was a brilliant team. Playing open-age football in the Manchester League they won everything, including the Gylcriss Cup, the blue riband of junior football in the area.

Jackie signed pro when he was seventeen. He could forget about plumbing. This was a big moment. You got your blazer with the Manchester United Football Club crest on it. He and Mark Jones shared a room at Mrs Browne's, and became great pals. Mark played for England Schoolboys. He was a Barnsley lad, a centre-half, a big powerful fellow, but gentle, a country-man who loved to go shooting. He smoked a pipe at eighteen and wore a trilby. He bred canaries and budgies which he kept in an aviary at home, and was engaged to June, his childhood sweetheart back in Barnsley.

The digs weren't great. Mr Browne liked a drink; pissed, he would fight with Mrs Browne and shout at the two lodgers. They told Bert Whalley. Bert moved them to Mrs Watson's.

Mrs Watson ran a boarding house at number 5 Birch Avenue, beside Lancashire cricket ground. There were two big houses knocked into one which meant she could cater for about twenty lodgers. When Mark and Jackie moved in, the house was used mainly by commercial travellers and long-distance lorry drivers. It was a relaxed, warm place, as such places go. Albert Watson was a character, in his sixties, but still game for a laugh. Too game, as things turned out.

Mark and Jackie spent a lot of time at the pictures, using their free passes to go to the Gaiety, Odeon or Oxford cinemas in town, or the Trafford at Trafford Bar just up the road from the digs. David Pegg arrived from Doncaster in the summer of 1950, a Yorkshire lad who'd come with a big reputation after playing outside-left for England Boys. He was a cocky lad, a flash dresser with an eye for the girls.

Mark and Jackie progressed through the reserves, both making appearances in the '51/'52 Championship side, Jackie just once, making his debut at right-half the same day as Roger Byrne at Anfield. Mark Jones played three games at centre-half when Chilton was injured.

United went back to North America in 1952. Mark, Jackie and Denis Viollet were in the party, as was Roger Byrne, now an established first team player. They sailed on the *Queen Elizabeth* from Southampton for a tour that would last eight weeks. One night on the outward sailing the United players were invited for dinner in the *QE*'s first-class restaurant.

Champagne was sent to their table by a large, rotund gent with silver hair who raised his glass to toast them. Louis Edwards was sitting on the ship's first-class balcony, cigar in hand, a jolly smile on his face.

Louis was a friend of Matt's, a butcher, co-owner with his brother Douglas of Louis C. Edwards and Sons (Manchester) Ltd. As far as the lads were concerned he was a wealthy 'face' they'd seen around the ground on match days.

Edwards and Busby had first met a couple of years previously at the Opera House where they were introduced by a mutual friend, Tommy Appleby. Edwards and his wife Muriel became close friends of Matt and Jean. Unless the show was really special Matt would often be bored by the interval, and, since the backstage stargazing held little appeal for him, he and Louis started slipping out halfway through the programme to find a quiet pub somewhere adjacent to the Opera House where they'd talk about their respective businesses. 'Champagne' Louis was easy company. He hung on Matt's every word. Many of their conversations focused on money, the way it could screw up a football club, as it had for Matt in the cases of Johnny Morris and Charlie Mitten. You couldn't buy success, Matt explained to Louis, but unlike other businesses where success generated more money, in football it usually generated more problems about money. Players started out happy for a first team place, then when success came they started looking for material reward. If they played for England and listened to the gossip in the international camp the going rate elsewhere became *your* problem.

The death of James Gibson and the succession of Harold Hardman to the chairmanship at Old Trafford had made matters worse. Hardman had no money and didn't like extravagance of any kind. Busby didn't want to go on a spending spree in the transfer-market unless it was unavoidable, but he wanted the best for his players, the best hotels and travel and other perks, like Blackpool and golf at Davyhulme. He didn't want to be profligate, he wanted to do things right. They had to think big. Floodlights, Europe, a large squad of players of first team quality. All these things cost money.

Louis Edwards understood. Hardman was sceptical. Louis

172

was a big thinker himself. He was also connected in a way to the United tradition as Busby cherished it, the family club for Outsiders. Louis's eldest sister Beatrice had married Louis Rocca's cousin Joe in 1926. Edwards was almost family.

The United States and Canada gave the new English champions a big welcome. They played to huge crowds, 35,000 came out to watch them play Stuttgart at Yankee Stadium. Spurs and Atlas from Mexico were also touring America that summer. The weather was warm, the settings glamorous. United went to Hollywood to tour the studios, meeting Bob Hope and other stars. They played Los Angeles, Montreal, Toronto, Chicago, Vancouver and Detroit. The hectic schedule didn't detract from the enjoyment.

'When we got back to Mrs Watson's there were these new faces,' Jackie recalls. Duncan Edwards and Gordon Clayton had joined the family. 'We were a bit disturbed, somebody had broken into our little circle, we were a bit jealous, probably a bit too hard on them,' Blanchflower admits.

Gordon Clayton remembers the day he and Duncan arrived in Manchester: 'It was Monday, June ninth 1952. We came by train together. Bert Whalley met us at London Road Station and took us to Mrs Watson's. We both started work on Wednesday, June eleventh. I went to a factory in Altrincham, Duncan went as an apprentice carpenter in Trafford Park. I lasted eighteen months but Duncan hated it. He wanted to play football and he was so good there was never any doubt about him making it. He was never going to be a carpenter. So he went on the ground staff – on the brush we called it – after a while.'

Gordon Clayton came from Cannock, a small town in Staffordshire mining country. Duncan was from Dudley. Gordon played in goal for Staffordshire Boys, Duncan left-half for Worcestershire. They were both eligible for Birmingham Boys, which is how they met and became inseparable friends. 'I was fourteen and a half when I met him, we were the same age, born within a month and two days of each other, he on October first 1936, me on November third,' Gordon reflects.

'We both trained at Wolves on Tuesday and Thursday nights. Stan Cullis had cottoned onto the youth policy thing, so had

Chelsea and a few other clubs. They all wanted Duncan. He stood out. He was built like a man, not tall, but his torso and legs, bloody hell. I mean I can show you photographs, you look at him and you look at me and there's no comparison. And yet I was regarded as a well-built young man. He was something else. He had this incredible urge to play. Duncan was a very dominant personality as a schoolboy. People used to say he was arrogant, he was big-headed, but he wasn't really. As kids you think that when somebody's got extraordinary talent.'

Edwards's talent was extraordinary. He played for England Schoolboys a year under age and captained the side the following year when Clayton was selected in goal. 'We were both Wolves fans. They'd had a great team in the late Forties and early Fifties: Billy Wright, Johnny Hancocks, Jimmy Mullen. We didn't know each other but Duncan and I used to stand on the terraces. I suppose we should have signed for Wolves, but I think Joe Armstrong got to the Edwards first and that was it.' Clayton smiles.

Gladstone Edwards was a metal-polisher. He and his wife, Sarah Ann, had two children born to them. Carole Anne, born when Duncan was ten, died after fourteen weeks. Sarah Ann fed Duncan on Ostermilk and rusks. He was always a big lad, nine-and-a-half pounds at birth, putting on two pounds every week. He was a healthy, well-behaved boy. He had an insatiable appetite for football, taking his ball everywhere, even when the Edwards were visiting friends. Gladstone would warn him not to bring a ball, but Duncan would always manage to hide one somewhere on his person. When he was ten he was playing with grown-up men. Later his mother would recall the constant cries outside the house: 'Come on Dunc, we're picking sides.' The only argument was about who'd get Dunc.

Duncan, Gladstone and Sarah Ann were invited to Manchester. When he came back Duncan urged Gordon to accept the invitation he'd been sent. 'They're different, they look after you, you'll enjoy it,' he told his friend.

'I went with my mum and day,' Gordon says, 'we were met by Bert Whalley. In the letter he sent us he said we'd recognise him by the flower in his buttonhole. "I'll be standing at the barrier, I'll have a blazer on and a flower in my buttonhole." And he did.'

Gordon remembers the taxi-ride to Old Trafford: 'The first thing that struck me coming from Cannock was the size of the place. "This is *big*," I thought. Then when we got to the ground there was this smell. It was the fumes from Trafford Park. I'll never forget that Old Trafford smell. When I think of Manchester United I always get that funny smell.

'Bert was a lovely man, we'd made our mind up in the taxi really. I was never going anywhere else. This was it, Manchester United, the '48 Cup-Final, Carey, Pearson, Rowley, there was something different about them, something vital and exciting. Of course they'd just won the League but it was the people, the idea of Matt Busby who was a god. And yet Bert was so human. When we walked into the ground we met Jimmy Murphy. He was in a little office with a kitchen off the back. Jimmy looked like a bull-dog, his face was like a bull-dog's but again there was a warmth about him, you felt he was genuinely happy and pleased to see you.

'Bert showed us round the ground and then said: "Come on, I'll take you to the place you're going to stay if you come to Manchester United." That was Mrs Watson's.'

Clubs weren't allowed to sign boys until after the last international of the season. England Boys beat Wales 5–1 at St Andrews, Birmingham City's ground. 'I'll never forget the scene outside the ground after the game,' says Clayton. 'We came out of the dressing-room and there was a compound wired off just outside the Players Entrance. All the mothers and fathers were there and all the scouts. Reg Priest, United's Midland Scout was standing with Jimmy Murphy and Bert Whalley. All eyes were on Duncan. We walked over to Bert and Jimmy. That was when the others *knew*.'

'Duncan said he'd meet me on the train. "I'll save you a seat," he promised. He got on at Dudley, I got on at Stafford. I can see it now. The train is pulling in to Stafford and he is hanging out the window waving. He'd saved me a seat. The train was empty. But he saved my seat!'

Their first day at old Trafford was a come-down. Especially for Duncan. For the first time in his life he was anonymous. They walked into the gym, a plain boarded room with wallbars screwed to the wall and two punchballs hanging from the ceiling. Chilton was working one. 'He'd been a boxer in the Army and he was stood at this bloody Speed Ball smacking it,' Gordon remembers. 'Mark Jones was working on the other one. He was obviously modelling himself on Chilton.' Neither man paid any attention to the two kids.

They were small news in Mrs Watson's as well. Gifted youngsters were no novelty at United. You began at the bottom of a well-populated hierarchy. The next morning Gordon Clayton encountered more indifference: 'I showed up for work at the factory. The manager, Albert Hall, showed me round. The word had clearly gone round – "another United player" – they used this place a lot. I walked into the section I'd be working in and a fellow says to me, "Hey young 'un, what religion are you?" I said, "I'm C of E." "You might as well pack your fucking bags now, you've no chance here. You've got to be a Catholic to play for United." This was the first time I'd ever heard there was any suggestion of religion coming into it. But the guy was proved wrong. It was a fallacy. Matt and Jimmy were Catholics, but Bert was one of The Big Three and he was a Sunday School Preacher, a Methodist. I went a couple of times with Duncan. What he'd do, he'd invite us to his house for Sunday tea. We'd automatically go home to the Midlands at weekends, but if you were staying Bert would often ask you round for afternoon tea.

'We'd have tomatoes and ham salad and afterwards we'd go to the Church service. He did it with all the lads.'

Whalley would also invite the senior players to his Sportsman's Services. Henry Cockburn and Johnny Aston attended several, reading the lesson occasionally.

The beginning of the 1952/53 season was difficult for Manchester United. They were Champions, but the magnificent drive which won the title also drained the final drops of inspiration from what was in essence the '48 Cup team. This period, between August and the end of October when United languished at the wrong end of the League table, tested Matt Busby as he'd never been tested before. His first great team was finished and he knew it. There were some promising young players at the club, Duncan Edwards being by far the most exciting of them, but the distance between promise and fulfilment was vast. So much could go wrong, as Busby and his staff knew.

The case of Cliff Birkett, the wonder-boy of 1948, proved the point. Birkett had made his début at seventeen playing nine games towards the end of the '50/'51 season. The promise was never fulfilled. Birkett never added to his nine appearances. Maybe he was pushed too soon. Maybe his temperament was wrong. What was undeniable was the degree to which even the best judges could be wrong about a youngster's chances of making the transition from reserve to first team football. Placing all your faith in breeding your own players was a gamble. Ability could be assessed, but character was the x-factor; you could never be sure how brilliance would respond when it was faced by the rigour of first team conflict.

Hence the appeal of the transfer-market where you could buy the finished article. Costly players may not be perfect, but you knew what you were getting. Most of the time.

United paid a record transfer fee for a goalkeeper to acquire Reg Allen from QPR in 1950. Allen proved himself worth the money, but by the autumn of 1952 Reg was a sick man. He'd been a prisoner-of-war for four and a half years, an experience which left him suffering from manic depression. The symptoms had manifested themselves from time to time after Reg joined United. Sadly, on 4 October, during United's important away fixture against Wolves at Molineux, Reg cracked. He'd been playing brilliantly and there had been talk of an England cap. At half-time in the Wolves game Allen disappeared. Jackie Blanchflower, who was twelfth man, explains what happened: 'Reg was desperate to play for England. At half-time someone brought a paper into the dressing-room with the England team in it. Bert Williams, Wolves 'keeper had been selected. Reg just left. Nobody realised until we were ready to go back out onto the pitch. We thought he was in the bathroom. But he'd gone. There were no subs in those days, so that was it.

' "The Boss" was amazing, he never panicked. Johnny Carey went in goal and Busby told the press afterwards that Reg had got pheumonia.' United lost 6–2.

United gradually hauled themselves up the League table to finish the season in eighth position. Seventeen-year-old David

Pegg made his début for United at home to Middlesborough on 6 December. Pegg kept his place for most of the season. In March 1953 Busby paid £29,999 to buy Tommy Taylor, a twenty-one-year-old centre-forward from Barnsley. Taylor had made a sensational start to his career in League football, scoring twenty-six goals in forty-four games for Barnsley, and was coveted by every big club in the country. Busby was happy to break United's record in the transfer-market. In order to spare Taylor the pressure of a £30,000 price-tag Busby agreed with Barnsley chairman, Joe Richards, that the cheque be made out for £1 short of the true figure. A pound note changed hands to seal the deal.

On 4 April, in the second of United's three Easter games, Matt Busby introduced seventeen-year-old Duncan Edwards to First Division football. It proved to be an inauspicious début, United losing 4–1 at home to Cardiff City, their solitary goal scored by Roger Byrne who, having started the season at outside-left, was now established at left-back.

Duncan Edwards played just one game in the first team. His main task that season was to help United confirm their reputation as the best club in the country for young players to join by winning the newly inaugurated FA Youth Cup. It is, perhaps, more accurate to use the word establish in place of confirm, for Busby's successes had been achieved with a mature team and some sceptics doubted the propaganda coming out of Old Trafford about 'youth'.

David Pegg showed distinct promise in the first team; another seventeen-year-old, John Doherty, had played a handful of games and was being much talked about; but Mark Jones and Jackie Blanchflower had just two games between them that season. Roger Byrne was an undoubted success but at twenty-three could hardly be described as a symbol of a flourishing youth policy.

So winning the FA Youth Cup was an important target for Busby and Jimmy Murphy. Facing criticism from shareholding supporters at United's AGM, Busby had made large claims about the future, asserting that the club had £200,000 worth of youngsters in the reserve and youth teams. He hoped the FA Youth Cup would substantiate this claim. United progressed to meet Wolves in the two-legged final.

John Doherty, a key member of the side, was injured before the first leg at Old Trafford, and a replacement was urgently required. Bert Whalley was sent to Ireland where the renowned soccer nursery, Home Farm, was said to have a prolific teenage goalscorer who would suit.

The story of how United signed Liam Whelan illustrates the haphazard, unscientific nature of scouting for talent. Billy Behan recounts: 'Bert came over with some other fella's name – I forget it now – but I explained to him that the kid was really a centre-half who was only scoring goals in schoolboy football because of his size.' Billy Behan watched schoolboy football every weekend, Saturday *and* Sunday. He knew every useful kid in Ireland, which really, in those days, meant Dublin. Behan *was* a genius, a rare example of reality in a business coloured by myth. The Republic of Ireland has, arguably, produced only five great players since Behan began working for United, informally at first, when they signed Johnny Carey in 1937. Beginning with Carey, Manchester United were gifted all the other greats, Liam Whelan, John Giles, Tony Dunne and Paul McGrath. Only Dunne – £4,000 – and McGrath, at around £30,000 – cost United fees. Behan's method was painstaking. He would go back time after time to see his man play, on all kinds of pitches, in big games and small.

What did he look for? 'The basics,' he muses now, 'control, passing, and the ability to read a game, they're the three essentials. The great players always read the game correctly and were good enough to do something to keep it going if it was going well or change it if the game needed changing. Ability in itself was never enough.'

Liam Whelan had the basics and a bit more. He had beautiful control, scored goals and was a tall strong lad not easily intimidated. But he was deemed to lack pace, a judgement Behan disputes: 'The acid test of pace is, do they get back at you once you've gone past them? They never got back at Liam, the defenders were dead once he'd done them.' Bert Whalley took some convincing. 'Well he'd been sent with this name, and I said, "Look, take Liam, he'll do the job for you." But Bert went back to consult Jimmy Murphy – I think he was a bit afraid of Jimmy – in the end they got in touch and Liam went over.'

Almost twenty-one thousand people attended the FA Youth Cup final first leg against Wolves at Old Trafford, for Busby's optimism had generated great expectation in Manchester. That night, 4 May 1953, the most optimistic expectations were surpassed. Before an enthralled crowd, Jimmy Murphy's boys gave a devastating display to win 7–1. Liam Whelan scored and did so again in the drawn second leg at Molineux. But it was the game at Old Trafford that sent a signal to the football world.

Something extraordinary was fermenting in Manchester. The names of Edwards, Colman, Pegg and Scanlon began to be mentioned in Manchester and further afield. Busby's New Idea was not mere talk. He *was* breeding his own players and they were special, had to be to humiliate the Wolves, who were once more a power under Stan Cullis.

The United team for this historic game makes interesting reading:

Clayton

Fulton   Kennedy

Colman   Cope   Edwards

McFarlane   Whelan   Lewis   Pegg   Scanlon

Eddie Colman, Duncan Edwards, David Pegg, Liam Whelan and Albert Scanlon became established first team players. Ronnie Cope played only a single first team game before the Munich Air Disaster. Of others in that great youth side, football would hear very little. And that was a vintage year. The failure rate was high. United went on to win the first five FA Youth Cups. A glance through the teams shows that most who helped to win this prize never went on to play regular first team football.

In 1953 Wilf McGuinness captained England Schoolboys. Wilf played right-half, and was one of the most coveted schoolboys in Britain. Wolves, Manchester City and all the big Lancashire clubs wanted his signature. 'I hadn't decided where I was going until I saw United play Wolves in the Youth Cup Final. I'd followed both the Manchester clubs. City had some good players: Roy Paul, Jimmy Meadows, Don Revie and Bert

Trautmann, so I'd go to Maine Road and Old Trafford on alternate weeks. I'd also been to Wolves to look around and it was great. But the 7–1 victory in the Youth Cup Final really swayed me.

'United murdered them. They had Duncan, Eddie Colman, David Pegg, Albert Scanlon and Billy Whelan. I looked and I knew Eddie Colman had played for Salford Boys and Lancashire, but hadn't played for England. I thought, if they can improve me that much I'm bound to make it. I thought they would make me play better than him because I have played for England and he hasn't. When I saw Duncan Edwards I thought thank God I am not playing in his position. I thought if they can get a side to play this great, this is what I want to be in with. They must make me. That decided me.

'I played for Manchester Boys football team for two years running. I was captain. I was wing-half by then. In my first year I started as a forward because I was a year younger than the rest and most probably couldn't get about as much. We played most of our games at Newton Heath Local. It was the first enclosed ground I played on which was great. It didn't matter what the pitch was like, and the pitch didn't have much grass on it, in fact we used to go up there to watch St Pat's and usually St Anne's playing on either Good Friday or Easter Monday morning in the Catholic Final. They don't have those sort of things now. We used to love going to see that. So I played my football with Manchester Boys, and then as a 14-year-old I got picked to captain England Boys 14-year-olds who played against Northern Ireland. Jimmy Melia was in the Lancashire Boys team, he played afterwards for Liverpool. He was the only other famous boy. The year afterwards was when Bobby Charlton came into the team. I first met Bobby when Manchester Boys played East Northumberland at Maine Road in a cup competition when we were both 15. I can remember beating them 3–0. I was the captain most of the time of everything I played in and I was a bit cocky. I saw this young lad, he came up to me after the game when we had beaten them, and I thought, who is this little lad? He said, "We may both be going to United," because Joe Armstrong had got him. "My name is Bobby Charlton," and I thought who the hell is Bobby

Charlton. He was very weak looking in those days, he made little impression. I thought, well, he is not a bad little player. Joe Armstrong had told him to make himself known to me.'

Bobby had already decided: 'I had made my mind up early really. I had played for East Northumberland boys and actually it was a headmaster in our Jack's school who wrote to Man. United and recommended that they come up and see me. This was before I got picked to play for England boys. I was playing for East Northumberland boys and we played a match at Jarrow on a frosty morning in January, and my dad said there is a scout from Manchester United at the game, and after the match he came to see me. I was so committed to becoming a footballer. I was good at it and I found it easy.

'Joe Armstrong came and he said, "I would like your son to play for Man. United." Now in those days the ultimate was that somebody asked you to go for a trial, so to ask you to go was good. So I said, yes, and I said yes in January even though I couldn't sign until I left school. I still had to go to school. After that, within a couple of weeks, I was picked to play for England boys, and I was in the trials and scored a couple of goals and played for them and then every club started to knock at the door, but I had made my mind up. I don't know whether I had made my mind up because Man. United had the reputation of having the best scouting and coaching system or whether I just wanted to be a footballer and the first one that came along was going to get me.

'A couple of years before, I had listened to the radio when United won the Cup in 1948. They'd won the greatest Cup Final ever played, so that created an aura round them and Matt Busby.

'I watched football, me and our Jack used to go to Newcastle – it was 15 miles. We went together, the two of us, we very rarely went with our family. We had the Milburn family connection, but we just paid to go in. School? It was alright to start with, then as football took over it became less and less important.

'I set off to Manchester at fifteen on my own. I thought it was a great adventure. I was quite used to travelling: when I was 10 and 11 my Uncle George, who played for Leeds United and was the trainer at Chesterfield, used to invite me down for my school holidays, so I went for four or five weeks and I used to watch them. I had travelled on the train on my own when I was ten, but when I arrived at Manchester, Manchester was black, the buildings were black and of course there were steam trains, and I am opening a window to try and see what a fantastic place I am coming to, and the smoke! Jimmy Murphy met me. When we were in the taxi going to my digs, which were at Old Trafford, he said: "We have got this player Jeff Whitefoot, a midfield player, he is going to be great, and we have just signed a young lad from Dudley in the Midlands called Duncan Edwards and he has a great right foot and a great left foot, he is strong in the tackle, he is great in the air, he reads the game and he can play in any position, and he is fast and has tremendous enthusiasm." And then he must have realised that he had gone too far, so he said, "And when I knock all the rough edges off him I am going to make him a decent player." And I thought, "Bloody hell."

'I stayed at Mrs Watson's. It was a big house where travelling salesmen used to stay. It was near Old Trafford cricket ground. There were ten to twelve of us staying there at various times because you could walk to the ground. The atmosphere was brilliant.

'My parents had been told that all you had to do on the ground staff was sweep up and clean up toilets and all that, and my Mam and Dad said they didn't want me to do that. The first three weeks I was down I had to go to school. I'd been to grammar school so my parents wanted me to carry on to get my GSE. I thought, alright, so I transferred to Stretford Grammar School. The whole curriculum was completely the opposite to the one at home, and not only that, they wouldn't let me play for United. I had come down to play for United, I hadn't come down to go to school, so they said, you can't play for United, you have to play for us on a Saturday morning. I had been there for about three weeks and then the season started and I said to my Mam, "I have to leave." So I left. But you had to work or go on the ground staff, so the compromise was I went to work. I didn't go on the ground staff. I went to train as an apprentice engineer and I did that until I was seventeen.'

A new generation was arriving as Manchester United's first great Busby era was drawing to a close. It may, perhaps, be stretching things to say that Matt Busby's first United team was great. In seven seasons a Championship and an FA Cup had been won. The record was not spectacular. Something had been missing. The departures of Johnny Morris and Charlie Mitten, neither of whom had been satisfactorily replaced, were costly. Busby nevertheless came as close as any man could have done in the circumstances to translating James Gibson's pre-war dream into a post-war reality. He had bought no mediocrities and the cultivated football he inspired was played by a Manchester United team largely composed of Manchester players.

The ultimate test in football management is to measure achievement against resources. Busby passes with Honours. The positional switches that transformed Johnny Carey, Henry Cockburn, Johnny Aston and Chilton from journeymen pros into international players was the work of a great conjurer. This is not the stuff of legend, rather proof of Busby's football wisdom which mocks the canard that he was 'merely' an expert in man-management. That cliché is self-defeating anyway, for, as Busby knew better than anybody, football is played by men. The footballer is not separate from the person. On the contrary football, as he uniquely understood it, was an expression of character and spirit, not simply a display of skill.

During seasons '53/'54 and '54/'55 Manchester United did no more than maintain a respectable position in the First Division, finishing fourth and fifth without ever threatening the Championship contenders. In '53/'54 Burnley beat United 5–3 in the third round of the FA Cup; the following season Manchester City eliminated them in the fourth round.

Those were bleak years for English football. In November 1953 the brilliant Hungarian team, inspired by Ferenc Puskas, came to Wembley to beat England 6–3. An illusion was shattered. The smug consensus that the English game was 'the best in the world' no longer held. England's humiliation was complete in Budapest the following May when Hungary won

184

the return game 7–1. The more enlightened in the football community, Matt Busby and his old Army comrade Arthur Rowe among them, had long suspected that the 'best game in the world' was stagnating. While English football stood still, devoid of energy and imagination, elsewhere, in Europe and South America, the game was developing towards a new, more vivid and inspiring realisation of its potential.

In the wake of the Hungarian débâcle a Great Debate raged: on one side a minority who believed that England had much to learn from this traumatic experience; on the other the majority who took the view that the Hungarians were 'special', a group of magicians from whose performance no definitive conclusions could be drawn. Arthur Rowe was among the more vocal critics of the domestic game. He argued from a position of some strength. The Spurs team with which he won the First Division in 1950/51 had placed a heavy premium on the un-English virtues of skill and movement, the weapons used by the Hungarians to destroy England. Arthur Rowe had played football in Hungary before the war and learned from the experience. The football he had known in England reflected the leaderless, pre-Busby past, when managers sat in their offices and the best players made it up as they went along. Gifted individuals dominated the game. Skilful forwards faced powerful defenders in a series of personal battles. English football had never been, in any formal sense, a contest between two units.

Coming to football with fresh minds the Hungarians had, like many other nations, redefined the game. The emphasis was placed on passing and movement. A more fluid and imaginative version of 'the best game in the world' was possible if the ball was the instrument of collective rather than individual will.

The style advocated by Arthur Rowe became known as push-and-run, and had the merit of being the product of an open mind. It was not *the* answer, but a step in the right direction. England Manager Walter Winterbottom had lots of ideas but little credibility in the professional game. And no power. A decent man, much maligned, Winterbottom's job

185

entailed making do with players produced by the Football League system. His answer to England's problems was more coaching. Others wanted players to be fitter, more dedicated to developing skills.

Matt Busby kept his own counsel. He was familiar with English football's weaknesses. The Great Debate would change nothing. He was not interested in abstractions. As with the perennial arguments about the maximum wage and the retain and transfer system, Busby was disinclined to try to change the world – except the part of the world he controlled. A few weeks after England's Wembley defeat Matt Busby entered his brilliant FA Youth Cup winners in an International Youth tournament in Zurich, Switzerland. His solution was not to ape the Continentals but to learn how to play against them. While playing for Liverpool he had toured Europe and was as aware as Arthur Rowe of the sterility of the British game.

Busby could do nothing about the real problem which he knew to be the Football League itself. From its inception professional football in England had set its official face against elitism. The game would not be run in the interests of 'a few rich clubs, a few rich players, who were in a class by themselves'. In 1900 the Football League had adopted a resolution which placed a ceiling of £4 a week on wages. Their intention was to 'control the professional game, protect smaller clubs from losing their best players to rich clubs and stem the destructive greed of players who used the game simply as a means of enriching themselves'!

Thus, unlike Europe and South America where the best players gravitated to a handful of powerful clubs, in England they were scattered all over the place, isolated from each other, big men in small towns bearing the burden of ordinary clubs' expectations. Tom Finney at Preston, Stan Matthews at Blackpool, Wilf Mannion at Middlesborough, prisoners of gents like Nat Buck. Great players were born not made was the wisdom of that age. Matt Busby did not agree.

Nor did he subscribe to the notion that 'our players simply aren't good enough'. Any manager of a top English club had a variety of riches to choose from. There was as little point in playing football without the quintessential English qualities of strength, courage and determination as in trying to do so without the wit and imagination of the Scots and Irish or the fervour of the Welsh. The ideal was a blend of all these influences, the mixture that Matt Busby had at his football club. He was intent on creating his own elite, and so, his scouts trawled England, Scotland, Wales and Ireland, North and South, to find the best young players and bring them to Old Trafford.

In May 1954 Manchester United Youth Team travelled to Zurich as holders of the FA Youth Cup. Wilf McGuinness and Bobby Charlton had joined Edwards, Colman, Pegg and Scanlon in that elite young side, which again defeated Wolves, winning the second leg of the final 1–0 before 28,000 at Molineux, having drawn 4–4 at Old Trafford. The importance Busby attached to the tournament in Zurich is vouched for by the fact that he, Jimmy Murphy and Bert Whalley accompanied the squad on their first venture into the unknown.

Bobby Charlton, making his first trip to Europe, testifies to the value of the experience: 'The Zurich tournament was a vital part of our education. We played against Italians, Germans and Yugoslavs and learned about their different ways of playing. We went three years on the trot and won the first two tournaments. Then we lost 1–0 to Genoa in the Final. They never came out of their own half, except once, and we thought there's something not right here. We'd never encountered anything like this at home. But they knew what they were doing, defending in typical Italian style. They wouldn't let you past, it was frustrating but an amazing education.'

The more basic education took place back home. Charlton experienced the process from beginning to end: 'Bert and Jimmy were like brothers. You never seemed to talk to one without the other. Bert would do the general things and Jimmy would pick out the young players they thought were important.' Charlton was one of those: 'I spent a lot of time with Jimmy. I was a good long passer of the ball and loved to hit spectacular cross-field passes. You thought *that* was what the game was about, the spectacular. Especially at United where there were so many brilliant players.

'I had this conceit that I could knock the ball forty or fifty yards and pinpoint it. And he would point to the risks, "The full-back can run thirty yards and intercept that pass," he'd say, "and look at the number of our people you've put out of the game." The other thing I hated was passing the ball first time. I always wanted to keep it. As soon as I'd got it I'd think, right that's me, I'm going to play. You see that's what you'd been able to do as a good schoolboy player. So he had to bash that out of me. He'd have me in on a Sunday morning, just the two of us in the middle of the field and he would have me knackered running back and forward knocking the ball back to him first time.

'Maybe some people would have thought this was ridiculous, but I accepted it. I wanted to be a professional footballer and this is the way it had to be. Jimmy was knocking the bad habits out of me. Jimmy made me a professional. From being an amateur schoolboy who thought he was a good player I suddenly discovered what it was all about. "Keep it simple, give it to a red shirt," he'd insist. "The time will come in games where you'll *have* to do the difficult things." He was right, of course.'

The principle Busby and Murphy worked from is exemplified by this work with Bobby Charlton, one of the most prodigiously gifted players in the history of the English game. The talent would develop once the basics of team play were instilled. The qualities of greatness were natural to a degree, acquired in other respects from childhood experience on streets and playing fields. You didn't make players by giving them gifts. The talent was there to begin with. Your job as a teacher was to nurture it, to preach the simple realities of the professional game, the basics of team play which, once grasped, would enable the gifted young to grow and mature alongside others of their ilk. Busby and Murphy didn't need to go abroad to discover the secrets of football. From the very beginning they had preached the gospel of movement and skill allied to simplicity.

The great players did the simple things well. In all the talk of the great Hungarians nobody had noticed that ninety per cent of the football they played was simple – superbly executed, but simple. The right pass, delivered to the right player at the right time. There was no score in football, just a simple melody – the rhythm of the team – from which the great players improvised when they had to. There would be a time for Bobby Charlton's great long passes, but first he had to learn the melody.

Charlton's education began at fifteen in United's fifth team: 'We had five teams. I started in the Altrincham League playing against local teams. We were winning by eighteen to twenty goals a game.' This was where the brilliance could be expressed without fear of losing. That was important, a way of gaining confidence, of exploring the limits of your talent. 'I was scoring regularly but I couldn't get into the fourth team,' Charlton explains. 'They seemed to have a set pattern or time-scale. You wouldn't progress until a certain amount of time was spent in the Altrincham League. Then you moved on. Real progress was getting to the "A" team, that was the third team. They played in the Manchester Amateur League. You were sixteen and this was open-age football with big dockers and guys from factory teams kicking lumps out of you. But it was another fantastic education.

'Getting into the FA Youth Cup team was the ultimate. Playing at Old Trafford instead of park pitches, the buzz of the crowd.' Charlton shivers at the wonder of those Youth Cup games. 'Jimmy created an atmosphere before those games. They were a matter of life and death. He and Bert would always say, " 'The Boss' is coming." Matt Busby, he was like a god. You'd be conscious of him sitting in the stand, you wanted to show him how good you were.'

Busby had the same electric effect when he appeared during training, as Wilf McGuinness recalls: 'Bert Whalley and Jimmy would supervise the training. Then when the five-a-side started – it was actually 20-a-side most mornings – Matt Busby would appear. As soon as he came out there was a feeling about the place. Some people would mess in the five-a-sides, but there was no standing about when the Boss appeared. It was like a bloody Cup Final. Everybody wanted the ball, they wanted to show him what they could do. That's how it was with me and all the others: Duncan, Eddie, Bobby, no matter who you were, first team or not you wanted to show him. Where's that ball, let me get a tackle in, let me do something good, and all of a sudden you were ten feet tall.'

This was Matt Busby's reality in the years '53/'54/'55. Outside, the Great Debate progressed without him. Those seeking a cure for the ills of the English game would surely not have approved had they glimpsed the daily routine at Manchester United. The young players with jobs trained at the Cliff on Tuesday and Thursday nights, the full-timers at Old Trafford, every day of the working week. Bobby Charlton, Wilf McGuinness, Jackie Blanchflower, Duncan Edwards, David Pegg, Mark Jones, Billy Whelan, all experienced life as vividly described by McGuinness: 'I worked for Richardsons Textiles in Manchester for my first year. I trained at the Cliff. It was beautiful, looking back, bloody awful at the time. The floodlights were dreadful, you could hardly see. The training kit was the worst imaginable. It was never washed, no one knows what disease could have spread all over the place. When you arrived you just grabbed what you could from the table. Those big heavy woollen sweaters, and the shoes we trained in ; big heavy things, you thought, how can I play in *these*. But it must have helped.

'Afterwards you'd get in the bath – forty of you – it was black within two minutes. When you got out you'd have to have a cold shower to get the muck off. Many's the time I remember standing there shivering, looking for a towel, practically in tears after a bollocking Jimmy had given me. He seemed to pick on me. I was cocky. I was his type of player – a battler – and he'd give me the sugar as well. But there was plenty of bollockings. He'd make me want to come back and prove him wrong when he questioned my attitude. He helped me tremendously, without Jimmy I wouldn't have been a player.'

When he turned pro Wilf tasted life in the big-time at Old Trafford: 'On Tuesdays we'd have the practice match and that

190

was for real. The other mornings you'd run the track, a few laps to loosen up, then ten sides of the pitch, a few sprints, a bit of gym work – or straight round the back for the game.

'We used to play on the car-park, which was half cinders, half tar,' McGuinness recalls. 'There was a thick wooden fence along the railway where the crowd used to queue on match days. The concrete wall of the stand was on the other side.

'When you were playing you had to look out for yourself. You'd have to duck under a player against the fence or the wall. If you didn't you'd get hit. You might think it wasn't conducive to good football, but you had to think quick and be tricky. If "The Boss" or Jimmy weren't there, Bert, Tosher Curry or Bill Inglis would supervise. Bert was the gentler of the coaches. He would put his arm round you and have a bit of a chat. He was North Manchester, Bert. He was a gentleman, a lovely man, hard-working. They all fitted in: Bert, Tosher, Bill and little old Arthur Powell who we used to take the mickey out of a lot. He was part of it, not just football people as such, we had "nice people" who looked after you. We didn't have "Hammerers" lower down.'

The games, twenty-a-side, were epics. In essence the improvised football of childhood on the streets recreated in the shadow of the Old Trafford Grandstand. The School of Football Excellence Manchester circa 1950–8.

Only the strong survived. Talent got you into this academy but you needed character to graduate, and every day your spirit was exposed and tested in one way or another. The Cliff, with its muck, dodgy floodlights, cold showers and bollockings, was not for faint hearts or tender egos. There were dozens of youngsters fighting for recognition, among them some of the toughest and most gifted in Britain. Then when you progressed to the cinders and tar beneath the Old Trafford Grandstand life was even harder. Matt Busby had broken down many of the barriers between the first team and the others, so on the pulsating stretch of ground between wooden railway fence and concrete Grandstand wall the youngest pro mixed it with renowned internationals. No concessions were made in these glorified street games. You made or broke. If you looked like making, Jimmy would have you back in the afternoon. Bert would put his arm around you if you looked like breaking. There was no soft option.

11

Red Devils

'It was an intimidating atmosphere at
Old Trafford in those days. There
were so many great young players
desperate to get in the side.'

John Giles

For two years Matt Busby was patient. There was no dramatic
transition from old to new. In October '53 Duncan Edwards
established himself in the first team when Henry Cockburn
broke his jaw in a floodlight game in Kilmarnock. Edwards was
the exception to every rule. Jackie Blanchflower and Denis
Viollet came into the side at the same time. Jeff Whitefoot was
now also a regular. Tommy Taylor was proving to be worth the
£30,000 he cost. Bill Foulkes was in at right-back, straight from
the pits at St Helens where he worked until he was twenty. Don
Gibson and David Pegg played occasionally.

Chilton hung on, playing every game that season. Mark
Jones was waiting in the reserves. Jack Rowley wasn't ready to
quit. Competition was fierce now at all levels of the club.
Potentially great players were grateful to get into the reserves.

Wolves won the Championship. The Great Debate went on.
The following season Chelsea won the title with fifty-two
points, the lowest total in history. The FA Year Book for 1953
carried an article headlined 'HAS FLOODLIGHT FOOTBALL GOT A
FUTURE?' The sceptical conclusion was that this 'gadget' probably didn't have anything to offer the best game in the world.
Meanwhile, the radical Arthur Rowe had sunk without trace to
manage Crystal Palace in Division Three South.

While the first team stayed respectably on the fringes of the
Championship contest, United's reserve and youth sides were
winning everything by incredible scores. Ten to fifteen

thousand attended reserve games at Old Trafford. The figure was higher for the FA Youth Cup. The youngsters were growing up spectacularly, their hierarchy reflected in Mrs Watson's lodging house. Jackie Blanchflower, Tommy Taylor and Mark Jones were the leaders. A couple of years older, with first team experience under their belt, Jackie, Mark and Tommy presided at meal times and organised the entertainment. Bobby Charlton, for one, appreciated this system: 'It was a godsend. We all knocked around together. Mark was the father figure. He smoked a pipe and had a sort of presence. To us he was an old man – he was only 22. He was just old fashioned. The pictures were our favourite entertainment. Mark, Jackie or Tommy would pick up the evening paper and say, "There's a good film on at the Gaiety or the Theatre Royal," and we would all say, "Right let's go." We'd get the tram into town and we would all walk back together afterwards.'

Gordon Clayton explains the routine: 'Sometimes we'd go to a dance, but mostly it was the pictures to begin with. We never went out after Wednesday except to the cinema. Friday night was Picture Night every week. We'd either go to the Trafford or Town. We had free passes for the Trafford and the Gaiety and the Oxford in town. Mark was the "Guvnor". He was a big Barnsley Chop, a lovely man. I can see it now. "Swing those arms," he'd say. On Friday nights we got back to the digs about half-ten or a quarter-to-eleven and there would be the cornflakes and milk on the table and we'd have them and then away to bed.'

Clayton and Duncan remained close. 'We stuck together,' Gordon confirms. 'Duncan was a little bit introverted when he came to Manchester first. With being a big lad he'd got this reputation where we came from of being a bully. But he wasn't. The only thing he wanted to do was play football. He wasn't interested in anything else. He wouldn't go to the bank on his own, for example. He hated filling in forms and stuff. Even at that age Duncan wasn't interested in the material things of life.

'Duncan had a mind of his own. He wasn't a mixer as such. He was shy with people. The pictures was the one thing he

194

loved, especially after he got in the first team and became well known. He'd go straight from one picture-house to the next. Couldn't get enough of films.'

Wilf McGuiness describes Edwards as 'a big softie . . . but this was off the field. He was a nice lad, Duncan, talked with this great Brummie accent. You will hear all sorts of stories about how great he was on the field and to us players he *was* that great. A big giant, he was. In training we would start off jogging, and chatting. Duncan would come out with his polo-neck sweater, big woolly sweater, shorts, no tracksuit bottoms, even on the coldest morning, and those big thighs. I can picture him now, just running flat out, not on the track like us, he went round the grass. He'd start by pounding out 10 laps and that was for warm-ups. He was powerful and he'd let us know. Duncan was something exceptional.'

'Duncan knew he was the best player,' Bobby Charlton confirms, 'but off the field he could be fun, although he palled with Big Gordon and went his own way in lots of ways. Even when we got older he didn't drink. It was always football, what was best for his football. He lived for that.'

As they got older they explored the more exotic delights of Manchester life. The Locarno Ballroom in Sale was a favourite Saturday night venue. 'Some were in the first team, Duncan, Tommy Taylor, maybe David Pegg and Jackie Blanchflower; me, Eddie and Wilf would be in the reserves, but we'd all meet up on Saturday nights,' Bobby recalls. 'If I was in the reserves and they were playing at Villa Park or West Brom I'd wait at the Bridge Inn near Sale until about nine o'clock. They'd come back and we'd go to the Locarno.'

Town was the alternative, Wilf McGuinness explains: 'There were lots of places in town. We'd have our fads. The Plaza at lunchtimes – it was sixpence to get in – that was one. And of course on Saturday nights the Plaza was one of *the* places. Jimmy Saville was the assistant-manager. The Cafe Royal opposite the Midland Hotel was a restaurant, but we went to the bar downstairs. We had lager and lime, big drinkers. Double Century Ale was another drink we used to have. There was the Sportsman's in Market Street, that was a pub; the Bodega was a jazz club we used to go into and the Zanzibar was a little coffee-bar. Jackie and Tommy were older. We'd be on the last bus – none of us had cars in those days – and we'd see Jackie and Tommy staggering about well gone.'

Jackie Blanchflower and Tommy Taylor became close friends. Mark Jones would go home to his sweetheart, June, in Barnsley every weekend. Jackie and Tommy would hit town.

'Tommy and I were pals for five years. I can't explain it to you. We had similar interests, a bet, the dogs, a few bevvies,' Jack reminisces. 'On Saturday night we might go to the dogs at Belle Vue, or for a Chinese, then go and have a few drinks in the Continental Club or somewhere. The Continental was a night-club, with cabaret, dark, always packed. Sometimes we'd go to the Ritz off Oxford Road. Eric Morley was assistant-manager there. Jimmy Saville would come over from the Plaza. Some-times Bobby and Duncan would come, but they weren't old enough to have a drink.'

Paddy McGrath had moved back to Manchester in 1954 to open the Cromford Club. This was a classy place, Wilf explains: 'Paddy's club was respectable, it was always the sportsman's club. You could get a meal and a drink. The Cromford was big-time.'

Eddie Colman loved the Cromford once he started courting Marjorie. Everyone loved little Eddie. 'We used to go to town together before he met Marjorie,' Wilf recalls. 'I never met anybody with as much personality as Eddie. He just bubbled, I loved him, we all did. Me, him, Bobby and Shay Brennan, who was another Manchester lad, would go to our house on Friday after training. Sometimes Gordon and Duncan would come. Friday was fish day. My father got the fish cheap in the Market and my mum would give me a few coppers to run down the chip-shop for chips. We'd all have our fish'n'chips and then go to the pictures in town.

'Sometimes we'd start off at Eddie's house on a Saturday. Number 9 Archie Street, Salford. *Coronation Street* is based on Archie Street, but they didn't have a pub. There was a little off-licence at the corner. We used to sit in the parlour with Elizabeth, his mum, and Dick, his dad, and they'd send down for a jug of beer. We would have shandies. It was our first taste of beer really.'

196

David Pegg would be there as well. He and Bobby were big pals. 'David was a ladies' man,' Wilf explains, 'a good looking lad with Victor Mature eyes, a right Yorkshire lad, confident.'

Today, thirty-five years later, Bobby Charlton, one of the most eminent and respected men ever to emerge from British sport, speaks in wonder of those evenings, those times, the lads he grew up with: 'It was paradise just before the first team started to win the title.' Eddie was the angel in this heaven. Cheeky and streetwise, nothing impressed or bothered him. He hadn't played for England Boys, so what? 'I remember when we started some great England schoolboy came – it could have been Duncan,' Bobby smiles, 'and Eddie pulled him right down to size. Tackled him, got the ball, sold him a dummy, nutmegged him, so that was the message. He'd strut, always laughing, always cool. A Salford lad.

'I had come from the North East which was, I suppose, a bit parochial and Eddie was the flash little townie. He was the first person I ever saw in drainpipe trousers. But he was brilliant. I was very close to Eddie, of course we were all close at that time. We'd go to Wilf's or Eddie's. I think the parents were frightened we weren't getting fed properly in the digs. At holiday times I'd always stay at Eddie's in Archie Street. Christmas I'd always be invited. We'd play on Christmas morning, then go back to his place for the turkey. His family were nice. His mum was a little fat woman, Elizabeth. His dad was a working lad. It was a tiny little street, a fabulous community spirit. We have it in the North East, but not like round there.

'If we played in the reserves on Christmas morning it was usually at Bury, Bolton or Rochdale, somewhere local. We'd have our dinner and then every house in the street would have the doors open. People would be in and out, down to the off-licence for jugs of beer, a real party. Eddie would say, "You've got to hear my Uncle Billy singing, he wants to give you a song, he's the best singer in the world." So Uncle Billy would sing, it was hilarious and non-stop. We'd have a match the next day, so we'd try to get to bed at twelve o'clock. But it was impossible to sleep. Someone was always coming up the stairs saying, "Grandad's here," or whoever. There were some amazing characters in the house.

197

'Eddie's grandad was about four foot eleven. He lived two streets up, he had a little bushy moustache and he was always talking about the First World War. He had a little voice, "The lads I fought with, Bobby, were the bravest lads you've ever seen. I remember marching past the Corn Exchange after the war and Lord Kitchener was there taking the salute. And I just happened to hear him say, 'Bigger men I may have seen, but smarter men I have never seen.' " He'd tell us stories about the war, all kinds of daft things, but he was funny. It was wonderful. Eddie was a complete original. It ran in the family.'

'Wherever Eddie was there was fun, it shone out of him,' Wilf McGuiness confirms. His character was formed by hard times, for Salford had suffered brutally during the depression of the late Twenties and early Thirties. His father, Dick, was unemployed for five years. Dick could play ball. In 1933 he scored a hat-trick to help Ordsall Centre to victory in the Salford Unemployed Cup Final at Old Trafford. The prize was a pair of heavy working boots and a new suit for scoring three goals. Dick pawned the suit for £1. Eddie was a villain growing up, 'a real one', Dick would later assert, but football made him blossom into a lovable rogue. He'd wear a cloth-cap and striped college scarf to training. Drainpipes and the latest gear to the Locarno or Town. 'He was the same lad, even when he made the First Team.'

Duncan changed. He was a shade more introverted, Gordon thinks: 'He never really enjoyed a big group. He'd go to the Locarno but he wouldn't dance. He wasn't one for the "birds". He had a dabble here and there like the rest of us but he was very shy with girls. At the Locarno Duncan would be on the edge, just standing there looking.'

One night Gordon and Duncan went to the Derby Street Ice House, a skating rink. There Duncan saw a girl called Molly. 'She was his first love,' Gordon says. 'He was a strong character and as soon as he set eyes on her you knew that was it. Molly was a nice girl, very nice, a bit up-market for us. Not what you might call a footballer's girl.'

Duncan didn't hesitate: 'There was no sophistication, he just went over and started talking to her. I don't think she was too keen at first. But she was the best thing that could have happened to him. He was famous, it was difficult to go out. Now he could go round to Molly's and sit with her. That's what he loved to do.'

Duncan and Molly would go to the pictures or play records in the evening. 'He became an England player very quickly, became more self-assured in public, got a bit of dress sense. But he never changed with me,' Gordon adds, 'he was a good friend, there was nothing he wouldn't do for you. He grew up, we all do, but it was a gradual process.'

Trouble was brewing at Mrs Watson's during Christmas week 1954. Mrs Watson had caught her husband, Albert, in bed with one of the maids. He was in the doghouse. A keen card school had formed among the United lodgers and Jackie Blanch-flower, Tommy Taylor and Billy Whelan were among a group of the players staying up half the night playing poker. Matters came to a head on Christmas Day. The boys were late home from their match to find the table was set as usual, but with Spam instead of turkey on the menu. 'The food was normally good,' Gordon Clayton declares, 'but that was the limit. Jackie called a meeting. We couldn't put up with this. We were Manchester United players, the Busby Babes having Spam for Christmas Day! Old Albert was sixty-five, it was his fault really.'

By the end of the season this branch of paradise was closed. They moved out to separate houses: Gordon with Duncan, Bobby with David Pegg, Tommy and Jackie. Mark Jones was marrying June. He was all right.

In April 1955 the French daily sports newspaper *L'Equipe* convened a meeting of sixteen top European clubs to discuss the idea of a champions' cup. As a result of that gathering at which Chelsea, England's champions-elect were represented, the European Cup was born. The first draw took place the following August. Chelsea were not, however, among the clubs participating. Although willing, the London club had been advised by the Football League that what was deemed to be yet another new 'gadget' would interfere with their domestic commitments. Elitism, the coming together of the best clubs and the best players, remained the appalling vista it had been fifty years before and ever since. The best League in the world had no need of a European Cup. Football was about Aldershot as much as Chelsea.

In Manchester, Matt Busby continued to proceed with prudence. The departure of Chilton, Henry Cockburn, Stan Pearson and Jack Rowley meant the transformation from the old to new was finally complete. Roger Byrne, the new club captain and England left-back, was maturing into one of the great defenders of all time. He was quick and clever. Roger wasn't a tackler, he simply couldn't be passed. He was everything the old full-backs had not been. He dispossessed clinically, timing rather than lunging was the essence. Going forward, he was as effective as most wingers. Defence, as practised by Byrne, was cerebral, a matter of concentration, reading the danger and moving swiftly to cut it out before any threat developed. Mentally he was hard; physically lithe.

Like Johnny Carey, the symbol of gracious thoughtfulness, 'Gentleman Johnny', Byrne projected a certain sense of Manchester United. The new mood was different. As embodied by its new captain, Busby's club had a bit of a swagger, more than a hint of disdain, was more powerful than gracious, possessed the arrogance of the new generation, convinced that it had found a better way – of playing left-back, of living, of expressing itself. Something was happening to England, to the world outside. Youth was beginning to assert itself, old values were being rejected, respect for the past was no longer automatic.

Bill Haley's rock'n'roll was the first hint of rebellion. Throughout Britain theatres had their seats ripped out as youngsters gyrated to the sound of Haley and his Comets. Teddy-boys with carefully coiffed hair, wore velvet collars on the long draped jackets, bootlace ties, drainpipe trousers and crêpe-soled shoes. They were angry and menacing. James Dean, Elvis Presley, Little Richard and Jerry Lee Lewis were other harbingers of a New Age, more threatening than Haley and the Comets who were soon to be dismissed as too tame.

In Liverpool John Lennon was at Art College. For now, rebellion was an imported product, America the source. But it was on the way. Soon popular culture in Britain would reflect the anger of the playwright, John Osborne, who 'damned England' for its stultifying post-war conservatism.

'The Fifties were a time of austerity, of punative conventions, of a grey uniformity,' the Bohemian George Melly has written. Manchester, living up to its proudest tradition, was about to change all that. The world's first great industrial city was fond of declaring: 'What Manchester does today the world does tomorrow.' By times a seemingly idle boast, this claim was about to be rendered credible again through the unlikely medium of professional soccer. Although, remembering Billy Meredith, Ernest Mangnall and J. H. Davis, and football's inspiring contribution to this extraordinary city's sense of itself, the events of the next three years were not all that surprising.

Roger Byrne would not have approved of Teddy-boys and the destruction of cinemas. He did, though, make a similar kind of statement whenever he faced Stan Matthews and Tom Finney, the legends of post-war professional soccer. The 'Matthews Cup Final' of 1953 engraved the Blackpool winger's name on England's contemporary roll of honour. Gordon Richards won the Derby that same summer. In 1953, Coronation Year, a British Expedition led by John Hunt conquered Everest. Roger Bannister broke the four-minute-mile barrier in 1954. Sportsmen were the heroes of the age.

Matthews, Finney, Richards, Bannister, Hunt; all were of a certain type, conventional English heroes, modest, self-deprecating, suburban heroes with whom the mums and dads could identify.

Byrne versus Matthews or Finney was a sign of changing times. In '53, '54 and '55 Roger faced the great men. And every time he stalked them down: as quick as they were, as confident, as smart or, his gait suggested, smarter. Watching in the stand, Busby understood. He had found his new leader. Theirs had not been a cosy relationship. Byrne was not Carey.

'Roger was a cantankerous type at times,' Jackie Blanch-flower says. 'He was stubborn, his own man, who did things his own way. He'd stand up to Matt in training. One day they had a row at the ground. Matt was insisting on something Roger disagreed with and Roger swiped the ball out of the Boss's hands to make his own point. But he was a hell of a player, the fastest thing we'd ever seen.'

'Roger Byrne was something like I imagine a cricket captain

to be,' Wilf McGuinness explains, 'he was a bit aloof from the rest of us. He had gone to night school to qualify as a physiotherapist; he was more intelligent, if you like, than us. We were silly at times, we were only growing up; he had grown up. Roger was an adult, we were only young lads, babes, the Busby Babes.' That phrase began to enter the language in 1955, inspired first by the FA Youth Cup team's achievements. Roger Byrne was not a 'Babe'.

Wilf made his début early in the '55/'56 season. He was seventeen, still a youth player, still cocky. Byrne put him in his place one day. 'He could be fiery on and off the field,' Wilf allows. 'We were playing somewhere just after I got in the side. We were in the hotel before the game and there was a spare chair in this room we were in. It was Roger's, but he'd left the room and I didn't know, so I sat down. When he came back he said, "Up you get." He was captain but I thought, "No way, you can get lost." I thought he was just pulling rank and I was going to get a bit aggressive about it. He clouted me round the ears, then I got a nudge from the side which explained the situation. I felt as though I'd been a bit of an idiot by not getting up.'

For all its essential decency there was a pecking order in the Old Trafford dressing-room. The Home team room was for senior first team players. The Away dressing-room for youngsters, however brilliant. 'You knocked on the door if you wanted to go in there,' Wilf recalls. 'We, myself, Eddie, Bobby were in the reserve room, we were the lads still.'

Manchester United were not expected to challenge for the First Division title at the beginning of the '55/'56 season – they had too many youngsters – but everyone knew they were an exciting prospect for the future. When they won only three of their first eight games, speculation about the lack of experience in the side seemed correct. By late October they were top of the table.

Tommy Taylor had missed six of the first seven games through injury. Duncan Edwards also missed half-a-dozen early games. Once they were fit, United began to soar. Little Eddie made his début at Bolton in November. The following Saturday United welcomed reigning champions Chelsea to Old

Trafford. Tommy Taylor scored twice, Roger Byrne once in a comfortable 3–0 victory. Suddenly the English game had changed. The dark night of stagnation was over. Matt Busby's Manchester United was about to make its contribution to the Great Debate.

Losing only once between New Year's Day and the season's end, United won the Championship by eleven points. On 7 April a post-war record crowd of 62,277 packed Old Trafford to watch Busby's team formally claim the title by beating Blackpool 2–1. Only 22,000 had attended the Chelsea game a few short months previously. Fans and sportswriters alike had been unprepared for the revolution. There was no slow dawn to this new age, instead a dazzling explosion of light and energy which took the breath away.

No seats were ripped out, but grey uniformity was swept away, and England's football past was damned with more daring certainty than even Osborne could have wished for.

The new champions were called the 'Red Devils'. It was an apt description, for their vivacious roguishness was one of their most attractive qualities. Denis Viollet who scored twenty goals that season brought another distinctly Manchester dimension to the side. Denis was a devil, a rogue, smooth, elegant and sophisticated, as were the Manchester nightclubs he loved to frequent. Denis was a Manchester lad to his marrow. Not for him the coffee-bars or Ice Rinks or the innocent cavorting of Sale Locarno. The Cromford Club, perhaps, preferably the velvet promise of the Queens and Continental Clubs where the real action was. He was a loner. Liked by the lads and liking them, but to them he was elusive, mysterious, Town, after the last bus had long since gone. And that's the way he played his football, beautifully balanced, subtle, a gliding, powerful presence, composed and deadly when the opening came. David Pegg was Manchester too, sharp, brazen, young and handsome. A lad.

Devils, yes, powerful ones. Duncan Edwards dominating everything around him, physically, spiritually, a force of extraordinary impact. So hungry for the ball that sometimes, as Jackie Blanchflower recalls, 'he would brush you aside to get possession'. Duncan broke up attacks with ruthless authority, the diffidence of dance-hall and bank-counter transformed into imperious conviction. When a goal was needed, a defeat looming, other spirits beginning to tire, his was the galvanising extra drive that turned the issue in their favour. The others were in awe of him, all except little Eddie, the Salford urchin who wasn't in awe of anyone.

Tommy Taylor scored twenty-five goals that year, leading the forward line with lusty vigour and delicate touch. His pal, Jackie Blanchflower, added another virtue to the whole, poise and intelligence, wry Manchester humour. A team of many talents for a city of many faces, a city made up of outsiders. A city where rogue and priest could sit together with rabbi and inventor, each feeling they belonged as truly as Beckett, Barbirolli and Alex Bird. Cottonopolis. Here the first Catholic church bells rang after the Reformation; here, half-a-mile from Old Trafford, on Stretford Road, the illiterate Polish Jew, Michael Marks, joined Tom Spencer to open their first Penny Bazaar in 1894. Men of many kinds dared to dream.

Matt Busby had dreamed long and quietly. As he sat in the stand watching his 'Red Devils' he experienced something much more profound than professional pride. He thought of Alex James, of the glorious vision of his bleak childhood, the light that first entered his soul beneath the pit-head bing in Old Orbiston. Matt didn't *think* of that so much as sense the old magic of the past surging through his blood. The feeling of fulfilment was chilling.

Matt hadn't expected this so soon. He was pleased and a little frightened. They'd won the Championship by *eleven* points. Their average age was twenty-two.

Busby knew there was more to come. United won the FA Youth Cup for the third year running in 1956. McGuinness, Charlton, Alex Dawson, Mark Pearson and Kenny Morgans played in the side that beat Chesterfield in the Final. They looked as good as their predecessors. McGuinness had already made his first team début. Bobby Charlton had almost got in at Easter. He looked an unbelievable prospect.

Reflecting on that time, Bobby outlines his fears: 'I was scoring goals and everybody kept saying you'll be in the first team soon. But I looked at them and I thought, "How am I going to get in?" I was an attacking inside or centre-forward. And we had Tommy Taylor, Denis Viollet, Billy Whelan, John Doherty, Colin Webster. I'll never forget the Easter they won the first Championship. I'd been playing well and scoring goals, so I thought with three games over Easter somebody's bound to get injured and I'll get my chance. They went to Newcastle on Easter Monday and drew 0–0. I'd played in the reserves at West Brom on the Saturday and scored five or six goals in a 9–1 win. The next Friday I was waiting for the team-sheet to go up thinking, "This is it," but the Boss kept the same team.'

When Busby, Jimmy Murphy and Bert Whalley assessed their incredible riches that summer the biggest problem they seemed to face was keeping restless players worthy of First Division football happy in the reserves. Almost every position was up for grabs. Thinking about how good this side, which had finished eleven points clear of the rest, might become when the average age was twenty-five, Busby and his staff were left speechless.

The Football League tried to intimidate Manchester United out of entering the European Champions' Cup. They were reminded of their first duty – to the Football League – and warned that no excuses could be accepted if this 'gimmick' called the Champions' Cup caused any disruption to their First Division programme. The League was politely but firmly rebuffed.

Busby had no difficulty persuading his Board that Europe was a wise option. By now he dominated board meetings although the protocol insisted that he sat in only to advise. Alan Gibson obeyed his father's wish and voted with Mr Busby. The chairman, Harold Hardman, was a flinty little man, Manchester's rigorous English Masonic face, and he and Busby were respectful rather than fond of each other. Hardman did not approve of the characters his manager socialised with, but he did approve of the football club of which he found himself the titular head. He remembered the bad old days and continued to watch the pennies, but as he wryly remarked, 'Our manager advises us and then tells us what to do.' The quote is apocryphal yet an accurate reflection of Busby's unique influence. No other manager before or since ever wielded the power Matt Busby did at Old Trafford.

His rationale for engaging in European competition was threefold. First it would provide money to pay for the floodlights United had still to install, and for the large, ever-expanding wage bill rising in proportion to the number of First Division quality players on United's books. Second, the extra competition, seen as a problem by the Football League, was a blessing to Busby – players could be kept happy and gain experience playing in the Champions' Cup. His final reason was more abstract than practical. He understood how irrevocably the balance of power was shifting away from the English game, and saw that football in the future would be an international game. The world was contracting, travel was easier, people were curious about abroad. As a football man he was intrigued by the international game. Football as played by the Hungarians was his kind of game.

Billy Whelan beat Bobby Charlton into the first team. Whelan started the '56/'57 season at inside-right in a side that began the defence of its title confidently by running up a sequence of twelve games without defeat. Bobby Charlton was desperate. At the end of September Edwards and Taylor were injured during an away victory at Highbury.

'I always remember that week,' Charlton declares. 'Three weeks before, I'd been injured at Maine Road in a reserve match. I twisted the ligaments in my right ankle – it's still bigger now. It took me two weeks to start running again. The week the lads got injured the Boss says, "How's your ankle?" And I knew this was my chance. So I said fine. It was sore as hell, not when I ran, but when I turned on it or tried to kick the ball. But I knew I had to get in. I was desperate. I played against Charlton at home, and scored two goals. I never kicked the ball with my right foot all day.'

That level of enthusiasm existed throughout the club. 'I was left out again when Tommy was fit,' Bobby recalls, 'but I got fourteen games that season which meant I got a blazer. You had to play fourteen games to get a blazer.'

Charlton, desperately worried about his future, was eighteen. He scored consistently whenever he played, including a hat-trick in the return fixture with Charlton at The Valley. Bobby was the young player with everything: power, wonderfully fluid movement and two great feet. He could score goals and link up in general play to devastating effect. His long gloriously flighted passes raked holes in the opposition defence. He could shimmy past defenders and once away was uncatchable. Bobby Charlton was a sensation. And he could hardly get a game.

John Giles had arrived at Old Trafford. John was, in Billy Behan's opinion, the best schoolboy footballer he had ever seen. A stocky, well-built little Dubliner, Giles was beautifully balanced, had two good feet and remarkable vision. From a renowned Irish football family, Giles was also impressively self-possessed for a youngster. Watching Bobby Charlton play for United's reserves caused Giles to doubt himself. 'I'd never seen anything like him,' John says. 'I remember sitting in the stand at Old Trafford one night watching the reserves with my dad. I don't know who they were playing, but they won something like eight or nine nil. Bobby scored five. I'd never had the slightest doubt that I'd be a player, but I turned to my Dad and said, "I don't know about this." '

Dickie Giles, a great old football man himself, offered his son reassurance. It was badly needed. 'Bobby was unbelievable, even in training. It was an intimidating atmosphere at Old Trafford at that time. There were so many great young players desperate to get in the side.'

The team matured as expected. Confidence now infused all the other qualities. Wherever they played attendances were inflated. This was particularly true of London. A crowd of 62,000 saw United win at Highbury; 57,000 turned up for the Spurs fixture at White Hart Lane. There was never any doubt that the Championship would be retained. Everywhere they played they attacked. They loved the applause: Colman, Byrne, Taylor and Viollet responding with deft little improvisations. There was something inspiringly joyous about this team. They were exhilarating, carefree, unconventional. And British, not Hungarian. Of this Britishness – or more accurately *Englishness* – the intimidating competitiveness of Duncan Edwards was a perpetual reminder. He *didn't* play to the crowd. He hardly seemed to notice.

By early '57 they were clear at the top of the Division. When they claimed the title they were eight points clear of Spurs their nearest rivals.

A legend was building around this astonishing young team. A popular songwriter penned the Manchester United Calypso in the idiom of the time:

> If they're playing in your town
> Be sure to get to that football ground
> If you do, then you will see
> Football taught by Matt Busby
> At Manchester . . . Manchester United
> A bunch of bouncing Busby Babes,
> They deserve to be knighted.

Busby was prepared to settle for the First Division/FA Cup Double never achieved in modern times.

Europe was another target. United slaughtered the Belgian champions Anderlecht in their preliminary round tie. Duncan Edwards, like Colman and Charlton, still doing National Service, was unavailable for the first leg in Brussels. Floodlit football was still a rare 'gadget' in England. This was United's first competitive floodlit match. Busby advised them to keep the ball on the deck. He hadn't had time to watch Anderlecht, so he told the players not to mind reputations – the opposition had six Belgian internationals – and play their own game. This was good enough for a 2–0 victory.

European football did not excite public imagination in England, and the national press devoted little space to this initial engagement. The return leg in Manchester was played under City's lights at Maine Road. United won 10–0. Denis Viollet scored four goals, Tommy Taylor was second best with a hat-trick, and Billy Whelan scored two. Forty-four thousand Mancunians attended. The story made the headlines. Some cavilled that it was only Anderlecht. The Belgians' captain, Mermans, offered a sobering perspective for the sceptics: 'The best teams of Hungary have never beaten us like this. They are fantastic.' Reminding the jounalists that Anderlecht had recently beaten Arsenal, Mermans concluded, 'They should pick this whole team for England.'

It is fascinating to note that Billy Whelan was the only non-English player in United's side that night. Bobby Charlton would have made a good substitute were England inclined to heed Mermans's advice. In this context the Englishness of Busby's great team is remarkable. Most great Football League teams had had a couple of Scots in key positions. Busby had none. The Welshman Kenny Morgans would emerge within a year to contest a first team place, Jackie Blanchflower was a regular deputy for the wounded in midfield or at centre-half but the team now writing its legend was distinctly English in nature. Ironically the city that now adored them was the least English of all the cities in the land.

United beat Borussia Dortmund 3–2 in the first leg of the next round. Seventy-five thousand spectators saw the game at Maine Road – the 'gimmick' was catching on. Swagger cost United dear when, after leading 3–0 they allowed the Germans two late goals. They battled to secure a 0–0 draw in Dortmund. Honved, the powerful Hungarian club side containing five of the national team, were presumed to be United's next opponents. The Hungarians had defected en masse before Budapest's '56 Uprising, so Honved were forced to play their 'home' leg of this tie in Brussels where Bilbao of Spain beat Puskas and his team 6–5 on aggregate.

Bilbao, beaten only once at home in three seasons, won the first leg 5–3. Northern Spain was a tough spot in January, and the trip over was a nightmare, snow rendering Bilbao airport treacherous and deserted when United arrived. The journey home, which began with players and officials helping to wipe snow off the wings of the plane, was warmed by thoughts of a magnificent goal Billy Whelan had scored late in the game to give United a chance in the return leg. Trailing 5–2 the cause looked hopeless, until Duncan broke up a Bilbao attack, found Whelan wide on the right and the tall Irishman ran zealously at the Spanish defenders before striking the ball to the far corner of the net with wicked power. This valiant final flourish was a mark of the courage which underpinned all else that was splendid in Busby's team.

On 6 February 1957 Bilbao came to Manchester. The city was

intoxicated. Seventy thousand went to the game at Maine Road. The whole city felt a rare enchantment. Those early European nights in Manchester were almost indescribably glamorous. It was as if the lights that lit Maine Road had cast their glow on everyone in the city, transforming Cottonopolis into a vast theatre. Drab mid-Fifties existence was lent enchantment by the beams of light which reached deep into the heart of the city, a couple of miles from Maine Road and reflected outwards to the suburbs. The roar of 70,000 voices echoed through the streets, never more passionately than the night the 'Red Devils' beat Bilbao.

Inside Maine Road the pitch was a pool of light and colour. The atmostphere tense, the play frenzied. The Basques were tough, they'd come to battle, selecting an extra defender, Etura, to replace Uribe who had scored two of their goals in the first game. The early goal didn't come. Edwards, driving forward more fiercely than any, created the chance for Denis Viollet to score just before half-time. Bilbao, galvanised by their international centre-half Jesus Garay, didn't buckle. They were Basque, unlikely to shirk the bruising physicality, of which, the dimmer English minds imagined, Continentals were scared. Switzerland had taught Busby and his players differently. The Spanish and Italians were better at kicking as well.

In the seventieth minute Tommy Taylor levelled the scores. Five minutes from time a night of magnificent drama ended triumphantly when Johnny Berry stroked home a chance created by Taylor's characteristic surge past Garay on the right. Manchester United were through to the semi-finals of the Champions' Cup. The players left the field to a tumultuous, almost hysterical ovation. Bilbao's captain, Piru Gainza acknowledged the victors: 'They play with such passion we were simply overwhelmed.' The Spaniards had been on a bonus rumoured to be several hundred pounds a man. The 'Red Devils' received appearance money of £5 each and £3 win bonus. The maximum wage had increased to £15 (£12 in summer). For adding to the folklore of their city, while restoring some of England's diminished prestige, the legendary 'Busby Babes' received £23 in their wage packets the following Friday. This was a good week.

210

The Double of League and Cup had not been achieved since 1897 when Aston Villa won both. The feat was deemed impossible in the modern game. By April United were favourites to make history by adding the FA Cup to the Championship already secured. After beating Birmingham City in the semi-final, United were due to meet Aston Villa at Wembley. They were long odds on to do the impossible. In fact the football world was now speculating about the unprecedented Treble with the European Champions' Cup added to the domestic spoils. The emergence of Billy Whelan and Bobby Charlton had lowered the average age of the side to twenty-one.

The lads had moved on from the Locarno and coffee-bars to Manchester's more exotic after dark venues. The Queens, Continental and Cromford Clubs were favoured on Wednesday and Saturday nights. One or two got motor cars, David Pegg a flashy little sports job. Jackie Blanchflower and Tommy Taylor kept to their Saturday night routine: dogs, Chinese, Ritz and Continental or Queens. Part of this ritual was a morning of punishment on Sundays at Old Trafford. Sandy Busby, Matt's son would often see them there: 'You could set your watch by Tommy and Jackie every Sunday,' Sandy recalls. 'They'd pound out 22 laps flat to the boards, no half-pace stuff. That got rid of the ale. It was completely voluntary.'

Sandy was a useful pro playing wing-half for Blackburn Rovers, then a good First Division side with England international Ronnie Clayton and Bryan Douglas their star players. Sandy was one of the lads, particularly popular with the characters who, like himself, enjoyed a flutter and a pint. At Paddy McGrath's Cromford Club you could play blackjack and roulette. Tommy Taylor, Jackie Blanchflower, Eddie Colman and David Pegg were regulars. Roger Byrne was not a man for the nightlife but he held his wedding reception in Paddy's club, as did John Doherty, another streetwise lad.

Matt and Jean Busby would sometimes drop in to the Cromford, but their usual Saturday routine was a meal with Louis and Muriel Edwards at the Bridge Inn where Bobby used to wait for his mates a year or so before. Matt had, as Sandy puts it, 'found his director'. To become a director of Manchester

United was a great honour now. The Board needed new blood, many names were being touted, though none impressed Matt, and some alarmed him. Louis was his nominee. Willie Satinoff, whose family owned a Manchester clothing company, was another possible Busby candidate. Both were close friends of his who could be relied upon to support his decisions.

Of the two, Louis Edwards, being the more malleable, was the most reliable. But Willie Satinoff was smart, and, like Busby, a racing man. Willie was a snappy dresser, lean and popular. He would make a good director but not a good stooge.

Real Madrid, holders of the Champions' Cup, were United's European cup semi-final opponents. The first leg in Madrid drew 125,000 to Real's fantastic Bernabeau Stadium. The wealthy Spanish club had gathered a collection of the finest players in their country and had the world's greatest footballer, the Argentinian Alfredo Di Stefano. This was the kind of thing the merchant blunderers who ran English football were against, the old enemy elitism. Busby had seen Real play. His usual form was to play down the opposition, talk about United's strengths rather than dwell on the possible dangers from the other side. Bobby Charlton explains the difference after the trip to see Real: 'Usually he would not talk about great players in opposing teams, not wanting to frighten you. But now he couldn't contain himself. This player Di Stefano he'd seen had just about everything from what he told us.' Alongside the Argentinian, Real fielded Raymond Kopa, the great French right-winger, with Gento, a magical Spaniard on the left. Spanish internationals Rial and Mateos also played in the forward line. Behind these aristocratic forwards Real had a classically tough Spanish defence, internationals Munoz, Marquitos and Zarraga. Soon they would add Ferenc Puskas to this elite.

'MURDER IN MADRID' was the way the *Daily Herald* headlined its report of the game. The opening two sentences convey a sense of occasion. 'Real Madrid got away with murder before 125,000 witnesses at the Santiago Bernabeau Stadium here today. They hacked, slashed, kicked and wrestled their way to a 3–1 victory in this European Cup semi-final first-leg.' Tommy Taylor scored United's goal, but the Spaniards were too worldly for the young 'Red Devils'.

212

Manchester United switched on their new floodlights for the first time for the second leg of the semi-final in which Bobby Charlton played and scored in front of a crowd of 65,000. The score, 2–2, meant United had failed in their first attempt in Europe, but it was a brave and honourable defeat at the end of an adventure which had transformed English football for ever, enabling 'the best game in the world' to measure its best against reality. As Matt Busby depicted the Real Madrid experience it was a contest between a great mature side and one destined for greatness. He was satisfied and in no doubt that his young team's day in Europe would come. The Double remained, a historic goal for all the great English club sides in the twentieth century, now a consolation prize for the 'Red Devils'.

The previous year Manchester City had won the FA Cup. Some of their players had swopped their tickets for a new Vauxhall Viva apiece. The official Football Association ruling restricted each player to twelve Cup Final tickets. All club representatives agreed to this rule at Football Association meetings, then all went back to their clubs and permitted the rule to be broken, so that traditionally players were given a hundred tickets for the great day. This handsome allocation would find its way onto the black-market. Thus, the heroes would be rewarded. Nothing much, if at all, had changed since Meredith's days.

Year by year Matt Busby had found himself sucked into this moral quagmire. A few quid in an envelope to the father of a talented youngster for scouting, no bribe intended. The public position was that Manchester United would only sign young-sters who really wanted to play for them. The fact was that a really determined and acquisitive parent could easily squeeze a little cash out of the system provided he wasn't too greedy.

According to Jackie Blanchflower, the Manchester United first team squad were each given a hundred tickets by the club before the 1957 Cup Final. Some players looked after their relatives and close friends and handed the rest to a man who promised them a new car each in return. Their benefactor's *bona fides* seemed to be OK for he was known to be a business associate of 'The Boss's' pal Louis Edwards. The motor cars never materialised and the tickets were not returned. The Babes had been done.

Robbery was the cry again after the Cup Final. Six minutes into the game Villa's Irish international winger Peter McParland floored United's 'keeper Ray Wood with a resolute challenge which many claimed was unacceptably reckless. Wood left the field concussed, with what was later diagnosed as a fractured jaw. Jackie Blanchflower, an international colleague of McParland's was close to the incident: 'Woody was a good 'keeper, but he didn't like to come off his line. "Puffer", we called him, he always had a fag in his mouth. He was a good lad, who could laugh at himself. Old Tosher used to tell him that if a barrel-load of hay went past him he wouldn't catch it. When I see him now I say,"Woody you were the second worst goalkeeper I ever saw in my life." He always asks, "Who's the worst."

'Peter was a naive lad. Villa told him that Woody was suspect, to "get in and let him know you're there" early on. Peter headed a ball from the edge of the box and kept running. For once Woody came off his line to gather it. I can see it now. I'll never forget, Ray braced himself for the challenge and then tried to get out of the road but Peter caught him. We were only about five minutes into the game. It was a sickener.'

With no substitute allowed, United were down to ten men. 'Roger asked Bobby to go in the goal but he didn't fancy it, so I went in,' Jackie recalls. At half-time United were level after winning most of the first half battles. But Wembley was a bitch with an extra man against you and McParland scored twice in the second half. Apparently dead, with Ray Wood, dazed, back in goal, United rallied desperately, Tommy Taylor rewarding them with a goal close to the final whistle. But too late to breathe life into the deflated Double dream. Busby was composed in the dressing-room afterwards. He had long argued for substitutes to be allowed, especially for goalkeepers. But this was yet another 'gimmick' the Football Association would not countenance.

This sad climax to a glorious season saddened the nation, the majority of whom, though not *au fait* with soccer, had been enthralled by the blaze of youthful colour Busby's 'Red Devils'

214

had ingrained in England's image of itself. Fate as much as Peter McParland had struck down the young heroes. It was the way of the world, courage fated to lose even when triumph seemed inevitable. More than a Cup was lost in many hearts that day.

In the Catholic/Irish enclave of Collyhurst one fifteen-year-old was particularly sad. Norbert Stiles was due to sign for United the following week. He was a fan. United was his life. 'I lived for them,' he explains. 'My earliest memory is sitting on my dad's shoulders at Old Trafford as a six-year-old watching the '48 team; Carey, Mitten, Rowley. I remember Johnny Carey scoring a fantastic goal against Chelsea when they won the Championship in '52. He hit a fantastic shot past Reg Matthews.'

Nobby's dad, Charlie, was the local undertaker. He was Paddy McGrath's childhood friend. 'People thought we had money,' Nobby remembers, 'but my grandfather owned the business, my dad was on a wage like everyone else. My mum was a sewer in the mill.'

Nobby and his older brother, Charlie, went to St Pat's School. His grandfather was a Byrne from Wicklow in Ireland. 'He came over to work on the railways. His sisters went into the convent for food and shelter. We were Catholics and very conscious of it,' he explains. 'We wore shamrocks on St Patrick's Day and sang "Faith of our Fathers" (an Irish hymn) rather than "God save the Queen". We had a great sports teacher called Mr Mulligan who got me involved in football. I was small, but I played inside-forward for Manchester Boys and wing-half for England Boys. You were either City or United, I was United from the start.

'Charlie and I used to play on Saturday mornings, go back home for boiled chicken and dumplings and we'd be at Old Trafford by one or half-past. We stood at the score-board end. Eddie Colman was my idol. I used to try and copy him, coming side on and shimmying, but I was nothing like him. We didn't have a television in those days. I remember myself and Charlie walking down Oldham Road to watch United play on *Match of the Day* in a television shop. We'd stand outside the window freezing. The night they lost 4–0 to Bristol Rovers in the Cup I was gutted.'

215

Nobby captained Manchester Boys. Bob Wilson and Bobby Tambling were in the same England Boys team. 'Another lad, Peter Bullock went to Birmingham. I think only the four of us played League football,' Nobby says. He was coveted by all the big League clubs when Joe Armstrong came to the house. 'He was a gentleman, he always got the mothers first. He went to Lourdes and brought my mum a Miraculous Medal.' Wolves and Bolton both offered Nobby's dad £4,000 for his signature, a sum that was the equivalent of five or six years' earnings in those days. 'My mum would have liked a television and a fridge. But they didn't tell me about the Wolves or Bolton money. My dad said, "Where do you want to go?" I said United. We got no money from United. I didn't want any.'

Nobby Stiles signed for United for £3. 5s a week and £1 expenses which Joe Armstrong gave him in an envelope each Friday. 'I kept the pound for myself and gave the wage packet to me mum.' That pound was probably an illegal payment.

The disappointments of 1957 were the spur for the new campaign. Looking back, Matt Busby and Jimmy Murphy would remember the summer of '57 as a blissful few months. But the Wembley defeat rankled, the frustration a reminder that their work was far from complete, that nothing could be taken for granted. Sport's oldest lesson – life's perhaps – that the day you think you've cracked it is the day you start to fade was the foremost thought in the minds of these two old pros.

Bobby Charlton was bitterly disappointed to find himself back in the reserves at the beginning of the '57/'58 season. He'd played in the Cup Final because Denis Viollet was nursing a groin-strain. Now Viollet returned, with Billy Whelan in the other inside-forward spot. Playing at Bolton in the reserves one afternoon around this time Bobby took a throw-in on the halfway-line. With a couple of minutes to go United led 1–0. Bobby's throw was careless, across field rather than down the touchline. A Bolton player intercepted and thirty seconds later the scores were level. Jimmy went berserk in the dressing-room. 'He gave me a terrible roasting,' Charlton recalls. 'I was embarrassed in front of the other players. But I never threw a ball across the pitch in that situation again. It was a lesson in professionalism and even though this was a Central League match they all mattered to Jimmy. That's what made me a player. Little things, the difference between being a schoolboy and a pro.'

Nobby Stiles was soon singled out by Bert Whalley for Jimmy's special attention. 'He made a huge impression on me,' Nobby says. 'When I went there I was overawed. The players were so good, you'd see them in training and games and think, "I'm never going to get this." Maybe I was Jimmy's style of player, but they were all his style . . . Duncan . . . Bobby. The "simple things" he'd say and for the first six months I thought, "I'm seeing all these brilliant players and it doesn't look simple to me." I remember seeing Bobby score an unbelievable goal, an overhead bicycle-kick. But Jimmy made me see that if you got the ball and gave it to a red shirt the game progressed from there. Football is about getting it and giving it. And the passion he spoke with was amazing. Jimmy would talk about "fire in your belly". "See this red shirt," he'd say, "it's the best in the world, when you put that on nothing can beat you." I would have gone through a brick wall for him. Bobby and Wilf will tell you the same. It wasn't just the passion, he gave me confidence because I could relate to the game as he explained it to me. People say to me I was this or I was that, but what they don't realise is, if you play for Manchester United and England you've got to be able to *play*. Jimmy gave me the understanding. They seem like small things but they added up.'

The basic football education was mixed with experience of dressing-room life. This could be very intimidating, as John Giles explains: 'We were in awe of the first team players. I mean you wouldn't go in the first team dressing-room unless you had work in there. Running round the track at training in the morning I'd be scared stiff of them. Duncan Edwards would come thundering past and you'd just get out of the way. They wouldn't notice you. But you had to be fair to them, Duncan, Tommy Taylor and David Pegg were only young lads themselves, 21 or 22 and at that age you're not as good with young fellas as you would be when you got older.'

Eddie Colman, John remembers as the exception: 'Eddie was very friendly, he'd have a chat with you, know your name.'

Eddie was Nobby's idol: 'I just looked at him from afar, I

217

couldn't take my eyes off him. He used to wear a pork-pie hat. I would love to have been able to go up to him and say, "you are my idol," but I used to blush like anything when I'd meet him.'
David Gaskill, a young goalkeeper, was the head ground staff boy. Nobby remembers being pushed around by Gaskill: 'David, Mark Pearson and Alex Dawson were a bit senior to me. Gaskill had played in the first team in the Charity Shield so he thought he could give the orders. He'd say, "Get that brush, brush this, brush that." I'd say, "Who are you, you do it." We used to strip in the ballboys' room. Going in the first team dressing-room was a big deal. I remember Mark Pearson and Alex Dawson getting hold of me one day. They wanted the first team's autographs. They were scared of going in there 'cause the lads didn't like signing. It's the same these days. I see apprentices at United today and first team lads tell 'em to sod off. It's a testing time for a kid. Anyway I took Mark and Alex's books in and I went to Mark Jones and Duncan. They were gods in my eyes, so I said, "Will you sign this please," and Mark said, "Piss off." I knew if I went back to the ballboys' room without the autographs I'd get battered in there so I said, "*Please*, Mark, sign it," and he told me to piss off again. And then he said, "Alright, give it here." He said, "Aren't you the young fella who played for England Schoolboys at Wembley a few weeks ago? I said yes, and he said, "Well done, keep it up," and I walked out feeling great.'

12

Tragedy

'When I saw the fear on Roger's face
it frightened me. He was a strong
man, not easily prey to fear.'

Harry Gregg

Manchester United began the season 1957–58 as expected,
remaining unbeaten for six games, five of which they won
handsomely. The only blemish on the record was a 3–3 draw
away to Everton at Goodison Park. Then things went badly
wrong. They lost three of their next four games; 4–0 at Bolton,
1–2 to Blackpool at home, and critically, 3–1 away to Wolves
at Molineux. In between on 25 September United travelled to
Dublin to play the great Irish club Shamrock Rovers in their
opening European Cup fixture. The result of the second leg of
this tie, a narrow 3–2 victory at Old Trafford, testifies to Rovers'
ability. This was the best club side in Irish history. Forty-five
thousand packed Dublin's Dalymount Park for the first game.
For Billy Whelan who'd been born a mile away in Cabra this
was a very special night. He scored two goals in a 6–0 victory.
On this sultry early autumn evening the 'Red Devils' cast their
magic spell upon this Georgian city which loves the English
game and had a proud soccer tradition of its own. Busby loved
Dublin, sensing a part of his past in its carefree, infectious
informality, and Dalymount was one of his marvellous nights,
his young side doing him proud with football that was elegant,
precise and, for those of us who watched from the terraces,
unbelievably grand.

We had seen other English teams: Stan Matthews, Tom
Finney, Wilf Mannion and Len Shackleton, the 'Clown Prince'
of contemporary legend. Before television these men were
faces on the little black and white cards we collected from

sweet-cigarettes. The Charles Buchan Football Monthly magazines would feature stunning photographs of Nat Lofthouse and Tommy Taylor leaping to impossible heights to head goals which we could only imagine and wonder at. When they came to Dublin the photos came alive, your blood ran cold with a shiver of delight. The 'Red Devils' were different to those who'd come before them. No baggy shorts, but neat white pants, hitched up to show the perfect muscles on thighs of unimaginable power. They wore v-necked red shirts without the old collars of Matthews and Finney, trim and dashing, an emblem of the gods whose lithe bodies they adorned. Football never came to life so vividly, with such awesome beauty, as it did in Dublin that night in '57. One goal remains in memory: a long crossfield pass from Edwards finding David Pegg who'd drifted to the right-wing. Pegg was clear with only the Rovers' 'keeper to beat. He paused for an instant as the 'keeper moved forward to narrow his angle, then from twenty-five yards and wide the god floated the ball, tantalisingly, over the head of his foe to the far corner of the net. Exquisite. Perfection executed with impossible grace and assurance. They lived up to their legend that night. More than that, they were – or seemed – unearthly, handsome creatures from another planet, more heroic than any movie-star we'd seen or could imagine. The following Saturday they lost to Wolves in the League.

European football was a glamorous distraction. The emotional exertions of the previous season now appeared to cause delayed reaction. For a few weeks the champions lost their focus, and Wolves took over at the top of the First Division. Busby didn't panic. As he'd explained to Billy Behan in Dublin, his side was young, its final composition yet to be decided. Some of the promising youngsters had gone, or soon would. Jeff Whitefoot and Don Gibson had been transferred, the latter to Sheffield Wednesday in his own interests after his marriage to Matt's daughter. When Gibson played poorly in a game at Old Trafford shortly after news of his romance became public the fans had jeered him. John Doherty left for Leicester soon afterwards.

'Matt felt that they were still only kids, despite winning two Championships,' Behan explains. 'He talked to me about

Bobby Charlton, and Liam Whelan when he was in Dublin. Bobby wasn't even in the team. "I've got these two and they're going to be as good as Puskas and Di Stefano," Matt said. The problem with Liam was shyness, Matt felt he would become a truly great player once he came out of his shell a little and asserted himself more. Liam had scored 28 goals in the First Division the season before, yet Matt believed there was more in him. Bobby was even more exciting, but he was only 19.'

Busby's concern for Whelan, his sensitivity to his young players' growing personality, is evidence of how closely he observed every nuance of life at Old Trafford. Even at a time when prosperity looked assured his own ambitions and expectations were focused on horizons way beyond anyone else's. A player who had scored twenty-eight First Division goals was not the finished product. The team likewise. Champions two years running, young legends in the country outside Old Trafford, they still had a long way to go to satisfy his aspirations, so when they lost two more home games in succession to Spurs and Chelsea at the end of November, Busby acted ruthlessly. Twenty-five-year-old Harry Gregg, a Northern Ireland team-mate of Jackie Blanchflower's was signed from Doncaster Rovers for £23,500, a British record for a goalkeeper. Busby inquired about Harry's character, and, assured that all was fine, closed the deal. Gregg was an unorthodox 'keeper who, unlike Ray Wood, loved to dominate his penalty area, indeed was prone to wander further afield, pushing outside the eighteen-yard line to marshal his defence. He was introduced to the side for the home game against Leicester City on 21 December. In a dramatic response to the autumn's disappointment, Busby dropped four players. Ray Wood, Johnny Berry, David Pegg and Billy Whelan. Kenny Morgans, an eighteen-year-old from the previous season's FA Youth Cup winning team, replaced Berry. Bobby Charlton came in for Whelan; Albert Scanlon for Pegg. Leicester were demolished 4–0 to set up a sequence of seven unbeaten games which put United back in the title race. Nobody could be sure of their place was the message Busby sent to his young champions' dressing-room. Jackie Blanchflower had discovered the truth of this a couple of weeks earlier. Jackie had kept his friend Mark Jones in the reserves for three

221

months, yet an international appearance for Northern Ireland allowed Jones to reclaim his centre-half position and put Jackie back in the reserves.

United had progressed in the European Cup, eliminating Dukla Prague 3–1 on aggregate, the 3–0 home leg victory proving conclusive. Red Star Belgrade awaited England's champions in the quarter-final.

United's FA Cup campaign began away to Workington, perennial strugglers at the foot of the Football League. On an icy pitch before 21,000 excited home supporters the Football League's poorest relation led 1–0 at half-time. Legend had touched Busby's great young side. There was a streak of *hubris* which could colour their performance on occasions. Workington benefited from this that day as Bristol Rovers had benefited a couple of seasons before. Denis Viollet solved the problem with a second-half hat-trick.

United beat Red Star 2–1 with goals from Eddie Colman and Bobby Charlton in the quarter-final first leg at Old Trafford on 14 January. The second leg would be a battle. Three days afterwards United were due to play Wolves at home in a game that would, it was felt, decide the Championship. Important though Europe was, winning three Championships in a row, as Herbert Chapman had with Arsenal before the war, was the goal Matt Busby secretly treasured. That ambition was nourished by two spectacular victories in the League games which preceded the trip to Belgrade for the return match with Red Star. First Bolton were beaten 7–2 at Old Trafford on 18 January, Bobby Charlton scoring three of the goals, and then on 1 February 63,000 packed Highbury to see the 'Red Devils' play Arsenal. United took a 3–0 lead, lost it in the second-half, scored two more to which Arsenal once again replied. The final score was 5–4, the match a classic, Busby's team living up to its reputation for brilliance and a daring that bordered on recklessness.

The Manchester lads loved going to London and showing off, and the big city loved them. They were cavaliers from the North which was grey and boring, or so the Cockneys liked to claim. Disproving that myth was a pleasure for Busby's team. For Busby too. He felt himself to be a Mancunian now. This was no denial of his Scottishness, rather a reflection of the precious sense of place he possessed after almost thirty years in Cottonopolis. Matt had been offered jobs elsewhere, by Spurs and Real Madrid, the latter promising him unimagined financial reward, and though he had been flattered or, more accurately, pleased to have his work acknowledged, he was never tempted.

Manchester was his place. The city allowed him to be what he was, the serious, dutiful Catholic, the man exemplifying the boy, observing the imperatives of behaviour and obligation to caste his mother Nellie had preached to her children. This was Matt the public man. The private man could exist with equal facility in Manchester. This man was the grandson of Jimmy Greer: Irish, human and, yes, a touch feckless, expansive, defying the conventions of Miners Row. This Matt remained hidden from public view. The deception was essential. First a Catholic, then a professional football man, his life had been a long struggle against prejudice of one kind or another. The public mask remained in place, but the other part of his spirit was indulged in his friendships – Paddy McGrath, Willie Satinoff, Louis Edwards, Johnny Foy – and his love of a gamble. Johnny Foy, the bookmaker, was one of those used by the professional gambler Alex Bird to place his bets. Bird had hurt the big bookies far too often, and they were wary now of accepting his bets, so a network of surrogates existed to spread Bird's money around the big bookmakers. Foy was one of Bird's men. Bird didn't have many bets, rather he specialised in two-year old horses whose ability he measured by the clock.

In an age when racecourse timing systems were universally inaccurate – a flaw reflected in the official form-book – Bird had the advantage of the correct time which he calculated on the course with his own stop-watch. Armed with the best information, Britain's biggest punter waged war on the bookies. Matt's arrangement with Johnny Foy allowed him to be privy to Bird's bets, and for several years he followed the system investing up to £50 a time on Bird's selections. The bets were substantial as were the wins and losses.

This indulgence was merely a distraction. The truest reconciliation of Busby's public and private selves was his 'Red

Devils' on a day such as the one at Highbury on 1 February 1958. The style was pure Busby, pure Manchester: Roger Byrne and Duncan Edwards, clinical, powerful, ruthless; Eddie Colman, daring, expansive; Denis Viollet, smooth, elusive, clever; Tommy Taylor and Mark Jones, as tough and brave as the navvies on the Ship Canal.

Busby hated the sobriquet 'Busby Babes'. It proposed innocence, naivety, callow youth, and this was not his team. 'Red Devils' was closer to the truth. Sometimes, Busby confided to his pals, he'd wish the other team to score first, to rouse their anger, make them stretch to the limits of their courage and talent. At Highbury this desire was fulfilled.

The Manchester United party left for Belgrade on Monday morning with no member of the Board accompanying them. Tragedy had struck at Highbury two days earlier when a United director, George Whittaker, collapsed and died of a heart attack, and Harold Hardman rarely travelled abroad anyway. Now he and his fellow directors stayed behind for Whittaker's funeral. Louis Edwards had intended making the journey to Yugoslavia, but he too remained in Manchester to pay his last respects to a man who, ironically, had vetoed his election to the Manchester United Board a few weeks before. Whittaker had blocked the nomination, much to Matt Busby's annoyance, but this battle was for another day. Red Star and Wolves the following Saturday were the more immediate concern.

Boarding the plane for the outward trip the players were surprised by the unusual interior. The twin-engined Elizabethan had seats facing back and front, unlike the Viscounts and Dakotas they were familiar with from previous trips to Europe. The layout suited the card-school, among them Harry Gregg, who loved his game of poker. Arriving at Old Trafford he found plenty of kindred spirits – Ray Wood, Billy Whelan, Johnny Berry and Jackie Blanchflower were enthusiasts, poker the favoured game. Busby kept an eye on the card-school. He didn't like the sometimes heavy gambling which could drain the team's emotions. Money won from friends and colleagues was not the same as takings from a bookie. But cards killed the boredom of coach journeys, hotel rooms and lodging houses and was better than the alternatives: boozing and ladies.

Belgrade was miserable. The hotel was spartan. People queued for food, for everything, it seemed.

A slight doubt over Roger Byrne's fitness had earned Geoff Bent a rare trip with the first team. Bent, a Salfordian, had played a dozen games as Byrne's deputy in the previous two years. Although yet to play a first team game this season, he was generally acknowledged to be a player of sufficient quality to get a place in most League sides.

Roger Byrne was cleared to play. United expected a battle. Within ninety seconds the pressure eased when Denis Viollet took a simple chance to make the score 3–1 on aggregate. By half-time United looked assured of their semi-final place. Two brilliant goals from Bobby Charlton left Red Star trailing 5–1 in the tie.

Two minutes into the second half Red Star scored, and then again eight minutes later from the penalty spot to bring the score to 5–3. The expected battle began. For thirty-five minutes the Yugoslavs laid siege in United's half. Gregg made spectacular saves on his line and ventured outside his penalty area when necessary. Four minutes from time he advanced to gather a ball on the edge of the eighteen-yard box and stumbled a yard too far. Red Star's international forward, Kostic, tried to flight the ball over the wall of red shirts. It clipped Viollet's head and looped beyond Gregg's desperate reach. The final minutes of acute anxiety were fraught with the suspicion that the referee would succumb to the home crowd's hysteria by awarding another penalty for any incident in the box. Time ran out. In the dressing-room they slumped, relieved. They had survived, having typically flirted with danger.

Early evening. The day victorious, the night was theirs to savour. The banquet would be endured, the dignitaries' self-regarding speeches mocked on the players' table. Barely suppressing their titters, they would wait for the Present. In Madrid the year before they'd got a gold watch each. Here in Belgrade it was a cheap trinket. The waitresses were gorgeous, Slavic, teasing these English footballers. The Red Star players were older, harder, less exuberant. Eddie's eyes twinkled mischievously at all, the benign urchin, irrepressible even in

225

club blazer and tie, the uniform of formal club occasions. Outside the banquet hall the reporters filed tomorrow's story, frustrated by the Yugoslav telephone system, as they searched for new words to describe another performance that mixed the brilliant with the valiant. George Follows of the *Daily Herald* informed his readers that this had been the best football United ever played. Tom Jackson had commanded the front-page lead in the early editions of that afternoon's *Manchester Evening News* to report 'UNITED SNATCH 3-0 CUP LEAD'. The second half altered the scoreline but not the end result. United were through to the semi-finals of the European Cup once more.

After the banquet Matt took them to a private room in the hotel. He ordered beers and whisky for himself and the other non-playing members of United's party. As on other nights in Europe they gathered for a couple of private hours together getting gently intoxicated. Jimmy Murphy was away with the Welsh international side he managed in his spare time. They'd had a couple of good nights previously in Europe when Jimmy played the piano for a singsong, mixing the popular with his own renditions of Chopin and Bach. 'The Boss's' contribution was always the highlight of those rare hours of music, his song the old Harry Lauder classic 'I Belong to Glasgow'. The lads would join in for the chorus but only Matt knew every word of the verses, his rich baritone voice touching its most emotive note when he reached the line 'I'm only a common old working man, as anyone here can see. But when I get a couple of drinks on a Saturday Glasgow belongs to me.' A song in memory of his youth and Jimmy Greer who took him to the Glasgow Empire to see Lauder sing this anthem of the Scots working-class on Saturday nights now evoked with real feeling.

In Belgrade the card players were getting restless. Tommy Taylor, David Pegg, and Bobby Charlton repaired to the hotel bar, disappointed like Denis Viollet that Belgrade offered no exotic nightlife. 'The Boss' reminded them of Wolves on Saturday and put them on their honour to be in bed by a reasonable hour.

The card school went on to the very small hours with Harry Gregg winning. They were playing for dinars, the local currency – 3,000 to the £1 or something. The tension of the poker hands was occasionally broken by the unreality of the bets. 'I'll open for three thousand.' 'I'll make it six thousand to play.' It sounded big-time. They laughed at the daftness of it.

They left Belgrade in mid-morning, tired, flat, anxious to get home. They were due to stop at Munich to refuel and arrive in Manchester at six o'clock. Wolves and the Championship loomed larger as the Elizabethan droned across snowbound Central Europe. Munich airport was starkly anonymous as they drifted in to land. The card school was in abeyance because of a dispute that had arisen over Harry's insistence that they continue playing for dinars, a large wad of which he'd been unable to spend at Belgrade airport. He promised to play for sterling once they'd taken off again from Munich.

Captain James Thain was in command of the charter flight. His friend Captain Ken Rayment was co-pilot. Because they were friends a certain informality was present on the flight-deck of 609 Zule Uniform, and they had agreed that Thain would fly the outward journey with Rayment taking charge for the trip back to Manchester. BEA regulations forbade captain and first-officer from changing seats, insisting that the captain stay in the left-hand seat. Thain, however, remained in his original position because he found it difficult to monitor the instrument reading from the left-hand seat, as they were not duplicated on the panel in front of him. Rayment consented to this arrangement despite the fact that as pilot for the return flight one must assume he needed to see the panel's reading at least as much as his co-pilot.

The passengers were not due to disembark at Munich. Refuelling would take only twenty minutes or so. On their first attempt to take off after completing the refuelling the aircraft came to a halt after forty seconds. The engines had sounded an uneven note which suggested there was boost surging, a problem which Thain subsequently claimed 'was not uncommon with Elizabethans at the time, particularly at airports like Munich because of their height above sea-level'. One cause of boost surging was opening the throttles too quickly, Thain explained, 'Ken said that at the start of our next run we would open the throttles a little before releasing the brakes and then continue to open them more slowly.' It was Thain's opinion that

227

despite the uneven engine sound there was 'not much danger that the take-off power of the aircraft would be affected because the Elizabethans were very powerful in their day and you could actually take off on one engine'.

At 14.34 hours clearance was given for another attempt. Again Thain aborted take-off forty seconds after it began, and the plane taxied back to the airport building for Thain to consult BEA's station engineer at Munich. Twenty minutes of anxiety ended for the passengers when Captain Rayment told them there would be a short delay as there was a technical fault. It was snowing quite heavily. The party left the plane for a cup of tea while the problem was being sorted out.

Matt Busby seemed tired but relaxed. He had been in hospital for a minor operation the previous week, now he was weary and had slumbered through the Belgrade–Munich leg of the journey. Getting home was everyone's priority, the prospect of an overnight stay in Munich unappealing. While they were getting refreshments in the café someone speculated that they might have to travel back to England by ship via the Hook of Holland if the weather deteriorated further. This suggestion was greeted by groans of dismay.

Thain and Rayment remained in the cockpit of the aircraft. Station engineer William Black came to join them to discuss the problem. The fate of Flight 609 was decided in the next five minutes.

Black confirmed that boost surging was common at airports like Munich and recommended the procedures for overcoming it. 'We told him we had tried these without eliminating the noise,' Thain later explained. Black said that the engines could be retuned but it would mean an overnight stop. Thain's reply was 'that I didn't think this was necessary because the starboard engine had performed normally'. Thain and Rayment had, in effect, decided to take a chance rather than the more prudent course of having the engines checked and retuned overnight. 'We talked about the snow and looked at the wings from the flight-deck. We had lost the film of snow we had noticed before our first departure and decided there was no need to have the wings swept,' Thain reported afterwards.

The passengers had only been in the terminal building about ten minutes when they were recalled to the plane. There was some tension among the party, but this was not the first time they'd been involved in airport drama. Twelve months previously they'd swept snow off the wings in Bilbao, and that journey home had been interrupted by an emergency landing in Jersey.

At 14.56 Captain Rayment was given permission to taxi out to the runway. A passenger count revealed that someone was missing. Then the plane doors were re-opened and Alf Clarke, who had been phoning news of the delay to the *Manchester Evening Chronicle*, entered to derisive cheers. At 15.03.06 the Elizabethan began rolling. Harry Gregg glanced at Roger Byrne sitting at the window seat diagonally across the aisle from him. 'When I saw the fear in his face it frightened me. Roger was a strong man, not easily prey to fear,' he says.

'The first two attempts to take off had been quite unnerving for me, possibly more frightening than the third time as I had been watching the wheels sticking in the slush. When we got back into the plane some of us were quite nervy. I saw the steward actually strapped into his seat when we got on which was not very reassuring! Alf Clarke was late getting back to the plane and we had to wait for him. I was quite worried by this time. I sat very low in my seat, opened my trousers and my collar and sank down into the seat with my legs up. I tried to crack a few jokes, but Johnny Berry, who was sitting near me, was too anxious to be amused by them and said he thought we would all be killed. Billy Whelan, who was sitting next to him, said "Well if that's going to happen I'm ready for it."

'We set off once again and I remember looking out of the window and seeing a tree and a house passing by; and suddenly we were passing places we had not done before. Everything went black all of a sudden and sparks began to fly. I was hit hard on the back of the head and I thought the top of my skull had been cut off. The plane seemed to turn on its side, sort of upside down. There was no crying. There was just silence and blackness and then for a second there was daylight again. I thought I was dead so I sat there quietly and a strange idea

229

passed through my mind. I remember thinking I had had a great life and a wonderful family and I couldn't speak German!

'There was a great hissing noise all around me and I realised that I was still alive and lying on my side in my seat. I unfastened my seatbelt and began to climb out. There was still no sound apart from this tremendous hissing. Captain Thain suddenly appeared holding a fire extinguisher and told me to run for it. I was about to take his advice when I heard a child crying so I crawled back into the wreckage. People outside were shouting, "Get out, get out, run for it." I shouted to them, "Come back you bastards, there are people alive inside." I found the baby and started to carry it out. The radio operator took the child from me and I went back into the débris and found her mother but she was in a bad condition. I found Albert Scanlon who was badly hurt and I tried to get him out too, but he was trapped by his feet and I couldn't move him. Peter Howard, the *Daily Mail* photographer, was with Albert keeping him company. I ran round to the back of the plane and found Bobby Charlton and Denis Viollet lying in a pool of water. I thought they were dead and dragged their bodies, like rag dolls, into the seats which had been thrown about twenty yards from the plane. I started calling for Jackie. As I searched for him I saw the tail end of the plane ablaze with flames. I found Matt Busby, who was conscious but holding his chest in pain. He was propped up on his elbow and did not look too badly hurt, although his foot was broken. I left him and found Blanchie, who was sitting up to his waist in water. Roger was close by him. Jackie's arm was in a bad way and bleeding badly, so I tied a tourniquet on it with my tie. I pulled so hard on it that I snapped my tie in half but managed to tie his arm with the bit that was left.

'Suddenly a man in a long overcoat arrived carrying a syringe. I shouted to him to go and help the injured in the aircraft but suddenly there were some explosions from the burning half of the plane and the force of them threw this doctor off his feet. He was a strange sight falling on his backside in the snow, with his legs in the air still holding that syringe in his hand.

'I turned round and got the shock of my life for there were Denis and Bobby standing, just watching the fire. I was so relieved as I had been sure that they were dead. Shortly after

230

this, when it looked as though the rescuers had everything under control, I sank to my knees and wept, thanking God that some of us had been saved. I had never seen death before and never wanted to see it again.

'Things began to happen fairly rapidly and Denis, Bobby and I were put into a Volkswagen van. I sat in the front with Bill Foulkes who appeared to have come through unscathed. Johnny Berry and Jackie were lying in the back with Matt, all were badly injured. As we set off, the driver was obviously in a great hurry and driving so rapidly that Billy felt something dreadful was going to happen. I remember him getting up and belting the driver who appeared to take no notice; but he got us to the hospital.

'In the hospital they gathered all the survivors together and those of us who could walk were asked to identify the others. We were given some soup to warm us up but I remember that even that had a disinfected hospital smell. I remember hearing over the intercom in the hospital that we had lost Frank Swift. The whole atmosphere was so unpleasant, and there was nothing that Foulkesy and I could do and we decided to get out, although I had a cut nose which I did not want treated. As a result my nostrils are now of different sizes.

'We went to a hotel in Munich where the manager gave us each a warm coat and some other clothes. Somebody also gave us some whisky. I remember looking out of the bedroom window and seeing the snow piled as high as the cars. I thought about what the snow was burying at the airport.'

Jackie Blanchflower never lost consciousness. 'It was like going down a cobbled road. The plane broke in half at the card tables. I was thrown out the top. The front part of the plane kept going. I saw it twisting round, then it stopped and a little puff of fire was coming out of it. I was lying in the slush. Roger Byrne was lying right across my feet with his eyes open. He was just in his vest and underpants, no socks or shoes on. I started talking to him. Then Harry came.'

Wilf McGuinness had been due to travel to Belgrade. His name was on the list pinned up by Matt Busby the previous Friday. 'I was to report on Monday morning but on the Saturday my knee locked in the reserves. I was carried off and

231

Ted Dalton thought I had a cartilage problem when I went for treatment on the Saturday morning. So that was me off the trip. I went to a specialist on the Monday and it was a cartilage. He told me they'd operate on Friday.'

McGuinness was not immediately alarmed when news of an accident at Munich reached Manchester in mid-afternoon. 'I think it was about 3.30 when rumours started going round. I was with a pal of mine who worked on the sales side of the *News Chronicle*. We were walking along and we heard about a plane crash. They'd clumped something on the runway. I felt they were probably making something out of nothing. The plane hadn't been in the air so I thought they're alright. We went to my pal's office to check out what had happened. At first all we got was news of surivivors: Harry Gregg, Denis Viollet, Bobby Charlton and Bill Foulkes. These were the first names we got. I was in a bit of a state of shock. We drove home.

'It was about six o'clock when I got home. My mother and father said there are deaths. So I went with my parents to Mount Carmel to do a novena. I prayed. I remember crying and praying – mainly for Eddie Colman and Billy Whelan. I remember saying to God, "I'll do anything if they're alright." '

Gordon Clayton was also out through injury. He'd played two first team games the previous season but the arthritis that would subsequently finish him had just been diagnosed. Gordon was in their old haunt, the Ritz Ballroom, at an afternoon Tea Dance, when the news came through. 'I was sitting on the balcony having a coffee with Jackie Lynch who managed the Ritz. I didn't believe it. There's always someone saying something like that. But I went out to get a paper, and came back and said it's true.'

The first person Gordon thought of was Mark Jones's wife, June, who was expecting a baby. 'I got a taxi from town to their house on Kings Road, Chorlton. June wasn't in. It turned out she'd been in the supermarket when someone blurted out, "The Manchester United plane's crashed." The next person I thought about was Jackie's wife Jean. They lived on Ryebank Road. So I went round to Jean. I stayed with her that night, answering the phone and dealing with callers to the house. It was bedlam. Jean was in a terrible state. We knew Jackie was alive, but we'd no idea in what state. So we just waited for a phone call.'

John Giles and Nobby Stiles were at the ground. The afternoon's work was over. The ground staff lads were waiting for Arthur Powell to let them go. Arthur was keeping them in suspense. Bill Inglis and Arthur came into the reserve team dressing-room together. 'Sit down, lads, I've got some bad news for you,' Bill said. 'The plane has crashed.' They didn't have any details but the two dressing-room old-timers didn't think it was too serious. 'We'll let you know later,' Arthur told the lads.

'We sat joking among ourselves,' Nobby recalls. 'We thought they'd have broken arms or something. "We might get a game in the 'A' team now," someone said.' There was no further news so Arthur let them home.

'I got a bus into town,' Nobby remembers. 'I got off at Piccadilly to get the 112 up Rochdale Road to home. I bought a paper. It said, "Many Dead." I'll never forget it. I got off at Cassidy's pub, my stop. There was a church there so I went in and prayed. I just cried. I was a punter, a supporter, I wasn't just praying for United, I idolised them.

'When I got home everyone was devastated. It was a rough area ours, little terraced houses with the front doors always open. We listened to the radio all night. People were in a state of shock.'

Paddy McGrath heard the news in a phone call from his brother. The sportswriter Frank McGhee called later to tell him that Matt had been pulled out of the wreckage but they didn't know if he was dead or alive. Paddy crossed Manchester to the Busby home in Chorlton. 'The city was quiet. It was strange, a kind of depression I had never seen, even during the war.'

Sandy Busby arrived at Victoria Station on his way home from training at Blackburn Rovers where he was reserve wing-half under Johnny Carey's management. 'I saw the billboards at the station but I thought it was just publicity, just something to sell papers. Then I thought, I better phone home just in case.' Two friends of Matt and Jean's from Bellshill were down on a visit. 'My Auntie was a bit of a panicker. She said,

"Get home quick, get a taxi." ' When he arrived home Sandy realised the seriousness of things for the first time: 'Me mam was in a state of shock. She was just sitting on the sofa and no one could get any sense from her. I wasn't religious, but I ran upstairs to my bedroom and knelt down and prayed. All of a sudden my Uncle Johnny came running up the stairs screaming, "He's alive, he's alive." ' A phone call had assured them that Matt was alive. 'As soon as me mam heard me dad was alive she was right.'

Jimmy Murphy arrived at London Road Station just before four o'clock. His taxi driver smilingly surmised that United would win the European Cup this year. Jimmy nodded. Wales had played Israel in Cardiff the night before, and Jimmy's mind was already on the coming weekend's work. The game with Wolves preoccupied him. He wondered if all the players were fit after Belgrade. At Old Trafford, Alma George, Matt Busby's secretary, broke the news:

'The fingers of the clock on the wall pointed to four o'clock when I first heard of the tragedy, and they were pointing at four o'clock when I went home the following morning. Don't ask me what I did. I was living a nightmare. All I know is that there was a bottle of Scotch in my cupboard and the following morning it was empty – and that was extraordinary. I am a beer drinker yet I must have drunk a bottle of whisky without knowing.

'Like everyone else I was too numb to take in the awful grief. Agony piled on agony as the hours ticked by. Thousands hurried down to the ground to see if they could help; the police threw a protective cordon around relatives and friends who had lost their loved ones. Those of us left at the ground did our best to calm and console the grief stricken. But what word of sympathy could I find to comfort the bereaved? There was nothing to lift the despair. I did not sleep that night.'

When news of the tragedy broke, a pall of grief spread across the nation. The novelist H. E. Bates reflected the mood of early evening when he later wrote:

> Late on a cold February afternoon, I was driving home from London when I suddenly saw, under the first lighted street lamps, one of those blue and yellow news placards

234

that are designed so often to shock you into buying a newspaper you don't particularly want and that nine times out of ten, you would be just as well off without. MANCHESTER UNITED AIR CRASH, it said. My immediate reaction was, I confess, a mildly cynical one. The announcement seemed to me to belong to precisely the same category as WINSTON CHURCHILL IN CAR CRASH – the car crash almost invariably turning out to be nothing more than a tender argument between the starting handle of an ancient Austin Seven and the great man's Rolls somewhere in the region of Parliament Square. I am getting too old, I thought, to be caught by newspaper screamers.

At six o'clock, out of pure curiosity, I turned on my television set. As the news came on, the screen seemed to go black. The normally urbane voice of the announcer seemed to turn into a sledgehammer. My eyes went deathly cold and I sat listening with a frozen brain to that cruel and shocking list of casualties that was now to give the despised word Munich an even sadder meaning than it had acquired on a day before the war when a Prime Minister had come home to London, waving a pitiful piece of paper, and most of us knew that new calamities of war were inevitable.

Jimmy Saville had been preparing for that night's Manchester Press Ball at the Plaza. 'I put a notice outside the Plaza. It just said, "Press Ball cancelled". Then I locked the door and we sat around, my staff and myself, listening to reports as they came through on the radio. We had to put the radio in the middle of the floor before it would work properly – something to do with the aerial. All around there was food prepared for the guests and though we were in a ballroom, dancing was the furthest thing from our minds.

'Even as we heard the news bulletins it was hard to conceive that such a terrible thing had happened. We stayed there all night. It was one of the most shattering experiences ever to confront a city – the biggest disaster Manchester had ever known.'

In Manchester the agony was personal. People wept openly in shops and bus-shelters. Most were too numb with shock to cry, an aching disbelief seeped into the communal soul.

At ten past ten that evening Dick Colman took a call from Jimmy Murphy at Old Trafford confirming that Eddie was one of those dead. 'I told the family and left the house,' Eddie's father later recalled. 'I don't remember anything from that moment until I suddenly realised I was standing in Piccadilly Manchester sometime after three in the morning, soaked to the skin wearing my slippers. I didn't sleep or eat for two weeks.'

The Busby house was full. Jean recovered enough to begin thinking of others. Sheena was sent round to Tom Curry's house. Tom was one of the first confirmed dead. Frank Swift was among the eight journalists killed. His wife, Jean, and daughter were in the Busby house. 'We heard about Frank and I asked his daughter's boyfriend to take them home and tell them,' Paddy McGrath recalls. Johnny Carey arrived from Blackburn. Henry Rose was another killed instantly. His girlfriend arrived at the Busbys' not knowing of Henry's fate. A doctor was called to sedate her.

The scale of the Munich Air Disaster became clear overnight. The following morning newspapers reported twenty-one dead, among them seven players, coach Bert Whalley, trainer Tom Curry, secretary Walter Crickmer, and Matt Busby's business-man friend Willie Satinoff. Busby and Duncan Edwards were reported to be fighting for their lives.

The players killed were: Roger Byrne, David Pegg, Tommy Taylor, Eddie Colman, Mark Jones, Billy Whelan and Geoff Bent. The journalists who perished were: Alf Clarke, *Manchester Evening Chronicle*; Tom Jackson, *Manchester Evening News*, Don Davis, Old International of the *Manchester Guardian*; George Follows, *Daily Herald*; Archie Ledbrook, *Daily Mirror*; Eric Thompson, *Daily Mail*; Frank Swift, *News of the World*; and Henry Rose of the *Daily Express*, renowned for his populist prose. Rose, a Jewish Mancunian, was a roguish iconoclast, who often irritated Busby and his team. But this colourful character was as much a part of the city as the players he wrote about. Busby's fondness for Henry had been evident a couple of weeks before when he'd attended a party to celebrate Rose's twenty-fifth year on the *Express*.

Wilf McGuinness turned up at Old Trafford on Friday morning: 'We were in the dressing-room. Bill Inglis came in and we all just sat there looking at each other. We didn't speak, say how sad it was or anything. We just stared at each other.'

13

Going On

'Although we mourn our dead and grieve for our wounded we believe our great days are not done for us. Manchester United will rise again.'

Harold Hardman

On Friday 7 February the Manchester United Board met at Alan Gibson's home in Bowden, Cheshire. The death of George Whittaker had left the club with just three directors: Gibson, Harold Hardman and William Petherbridge. All attended this meeting convened at the home of James Gibson's son. Condolences were extended to the families of the deceased and injured; Walter Crickmer's assistant Les Olive was appointed acting secretary, and the minutes record: 'It was proposed, seconded and carried unanimously that Mr Louis Edwards of "Caudebec", Alderley Edge, Cheshire, be and is hereby appointed and co-opted as an additional Director of the Company.'

The Busby family, Jimmy Murphy and a party of relatives and friends of the dead and injured were already in Munich when the board meeting concluded in Cheshire. Dr Georg Maurer, Chief Surgeon at Rechts der Isar Hospital, told Jean, Sheena, Sandy and Jimmy Murphy that Matt's chances of survival were no better than fifty-fifty. His chest had been crushed and he had suffered massive internal and external injuries. He was in an oxygen tent, his breathing assisted by a tracheotomy because his left lung had collapsed. When they took the lift up to the Intensive Care Unit Sandy walked anxiously ahead of the group in the company of a nurse. 'I was walking along looking in each room to see if I could recognise anybody. I walked past one room and this poor old man was in a plastic oxygen tent. I was three yards past and then I realised it was my dad,' Sandy recalls. 'He was a strange green kind of colour. I ran back to get hold of my mother to warn her what to expect.'

Busby was hovering between sleep and consciousness. Jean held his hand. He seemed to acknowledge their presence. Sheena and Sandy begged him not to leave them. Twice he was given the Last Rites. After he slipped back to sleep Jean, Sheena and Sandy went to comfort the others of their 'family'. Duncan was the most critically injured. As with Matt, Duncan's injuries would have killed other men instantly, but both men were immensely strong physically, both had unusual depths of spirit. In Edwards's case that was all that was keeping him alive.

Jimmy Murphy stood soothing the young giant as the Busbys arrived at his bedside. In a fleeting moment of recognition Duncan had responded to Jimmy's presence by asking, 'What time is kick-off on Saturday?'

Sandy Busby and Duncan had been pals. On dark nights at the Cliff they'd trained and larked about together. At the bedside in Rechts der Isar the horror of the scene was intensified for Sandy by memories of happier, carefree times he'd spent with Duncan. 'He was a real Brummie,' Sandy reflects, 'his favourite expression was "chief", "All right chief" he'd greet you. He was shy with strangers but with the lads he was great, he was always a young lad at heart, even when he was in the England team.

'He believed in himself, that he could do anything. We were training at the Cliff one night and there was a young amateur lad called Alan Walsh who was a crack gymnast. So we're running round the track and we say to Alan, "Do us a somersault." Off he goes down the pitch and does this incredible somersault. Big Duncan is looking at this and says, "I can do that." Of course he had a go and landed on his arse.'

Sandy used to travel to the Cliff by bike, and Duncan loved tearing around the training ground on the bike. One night a tyre was punctured when Sandy went to get it to go home. Duncan was missing. 'I could have strangled him,' Sandy says. 'Next time I saw him it was "All right Chief." '

For Duncan Edwards it would never be all right again. Five

days after the crash he was put on an artificial kidney. He fought for two weeks but, at 01.12 on 21 February 1958 the greatest footballer the British game had known died. He was twenty-one. Dr Maurer said, 'I do not think anyone other than this young man could have survived so long. His resistance made us admire him.' Duncan's last words were those he'd whispered to Jimmy Murphy asking about kick-off time for the match against Wolves that would decide the Championship.

News of Duncan Edwards's death deepened the sense of loss at Old Trafford. He more than anyone had been the symbol of indestructible youth, the most awesomely vigorous of the 'Red Devils'. 'We thought Duncan was going to come back,' Wilf McGuinness confirms, 'his death was another shattering blow.'

The coffins returned from Munich to rest in the gym at Old Trafford, where the players now gone had played endless games of head-tennis. It was to this macabre setting that Jimmy Murphy returned from Munich to ensure the club's survival. Jimmy buried his grief, as, in previous times he had concealed the warm, sensitive core of his nature, in order that he should do his duty better. Life must go on, was Murphy's slogan as he deployed the full force of his formidable personality to wake those left at Old Trafford from the nightmare around them. Time would take its toll of Jimmy's emotions, for the essential generosity of his spirit could not, any more than the grief, be concealed for ever. For now the business of football had to proceed.

Jack Crompton left his coaching job at Luton to return to help at old Trafford. One of Crompton's first tasks was to oversee the unpacking of the 'skip' containing the playing kit from the Red Star game. 'Jack did a brilliant job after the crash,' Nobby Stiles vouches. 'His enthusiasm lifted us. He brought weights and different routines. The club had to go on and without Jimmy and Jack it wouldn't have.'

Nobby was still on the ground staff. He remembers opening the 'skip' retrieved from the scene of the crash: 'My job was to clean the boots. It was a heavy, shitty pitch and the boots were full of caked mud. When I finished I asked Jack if I could keep Tommy Taylor's boots as a memento. He said, "OK." I kept them for years, then I gave them to the club museum.'

239

The Football Association allowed United to postpone their fifth round FA Cup-tie until 19 February. Jimmy Murphy considered signing Ferenc Puskas, by now playing for Real Madrid and earning £800 a week in Spain. The maximum wage in England was £17 a week. Jimmy concluded that the Puskas idea was impractical. Instead he turned to Ernie Taylor, regarded by most informed judges of professional soccer as the real inspiration behind Blackpool's FA Cup victory in 1953. The '53 Final was remembered in folklore as 'Matthews's Final', but Murphy knew Taylor had been the player who made the difference. United paid £8,000 for the thirty-three-year-old midfield general. Paddy McGrath, who knew Taylor through his Blackpool connections, helped Murphy complete the deal.

Murphy was also keen to sign Stan Crowther, Aston Villa's hard-tackling wing-half who'd proved a tough opponent at Wembley the previous May. Crowther was not so keen. Villa Manager, Eric Houghton, persuaded the player to travel with him to Manchester to watch the Sheffield Wednesday tie, and Murphy went to meet them in the Midland Hotel. Four hours before kick-off Jimmy's Welsh fervour changed Crowther's mind. The deal cost United £23,000. Crowther was cup-tied, having played for Villa in the third round; his boots were in Birmingham. Eric Houghton sent for the boots and the Football Association agreed to waive their rule in relation to cup-tied players. Stan Crowther's boots arrived at seven o'clock.

There were 59,848 people inside Old Trafford when the gates were closed. Several thousand more stood silently outside. The atmosphere inside the ground was strange; some wept, others shrieked the names of those who had died at Munich, most waited hushed for the teams to appear. The match programme carried a message from Harold Hardman on its cover. Under the heading 'UNITED WILL GO ON' Hardman wrote:

> On 6th February 1958 an aircraft returning from Belgrade crashed at Munich Airport. Of the twenty-one passengers who died, twelve were players or officials of the Manchester United Football Club. Many others lie injured.
> It is the sad duty of us who serve Manchester United, to

offer our heartfelt sympathy and condolences. Here is a tragedy which will sadden us for years to come. But in this we are not alone. An unprecedented blow to British football has touched the hearts of millions and we express our deep gratitude to many who have sent messages of sympathy and floral tributes. Wherever football is played United is mourned, but we rejoice that many of our party have been spared and wish them a speedy and complete recovery. Words are inadequate to describe our thanks and appreciation of the truly magnificent work of the surgeons and nurses of the Rechts der Isar Hospital at Munich. But for their superb skill and deep compassion our casualties would have been greater. To Professor Georg Maurer we offer our eternal gratitude. Although we mourn our dead and grieve for our wounded we believe that our great days are not done for us. The sympathy and encouragement of the Football world, and particularly our supporters, will justify and inspire us. The road back may be long and hard but with the memory of those who died at Munich, of their stirring achievements and wonderful sportsmanship ever with us . . . MANCHESTER UNITED WILL RISE AGAIN.

H. P. Hardman

Jimmy Murphy had been unable to give a team to the programme editor earlier that day, so the spaces where the United team should have been named remained blank. The team announced on the Tannoy system just before kick-off was:

Gregg

Foulkes   Greaves

Goodwin   Cope   Crowther

Webster   Taylor   Dawson   Pearson   Brennan

Bill Foulkes captained the side; Harry Gregg, the hero of the Munich tragedy, followed immediately behind as the team took the field. The crowd erupted at the poignant sight of these two men, their presence underwriting the words Hardman had written in the programme. The day after the crash Foulkes and Gregg had returned to the airfield to collect some personal

241

belongings. Foulkes had found Eddie Colman's scarf and cap amid the snow-covered wreckage. Now life resumed. Old Trafford on the night of 19 February 1958 bore more resemblance to a shrine than a football ground.

The side that turned out alongside Foulkes and Gregg contained two débutants from the 'A' team: Shay Brennan, a wing-half converted to outside-left for the night and Mark Pearson, plucked from the youth team. The reluctant Crowther and the veteran Taylor joined five reserve team players to complete United's line-up. Sheffield Wednesday fielded a strong side including England Internationals Tony Kay, Peter Swan, Redfern Froggatt, and Albert Quixall, one of the game's outstanding young players, who captained the team. The visitors were overwhelmed by the emotion of the occasion. The team that perished at Munich had struggled to beat Wednesday 2–1 a couple of months previously. Murphy's scratch team won 3–0. Brennan scored direct from a corner in the twenty-seventh minute, added a second with half-an-hour to go and Alex Dawson ensured United's place in the sixth round a few minutes from the end of an extraordinary night.

Two days later in Munich Duncan Edwards died.

Jimmy Murphy took the United players to Blackpool the following week where, except for weekends at home, they stayed for the rest of the season. If United were to go on it would have to be away from Manchester and Old Trafford, the city still grieving, the ground still occupied by voices and faces of men whose loss was still almost unbearably shocking. Especially during the week where, in dressing-room, training-ground and in matches 'out the back' the ghosts of Tosher and Bert, Eddie Colman and Roger Byrne lingered tormentingly. And for no one more than Jimmy who ten years later explained: 'Even now the heartache is still there. The memory never fades. If I close my eyes and meditate I can still see them playing.'

A lesser man left to save another football club could have been excused for indulging the sorrow Murphy experienced in the weeks after Munich. There is no more remarkable testimony to the work Matt Busby had all but completed before the Munich tragedy than Jimmy Murphy's unflinchingly courageous commitment to the task he now faced.

Matt and Jimmy were never personally close, but they understood each other. What they shared was a love of the game and pride in what they had achieved at Old Trafford. They also shared values which, although ostensibly irrelevant to professional soccer, had formed the club they'd built together. Both were family men and United was a family club. Both of them were decent, paternal, each placing great store on loyalty. United's success had encouraged other clubs to covet Jimmy, yet he'd never seriously considered any of the offers. He was happy to serve Busby's cause because it was his too. Both men had played in the pre-war game and dreamed of something better, and that was what they had created at United. They knew each other's strengths and weaknesses.

Matt's patience and cunning, his football-worldliness was perfectly compatible with Jimmy's evangelical passion. Jimmy drove United at a certain fundamental level, Matt steered from the bridge; Matt found it difficult to express emotion, Jimmy impossible not to do so.

John Giles recalls a typical Murphy scene during a reserve game at Elland Road: 'We were playing Leeds and it was 4–4 at half-time. There was a lad called Barry Smith playing at the back for us who'd had a terrible first half. Jimmy gave us a right bollocking: "What the fucking hell do you think you're playing at. This fucking team are fucking useless, they haven't scored four goals all fucking year and they've scored four against us in the first half." Barry Smith said, "Sorry Jimmy." "I don't want your fucking sorry, get out there and fucking play. I don't want any more of that rubbish again." '

Yet Giles, like all the others who experienced their first taste of the pro game in this combustible environment, remembers Jimmy with respect and affection. 'He was good for me, when he talked you listened and he invariably made good football sense. The Boss would speak in general terms, Jimmy was more specific.' Giles also felt Murphy's wrath and the basic humanity from which the harshness was never divorced. 'I missed a penalty in a reserve game at Huddersfield one day. He gave me a terrible coating in the dressing-room after the match. I was only a young lad and I was going home to Ireland for the weekend. He must have sensed how upset I was because 15 minutes after bollocking me he put his arm round my shoulders and said, "Have a nice weekend and tell your dad I was asking for him." '

Wilf McGuinness provides further evidence of the co-existence of fervour and decency in Jimmy's soul: 'We were playing a German side in the European Cup out there and before the game Jimmy's saying to me, "These bastards did this in the war . . . that in the war . . . to us . . . to your parents . . . you go out there and remember what they are " . . . and then he stops, pats me on the back and says, "God Bless." '

Matt Busby, who never swore, indeed had a genuine distaste for invective, knew this side of Jimmy and tacitly approved. His football club couldn't run on dignity alone.

While Busby lay painfully convalescing in Munich, Manchester United ran on Murphy's raw passion. Everywhere they played United drew capacity crowds. Their FA Cup run became a crusade, the hopes of the nation invested in this squad of footballers, distinguished only by the red shirts they wore. A disproportionate share of the burden fell on the shoulders of Bobby Charlton, a nineteen-year-old rookie pre-Munich, now the principal source of Manchester United's inspiration. Coaxed by Murphy, Bobby delivered magnificently. Less than a month after the crash Charlton returned to face West Brom in the sixth round of the FA Cup at The Hawthorns.

West Brom were one of the best sides in the country. They had beaten the 'Red Devils' 4–3 at this venue earlier in the season. Vic Buckingham, their manager, promised to show no mercy for the new United. 'We will win six nil,' he promised. United defied this prediction drawing 2–2 having come close to victory. The replay at Old Trafford was scoreless until a minute from time when Ernie Taylor found Bobby Charlton on the right. The 'quiet kid' of a month ago swerved with elusive power past four defenders before slipping the ball across the face of the goal to present Colin Webster with a simple chance.

United's semi-final victory over Fulham followed another pulsating replay. Charlton scored United's two goals in the drawn game at Villa Park, and another in the 5–3 win that secured their place in another Wembley Final. Alex Dawson scored a hat-trick in this replayed FA Cup semi-final less than a year after appearing in the FA Youth Cup Final. Shay Brennan scored the fifth United goal, his 'A' team days a bare couple of months behind him. Shay was twenty. A decade before he'd almost fallen under the coach bearing the '48 team home triumphantly from Wembley. He found it hard to believe that this time he'd be on the bus.

After the cup-tie Manchester United retreated to Blackpool. The promise to go on was sensationally fulfilled. Viewed from Blackpool, the reality of spring 1958, the dreadfully poignant fusion of tragedy and triumph, seemed hazy. Bobby Charlton has no rational memory of those weeks: 'I never saw the whole thing in context,' he says. 'With replays and the backlog of fixtures caused by the crash we seemed to have a game every three days. Jimmy kept our minds on football. He just said we've got to keep the club going and that's really what the Cup run meant. We were almost proving to ourselves that Manchester United was alive.' Even now Bobby cannot talk about the tragedy. When it's mentioned, a couple of hours into the story of the pre-Munich club he so vividly describes as 'paradise', emotion wells in his body, his eyes detach from yours, unwilling to betray their hurt.

Like Murphy and Charlton, Harry Gregg and Bill Foulkes found solace by practising their craft in the desperate weeks after Munich. If they worked like men possessed it was because they were.

For Jackie Blanchflower and others there was no refuge from appalling reality. Jackie arrived back in England the afternoon of the semi-final against Fulham. 'It was six weeks after the crash. I came back with my wife, Jean, on the Belgrade Express and then by ship to Dover. The club sent a taxi to bring us to Manchester and the driver had the semi-final on the radio. I didn't want to listen to it. When I got home the replay was on television but I switched it off. It wasn't Manchester United to me.'

Manchester United was the friends he'd left behind. 'It's hard to explain to people who haven't been through it. I lost the will to play again. I can understand the Liverpool players after Hillsborough, John Aldridge saying he didn't care if he played again. When you lose people near and dear to you in a tragedy like that you lose your passion for the game. Tommy Taylor was the worst blow for me. I've never made a relationship like that since.'

In Munich the news of fatalities was kept from Matt Busby for almost a month. Professor Georg Maurer insisted that the shock of learning about Tom Curry, Bert Whalley, Willie Satinoff and the players he'd led on this great European adventure might sap his will to fight for his life. Jean, Sheena and Sandy lived anxiously lest they betray their dreadful secret. Frank Taylor, the only sports writer to survive the crash, recounts a visit to Busby's hospital room a month after the tragedy: 'Matt was a shattering sight. He lay silent, stretched full length as though asleep, the plaster on his right leg bulging the blankets. The bushy, once sandy hair was now grey and tinged with streaks of white. The eyes opened in recognition; the pale waxy face which belonged to a man of seventy brightened; a thin pitifully emaciated hand advanced haltingly over the white cover on the bed, found mine and gripped it weakly. "Hallo, my old pal, how are you, Frank lad?" ' Within minutes Busby had lapsed into slumber.

Busby knew that something awful had occurred. Lying weakly in his bed his powerful instincts still functioned. He didn't press the questions for in truth he was afraid to know the answers. Finally it was Jean who broke the news. Sheena and Sandy listened as Matt held her hand and listed the names of those who'd boarded Flight 609 with him. When he named a survivor Jean nodded and squeezed his hand. When he asked for those who'd died she shook her head. Words seemed pointless.

Subsequent claims that Matt Busby decided to quit football after the Munich air crash are inaccurate. Thinking aloud he talked to his family about the absurdity of the game's obsessive quest for results and trophies when measured against life's realities as they had just experienced them. Understanding power as he did, Matt Busby also reflected on his decision to seek the glory of European football, his defiance of those who argued against the new idea. He had been impatient, resenting the timid, narrow-minded counsels of caution. Europe had been his vision. This thought prompted reproach. However, on reflection, he recalled his young team's enthusiasm for the challenge he'd posed them, their hunger for the new experience, their desire to fulfil themselves beyond the parochial English game. They could have been the best in the world, but not unless they went in search of Real Madrid and others like the Hungarians of mythology. That was what he wanted, the dream his players shared.

Thus, remorse gave way to deep, abiding sadness. On 19 April 1958 Matt Busby left Rechts der Isar Hospital to return home. That afternoon Bobby Charlton marked his début for England against Scotland at Hampden Park, with a spectacular goal volleyed from a Tom Finney cross. The same day Billy Meredith died in Manchester aged eighty-three. Professional soccer's first great star died almost destitute. During his last years Meredith eked out an existence with small donations from the Professional Footballers Association. Thanks to Matt Busby and United he kept a roof over his head. He had met Duncan Edwards, Tommy Taylor and Eddie Colman who had called to see him to pay their respects. The Wizard and the 'Red Devils' had much in common. Like him their hearts were always full of football. They died on a maximum wage of £17 per week, less in real terms than Billy had earned fifty years before. In newspapers dominated by Matt Busby's return home and Bobby Charlton's stunning début for England, the passing of professional football's first hero was a small story. He would have understood, for nobody knew better the nature of the glory game.

Manchester United were in the FA Cup Final. Old Trafford was curiously still when Jackie Blanchflower went back a couple of weeks before the great event. There was much on his mind. He went to see the new club secretary, Les Olive, about one relatively minor matter. Jackie had encountered an Irish construction worker in Belgrade who'd saved some money he wanted to send to his family in Belfast. He gave Jackie the equivalent of £48 in Yugoslav currency asking him to convert the money to sterling and post it on when he returned home. Walter Crickmer had run out of Yugoslav dinars so Jackie had given United's secretary the Irishman's money agreeing to collect the £48 when he returned. Jackie explained the situation to Les Olive, who of course knew nothing about the arrangement. Jackie was unable to claim the money back, but sent £48 to the man's family anyway. Life had gone on.

Stan Crowther caught Jackie's eye: 'I heard him effing and blinding and I thought to myself, you won't last long when the Boss gets back,' says Jackie. 'He didn't.' Crowther was hot-tempered and profane even by dressing-room standards. He'd caused a couple of fights in training, on one occasion crunching Ernie Taylor to the ground in a practice match; another day, at Davyhulme Golf Club, he smashed a snooker cue in pieces on the green baize after missing a simple shot.

The week before the Cup Final Matt Busby returned to the ground. The staff gathered in Ted Dalton's medical room. 'The Boss' wanted to say a few words. He planned to say, as Harold Hardman had, that United would go on. He looked old, Wilf McGuinness thought, 'as if he'd been through hell. Before the crash he'd looked so strong, like a man who'd never suffered, now the suffering showed.'

With Jimmy Murphy and Jack Crompton on either side of him, Busby began to speak. A word or two came out, then he broke down. Sobbing, he allowed Jimmy and Jack to help him from the room.

Paddy McGrath, his close friend for over forty years remembers his first meeting with Matt after the Munich air crash. 'He was always very careful with his emotions, you wouldn't know what he felt. I'd gone to his house to see how he was one afternoon. It was a nice spring day and Matt was sitting out in the garden. He was still in a bad way . . . but he got up as I came across to him. We just hugged each other. There were tears in his eyes. But he said nothing. Never did talk about the crash. But it was always there. In his eyes. Always.'

14

Another Story

'Before Munich it was Manchester's club, afterwards everyone felt they owned a little bit of it.'

Bobby Charlton

The family passed into legend. Bolton had beaten United in the 1958 Cup Final. The five-week gap between semi-final and Wembley had left the driven team too much time for reflection. The return of Matt Busby, the sight of him breaking down in the treatment-room, had exposed the illusion of glorious survival masked by the victories over Sheffield Wednesday, West Brom and Fulham. Wembley on Cup Final day seemed appallingly incongruous to Harry Gregg. Fate rubbed salt in the wounds. Nat Lofthouse put Bolton in front after three minutes. The decisive second goal was a source of bitter controversy. Gregg parried a shot which he gathered at the second attempt, then Nat Lofthouse barged into him from behind, this dubious challenge causing the ball to slip out of his grasp over the line.

Fate could perhaps have been forgiven. The men who governed English football are another matter. They hadn't changed. Manchester United were due to play AC Milan in the first leg of the European Cup semi-final at Old Trafford on the Wednesday after the Cup Final. The Football Association insisted that this game be played without the assistance of Bobby Charlton, United's best player. He was required for a friendly international against Portugal at Wembley. It says much for United's residue of courage that they beat Milan 2–1. But this slender advantage was not enough, and the adventure that began in such magnificent style with the 6–0 victory over Shamrock Rovers in Dublin the previous September before being tragically disrupted at Munich finally ended in a 4–0 defeat in the second leg of the semi-final in Milan. Playing for his country at Wembley, his heart elsewhere, Bobby Charlton scored the winning goal with an explosive shot from thirty yards.

The following month Matt received the CBE for services to English soccer. In July, perhaps regretting the callous indifference to United's plight they had demonstrated by demanding Charlton's services against Portugal, the Football Association granted the club permission to accept UEFA's invitation to participate in the following season's European Champions Cup, but English football's other controlling authority, the Football League, protested. Wolves were the champions and according to Football League rules Manchester United were ineligible. This brutally insensitive decision was taken by the League's Management Committee, a body composed of club chairmen. Esteemed across the world, loved by the game's fans, their dreadful tragedy lamented in every home in Britain, Manchester United could not command any sympathy from the merchants who ruled the professional game. The laws were what mattered. Busby appealed – successfully – to the Football Association. The Football League remained firm. A major row broke out which wasn't finally resolved until a joint FA/League commission found against United. Matt Busby had always been a believer in the rules, but this particular application of football law, a few months after the Munich Air Crash had torn the heart out of his club, did nothing to reinforce his faith.

The years that followed were desperate ones for Matt Busby, CBE. It was a bad time for paternalism, on which Busby's vision of a football club was founded. His vision of the game itself was rooted in the same principle. Freedom and respect for the individual in order that he may serve the family better. Now people wanted to look after themselves, do their own thing. Manchester United football was about doing your own thing – up to a point. You were free to express yourself as a footballer but you had obligations as well: to the team, to the club and to the rules governing football which Busby presided over as humanely as he could. There was a paradox here; the great believer in individualism demanding that his men conform to the greater good, be obliged to serve loyally the common cause which was Manchester United. This wasn't simply Busby's paradox or his club's, it was the riddle at the heart of the game of professional soccer. Each player was different, each season presented its own problems, each match, each day; every time you went to work some adjustment was required, a subtle tilting of the scales was necessary, every nuance must constantly be observed. That was football management and Matt Busby understood it better than anyone. 'The Boss' understood people better than anyone, footballers at least.

The Sixties were challenging for him on a number of fronts. Munich had left him scarred more profoundly than the physical marks allowed. The man who defined the manager's role by putting on his tracksuit and working with his players was now office-bound or confined to the edge of the training ground, but when he appeared, whether tracksuited or not, the charismatic presence still worked. At least for those of us who were young like George Best, David Sadler, Johnny Aston's son – young John – Tony Dunne who was a little older and Nobby Stiles, then trying to break into the first team. Like Wilf McGuinness, now youth team trainer, and Bobby Charlton before us, we wanted to 'show him' on the odd occasion he came out.

The training ground bore reminders of the past. Most aspects of daily life contained their share of melancholy. He saw faces where once they'd been, heard the voices, the laughter and the banter of the great days when for a while the game seemed easy. Even the journalists he dealt with touched a nerve. David Meek of the *Manchester Evening News* where old Tom Jackson had been, Peter Slingsby instead of Alf Clarke. And no Henry Rose, the rogue with a vitriolic pen and a warm heart. Rose was the quintessential Manchester character, sceptical, funny, earthy and warm. On the day of the *Express* man's funeral Manchester's one thousand taxi drivers had offered their services free to mourners and the cortège had stretched six miles back. Matt was always wary of journalists, anxious to avoid unpleasant publicity, and despite the occasional incident the eight press men who died at Munich had played the game with him. They played to his rules, they belonged to his generation, had served in the war, known the hard times. The new men were a different breed, less amenable to flattery and the little tit-bit of exclusivity his pals from the past nibbled gratefully. They had to be watched.

Busby had decided to spend big to rebuild quickly. He didn't feel he had time on his side. He was in his fifties, physically and emotionally tired. The Munich side had burst on the scene, causing people to believe that a miracle had been worked. He knew how long the process had been, the best part of ten years had elapsed between Roger Byrne's arrival and the flowering of that side. Jackie Blanchflower and Mark Jones had come to Old Trafford in 1949, Johnny Berry in '51. Even the youngest – Duncan, Eddie and Tommy Taylor – had been at the club five to six years before the chemistry had begun to work the way he envisaged. Now he didn't have the time, the energy or even the will to start out again.

Prudence would have to be abandoned. Expensive players would demand high wages. Schoolboys were asking outrageous signing-on fees which he was having to pay under the counter. Matt had, as Harold Riley observed, always known what he was. Now he wasn't so sure. Riley's man of great principle was tarnished. Given the values prevalent in professional soccer as the Sixties began to swing he had no option if he wished to serve his club. Control of himself and the working environment around him had always been his secret. It was more difficult now.

This bothered him, on occasions causing torment. Sometimes the frustration showed. In early '61, with the maximum wage about to be removed, things looked particularly black. United lost 7–2 at home to Sheffield Wednesday in a replayed fourth round FA Cup tie. The first game at Hillsborough had been a 1–1 draw; this humiliation at Old Trafford was a shock. Busby's reservations about the transfer-market remained yet it was obvious as well that youngsters like Pearson, Alex Dawson and Jimmy Nicholson, all of whom played in this game, weren't good enough. The following week United played Leicester in the League at Filbert Street.

Sitting in his usual seat, the first one on the coach, by the door, Matt could hear the card-school a few rows back. On coach or train he always appeared to be in another world. He wasn't. He listened and observed, judging character, working out who was influential, who was strong, who was weak, who was honest, mean or generous. He told Paddy McGrath that sometimes he learned more sitting there than watching games. On the way to Leicester there was a brag school. They were playing for big stakes, a week's wages, more, changing hands at the turn of card. Matt hated high-stakes gambling in the club, not least because he believed it could affect a player's performance on the pitch.

The anger of the 7–2 Cup defeat in his mind, he sat raging as the coach pulled up at Filbert Street. He had been in the dressing-room for five minutes before he realised that the card players were still on the bus. Jack Crompton went out to get them. Busby said nothing. United lost 6–0. Afterwards he kept his head, and went to the boardroom for his scotch before returning to the bus for the journey home. They were at it again, animated bidding in fancy amounts. Matt got up from his seat, walked deliberately back to the card-table, picked up the deck of cards and flung them out of the window of the speeding bus. The high-stakes gambling would stop. Right now. Gambling being his own secret vice, Matt knew only too well how it felt to lose heavily. This compounded his anger.

George Best arrived in the summer of 1961, one of that year's intake of talented fifteen-year-olds. I had joined United in another batch the previous year. We were lucky. All young lads dreamed of playing for Manchester United, inspired by the same vision that had seduced Bobby Charlton, Nobby Stiles and the great young players who died at Munich. Alas, the club we joined was different, although not to innocent eyes like ours.

Matt Busby had been at Old Trafford for fifteen years. His two great sides were founded on certain principles: decent behaviour which allowed that professional footballers were human beings entitled to respect; pure football based on the individual skills and imagination of those people; talent that would blossom the more if character was allowed to develop in an environment free of profanity and bullying. The kind of professional footballers he wanted at Old Trafford were made

253

not born, or bought. From those values a sense of identity was created which was distinct to the Busby family. This was paternalism, Busby the father-figure, his own values and experience reflected in his football club. Those like Johnny Morris and Charlie Mitten who questioned too much or were disloyal had to go. Few were adopted: Jimmy Delaney bought for the '48 team, a Scot from Celtic, one of Matt's own; Johnny Downie, another Scot from Lanark up the road from Bellshill, Johnny Berry and Tommy Taylor for the 'Red Devils', specialists bought to plug the odd gap in the system.

Remarkably Matt Busby did not buy a single player between March 1953, when twenty-one-year-old Tommy Taylor came from Barnsley, and November 1957 when another specialist, Harry Gregg, was purchased from Doncaster. He believed that he could make players, and the record proved that this was no idle conceit. Moreover, Busby was convinced that players whose characters were formed elsewhere in the professional game could not be reconstructed to conform with the values prevailing at Old Trafford. His experience in the post-Munich era confirmed these views.

In September 1958 United bought Albert Quixall from Sheffield Wednesday for a British record fee of £45,000. Sheena's husband, Don Gibson, a Wednesday player, was a frequent weekend visitor to the Busby household. Week after week Gibson raved about Quixall, a gifted technician who'd played five times for England. Assured that Quixall was the right type, Busby took the gamble. When he travelled to Sheffield to complete the business he was shocked by Wednesday's price. The press had been alerted and gathered outside Hillsborough. Inside, Wednesday's shrewd general manager, Eric Taylor, who'd leaked the story to the press, informed Matt that the player would cost £45,000. Busby's prudence got the better of him and he refused to close the deal. He worried about the press outside. 'Tell them you can't afford it,' Taylor joked.

The truth was Busby felt United *couldn't* afford £45,000. This view was shared by Harold Hardman, his chairman. The club had been hopelessly under-insured for the players killed and permanently injured at Munich. As well as the eight who died,

Jackie Blanchflower and Johnny Berry were finished with football. Thrift was fundamental to Busby's nature and, contrary to the idea implicit in Eric Taylor's joke, United was not a wealthy club. When Busby returned to Manchester it was to Louis Edwards rather than Harold Hardman he turned for guidance. Hardman would have counselled prudence; Edwards encouraged Matt to take the gamble. Busby returned to Sheffield, accompanied, significantly, by Edwards, to sign Quixall for the record fee demanded.

Time would show the Quixall signing to be a mistake, both for United and for the player. 'Quickie' was a nice man, gentle, funny, extrovert, nothing like the dour Yorkshireman of popular repute. Sadly, this talented inside-forward didn't have the stomach for battle demanded of those who pulled on Jimmy's red shirts. In the vernacular of the professional game Albert was a 'cheat' lacking the competitive edge necessary at a club competing for high honours. Bought to lead the revival of England's most renowned football club for a fee commensurate to that task, Albert Quixall ended up suffering a nervous breakdown.

United had finished runners-up to Wolves in season '58/'59. The men responsible belonged to the pre-crash era. Harry Gregg, Bill Foulkes, Albert Scanlon, Denis Viollet, Wilf McGuinness and, more than anyone, Bobby Charlton. Bobby scored twenty-nine goals; Wilf missed only three games, establishing himself at left-half and winning an England cap. Old virtues did not disappear overnight.

In December 1959 Wilf McGuinness broke his leg. For several weeks he had been playing through pain in his shinbone, though X-rays had revealed no abnormality. He couldn't train but continued to play after spending his week on the treatment table. His form suffered and along with three other internationals – Gregg, Charlton and the former England amateur Warren Bradley – he was dropped. Desperate to regain his place, Wilf sought painkilling injections from the club doctor. Cortisone was drilled into his leg either side of the troublesome shinbone to enable Wilf to play against Stoke in a reserve match at Old Trafford. 'I went into the first tackle which was perfectly straightforward and my leg broke like a twig,' he recalls. 'I'd had a stress fracture all along but in those days they didn't have the equipment to do scans.'

Matt Busby bought Maurice Setters from West Brom to replace McGuinness for a transfer fee of £30,000. Setters was a hard man who'd turned down moves to Everton and Manchester City before United moved for him. He signed within ten minutes of meeting Busby, declaring himself 'thrilled' at the prospect of playing for Manchester United. Setters would prove to be a more serious mistake than Quixall. Burnley won the Championship that season, United finished seventh.

In November Matt Busby bought Noel Cantwell, West Ham's elegant Irish international left-back, for £30,000. United needed a leader, someone of Johnny Carey or Roger Byrne's calibre, and Cantwell looked the part. Noel was a tall, handsome, intelligent man, composed and imposing on the field, capable of commanding respect in the dressing-room.

Cantwell thought the place was a joke. His first few weeks in Manchester were spent in a hotel while he found a house for his family. In the afternoons he trained with us 'round the back' with Jack Crompton in charge. Johnny Aston was back at the club as youth team coach. The training was more or less the same as before Munich. Jack had introduced a couple of variations: a few weights and some bodywork exercises, basic stuff like 'tummies' (stomach exercises) and what might be called physical jerks. Then everyone went round the back for the five-a-side or twenty-a-side, depending on the numbers. George Best was unbelievable round the back. He was skinny, dark and quiet as a mouse, but this street game was life to him. Here, in between the railway fence and the concrete, he did things we'd never seen before. And *we* were the cream of young footballers in the British Isles, plus the first team and promising young men like Nobby Stiles, John Giles and Jimmy Nicholson, who everyone thought was the new Duncan Edwards.

Sometimes getting a kick was difficult. There was so much passion that fights would break out when someone was knocked to the cinder-strewn ground or crushed against the concrete wall. Harry Gregg and Bill Foulkes were particularly dangerous. Big 'Greggie' was daft. He always wanted to play 'out' – of goal that is – and of course he was fucking hopeless. The boys would take the piss out of him, teasing with the ball, maybe nutmegging him and then sniggering. Harry would chase the ball like a headless chicken, temper rising all the time.

The favourite joke was to pass the ball to somebody to allow Harry to catch the victim in possession. Whoever got caught hit the deck – or one of the boundary walls – suffering the wrath of Harry's cumulative frustrations.

Foulkesy was just a bully. He seemed to enjoy knocking kids down. 'Popular Bill', or PB as he was known, left the pits at St Helen's aged twenty. Miners were hard men was his message. He hated Harry, who felt the same about him, though no one was quite sure why this mutual dislike existed. It probably had something to do with Munich, that day on the airfield after the crash. The papers had described them both as heroes yet Harry would claim privately that 'you should have seen that big fucker run'. Conversely Bill probably resented Harry's implicit (occasionally overt) projection of himself as the keeper of the pre-Munich faith. He'd only been at the club a few weeks before the crash.

By the time I arrived in 1960 Munich was history. Nobody mentioned it. The clock on the wall over the forecourt bore the words February 6th 1958. That was all. This was a modest and, it seemed, entirely appropriate memorial. There was no need for an ostentatious memorial, the grief was profound. But it was not our grief, rather Bobby's, 'The Boss's', Jimmy's, the grief of those who'd belonged to another club.

One afternoon Noel Cantwell started chatting to me in the bath after training. 'Is that it?' he asked of the training routine. I told him it was. He was incredulous. I was Irish, he could confide in me. Doesn't anybody ever talk about the game here? Why isn't the training organised . . . what about ball-work . . . do you ever see Busby . . . doesn't anyone think about the game. Was that it? A bit of running, head-tennis and 'round the back' for a bloody free-for-all. The frustration poured out of him. He shook his head in disbelief as I assured him that, yes, that was it and no, there wasn't much talking about the game.

I was only a kid. Noel assured me that the first team

preparations were the same. Busby just came in, talked in generalisations and said 'go out and enjoy yourself'. Keep it simple, give it to a red shirt. 'Give it to a fucking red shirt,' Cantwell exclaimed. 'You don't need a manager for that. How do you find a red shirt if you haven't worked on it and talked about it?'

Noel had ideas. New ideas. He'd come from West Ham where he was the leader of a group of players who were questioning the way the game was played in England. The Great Debate of the early Fifties had developed, new ways of training were discussed, players had to be fitter, more tactically aware, you had to think about the game and talk about it. At West Ham Cantwell was the professor. Malcolm Allison, John Bond, Jimmy Andrews, Frank O'Farrell and Malcolm Musgrave would join him in an Italian café round the corner from Upton Park to discuss the game. This gathering would later acquire national fame as the West Ham Academy.

A revolution was taking place in English football, on and off the field. In 1961 the maximum wage was abolished after George Eastham took his case to the High Court. Eastham, a gifted footballer with an independent mind, challenged the legality of the Slaves Charter and won. It was to take another two decades to get rid of the retain-and-transfer system, meanwhile the concession of maximum wages was the compromise accepted by the Masters. They fought hard to keep the Slaves in place, but Eastham and Jimmy Hill, supported by Cliff Lloyd's Professional Footballers' Association, had right on their side. Newspapers, notably the *Observer*, facilitated debate. Queen's Counsel was enlisted to examine the contracts which had governed professionals' lives since the Edwardian era. The QCs laughed. Billy Meredith was vindicated, alas too late for him. Newspapers weren't unanimous, nor, astonishingly, were the professionals, a significant minority of whom felt, as in The Wizard's day, that 'we are lucky to be doing what we do and getting paid for it'.

But Bob Dylan was on the road, the Beatles were in the charts, Jack Kennedy was in the White House and free love was on the agenda. The times they were a-changing and the maximum wage was blown away by the winds of change.

The West Ham Academy was of its time. Others in football were thinking and talking as well. Burnley won the Championship in 1960 playing cultured Continental-style football under Jimmy Adamson, their captain, and Jimmy McIlroy, their gracious, articulate schemer. The following season Spurs won the Double. This historic achievement was gained in style, a victory for the thinking professional epitomised by Spurs captain Danny Blanchflower, Jackie Blanchflower's elder brother. Professional football appeared to be emerging from its Dark Age – the only Age it had ever known – in those early Sixties years. Blanchflower's Spurs, followed enthusiastically by philosophy don Freddie Ayer, symbolised the New Age. At United Cantwell was representative of the new, cerebral, professional game. Thought had become a fact of professional football life. Coaching had begun.

This is the most fascinating period in the history of the English game. Reflecting society at large, as it always had done, professional soccer allowed its best and brightest to have their say. Ignorance was the enemy; thought and freedom of expression would broaden horizons. The reactionaries who had dominated professional soccer in England were now fully exposed to the light of rational discourse. Men like Blanchflower, Cantwell, Allison and their followers were eager to learn from the Hungarians and Real Madrid who had won the European Cup for six successive years playing glorious football. In 1958 Brazil with Pele had won the World Cup, England finished nowhere once again.

The new men knew what was wrong, there was no argument now about 'the best football in the world'. That was a joke. According to consensus, the answer to English football's problems lay on the training ground. That was where players were improved, skills developed, fitness raised to new levels. The training ground should offer education, thought translated into action, you should work with the ball, always with the ball, that's how the Continentals did it, they always had the ball. And they were organised. The wonderful football Real Madrid played didn't just happen.

This was why Cantwell was so shocked when he arrived at Old Trafford. From afar Matt Busby's Manchester United had seemed a beacon of enlightenment. United had done it, played the football of the new men's dreams. Hence Cantwell's disillusion with the club he found himself leading on the field. Busby appeared to provide nothing but platitudes about simplicity and the importance of character. The fundamental disagreement between Busby and the school of which Noel Cantwell was representative was about the means to the end both desired. Could you plan good football or was it the product of the individual's imagination, great teams being those where the best players gelled instinctively to create a chemical unique to themselves rather than a formula that could be learned and passed on? The West Ham Academy believed in football's virtues, the positive, but once you started to think rationally about football what was negative became apparent.

In 1962 Alf Ramsey's Ipswich won the Championship. Alf Ramsey had thought about his team and come to the conclusion that his players weren't good enough to compete, in any positive sense, with their betters. His response was a formula which stopped good footballers playing. Ipswich were organised. United finished fifteenth in the First Division. Ramsey's team won 4–1 at Portman Road; United, on one of their few happy days that season, beat the champions-elect 5–0 at Old Trafford. Albert Quixall scored a hat-trick. In the same year United reached the FA Cup semi-final, losing to Spurs. At Leeds Don Revie was also thinking deeply about football. In 1963 Leeds won the Second Division, and United finished nineteenth in the First Division having narrowly avoided relegation. At Wembley Manchester United won the FA Cup beating Leicester City 3–1 with a scintillating display of football. David Herd scored twice, Denis Law once, a brilliant swivel and shot setting up United's victory. Paddy Crerand played superbly in midfield for United. The turbulent contradictions evident in Manchester United's fortunes on the field in 1963 reflected life in the dressing-room that season and, indeed, in the three preceeding years.

Manchester United was in transition, and nobody was sure exactly where the club was heading. The shambles of the League performances was indicative of the mess the club was in, but the magic of Wembley proved that Matt Busby was alive and well, still the great conjuror with tricks to play. The game had changed, his club had changed and so to some extent had he.

After Cantwell Busby bought David Herd, son of his old friend and City colleague Alec, for £38,000. In 1962 he broke the British transfer record again to buy Denis Law from Torino for £115,000. Paddy Crerand followed from Celtic for £55,000. United were big spenders now. The old network of scouts still existed, Joe Armstrong still charmed mothers, but Miraculous Medals were not sufficient to turn the trick these days. Parents had started thinking rationally as well. Nobby Stiles had come to Old Trafford because he loved United; Kenny Morton, the best schoolboy footballer in England was keen to come to United. And because of the club's renown his parents only wanted five grand, which was less than others were offering. Things having changed since Johnny Morris's day – and Charlie Mitten's – the Mortons got their money. Kenny never made it, leaving United for York City, on a free transfer, where he made nine appearances in 1965. He subsequently played three games for Darlington. Kenny was a nice lad, a vegetarian whose special meals were prepared in the digs. Barry Fry, *the* England schoolboy of his year, joined with me in 1960. United gave his dad a scouting job and a lump sum to come to Old Trafford. His dad never found any talent.

Billy Behan found Tony Dunne playing for Shelbourne in the League of Ireland. Tony cost £6,000 in one of the best deals United ever did. The old way still worked, but it was a back-up system to the more profligate norm of the post-Munich club. David Sadler cost £750 from Maidstone. He'd been a sensation in the England amateur team but no more than a curiosity when he arrived at Old Trafford in February 1963. David moved into digs with George Best at Mrs Fullaway's.

The abolition of the maximum wage cast everyone in professional football into the unknown. With the ceiling of £20 a week removed, the sky was the limit when negotiations began in the summer of 1961. The showman Tommy Trinder, Fulham's chairman, had been vocal in support of the players. Trinder's promise to pay his international inside-forward, Johnny Haynes, £100 a week went down like a lead balloon in most First Division boardrooms. Haynes was after all Fulham's only star. Matt Busby had a whole squad of internationals to bargain with. Trinder's sum applied to Manchester United's circumstances would mean a rise of sixty or seventy thousand pounds on the annual wage bill. Given Busby's other money worries this was unthinkable. His dilemma was more acute; during the struggle with the Football League he had backed his players: 'It's ridiculous what you boys are being paid. You should be on £100 a week.'

Players everywhere speculated. There was a lot of idle talk, much private worry. How would you know what the others were getting, would your valuation of yourself vis à vis them be reflected in your offer, how valuable were you to your club? In a business already inherently insecure, the maximum wage, for all its faults, had left everyone certain where they stood. John Giles was not especially money conscious. Charlie Hurley, who played for Sunderland, was fond of the folding stuff. On a close-season trip with the Irish international squad John and Charlie agreed to compare offers when the letters arrived. Giles was one of United's most gifted young players. He'd played twenty-three games that season. He was offered £25 a week plus £5 appearance money. Nobby Stiles, with whom John lodged in Collyhurst, enjoyed the same status at Old Trafford and received the same offer. When they turned up for pre-season training United's players discovered, after some huffing and bluffing, that all members of the first team squad had been offered £25 plus a fiver for appearing in the League and some nominal crowd bonus. Giles rang Charlie Hurley. Charlie was in bad form. Second Division Sunderland's offer was £60 a week which he had turned down.

When they checked with players from other clubs United's stars discovered that theirs was the lowest offer in the First Division. Most Second Division clubs had offered more. Liverpool, managed by Matt's friend Bill Shankly, were then in the Second Division, and their offer was the same as United's. Busby and Shankly had discussed the matter and agreed on the norm, yet there was no comparison between the clubs other than their two managers' canny natures.

Busby's offer was outrageous, and the players were bitter

262

when they met to consider what to do. They agreed that nobody would sign the new contracts. Later, Busby saw them in his office, one by one. He explained the offer in terms of team spirit and the club's finances, dismissing as wild talk the figures being mentioned elsewhere. He put the contract on the desk and, one by one, they signed. Big talk in the dressing-room was one thing, dealing with 'The Boss' in his office was a very different experience. His presence was overwhelming. You were not confronted, on the contrary, he was charming, solicitous, understanding your concerns, keen that you should understand Manchester United's interests as well as your own. He didn't make you feel bad, he made you feel important, you wanted to please him, do what was right for everyone, yourself and the club. *He* was the club. You signed. And felt like a shit for causing hassle in the first place. Then you thanked him. On the way down the stairs you tried to figure out a way to explain to the others what had happened. There were many sheepish-looking hard men around the dressing-room that week.

It is impossible to overstate the importance of his sheer physicality in circumstances such as these. Busby was no mere charmer. He was a huge man, immaculate in manner and dress. The voice, a deep, soft Scottish brogue, was a force in itself, the humility Harold Riley alludes to projected as vulnerability. There was a sanctity about this person, its power especially potent when you were alone with him, something indefinable yet invisible which, in purely physical terms, amounted to greatness. Munich had saddened his face perceptibly, the presence was stronger for that.

Busby's toughness was well known in the dressing-room. Those who didn't fall under his charismatic spell eventually saw a glint of steel. In this too he was subtle. An exasperated sigh was a bad sign. His eyes, never warmly engaged with yours, would focus coldly as it became clear that ground was not being conceded on the other side of the desk. There was rarely any shouting, just the simple observation that if you chose to have it your way there was nothing Manchester United could – or would – do. At the end of the day it was your decision. This club was bigger than anybody.

Once a decision had to be made Busby was swift and ruthless, as Johnny Morris and Charlie Mitten had discovered. Colin Webster, the wrong type, left in the early Sixties and in 1962 Denis Viollet was transferred to Stoke on similar grounds. Viollet had broken United's goalscoring record with thirty-two League goals in the season '59/'60. He'd captained the club and been close to Busby, as all his captains were, for a while afterwards. But Denis was too fond of ladies and the Manchester night life. After the usual Busby patience was exhausted, Denis, a popular man in the dressing-room, was exiled. One of the greatest players ever to play for the club, Viollet may also have suffered delayed reaction to Munich.

Busby sought to replace Viollet with Denis Law. The Scottish international was known to be unhappy at Torino. After a tip-off, Busby enquired about a price for a player he'd always admired since seeing him play against United in a youth cup tie at Huddersfield in the mid Fifties. The price was £115,000, way beyond the British record in 1962. The deal would place United in debt for the first time since Busby had arrived in 1945. Harold Hardman was not sympathetic when Busby broached the subject. The chairman had been at United since the Newton Heath days. He knew the cost of extravagance, remembered Walter Crickmer returning empty-handed from the bank unable to pay the players' wages. Spending on the transfer-market had not produced results thus far, Busby was reminded. Setters, Quixall, Cantwell, and Herd had not transformed United, nor was there any sign that better days were in the offing. Thanks to Alan Gibson and Louis Edwards Matt commanded a majority in the boardroom, but he needed unanimity to push the club into the red at the bank. For a couple of days he considered accepting an offer from his friend Johnny Foy and another Manchester bookie, Ely Rose, to underwrite the bid for Law. In the end Louis Edwards helped Matt persuade Hardman, and the three of them set off for a secret meeting with Denis in Switzerland.

Law was desperate to leave Italy and eager to join United. Torino, angry at his defiance, now sold his contract to Juventus. Presented with this *fait accompli* Denis packed his bags, returned to Manchester and sat tight for a month. He was threatened with a worldwide ban if he didn't abide by international football law. Busby assured Denis that if he kept his nerve the Italians would accept the £115,000. For an anxious month the situation remained deadlocked. Busby was not publicly involved. In August 1962 Torino blinked and the deal was closed. This was Busby's biggest ever bet.

The atmosphere of the dressing-room Denis Law arrived in was tense with a clear undercurrent of spite and resentment. Busby had originally put his tracksuit on to bridge the gulfs he so despised as a player. His presence would shape the character of his club's dressing-room. This was the soul of a football club. Now, in his absence from the United dressing-room, a situation amounting to anarchy prevailed. The rooms beneath the stand at Old Trafford were divided, unhappy places. There weren't so much gulfs as chasms between the various types sharing this unhappy epicentre of the club. Busby wasn't often seen during the week, and Jimmy Murphy devoted most of his energy to the youngsters. Jimmy's role had changed since Munich. He had changed himself. Like Matt, he was more on the fringe of things. Jimmy had been given the title Assistant-Manager in 1955, an acknowledgement of the work he'd done with the pre-Munich youngsters. Nothing changed except the title. Things did change after the crash. He didn't go to the Cliff on Tuesday and Thursday nights, except the odd time. Afternoon coaching sessions ceased, and with them the danger of Jimmy telling you to be back at two o'clock had passed. Now Wilf McGuinness and Johnny Aston did most of the work Jimmy and Bert Whalley used to do. The reserve team dressing-room was a more relaxed place on Saturday afternoons. Jimmy still promoted the same principles but although the message was the same the words lacked the fervour of the past. The dynamic presence of the thirteen years between '45 and '58 no longer imposed on the young and gifted who arrived at Old Trafford after Munich. Compared to others Jimmy Murphy was still a passionate man, compared to the demon pre-Munich he was a paragon of reason. He seemed kind, like a pastor rather than an evangelist.

Evangelism was for younger men, and Jimmy, like Matt, had aged. There was an air of melancholy about him as well. On Youth Cup nights he came alive, you saw a flash of the old fire, but nobody was ever reduced to tears as John Giles had been, or shamed as Bobby once was for throwing the ball away on the halfway line. There was no more effing and blinding. He was likable. He understood.

The first team dressing-room was dominated by Cantwell, Setters, Gregg, Foulkes, Crerand and amused by Albert Quixall the court jester. Denis Law kept to himself. Bobby Charlton said nothing. Nobby Stiles, Bobby and Shay Brennan were close, sharing rooms, playing crib for pennies on the coach and going for half-a-bitter or to the pictures on Friday nights away from home. For Bobby the years between 1960 and 1964 were strange. Effective wingers were always fundamental to Busby's team. Finding himself without an outside-left in 1960 Matt turned to Bobby whose range of gifts equipped him to play virtually anywhere. Thus, this potentially great inside-forward spent four seasons playing as a winger. Even though he won international honours at outside-left Bobby 'hated it'.

Reflecting reluctantly on United before and after Munich, Bobby admits that 'the happiest time for me was up to it happening. After that, well I wouldn't say it was a job, I still enjoyed playing – but nothing would ever really be the same. I hated playing on the wing, waiting, depending on other people. I wanted to get into the game, to get something out of it. I remember once at Notts Forest I didn't touch the ball for twenty minutes. So I started going inside to look for it and Jimmy was there saying stay wide. But I said, "Jimmy I'm not getting a kick," and he said, "You will."

'I hated it but I never really questioned it. If that was what The Boss wanted I did it.'

The chasm which existed in United's dressing-room divided those who felt like Bobby, Tony Dunne, now an established first team player, Nobby Stiles, still on the fringe of the side, Shay Brennan, Bill Foulkes and John Giles, and a group led by Noel Cantwell and Maurice Setters who were contemptuous of Busby, his staff, the training and United's way of playing the game. Harry Gregg was an active campaigner for his own party of one. Denis Law didn't get involved. Paddy Crerand who'd come from Celtic which he'd thought of as 'a joke' felt that the situation at Old Trafford was little better. David Herd listened and played. Quixall provided the banter.

For two months after Christmas 1963 Britain froze to a standstill. United didn't play a League or FA Cup match between Boxing Day and 23 February. This was a bad time for a club in ferment. Nerves frayed, old grievances surfaced, simmering resentment became open hostility. Angry voices rang on the training ground, frustration, which might otherwise have found an outlet in competitive football, now consumed the various factions inside Old Trafford. Fist fights resulted when five-a-sides got out of hand. Something had to be done. Harry Gregg went to see 'The Boss'. Everything had to come out in the open Harry felt, but 'everything' was not exactly what he meant. Everything focused on Jack Crompton whom the dissidents identified as the problem. Not daring to voice their opinions about 'The Boss' to his face, Jack presented the perfect target. Jack's training was a joke. Jack wouldn't let them have the ball. Jack didn't know the game. Jack would have to be sorted out. Nobody was thinking about the game at Old Trafford. That was Jack's fault. Harry felt 'The Boss' should know.

Busby knew more than Harry thought. He agreed to call a meeting to clear the air. Everyone could have a say, out in the open. The meeting was held in the first team dressing-room. Busby presided, Jack stood in the dock and listened as his régime was condemned. Cantwell and Setters had plenty to say. Harry weighed in. Most mumbled unconvincingly about their own pet theory: more ball work, more sprints, more weight-training, less weight-training, stamina work, speed work. Some declared themselves happy, others passed. Denis passed, saying he hadn't been at the club long enough to express an opinion. Bobby was quiet. Paddy was with Noel and Maurice. John Giles thought the whole exercise was a waste of time, he thought the players had too much to say. John understood the real problem which was the absence of authority, leadership, on a day-to-day basis, within the club. The hidden agenda was Busby, Jack was merely a convenient fall guy. Giles understood Busby, and respected him sufficiently to know that even though he wasn't around during the week the training was his training, Jack was simply doing a job. John knew that Manchester United's problems wouldn't be solved – or even addressed – by clear-the-air talks. Like Nobby he belonged still in the reserve team dressing-room, unconcerned with the politics of this debate.

When all had had their say Jack was given his. He was a quiet, unassertive man of the old school. If the new ideas about training and coaching hadn't been imposed at Old Trafford it was because 'The Boss' didn't want it to happen. Busby had exposed him to this ordeal, conveying the impression that he was neutral. Jack might have passed the buck to 'The Boss' when he began to defend himself. But Jack knew better.

'*Him*'– Jack pointed dramatically at Cantwell, his most articulate prosecutor, 'things haven't been right at this club since he walked in the door.' Cantwell had spread discontent. He'd undermined everything, he should get on with his own business and leave the running of Manchester United to those paid to do the job. Crompton's voice was calm. There was no hint of diffidence. He was sure of his ground. The opinion he expressed was Matt Busby's. The old fox now knew the score. The meeting had not really been about clearing the air so much as assessing the mood in the dressing-room.

Matt Busby knew all along about the dissidents' views, what he wanted to find out was how brazen they were prepared to be in expressing them in front of him, and more critically, how much support there was for the new thinking.

Wilf McGuinness was Matt's eyes and ears in the dressing-room, for, although on the coaching staff, he was still one of the lads. On Sunday mornings Wilf would come into Old Trafford to have a beer and a chat about the week's work with 'The Boss', Jimmy, Jack and Johnny Aston. Ted Dalton always joined them in Matt's office. 'I'd leave the ground about half-one,' Wilf smiles, 'and get last orders at the Quadrant.' The 'Quad' was still the favoured pub for United players. There on Sundays the previous day's game would be mulled over and arguments about the rights and wrongs of new ideas and old were conducted over pre-lunch pints of bitter. Busby was frequently on the agenda. Cantwell held court. Setters was pre-eminent. Gregg another insistent voice. 'Quickie' told jokes. Shay Brennan agreed with everyone. Shay was the most popular lad at the club. Close to Bobby and Nobby, just as comfortable playing crib with them as brag in the heavy gambling school, Shay was United as it had been before the crash, a typical Manchester rogue who loved the game – whatever or wherever it was.

In the 'Quad' circa '63/'64 the new men had much to discuss. Jack wasn't the only target. Bobby wasn't a player at all. Gilesy was a coward. 'Quickie' was a cheat and whenever Harry got too heated he was told that he was 'fucking mad'.

Knowing all this, Busby still hoped that things would knit together. His growing conviction, as United fought their relegation battle in the spring of 1963, was that he'd have to sort a few people people out. This was not a simple proposition. He liked Noel Cantwell. The big Irishman believed in the new ideas he was campaigning for. Matt knew exactly what the issues were and had discussed them with Cantwell, Setters and Paddy Crerand. He liked Paddy as well. Another aspect of Busby's character was evident at this time: his taste for rogues who made him laugh. On Saturdays he and Jean sometimes dined at the Cromford Club with the Cantwells, Setters and Crerands. Bobby Charlton and Denis Law both resisted joining this set. Bobby had too much respect for Busby: 'I would never have dreamed of asking him out for a meal.' Cantwell did. Busby accepted. Bobby thought he was 'too much of a gentleman' to refuse. Denis Law was a private man, full of banter during working hours, an occasional patron of the 'Quad', for four halves of bitter, but he wasn't into socialising with 'The Boss' – 'It wasn't on' – or the politics of the dressing-room.

Bobby was right about Matt's inability to say no to his senior players. Away from work he was a different man, and all that was formal was shed leaving only the charm. He was easy to get along with. After a few drinks and a steak he would have a laugh, talk about the old days in football, though not the recent past, and be a gregarious, unimposing presence in the Cromford. He loved the company of football people. Players or old pals like Joe Mercer, Bill Shankly or Jock Stein whom he would later get to know very well. Big characters, like Cantwell and Crerand also appealed to a side of him the public rarely saw. CBE or not, Matt Busby would, given a choice, rather spend an evening with a bookie or a streetwise Scot like Paddy

Crerand than a bank manager or a bishop. The golf course on a Monday afternoon allowed him the same kind of relaxation. The races or the dog-track yet another escape from the burden of being Matt Busby, Manager of Manchester United. His friendship with Louis Edwards was now firm and lasting. The chairmanship of United would be in Matt's gift eventually and Louis was his man – Louis Edwards, Chairman of Manchester United. It sounded good to both of them, the seal would be set on their friendship and Matt would finally control the football club he'd created. This happy prospect lent urgency to the task of solving the problems bedeviling United on the field and in the dressing-room.

Around this time there was considerable speculation within the game about a ring of professional players who, it was alleged, were conspiring to rig games and profit by betting on the outcome. As bookmakers accepted bets on single games as well as doubles and trebles it was theoretically possible for a relatively small group of players to exploit the fixed-odds system. Odds on an individual game were, however, short. Real profit would depend on rigging more than one game. A middle-man would also be required to place the bets and a bookmaker would serve ideally for this purpose.

These rumours of match-rigging were confirmed in 1963 when a number of professional players were tried and convicted in the courts. The football world was shocked by the extent of the conspiracy and the eminence of some of the players involved. Three Sheffield Wednesday players, Tony Kay, England's left-half, Peter Swan, another international, and 'Bronco' Lane were found guilty and sent to prison. They were among a number of professionals suspended from the game for life.

The match-rigging scandal touched Manchester United when two *Daily Mail* journalists travelled to Blackpool, where the team were staying at the Norbreck Hydro, to confront United goalkeeper Harry Gregg and some of his colleagues with allegations that they had been party to the conspiracy. Busby was deeply shocked when confronted with the accusation that a small group of United players had sold games. Unable to confirm the story, Busby persuaded the *Daily Mail* not to publish the allegations. He then convened a meeting of United's players at which he warned that anyone caught or even suspected of match-rigging would be out the door. The matter ended there. However, Harry Gregg claims that there was substance to these allegations and that he was asked to participate in throwing matches on a number of occasions between 1960 and 1963. Despite his refusal to participate, Gregg has told me that matches were thrown by some of his United colleagues and has named several players. One of those accused admitted that there was a lot of discussion about fixing games in the United dressing-room but says that the talk never translated into action. Others, innocent of involvement, acknowledge that on occasions there did appear to be something odd about United's performances.

It is impossible to be certain on the basis of hearsay evidence which may to some extent to be contaminated by personal grievance. However there is no doubt in my mind that Manchester United players did conspire to fix the result of at least three games during the '60/'63 period. It is widely accepted within the game that those who were convicted in the ensuing scandal were not the only prominent players involved in the match-rigging conspiracy.

Despite finishing nineteenth in the First Division, Matt Busby had some reason for optimism in the summer of '63. The FA Cup Final victory was encouraging. United had won in style. The miseries of the winter months faded as he watched the team demolish Leicester City, Crerand and Law playing with particular flair. Crerand had had a nightmarish start at Old Trafford. A beautiful passer of the ball, Paddy was as slow as Busby himself had been when he played, but sureness of instinct, clarity of vision and the most delightful imagination placed him in the classic mould of great Scottish wing-halves. His courage, physical and moral, was not in doubt. On his day Paddy's long incisive passes were delivered to devastating effect. Off form he looked cumbersome, trundling adrift of the play like a carthorse in a paddock of thoroughbreds. The spectacular passes looked bizarre when they failed to reach their targets, and the crowd would gasp at his folly. His early games for United had been undistinguished at best. Wembley saw the real Crerand. Busby was immensely supportive through the period Paddy struggled. 'I know what you're trying to do, keep doing it, it will come right,' Busby insisted. In difficult times like this Busby had the purist's vision and the guts of a tiger. The problem‚ was his, not Paddy's. He would take the stick in public.

Wembley had brought out the best in Denis Law, Matt's most expensive signing. Denis had looked the part all season. Even in a struggling side he scored twenty-three goals. Denis was more than a goalscorer. He was an inspiration, capable of lifting those around him, his cavalier thrusts at the opposition impudent and taunting sowing doubt in defenders' minds, a source of encouragement to his colleagues. In the box he was deadly, quick, brave, elusive, taking half-chances with the daring and sureness of a matador. No game was quiet, no cause lost, no crowd less than enthralled when Law was hungry for the game. He was fearless, wild, impetuous, a unique force in the English game. Law was the kind of player systems didn't produce. He was the product of life, a harsh Aberdonian childhood blighted further by squint-eyed deformity which caused him torment in schoolyard and neighbourhood. The magic of football was Denis's solace as it had been Mattha's and all the great players'. The thing of slumbering dreams, the glorious escape from the world, the triumph of a beautiful spirit over ugly material reality.

The great showman Law was extrovert at work – sardonic, amused, intelligent and alone once the job was done. In Law Busby saw the defiant spirit of his great lost team, the bit of devil, the grace, the brio which was to Matt professional football's ultimate vindication; the merchants and politicians could have the world, he lived for this beautiful, unsullied expression of life. He loved the game and, like all who do, knew there was nothing more to be yearned for than the sight of it played as it was in the imagination – and so often by his teams. At Wembley Law and Crerand allowed Matt to hope again.

Problems remained. After the FA Cup win another row broke out about money. Wage disputes were now a perennial cause of friction at Old Trafford. United were still the First

Division's poorest payers. The success at Wembley embol-
dened the lads. This time they *would* stick together. Although
heartened by the Cup triumph, Busby knew he was short of two
or three players of championship standard. He was not without
hope of finding them at Old Trafford, but more money might
have to be spent on the transfer-market. All the usual noises
were made in the dressing-room. The result upstairs was the
usual rout of the big talkers.

For the opening game of the 1963/64 season, away to
Sheffield Wednesday, Busby shocked football by dropping
three of his Cup-winning side. David Herd, Albert Quixall and
John Giles were omitted in favour of three youngsters, Ian
Moir, Phil Chisnall and David Sadler. Quixall was due to go
anyway. He'd been bought to do a job he was ill-equipped to
tackle, and though he was popular he lacked the appetite for
conflict. Jimmy Murphy and Wilf McGuinness were particularly venomous about the 'Golden Boy' of 1958. Busby admired
his skill but accepted that his staff were right. David Herd,
scorer of two Cup-Final goals, and nineteen the previous
League season, had been particularly stubborn during the wage
round, and dropping him was Busby's way of teaching him a
lesson. Giles was the most interesting casualty. Subsequently to
become one of the great midfield players of his generation,
Giles had played his last game for United. Within a couple of
weeks he was transferred to Leeds United, a decision which
Busby later admitted was his 'greatest mistake'.

John Giles was a model professional. Beautifully balanced, a
superb passer of the ball with both feet, he fulfilled all the
criteria Busby sought in his players, yet the chemistry between
them was never quite right. Giles, a piss-taker of renown in the
reserve team dressing-room, was serious and intelligent about
his football. He was, rather like Busby, careful about expressing opinions and tended to keep his own counsel. Above all
John was uncommonly self-possessed. When *he* went upstairs
football rather than money would be on the agenda. Busby's
charm was met with football logic. Giles saw himself as an
inside-forward, Busby wanted him on the wing. He doubted
Giles's lust for battle – a judgement which time would render
laughable, but which then was shared by the Cantwell/Setters

273

Debating Society and, significantly, Jimmy Murphy. Giles had had a run at inside-forward in '61/'62 but a virus infection, undiagnosed, left him weak although he kept playing. This period culminated with a disappointing display against Spurs in that season's FA Cup semi-final. 'I think he gave up on me then,' Giles confesses.

On reflection it is remarkable that for a couple of seasons Busby fielded a team with Bobby Charlton and John Giles, destined to develop as two of English football's greatest inside-forwards, as makeshift wingers. Charlton resented this, Giles did so more obviously.

After United's Cup semi-final win over Southampton in 1963 Busby decided to leave Giles out of the side for a league game. Busby's method of dropping players was well known at Old Trafford and offers another fascinating insight into the non-confrontational side of his character. Giles and his friend Nobby Stiles were frequent victims. 'He'd call you into the Referee's room on Friday mornings,' John recalls. 'This was a bad omen. "How do you think you're playing son?" he'd begin. Being young lads we'd be honest and say, "Not bad," or "Not so good."

' "That's right," he'd agree, "I'm going to give you a rest." '

After the Cup semi-final Giles was prepared, and when Busby collared him in the Ref's room to ask how he thought he'd played, John replied, 'Well.' And continued, 'How do you think I played?'

'Reasonably well,' Busby conceded.

'Why are you leaving me out then?' John responded. 'If I played reasonably well and we won a Cup semi-final and I'm still being dropped I've got no chance, have I?' The logic was unassailable.

Giles played at Wembley but the die was cast between Busby and himself. They were in many respects alike, tough men who guarded their emotions and were firm in their convictions about how the game should be played. The anarchic atmosphere at Old Trafford dismayed Giles who was, like others from pre-Munich days, concerned to play football for Matt Busby rather than seek undue influence through dressing-room politics or socialising in the 'Quad' or the Cromford Club. John was not alone in feeling an outsider at this time. Bobby Charlton,

Nobby Stiles, Tony Dunne and Denis Law also felt Busby was a prisoner of the self-appointed praetorian guard of senior players whose opinions were sought and acted upon. That's not quite the way it was, but it's how it seemed.

When Don Revie offered £34,000 for Giles, Busby accepted and the player was happy to leave. Paddy Crerand was a notable dissenter from the Debating Society's view that Giles had no 'bottle'. 'Bobby Collins rang me from Leeds about John,' Crerand confides. 'I told him I thought John was a great player and Leeds were getting a bargain.' A day or two before Giles left he met Wilf McGuinness in the car-park. 'Don't worry,' Wilf comforted John, 'The Boss might change his mind.' Giles laughed, 'He might, but I won't.'

Busby lived to regret this departure from the club more than any other in his career, but the fact that Leeds were struggling in the Second Division made Busby feel more sanguine about Giles's deal than he might have done selling to First Division rivals. The prudent Matt liked to bury the departed lest they come back to haunt his team and raise doubts about his judgement. The same consideration applied when Denis Viollet left for lowly Stoke City. Alas, for Busby, football had not heard the last of Leeds and Giles.

The 1963/64 season belonged to Denis Law. He scored thirty League goals, and ten more, including two hat-tricks, in an FA Cup run which West Ham ended in the semi-final. United finished second in the Championship. They might have won the title if Law had not run foul of referees and injury. English football was becoming faster and meaner. Hard men like Liverpool's Tommy Smith, Chelsea's Ron Harris and Spurs' Dave Mackay were among the most intimidating of a new breed of defenders who, unlike their muscle-bound post-war counter-parts, were as quick and, in Mackay's case as skilful, as the forwards they ruthlessly pursued. 'I think anybody doing their job up front was very lucky to play a full season without injuries,' Law concludes, reflecting on the Sixties. Leeds emerged in 1964 to add an even nastier dimension to the First Division. In Bobby Collins and Norman Hunter Leeds possessed two particularly wicked exponents of subtle yet terminal destruction. While Harold Wilson led the Labour

Party into government, promising to create a new Britain forged in the 'white-hot heat of technological revolution', League football at all levels was becoming leaner, more efficient, and gifted players who couldn't compete were a luxury those seeking to win could no longer afford. As Law points out; 'Every team has one or two hard men.' Denis met fire with fire. Nobody would bully him. Suspension, hefty fines and controversy resulted. Busby was criticised for failing to curb Law's retaliatory impulses but he knew that his man's aggression was of the essence. Publicly Busby expressed his disapproval, privately he allowed Law's nature to take its course.

Manchester United began to be respected again, but behind the scenes the gulfs remained. Many of the younger players had been infected by the poison in the air around Old Trafford in the five years after Munich. The club's character had changed. In the year after the FA Cup win things took a turn for the better. They needed to. An outbreak of thieving spread suspicion through the dressing-room. Heavy gambling in card schools and at Manchester's three dog-tracks was a plague now infecting the youngsters at the club. Contempt for Busby was not erased by the Wembley win. That season I was selected as twelfth man for the away game against Notts Forest. The journey by coach allows a glimpse of the mood prevailing. Busby sat in his usual front seat for the relatively short trip to Nottingham. Across from him 'Champagne' Louis, large cigar in large hand; beside him, Martin Edwards his public-schoolboy son, a pleasant, well-mannered lad. Further back the card schools; the serious brag for wads of folding money, and the crib players jousting for fun and pennies. I was sitting reading a newpaper somewhere between 'The Boss' and the lads at the back of the bus, feeling a little overawed at this first taste of the big time, when a folded sheet of paper fell on my lap, dropped from the seat in front. When I openened it I was shocked to see a vicious caricature of Busby drawn with great skill and care in ink. The image was a perfect likeness of him in stern-faced repose. The nose was drawn as a penis, the cheeks as two testicles. The caption read 'Bollock Chops'. This cruel depiction of 'The Boss' did not amuse a nervous eighteen-year-old. Terrified, I passed it back to the sender, a senior player whose name I can't remember. For those of us outside the cauldron of the first team dressing-room Busby was still an awesome man. I was a bit of a lad myself but this I simply couldn't comprehend. The caricature does, however, illustrate the depths to which Busby's stock had sunk among a faction in the club. Ironically, United won at the City Ground that afternoon.

The thief was eventually trapped but not before substantial sums were stolen over a period of several unhappy weeks. The culprit was caught when found in possession of marked money used as bait. Busby had personally taken charge of this episode, during which he made an uncharacteristically insensitive remark seized upon by those who sought to ridicule him. A meeting of staff was called to discuss the thieving. In passing 'The Boss' alluded to there being 'a nigger in the woodpile'. Denis Walker, one of the first black players to emerge in the professional game sat unperturbed at the offence. The sniggering at Busby's blunder lasted for a day or two, and the incident strengthened the view that he had lost his touch.

First team results, however, indicated otherwise, and United finished the season in style. Tony Dunne, replacing the injured Noel Cantwell, had made the left-back position his own, and was beginning to look like one of the best defensive full-backs in the game. That promise was fulfilled. Nobby Stiles established himself at left-half towards the end of the season. Maurice Setters, on the other hand, was on his way out. Setters was not Busby's type. At West Ham the season before, Busby had lost his temper after a defeat when he returned to the dressing-room to find Setters shouting the odds. Busby pulled him into the bathroom, out of sight but within earshot. 'Who the hell do you think you are? Why is yours the voice I always hear when I walk into the dressing-room?' Busby shouted. Setters began to reply. Busby told him to 'shut up and listen'. The hard man shut up. Busby knew almost every move his players made. Maurice Setters belonged to the work-hard-play-hard tendency. Important games the following day didn't always curb his taste for late night adventures, and he wasn't the only pre-match absconder from the Russell Hotel, United's London headquarters: Shay Brennan and later George Best were others who occasionally broke the eleven o'clock curfew. Busby could be forgiving of such behaviour – if you did your stuff the following day. Alas, Setters's desire to embellish his rugged play with skilful flourishes he rarely managed to achieve was less easily forgiven. Loose talk in the 'Quad' which parroted Noel Cantwell's intelligent analysis of the game, but lacked the coherence of real conviction, did nothing to endear Setters to 'The Boss'.

Billy Behan, United's Irish scout, believes that Busby had already made up his mind about Setters when the club visited Dublin to play an exhibition game against Shamrock Rovers in the spring of 1964. Before this game at Dalymount Park Setters was unnecessarily dismissive of a group of Dublin youngsters seeking autographs. Behan, who witnessed this scene was concerned about the effect on the club's image. A decent, mild-mannered man and a close friend of Busby's, Behan surprised the United manager with the vehemence of his complaint about Setters's abrupt refusal to sign the kids' autograph books. 'Don't worry,' Matt assured him, 'he's on his way.'

George Best made his first team début on 14 September 1963 against West Brom at Old Trafford. He played outside-right in place of the injured Ian Moir, who had himself taken John Giles's red shirt a few weeks earlier. Albion's left-back, Graham Williams, was a tough, experienced Welsh international, but George gave him a chasing. George looked younger than his seventeen years, he was a schoolboy among men, and he played like a schoolboy as well. He *was* a schoolboy in football terms, for nobody had told him how to play since he arrived at Old Trafford. George Best wasn't a pro.

Six months earlier, when Britain began to function again after the Great Freeze and football had resumed, George played for our youth team in the FA Youth Cup tie at Sheffield Wednesday. David Sadler also got into the side that night. We had a good team, we fancied that this would be our year in the Youth Cup. George had not been in the team. He played at Sheffield only because our regular outside-left was injured. We lost 1–0, with George contributing nothing. He fucked around

278

on the left-wing all night. We put the result down to him. He played like a schoolboy. He didn't do the simple things . . . give it to a red shirt . . . play it simple . . . the ball's made round to go round. Jimmy's gospel didn't apply to George. He hadn't got the message. We thought he was just another of those brilliant kids who could make the ball talk in the car-park but couldn't do the business when it really mattered. Car-park virtuosos were nothing new at Old Trafford, kids who could make the ball talk yet couldn't apply their technique to the real game. Albert Quixall could do anything with a football until you put opposition on the field. Football wasn't about technique, rather the application of ability to the business of winning. There was a lad called Barry Grayson at Old Trafford around this time, a Manchester and England Boy, whose skill was incredible. But he couldn't play, despite making us feel inadequate on Wednesday mornings. George was deemed to be in that category by his young peers.

He was also frail. Size had always been his problem. His father Dickie, an iron-turner in the Belfast shipyards, was a useful left-back in local amateur soccer. 'My mother was more sporty,' George remembers, 'she played hockey for a local team, I used to go and watch her.' He thinks his gift came from his mother.

Football is the first thing George remembers in his life: 'From day one I was always kicking a ball around. I always carried one with me.' He played for the school and Craigie Boys' Youth Club. He thinks he might have played once for Northern Ireland Boys, but his most powerful memory of schoolboy football is of failure. 'Size was my main problem. I remember getting into trials and the final sixteen who were picked for the squad, but I never got a game. Once there were seventeen of us left with a chance of making the final fourteen, and I was left out. It was a right sickener. I was too small. It didn't bother me, I was an inside-forward and I always scored goals.' Bob Bishop, United's Belfast scout, who saw the gift but wondered about the strength, has gone into folklore as the man who discovered the genius. 'That's not exactly what happened,' George recalls. 'A fella called Bud McFarland ran one of Belfast's most successful schoolboy clubs. He mentioned me to Bob. They thought I was

279

too small, so they set up a match against a team of lads who were a couple of years older than me, to see how I handled it. Our side weren't supposed to have a chance but we beat them and I scored a couple. That was it.'

He was offered a two-week trial at Old Trafford. 'I had just passed my final exams to be a printer. The idea was I'd come back and go into printing if things didn't work out.' George travelled to Manchester with Eric McMordie, another fifteen-year-old Belfast lad, whom he'd never met before they arrived to board the ship for Liverpool. 'We got a train to Manchester. The first thing that struck me was that nobody met us at Manchester, which I though they might have done as we were two kids away from home for the first time. We got a taxi from the station. When we got into the cab and asked for Old Trafford the driver said, "Which Old Trafford?" We nearly freaked out. We thought he was a nutter. We'd never heard of the cricket ground.'

They met Joe Armstrong at the ground. It was summer, boys were arriving at Old Trafford every day, some to start work as apprentice professionals, others, like George and Eric, for trials. You were insignificant. The place was huge, you felt small, embarrassed to be arriving with your secret dreams, your little case full of shirts and underwear, with your best trousers, carefully folded by your mum before you left home, neatly stacked on top of all the wordly goods you possessed. Your departure had been one of the most emotional days in your life and your family's. Your arrival was a non-event. Especially if you were on trial, hadn't cost a few grand or, in George's case, even a Miraculous Medal.

'Joe Armstrong met us at the ground. He introduced us to the Irish lads; there were quite a few of them at the time.' So there were: Harry Gregg, Jimmy Nicholson, Sammy McMillan, and Willie Donaldson, all from Northern Ireland. All seeming adult, self-assured, giants, composed and smartly dressed, fit, lean, at ease, belonging to this new world, everything you weren't.

'Joe took us to the digs, Mrs Fullaway's in Chorlton. We spent our first night there. We were both frightened to death. We weren't sure what was going on, it just felt strange. So we

280

had a chat and decided to see Joe Armstrong the next day to tell him we were going home.'

Eric was the most convinced that this was what they should do. George feels that if they hadn't been together they'd have stuck it out alone.

George's mum was delighted when he arrived home. Matt Busby got on the phone to find out what the problem was. Matt knew the feeling of arriving in a strange city with a little case and a frightened heart. He told Dickie Best that George was welcome to give it another go if he changed his mind. Two weeks later George came back, alone, to Mrs Fullaway's.

Boys from Northern Ireland couldn't sign as apprentice pros because of an agreement reached with the Irish FA designed to stop English clubs stealing the best young players from the native game. This deal sought to make it difficult for English clubs who were obliged to find proper work for the boy until he was seventeen when he could turn full-time professional. Like most football regulations this one made no sense and was widely disregarded.

The Apprentice Professional Scheme was one of professional football's New Ideas. Like all the other New Ideas this one was well intentioned. Instead of wasting two years 'on the brush', sweeping terraces, cleaning boots and scrubbing the dressing-room bath, or going off to work in a factory until they were seventeen, youngsters would start learning the game at fifteen, be imbued with the wisdom of coaches who would make players of them. George Best was denied this privilege: like Duncan Edwards, Bobby Charlton, John Giles and many other great players, he had to go to work in the real world for a while, losing out – or so it seemed – to the lucky fellows who spent their formative years in the pro game listening to men with ideas.

'I went to work for the Manchester Ship Canal Company as a tea-boy,' George explains. 'I hated it. I was just a messenger running around the place for anyone who wanted anything. We trained at the Cliff on Tuesday and Thursday nights with the juniors and amateurs. I wasn't very pleased about it because I hadn't come to Manchester to be a tea-boy. I stuck it out for a year.'

When he started training with the rest of us George made an

281

impression straight away. We had learned a trick or two, he still played the game as you would on the street. He was impudent, trying the kind of things you'd get away with on your own street against kids who couldn't really play. The dazzling little flicks, the nutmegs – poking the ball through their legs and skipping past their stupid, clumsy challenges – the mazy dribbles of your imagination, now made real in street or playground against kids who stumbled and fumbled desperately in your wake; past one, then another one, cut towards the goal, sell another dummy, shimmy past the last guy . . . then *bang* . . . into the back of the net. Except it wasn't a net, it was the schoolyard wall or the space between the lamp-post and the neighbours' garden-wall.

The first thing you learned as an apprentice pro was to forget that self-indulgent crap. This was the real world so you forget *your* little tricks and learn how to be a player. Every coach had his own idea of what being a player meant. They all agreed on one: it had nothing to do with childhood fantasies. The trouble with United in those days was – according to the sages in Busby's dressing-room – that nobody was thinking about the game, there was no coaching, it was a joke. The kids weren't learning anything. George was cited as a classic example of this. What a player he could be if someone got hold of him. But look at him!

When you looked, what you saw was a skinny kid doing all the things of street imagination. Nobody had told him that this wasn't on. So he nutmegged and dribbled, beat one man after another, then swerved the ball magically into the net, this net being attached to little five-a-side goals. Now he wasn't waltzing past clumsy kids on the street, but international footballers in a crowded car-park. The price usually extracted for this kind of thing was short, sharp and painful. You might be crushed against the railway fence, propelled into the concrete grand-stand wall or simply grounded on the cinder-strewn tarmac. Your flesh grazed, a bloody fire on your shin or thigh, the pain as intense as the embarrassment, you soon learned the lesson; don't try it on kid, the dreaming days are over.

Strangely, George was never caught. His body was frail but he possessed extraordinary flexibility of movement which enabled him to snake his way through a scrum of powerful bodies with the ball, impossibly, at his feet. His balance was perfect. He rode the most determined tackles comfortably. He was daring, an imp, certainly not a pro. He'd never get away with it on Saturdays. Nobody ever had. This was not what the game was about. There was a lot of talk about what the game was about at Old Trafford those days. And everywhere else. Organisation, efficiency, movement. Formations were coming into vogue: Alf Ramsey's 4–3–3, the Brazilians' 4–2–4, the Italians' sweeper system. These were the things football was about, they had to be learned, thought through, practised during the week instead of playing five-a-sides.

John Giles recalls a conversation typical of United at the time: 'We played Sheffield Wednesday in an FA Cup replay at Hillsborough one night. We'd drawn at home, '62 I think, and they were favourites to beat us. We won two–nil, Bobby and myself scored the goals. Mine came after a good move; I played a one-two with someone and got clear on goal. When we were coming home in the coach all the talk was about one-twos. "That's what the game's about," they were saying . . . "one-twos, give it and go" . . . it was rubbish. I'd just played the ball I saw, it was natural, you couldn't practise it or contrive situations where you'd learn creativity. You either had it or you didn't. If you had it nobody had to teach you how. You just did it. If you didn't have the instincts nobody could give them to you.'

George was quiet off the field. He was not noticed amid the banter of dressing-room life. He wasn't a lad. He wasn't coarse the way young men tend to be where they are together. George didn't swear. He was pleasant, laughed at jokes and piss-takes along with everyone else . . . but they were never his jokes and he was never the instigator of the piss-taking. We stripped in the Away team dressing-room, we'd graduated from the Ref's room. David Sadler, Jimmy Ryan, John Fitzpatrick and Bobby Noble knocked around with George. They were a mixed group. David and Jimmy were quieter types, the sensible tendency, 'Fitzie' and Bobby were lads.

George was always neat, trousers pressed, shoes polished, shirts clean. Most of us in digs were less attentive to appearance. We didn't have much money. Seven or eight pounds a week, four of which went to the landlady. After we'd sent a pound or two home and had a good weekend we'd be broke on Monday. Clothes were beyond our pocket. We made do. A bit of good gear for town on Saturday night – and match days – and anything you found near to hand most mornings. We tended not to hang our trousers up the night before. Shirts could last for three or four days. George took more care of these things. Appearance meant a lot to him.

He introduced shampoo and talcum powder to the Away team dressing-room. We'd wash our hair with the red carbolic soap cut in rough lumps by Arthur Powell for after training use. George would have Palmolive. And Silvikrin Shampoo. Also, in his little bag of toiletries, Johnson's Baby Powder, which he sprinkled lavishly over his skinny body with care while the rest of us were horsing around happy that the day's work was done. We were rough and ready. He, a touch refined but generous with money, good humoured, in no sense a goody-goody. Just gentler than most young pros are.

He arrived at Old Trafford a year after I did. During that first summer, '61, after he came back alone from Belfast, we took him dancing one Saturday night to The Plaza. It was one of his first nights out in town. The Plaza was still one of *the* places to go; Jimmy Saville was the Manager/DJ although he was about to open his own club, the Three Coins in Fountain Street. That first Saturday on the town we were twisting the night away to Chubby Checker. George never left his seat at the edge of the ballroom floor. Having been in Manchester a year I knew the scene, all the obliging girls. Manchester girls were very obliging, particularly if you played for United. There was a girl called Christine, a pretty little 'raver' in our terminology. I asked her to dance with George. He's just come from Belfast, I explained. She had a look. He was small, quiet, too small and quiet for Chrissie's taste. No way, she told me. I met her a couple of years later when every woman in Britain wanted to dance with George. She laughed ruefully and wondered if it was too late. It was.

After his début against West Brom, George was left out of the first team for four months. Busby had given him a taste, but as Wilf McGuinness explains, they were still worried about his size and strength: 'We knew George could play, but he was small and thin and we wanted to protect him. On Sunday mornings when we'd come in to have a chat about how things were going, the Boss would always ask about George. We decided to keep him out of the reserves, let him play in the "A" and "B" teams and the FA Youth Cup side which we thought was good that season. He was only seventeen and I think the Boss thought he needed another year.'

Back in the "A" team after his début George was worried: 'I found football easy in the "A" team but there were so many good players at the club I wondered if I'd even get in the reserves. For a while I thought this is a waste of time, that really every month I was at United was a bonus. I was playing inside-forward for the youth team. John Aston was outside-left and really I thought he was ahead of me. Bobby and Denis were in the first team, there was another lad called Phil Chisnall in the side at inside-forward. I couldn't see much hope.'

Despite the FA Cup victory and an encouraging start to the season, Matt Busby's authority was still being questioned by senior players. Setters, on the way, was not yet out. Noel Cantwell was club captain. Giles was gone, Bobby Charlton was still playing outside-left but not well enough to hold his place in the side, according to the thinkers. Harry Gregg conveys a sense of that period: 'There was a lot of talk about Bobby. Nobody disputed his talent but they said he was brainless, didn't know how to get in the game. Yet he was in the England side and the fans loved him.'

The notion that Matt Busby shared his senior players' opinion about Bobby Charlton, but was afraid to offend United's supporters by dropping him may seem preposterous. The fact that they believed this indicates his standing in their eyes at the time. Another glimpse of the chaos behind the scenes as United evolved through this period is provided by Gregg's memory of a pre-match break at the Norbreck Hydro in Blackpool prior to the 1963 Cup Final: 'We were having a few beers one night early in the week. I'd been left out of the side after the semi-final and there was a lot of piss-taking along the line of: "Don't worry, Harry, reserves are welcome to have a drink with us." Shay Brennan and Gilesy were the two worst mickey-takers. But it was in good fun. A singsong started that night. Matt and Jimmy were over in a quiet corner of the bar. Paddy Crerand sang "Kevin Barry" (an Irish rebel song) and young Sammy McMillan, who was in the squad and came from Belfast, sang "The Sash", a Protestant song about the Battle of the Boyne. When Sammy finished, Paddy threw his glass of beer in the kid's face. "The Sash" was like a red rag to a bull for Paddy with his Glasgow Catholic thing. But he was completely out of order, we'd only been having a laugh. The Boss saw the whole thing but never said a word.'

Later that night Harry kicked a hole in the door of the room Brennan and Giles were sharing after they'd made one joke too many about the big goalie's reserve team status. This time Busby did react strongly after a complaint by the Norbreck's manager. Pre-Munich Busby would have acted after the first incident involving Crerand and McMillan. Now he had mellowed somewhat, on the surface at least. This was all the denigrators saw. Mistaking patience for weakness. And, adding his forbearance of misbehaviour to the *laissez-faire* nature of footballing matters at Old Trafford, some influential dressing-room figures came to the conclusion that he was 'gone'.

15

Gone!

'If I walked past him and he smiled I
felt I was in the presence of a
superhuman being, which he was,
still is to me.'

George Best

News of Matt Busby's demise hadn't reached the new crop of youngsters at Old Trafford. 'The Boss' was as revered by us as he'd been by the 'Red Devils'. Like Duncan Edwards, Bobby Charlton and Nobby Stiles, George Best felt a buzz every time Busby was around: 'If we were playing a Youth Cup match I could feel his presence in the stand. I played for *him*,' George recalls. So did Nobby, still the fan for whom the red shirt meant everything, and Tony Dunne who'd seen the Munich team play in Dublin against Shamrock Rovers and now thought he was living a dream with a Cup winner's medal in his possession as well as a regular place in the first team. Tony was now playing left-back. Shay Brennan was at right-back, a good footballer, a Busby-lover, who stayed his distance from club politics.

At Christmas 1963 things seemed bleak for George Best. He hadn't played again in the first team since September. His prospects seemed grim when youth team coach Wilf McGuinness told George that he could go home to Ireland for the festive season. It was bad news if you were allowed home for the holidays. The message was that you weren't even required for the reserves. The first team were due to play Everton at Goodison and Burnley home and away over Christmas.

United lost 4–0 at Everton. On Boxing Day Burnley slaughtered them 6–1 at Turf Moor. Busby sent for Best. The phone call to Belfast shocked George. He was on the next plane. On 28 December he played outside-left in the return fixture with Burnley. United won 5-1. George was sensational. He scored a goal but it was the magical reproduction of his car-park genius that signalled the arrival of a startling new talent in the English game. Bobby Charlton moved inside to centre-forward that day, the beginning of the end of his existence on the margins of Matt Busby's teams. Bobby was one among many convinced that Best was special after this performance: 'John Angus was playing right-back for Burnley marking George. John was a good pal of mine, we came from the same part of the country. John was hard, and fast. He'd kick you, he was like an oak tree and brave. George murdered him, stuck the ball through his legs, turned him inside out. We'd heard about this great young player in the youth team but I'd no idea he was this good. There were so many you'd hear about, who were going to be this or that, but could never do it in the first team. I don't think John Angus ever really recovered from that match.'

That was it. George stayed in the side, on the right or left wing for the rest of the season. He'd leap-frogged the reserve team. United went on to finish runners-up to Everton for the title, and, for the first time since 1956/57, win the FA Youth Cup. George played inside-left for the youth team who attracted 27,000 to see them clinch the trophy against Swindon at Old Trafford.

George Best's life was transformed during the hectic months in the first half of 1964: 'I was stronger, especially my legs. I found first team football easy. There were so many good players: Denis, Paddy, Bobby, Nobby, Tony Dunne. I never felt any pressure. The Boss would say, "Keep it simple, go out and enjoy it." I did.' The stricture about keeping it simple was not applied to George. But it was still the founding principle at Old Trafford. In George's case a more relevant virtue of football as Matt Busby conceived it served: keep it natural.

'We weren't fancied to beat Manchester City in the FA Youth Cup,' George remembers. 'They had a good side. We played them in the semi-final, home and away, we won both legs. We drew at Swindon and beat them 4-1 at home. David Sadler scored a hat-trick. Those few weeks were the turning point for me. After the City game at Maine Road I was picked to play my first international for Ireland – against Uruguay in Belfast. That whole period was like a dream.'

The youth team went to Zurich for the annual international tournament. George got drunk for the first time on this trip. 'We headed into the city on the last night, we were going to hit all the bars. There was David and myself, Fitzie, Bobby Noble, Jimmy Ryan and two Manchester lads, Eddie Harrop and Dave Farrer. Eddie and Dave were big lads, they could drink, pints of lager. I had never drunk in my life, neither had John Fitz, we both got pissed. Fitzie was worse than I. I had three pints of beer, that was all it took. It was amazing, just pints of beer. I couldn't drink a pint of beer today if you paid me. The main problem we had was getting back into the hotel without the Boss or Jimmy spotting us. They used to sit in this little bar across the street from the hotel: the Boss, Jimmy, Jack Crompton, Wilf, and I think Louis Edwards was with them.

'I remember us being in a taxi and I was hanging my head out the window. I was going to be sick. The taxi-driver said he'd double the fare if anyone threw up in the cab. We got him to drop us off around the corner from the hotel. Eddie and Dave got on each side of Fitzie and me trying to hold the two of us up. We got in somehow without being seen. They dumped Fitzie in the bath first – to sleep it off – then they got me into my room. It was my first experience of a moving room. I thought I was going to die. I didn't have another drink for about three years.'

Manchester United had finished strongly in the League, and reached the FA Cup semi-final and the quarter-final of the European Cup Winners' Cup within twelve months of staring relegation in the face. The Wembley victory of 1963 had proved a turning point. Humiliation by Sporting Lisbon in the second leg of that quarter-final Cup Winners' Cup tie was the low point of an otherwise profoundly encouraging season. United won the first leg comfortably 4–1 at Old Trafford. Lisbon was regarded as a formality. Denis Law hit the post in the opening minutes, after that it was backs to the wall all night. At the end Sporting led 5–0. This tie was George Best's first experience of European competition. Busby, rarely angry in the post-match dressing-room, showed his emotions on this occasion. Two players, Maurice Setters and Phil Chisnall, a clever skilful inside-forward of whom Busby held a high opinion, were doomed by this dismal performance. Setters played only eight more League games for United before being sold to Stoke for £30,000. His departure allowed Nobby Stiles to claim a regular first team place at last. Chisnall played once more before being sold to Bill Shankly at Liverpool for £25,000. In the close-season Busby signed John Connelly, the English international winger from Burnley, and Pat Dunne, a goalkeeper from Shamrock Rovers. Connelly who cost £56,000 proved a superb buy.

Fast, strong, skilful and brave, Connelly played forty-two League games the following season scoring fifteen goals. Manchester United won the First Division Championship from Leeds on goal difference. Season 1964/65 saw the birth of a great side which will be remembered as long as soccer is played. Over the next four seasons Manchester United staged a glorious last stand for virtues to which Busby's whole football life had been dedicated.

English football was poised on the brink of its Golden Age, when, for a few years, men, great and close to greatness, competed for the game's most coveted prizes. England won the World Cup in 1966, a victory for Englishness as personified by Alf Ramsey, one of those who'd come to management with new ideas in the years when Busby was deemed to be 'gone'. Ramsey's way was one of many, he only one of many influential men during that period.

At Leeds Don Revie was creating another potent force which was to evolve from nasty negativism to grandeur of a kind in the years to come. Bill Shankly, Matt's passionate pal, had produced a great Liverpool side and at Maine Road Joe Mercer, another close friend of Busby's, was about to join forces with Malcolm Allison from the old West Ham Academy to build a championship-winning team of style and vigour.

Before this decade was over Everton, with Kendall, Ball and Harvey in midfield, would also emerge, Arsenal destined to win the Double in 1971 were in embryo.

In the Golden Age between the mid-Sixties and mid-Seventies one saw a fusion of great forces, a new breed of capable, charismatic coaches and managers, the inheritors of the power Busby had gained for those charged with the responsibility of putting teams on the field. The pioneering radical who had fought to define the role of the modern manager was now challenged by men whose right to impose themselves and their ideas, existed, primarily, because of the respect Matt Busby had won for professionals. Thus, Ramsey, Revie, Shankly, Mercer, Allison, Catterick, Nicholson, Clough, Howe, and Bertie Mee, Ron Greenwood at West Ham, Tommy Docherty at Chelsea, and in Scotland Jock Stein at Celtic who in 1967 were to become the first British club to win the European Cup. For the first time the power vested in the football club manager was wielded not by one or two but by a generation of extraordinarily capable men, their talents widely dispersed across the map of the Football League. Their philosophies varied, dynamic personalities and fertile minds were the common denominators.

Without players of commensurate talent these men of powerful conviction could not give expression to their conflicting ideas. In the mid-Sixties a generation of great players emerged to bring professional soccer to vibrant life in its Golden Age: Law, Charlton, Best, Stiles and Tony Dunne at Old Trafford. Giles, Billy Bremner, Norman Hunter, Bobby Collins at Leeds, soon to be joined at Elland Road by Terry Cooper, Peter Lorimer, Eddie Gray, Paul Madeley and Alan Clark.

At Anfield Shankly's vision materialised through Ian St John, Ian Callaghan, Roger Hunt, Tommy Smith and Ron Yeates. Manchester City had Colin Bell, Frannie Lee, Mike Summerbee. At West Ham Bobby Moore, Geoff Hurst and Martin Peters, three of England's World Cup winning side, sought desperately to keep their club abreast of the First Division challenges. They failed. In another age any of those teams might have prevailed to dominate the English game.

The Chelsea of Osgood, Hudson, Peter Bonetti, David Webb, McCredie and John Hollins was infinitely superior to the Chelsea of 1954/55 which won the Championship with the lowest number of points in history. Yet Osgood's Chelsea never came close to a championship, although they managed to win the FA Cup in 1970.

The powerful leaders and wonderful players were the two

elements which compounded to give this era unique splendour. Footballers of talent were fitter than their counterparts before them had ever been and more technically accomplished than the generation of players to follow. Thus, for a few years conflict was rendered vigorous *and* beautiful by a historical convergence of talent, contrasting philosophy and distinct personalities.

What once sufficed to lay hands on the Championship and the FA Cup was no longer enough. English football required more of its pretenders during these years than had ever been demanded before. English football between 1965 and 1975 was about many things. Every quality essential to sport at its most enthralling found expression in that era: great talent; passion; team play at its finest; the gifts of great individuals harnessed to a single cause; athleticism, pace, power, aggression; the absence of self-indulgence. Added to those positive elements were the darker realities of professional soccer which are just as real as its glorious potential: aggression rendered ugly, a means of vicious intimidation; the wicked leg-breaking tackle; the maliciously lingering boot, studs, a painful weapon, their use perverted by swift assassins like Hunter, Giles and Collins of Leeds, Arsenal's Peter Storey, McCreadie and Harris at Chelsea, Tommy Smith at Liverpool.

The removal of the maximum wage in 1961 also had a profound effect. For the first time professional footballers felt that their achievements would be reflected in their wage packets.

Despite all that had passed before, it can, I believe, be argued that the Manchester United team of 1964–8 came closest to reflecting the people, places and experience which had formed the man who sent it out to play. Football for Matt Busby, as for Mattha, was about the spirit. At its most glorious, football transcended the ordinary, the material. There was no formula, just people, expressing themselves through this tantalisingly simple medium. Football's properties – imagination, courage, grace and wit – were God's gifts, belonging to the humblest person, be he in Orbiston, Manchester, urban ghetto, mining village, the slums of Naples or the *barrios* of South America.

Set against the influences that formed Matt Busby, the

composition of his last great side offers a fascinating insight, showing the degree to which in his most trying phase in management he sought survival through the kind of people he trusted and knew best. Of the six bought players in the Championship side of '64/'65, four were Scots, one Irish and if you stretch the point, John Connelly, the Englishman from Burnley, was of Irish descent.

David Herd, son of Matt's old golfing partner Alex, contributed twenty-three League and FA Cup goals. Denis Law, the modern Hughie Gallacher, scored thirty-one goals in major English competition. Paddy Crerand, Busby the player reincarnated, was the magnificent orchestrator of midfield, controlling the rhythm and direction of United's attacking play. Pat Dunne in goal, bought for a modest £30,000, was in the bizarre tradition of Busby goalkeepers, occasionally inspired, often competent, never completely reassuring.

The rest of the squad was reared in the United family and of its ethos: Nobby Stiles, Collyhurst Catholic, a fan who played with the guts of Jimmy Murphy and the football wisdom of Busby; Nobby, the quintessential Mancunian, earthy, passionate and privately warm and modest; Shay Brennan, Manchester in another guise, the gambler, handsome, night-town man, his Englishness doused with Irish charm; Bill Foulkes, the miner who'd never really left the pit, taciturn, dependable, the block of granite in the bejewelled showcase, a surviving 'Red Devil'; Tony Dunne, Irish, clever, Dublin, one of Billy Behan's greatest discoveries, the best defensive left-back in a generation of outstanding quality; then Bobby Charlton, the kid from Mrs Watson's, another son of a mining village, a 'Red Devil', a Busby loyalist who had sacrificed four seasons of his footballing life without demur to serve United's cause which was life itself to him; on the fringe for the Championship season, David Sadler, elegant, in bearing and manner, a cut of the young Busby on the Merseyside tram before the war, the decent, intelligent, well-behaved model professional of Busby's imagination; John Aston, son of Johnny, showed enough promise to travel with the first team; John Fitzpatrick, a Scot, played a couple of games; Noel Cantwell, on the margins, though still respected by Busby, also played twice.

And then there was George Best, Irish, Protestant, the iron-turner's son from Belfast, who shared the values that had made United great in the past. Busby was his inspiration. Life's simple pleasures, digs, bowling-alley, snooker hall, cinema, the world of Chorlton. Manchester's innocent pleasures were for George as for the 'Devils', a glimpse of paradise in these teenage years. Zurich was exotic, football at Old Trafford with Busby looking on was heaven.

Footballers as people first, that was Busby's secret. Even the oldest of these men were boys to him. His job was to facilitate their development as human beings, their innate talent would then blossom. That was his formula.

The Championship was bitterly contested through the spring of 1965. Leeds and United drew clear in the closing weeks. In the FA Cup the two clubs were due to meet in the semi-final. This was United's fourth consecutive semi-final appearance. The first game at Hillsborough degenerated into a brawl. Leeds were ugly, spiteful, malicious, bent on intimidation. There was some irony here. Revie had not been a tough player. He was most remembered as the deep-lying centre-forward in the mid-Fifties Manchester City team which attempted to copy the Hungarians.

When he got the manager's job at Elland Road, Revie made a great public show of travelling to Old Trafford to seek Matt Busby's advice. Busby stressed the importance of a family atmosphere at a football club. This principle was acceptable to Revie who repeated it *ad nauseam* for years, and Leeds did become a caring club, caring, that is, about their own. Players in trouble, Billy Bremner being the most notorious, but not the only one, could always seek help and understanding from Revie. Flowers were sent to pregnant wives, a Christmas party was thrown for children of the Elland Road staff.

People were treated like human beings, but this value did not extend to opponents on the field. Revie didn't initially have the players to play the way Matt Busby believed you should, so football as played by Leeds was a war of attrition. That's how they clawed their way out of Division Two and immediately became a force in the First Division. Busby could pass on the relatively simple virtue of family, but courage and wisdom, the rare qualities that were fundamental to the creation of Manchester United, were not transferable.

Don Revie was a new thinker. Taking charge of Leeds he decided, as Alf Ramsey had at Ipswich, that with the players at his disposal success would more likely be gained by stopping others playing. When John Giles arrived at Elland Road in 1963 he was astonished – and heartened – by the difference between Revie's club and Busby's. The United he had left was at its lowest ebb: 'It was a huge transformation for me,' John recalls. 'First of all the spirit of the club, between the players, was great. Also the attention to detail. The first Friday morning I arrived they were actually talking about the next day's game. I liked it straight away. The atmosphere was different, people were consciously thinking about the game, small things like throw-ins, free kicks and corner-kicks were discussed and planned. People were intent on doing *something*. It wasn't all left to chance. I'd never known anything other than Old Trafford, but this felt right to me. I thought this is what you should be doing.'

The training was also different. Syd Owen and Les Cocker assisted Revie. They were new thinkers from the Lillishall Centre for Football Thought where a new breed of coach was learning what the game was all about. 'Everything we did at Leeds had a purpose,' Giles explains. 'The training sessions were much shorter and sharper.' He agrees there was a lack of respect verging on contempt for the game of the Forties and Fifties. 'We talked about the sloppiness of defending, full-backs allowing balls to be knocked inside them, letting wingers free, not being on the cover. What we wanted at Leeds was organisation. Properly organised, the good players would be better, the poor players – which we had a few of at the beginning – could at least be functional. Basically we would cut down the goals against and win games scoring fewer.

'Manchester United had great players, we didn't at that stage. So we paid more attention to detail, concentrated better for ninety minutes.' Bobby Collins was, Giles admits, 'a huge influence' because of his attitude and 'competitiveness'. Collins was a wonderful footballer in the Scottish tradition with a streak of malevolence in his soul. Standing five feet four inches, Collins was the most feared midfield player in England.

Thus, the scene was set for the semi-final brawl of 1965. The result, 0–0, was secondary. Football was outraged by the behaviour of both teams in what was judged the most ill-tempered semi-final for years. Busby and Revie shared the blame for allowing matters to get out of hand. Referee Dick Windle booked only two players. Denis Law scuffled with Jack Charlton. Law's shirt was almost torn off his back. Bobby's brother, Jack, did not belong to – or agree with – Leeds's malignant tendency. Collins, Giles, Hunter and Bremner were the warriors. Law, Crerand and Nobby Stiles didn't turn the other cheek. George Best, injured, missed the Hillsborough battle and the replay which Leeds won 1–0.

'We were gutted,' Nobby Stiles remembers. Out of the FA Cup, United now focused on their Championship contest with Revie's team. There were seven League games to go, and Leeds were favourites. The semi-final victory gave the new men a critical psychological edge. 'We went to Blackburn three days after the semi-final,' Nobby recalls. 'I always wanted to play, but I had no heart for it that day. Denis was the same, and Paddy; George was injured. Blackburn were a good side, Ronnie Clayton, Bryan Douglas. I remember walking on the pitch before the match and thinking the whole season could be over today. Bobby was the one. We had three world-class players in that side, for me Bobby was the best. He covered everything that day at Blackburn. He played them on his own, his spirit lifted us. People talk about his ability, but this was down to guts. We slaughtered them, 5–0. Bobby scored three. A fortnight later we went to Elland Road and won 1–0.'

United won six of those last seven games, losing only at Villa Park on the last day of the season when the Championship was already claimed.

I left Old Trafford that summer. This mattered little to anyone but me. The manner of my departure illustrates Busby's sensitivity to the smallest detail of Old Trafford life. He was 'The Boss' of old once more. I had been a promising youth team player but was neither strong enough nor good enough to make further progress in this born-again football club. I asked for a transfer. The Boss saw me in the office. There was a saying that nobody ever made it after leaving Old Trafford. This was an article of United faith. Busby reminded me of this. Players are desperate to come to Manchester United. They don't choose to leave. He'd reminded John Giles of the same fact of football life. As I was hardly going to make it in Manchester United terms I wondered why he bothered in my case. But he did. He wanted me to stay another year. I, concealing my awe, remained firm. There was a good reason for doing so. Noel Cantwell had marked my card. Birmingham City, then a First Division club, wanted to sign me, and Joe Mallett, City's Manager, was a pal of Noel's. He'd offered £8,000 for me, all I had to do was convince the Boss I wanted away. In the end I managed, politely, to hold my ground. The following week Matt sold me to York City, newly promoted to Division Three. The fee was £4,000. At Birmingham I might just have developed to disprove the adage that there was no football life after United. That was a long shot. York was safer from the club's point of view. I wouldn't come back to haunt him as John Giles had at Leeds. This was the kind of detail Matt Busby paid attention to. He was a hard man all right.

The summer of 1965 was George Best's last taste of normal life. He was famous in Manchester already, twelve months on his name would be known around the world. Fame was on the way. For now George lived contentedly with Dave Sadler in Mrs Fullaway's. Dave and Mrs Fullaway's youngest son, Steve, were George's mates. 'We just did normal things,' George somewhat wistfully recalls. 'We didn't really go anywhere special, we couldn't afford to.' Life was geared to football. 'After Wednesday we didn't go out. We used to play cards for pennies with Mrs Fullaway and Steve. I never dreamt of going out. Maybe the odd time for a game of snooker on Thursday, but not out as such.'

Out as such meant the bowling alley, the Temperance Snooker Hall in Chorlton or Steve's working man's club for a game of darts. John Spencer, later to become world snooker champion, eked out a living hustling punters who fancied their chances in the halls around Manchester. The Temperance Club was one of Spencer's haunts, and George was one of his favourite mugs. George was a good snooker player, the best of the footballers. Spencer always beat him on the black ball. First giving George fifty up and just pipping him. Always just scraping home on the final colour. The starts increased, sixty ... seventy ... eighty. The result was always the same: George parted with the money. A fair proportion of United's wages ended up in John Spencer's wallet. This was George's vice.

David Sadler remembers those days with great fondness: 'We were compatible. He was very bright, only interested in football and I mean that. He was easy to talk to. We could be in the same room for hours on end, playing cards, reading, not necessarily even talking to each other. But we were comfortable together. The club scene wasn't my thing, it wasn't George's either. It was bowling-alley, snooker or cards in the digs. That was it. He had no appetite for drink or gambling. The Boss hated the serious gambling so we just played crib or aces to kings for fun.' On the road George and Dave shared hotel rooms. All passion was spent on the game.

The European Cup was Manchester United's target in 1965/66. They remained a force in the League, eventually finishing fourth to Liverpool. Yet another FA Cup semi-final ended in disappointment when United lost 1–0 to Everton. Subconsciously everything focused on Europe. Munich was evoked in newspapers, but never mentioned within Old Trafford.

United progressed comfortably through the opening two rounds, then drew Benfica in the quarter-final. The Portuguese champions had been in four of the previous five European Cup Finals, winning twice. They were impressive though not invincible as Real Madrid had been. Eusebio was Benfica's great player, wonderful everywhere, a deadly striker on goal, a lover of the spectacular. He lacked the raw competitiveness, the hardness, of the truly great, but Eusebio on song was formidable. Coluna, Torres and Agusto were other fine Benfica players. In the first leg at Old Trafford, United took a 3–1 lead. Inspired by Eusebio, the Portuguese snatched a second and almost a third. One goal was little to take to Lisbon where Sporting had inflicted a 5–0 hiding a couple of seasons before. Benfica were a different class.

On 9 March 1966 Manchester United destroyed Europe's best side 5–1 in Lisbon's 'Stadium of Light', silencing the

298

75,000 crowd who watched in disbelief as their team was taken apart. Within minutes the tie was settled, George Best scoring twice, his second goal the stuff of fantasy, defenders lying in his wake, the 'keeper lured and passed, the ball guided insouciantly to the net. Harry Gregg, who'd suffered a severe shoulder injury that would finish his career soon after, played in goal that night: 'I never knew the team come together the way we did against Benfica. George was incredible but everyone played great. It was the perfect display of football,' he claims.

Manchester United were renowned again in Europe. The next morning United made the front page of most British newspapers. Their spectacular triumph had a resonance beyond the world of sport, for the memory of the Munich Air Crash eight years before lingered in the nation's heart. The image of the team that died was evoked, the club, so tragically stricken on 6 February 1958, had emerged from its grief to stride gloriously once more across Europe. The style, epitomised by George Best, was, as before, un-English: the new Busby Babes, as United were misleadingly tagged, were cavalier rather than stolidly British, vivacious, original and brilliant where other English sporting heroes had been no more than doggedly efficient. If the 'Red Devils', brashly confident, had been the precursors of Britain's cultural revolution of the late Fifties, the liberation of the young and gifted from the austerity of the post-war era and the conservative mores of previous generations, George Best now became, overnight, a symbol of the Swinging Sixties. Returning to Manchester the day after Lisbon, George was photographed wearing a sombrero as he descended the aircraft steps. The picture made the front page of Friday's *Daily Mirror*, the caption 'El Beatle' depicted him as no British sports hero had ever been before – the professional footballer, not as modest hero, but as pop star, 'the fifth Beatle', young, handsome, sexy and free. No slave had ever been this way before. A new image of professional football was cast at that moment. George became famous. Everywhere.

The Britain of staid tradition was no more. Carnaby Street, the Beatles, the Rolling Stones, Mary Quant, David Bailey, Terence Stamp, Twiggy, the icons of the new age were now joined by George. He was a celebrity. George became Georgie, no longer a back-page star, instead, a suitable subject for profile on the woman's page, in feature articles. Modelling the latest line in Sixties gear the lithe, athletic, dark sensuous figure was vital and authentic, striking, in a way that no male model could dream of matching. The transformation was instant in the manner of that age.

George was, perhaps, the most authentic hero of those years and paradoxically the least equipped for the fame he now experienced. A great athlete, he was, unlike many of his celebrated Sixties contemporaries, substance rather than shadow. Football was accessible to millions for whom Twiggy, the Stones and Mary Quant were mere names, the source of their celebrity vague and rather questionable. They were merely famous, George was the scorer of goals, the conqueror of muscular pursuers of malicious intent. Those dubious of other decadent manifestations of this liberated age, the haters of longhairs and mini-skirts, people who clung to the straight and narrow, who despaired of sexual promiscuity, could adore George Best. He was a footballer, the boy-next-door, a safe, morally acceptable fantasy for women, the man other men had dreamed of being, fellows who had never dreamed of being Beatles or Stones. George was a man of action, his talent, like his personality, easy to identify with.

The new superstar was nineteen, living in digs at Mrs Fullaway's in semi-detached Chorlton, getting high on penny games of crib, snooker and darts. 'That night changed it all,' George confirms, 'life started to become crazy.'

But first life became difficult. George tore his cartilage in a League game. The injury not immediately diagnosed, he played against Partizan Belgrade in the first leg of the European Cup semi-final in the Yugoslav capital five weeks after the humbling of Benfica. United lost 2–0. 'The Yugoslavs were terrified of us,' Harry Gregg claims, 'they'd read of the mighty Manchester United back in all our glory. They were mesmerised by the very name and that's how they played in the first half. But we were terrible. George played with his leg strapped up. He wasn't fit, yet he was still our best forward. Partizan were a different team in the second half, they realised they'd overestimated us and began to play.'

300

The calculated risk of playing George failed. He finished the game hobbling, a passenger on the left-wing. Gregg blames Busby for this defeat: 'Our team talk was the usual, go out and enjoy yourselves, play it as it comes. That's what we'd always done. We made no adjustments, which you have to do in the away leg of a European tie.'

The Yugoslavs did not make that mistake in the return game at Old Trafford: 'They were well drilled, physically and psychologically prepared to defend,' Gregg explains, 'they were able to adapt tactics to the needs of that particular situation.' Thirteen minutes from the end of a bruising, scrappy encounter which Best, his cartilage problem now identified, watched from a seat in the stand, United pulled a goal back through Nobby Stiles. A frantic final drive ensued, but no more goals. United were out of Europe. Busby was as usual philosophical. 'He was sick, we all were 'cause we knew we should have won on ability and chances, but he just shrugged his shoulders and smiled that resigned smile of his. I felt sorry for him,' Gregg recalls.

Gregg's criticism of Busby's approach to European competition is legitimate. A certain adjustment was required in the away leg of these ties for, relying on talent and spontaneity, United took no account of the fact that the opposition were bound to be more aggressive and inspired before their own fans and were bound to set out to kill the game away from home. The point about adapting psychologically was particularly relevant in the context of the humiliation inflicted by Sporting Lisbon in 1964 and to a lesser degree to their defeat by an ordinary Partizan side in Belgrade. Busby was culpable on both occasions but time would show that he had learned his lesson.

Money, the perennial problem at Old Trafford, caused a major dispute once more as England prepared to host the World Cup in the summer of '66. On this occasion Denis Law was the rebel. Remarkably, five years after the abolition of the maximum wage, no Manchester player was close to earning the magic £100 a week Tommy Trinder had awarded his beloved Johnny Haynes. The going rate at Old Trafford was half that amount, the club's renewed pre-eminence notwithstanding. Law had proved an outstanding acquisition, his brilliant goal turning the '63 Cup Final and the twenty-eight goals he scored in the Championship year being equally decisive. Denis was known as 'the King' by the Stretford End, a sobriquet deserved not just for the goals but for his ability to lift the side's spirit with electrifying interventions at critical moments in a game.

When his contract expired Denis decided to ask for a substantial rise. The public showman was privately taciturn, self-possessed, watchful, intolerant of fools. He rarely socialised except on Saturday nights when he and Diane went for a meal with Paddy Crerand and his wife. Denis was an Aberdonian, canny, unlike Crerand the genial Glaswegian, or Busby off-duty who enjoyed the gregarious company of the Cromford Club on a Saturday night. This was not Denis Law's scene. Nor did he care for publicity – journalists were always kept at arm's length. No colourful quotes fell from his lips. There was a considerable gap between the extrovert at work and the introverted private man. Even in the dressing-room he left the talking to others. He was his own man, popular but a member of no faction.

Denis conveyed his wage demand to Busby in a letter: 'To be honest, I didn't fancy facing him in his office, so I left the note with Ken Ramsden in the secretary's office,' Denis explains. He then went to Scotland for his family holiday. Ramsden, Les Olive's assistant, passed the letter to Busby.

'I was in Scotland when all hell broke loose,' Denis ruefully recalls. 'The press were on to tell me I'd been put on the transfer list. Next the Boss was on the phone telling me to get back to Manchester straight away.' Denis had imagined he was in a strong bargaining position. Right was also on his side. United were still the lowest payers in the First Division, with Shankly's Liverpool, champions for the second time in three seasons, similarly renowned for meanness.

Busby had phoned the Press Association on receipt of Law's demand. No player is bigger than Manchester United and Law will be on his way if he persists in his demands was the message which made banner headlines in all newspapers.

Arriving at Old Trafford, Law was greeted stonily: 'He was stern. You've caused a lot of problems for this club, he told me, a lot of heartache. Nobody's going to hold Manchester United to ransom. Then he reached into his drawer and pulled out a typed apology which he told me I'd have to read at a press-conference he'd called for later that morning. We'd always got on well. But he was a hard man . . . and crafty. He said he was protecting the wage structure at the club. But we did a deal which nobody knew about. He told me that if I apologised in public for the trouble I'd caused he'd give me half the rise I'd asked for. So I went out and ate humble pie.'

Far from causing Busby 'heartache', Law's letter was a godsend to the Boss. Rebellion about wages was perpetually simmering in the Old Trafford dressing-room. The side was full of international footballers' well aware of the money players at other clubs were earning. United were getting away with murder. The force of Busby's personality was the weapon. Law's challenge to the system did not provoke the anger implicit in Busby's public response. On the contrary, Denis had provided an opportunity, which Busby eagerly grasped, to relay a message to other putative dressing-room rebels: don't even dream of trying it on. If the King is dispensable anyone is. Denis, for his part, kept quiet about his increased salary, and began the following season the best paid player on United's books. Ruthless, clever and pragmatic, Busby's concern was for Manchester United. Other clubs could afford to indulge their one or two exceptional players; United, with a dressing-room full of outstanding players, could not afford to satisfy them all.

Alf Ramsey had promised that England would win the World Cup in 1966. He honoured that pledge. The nation celebrated. Football became even more fashionable. The sense of a nation revitalised was confirmed by its footballers' defeat of West Germany in a thrilling Wembley final. England was not any more George Melly's land of 'punitive conventions, austerity [and] grey uniformity'. The spiritual revival John Osborne had angrily demanded seemed to have taken place. The English were winners. Ramsey's team had restored self-respect to the national game. 'The best game in the world' was no longer an idle boast.

Ramsey did not, however, satisfy everyone. Although the consensus within the game was that he had done a marvellous job, dissenters were numerous and vocal. Many of us felt that the price paid for victory was unacceptable. The charge levelled at Ramsey was that he had sacrificed skill and imagination in order to win. Assailed by virulent rhetoric, Ramsey – soon to receive the first knighthood awarded to a Slave – affected indifference. A warm, respected and knowledgeable football man in the privacy of the dressing-room, Ramsey shared the professional's contempt for the media. His public persona – the stilted, monosyllabic language, the shadow of impatience on his face as he listened to questions formulated on the basis of received wisdom – compounded the impression of him and his football values as narrow, conservative, a denial of what was most inspiring in the game. His defence was that England had won. But why not in style his critics persisted? The style of Manchester United, Spurs or Liverpool.

The answer is obvious on reflection: England didn't have the services of the great Celts, like Law, Best, Mackay, Bremner, Giles, Blanchflower, and all the others of that ilk whose flair fertilised the great English League clubs, creating an illusion as to the true nature of English football. Ramsey had nothing against brilliance of the kind his critics alluded to, he simply didn't believe England possessed players capable of fulfilling the glorious aspirations of those who damned him. Alf Ramsey was an Englishman. His World Cup winning team applied the traditional English virtues of discipline, resilience and stomach for conflict, personified by Nobby Stiles, to the task in hand. Winning.

Alf Ramsey was eventually vilified out of office. George Best is one of those who identify the World Cup victory as the beginning of English football's Dark Age: 'After 1966 the game stopped being a pleasure, the fun went out of it,' he claims. Denis Law disagrees: 'I was one of the people who mistakenly blamed Ramsey. He wasn't the problem, it was the people who copied him who are to blame.'

Ramsey was a thinker with a first-class football mind. The problem for the game was the second-raters for whom the formula invented by Ramsey, to make the most of the talent at his disposal in order to win the World Cup, became the means to lesser ends.

Although ostensibly of little consequence to Manchester

United, England's World Cup success did affect the lives of four men at Old Trafford. Bobby Charlton returned to the club, his place in football history ensured by his magnificent performances embellished by unforgettable goals in England's hour of need against Uruguay and Portugal. He was a greater player, more certain of his powers for the experience. Nobby Stiles was similarly confirmed. His real stature had never been doubted by Busby or his colleagues at Old Trafford. The public caricature of Nobby the Destroyer was an outrageous underestimation of his true talent. In fact he never kicked as such, never went over the ball in the wicked manner of the game's real destroyers. He projected aggression and occasionally mistimed tackles to spectacular effect. His true qualities were virtually impossible to identify unless you were out there alongside him. Given a man-marking job to do he was an unrelenting foe. The skills required for this task were mental rather than physical, and concentration was the key. Cover every move, wear your man down psychologically. Break his spirit, not his leg. Thus Ramsey had deployed Nobby to neutralise Eusebio in the World Cup semi-final. Busby was persuaded to set that kind of task for Nobby: 'Let's make it a ten-a-side today,' was the order if the circumstances required it. Nobby was a guaranteed deliverer.

But that was only one of his gifts. He was a superb reader of the game, assessing danger to make critical interventions which looked easy from the stand. In a team which instinctively reflected the Boss's taste for fantastic self-expression he was the watchdog when United didn't have the ball. When the gifted were self-indulgent Nobby remonstrated with them, using invective to remind Law, Best and Charlton what this fucking game was also about: marking at corner-kicks, picking-up at throw-ins and battling for the cause to the bitter end. He was a consumate professional with unfathomable depths of spirit, real football intelligence and, behind the frantic gesturing, a cool understanding of the ebb and flow of the game around him. He could also play a bit.

Off the field Nobby was a quiet man, with a goonish sense of humour and generous nature. His nickname 'Happy' was an affectionate allusion to Nobby's ability to project disgruntlement when the job demanded it. The snarling character of international repute was a role he played, a necessary affectation. Someone had to be the 'Baddie', the joke in the United dressing-room concerned the gap between perception and reality. Nobby's giggle was one of the most recognisable sounds on coach or train or minutes after the most intense encounter on the field.

If not exactly an unsung hero, Nobby Stiles was a truly great footballer as essential to the team as the men whose names – Law, Charlton, Best – evoke the memory of Busby's last great days. The World Cup completed Nobby's education, and he returned to United with an honours degree in the art of containing international forwards. This final move from distinction to greatness was not, however, reflected in Nobby's wage packet. With the England team he discovered what others less well-endowed were earning at clubs United always expected to beat. He also knew that he was one of the lowest-paid players in Manchester United's first team. Mindful of the Law row, Nobby decided against a similar confrontation. The Boss did not offer a better deal.

Wilf McGuinness also benefited from that World Cup summer. Wilf's success with United's Youth Cup team had won him the job of managing England's youth side. A member of Alf Ramsey's staff, he helped behind the scenes as the England senior team prepared for the World Cup. At twenty-eight he was uniquely experienced for a professional of his years. Busby's remained in most respects the seminal influence on Wilf's thinking about the game, but Ramsey had also impressed him. He returned to United believing that a balance could be achieved between football's two fundamentally conflicting philosophies; self-expression and team organisation. He thought, as many did, that what Matt Busby preached could be reconciled with the new thinking Alf Ramsey had imposed on the successful England team.

Although not directly involved, George Best was the player most dramatically affected by England's triumph. England's most famous footballer was a convenient medium through which to explain and exploit the sport that had captured the nation's imagination as England won the cup. Millions of people had been moved by the World Cup drama. They didn't know much about football but they knew what they liked. The academic arguments about Ramsey and 4–3–3 were meaningless to the nation at large. English success could not be gainsaid. For most, George Best equalled soccer, and he was deluged with offers of all kinds, commercial and personal. His agent, Bagnal Harvey, handled the business. George took care of the personal.

George had always liked girls. He didn't talk dirty about women or come on like a stud, but he never passed an opportunity by. His friendship with Jimmy Ryan, the closest pal to him apart from Dave Sadler, had foundered when George stole his pal's beautiful girlfriend. One night at a party George and the girl went missing. He was seventeen. Three years later he and Jimmy still weren't speaking and any dull morning at Old Trafford could be enlivened by winding up one or other of the two Romeos. Lisbon changed everything for George. Girls were the most welcome thing in his life. After the World Cup a better class of lady became available to him. Beauty Queens and models were his speciality.

It was rather difficult to pursue this hobby living in digs. Going to the bowling-alley, which he still loved to do, also became complicated: 'Wherever I went people recognised me, which was fine. Then I started getting hassled, serious stuff, guys wanting to fight, in pubs, even restaurants. I was in an incredible situation. I was getting ten thousand letters a week so I had to employ three girls just to answer the mail. I was driving a Rolls Royce, going out with Miss England and living in digs.' Mike Summerbee and George became good pals. Summerbee had recently joined Manchester City. 'Mike and I decided to get a secret flat. I ended up leading a double life, half the time at Mrs Fullaway's and the rest of the time in the flat.' United didn't allow single players to live alone. Digs were the order of the day. The Beatles would never have stood for it, and George resorted to subterfuge. But never after Wednesday.

One thing never changed. George Best remained in awe of Matt Busby: 'I never bothered about money, I was earning enough outside the game anyway. When my contract was up I just signed a new one for whatever he offered. Playing was still

307

the greatest thing in my life. I never worried about a match. I was strong then, particularly my legs. There were a lot of kickers in the First Division: Chopper Harris, Hunter and guys like that, but they didn't bother me. I remember one game against Chelsea. I'd gone past Harris in the box and he took a whack at me. It was a definite penalty and although I was knocked off balance and nearly fell, I can remember thinking in that split second; don't fall, if you stay on your feet you'll score. Which I did. I suppose it was pride, I didn't want to give him the satisfaction of stopping me. The best way to sicken him was to keep going and score.'

Dave Sadler testifies to George's extraordinary courage: 'Well at that time he was a complete man. He was so brave, so strong in comparison to his size and build. If he got injured he'd still play. In my opinion he was without doubt the greatest player I ever saw or played against.'

George still played for Matt Busby: 'If he wasn't at a game for some reason, if he was ill or away watching a player I'd be disappointed. He never said much after a game, "Well done son" would make me feel great. In fact the best compliment he ever paid me was to say I was the best tackler in the club. "Sometimes I'm frightened for you," he said.'

By Christmas over one million people had watched Manchester United play. England's World Cup victory had drawn a vast new audience to League football. Best, Law, Charlton and United were the star attractions. By April a million people had passed through the turnstiles at Old Trafford alone, and United's average home attendance was a post-war club record of 53,800. The huge crowds were not disappointed.

The 1966/67 season began unspectacularly. Alex Stepney, bought from Millwall for £52,000, was the new goalkeeper. United lost three of their opening seven games, and Busby began to experiment. John Connelly was sold to Blackburn. George Best moved to outside-right, John Aston replacing him on the left wing. Dave Sadler took David Herd's place at centre-forward. Shay Brennan was dropped; Tony Dunne took the number two shirt and Bobby Noble, a member of the '64 Youth Cup winning team, won a regular place at left-back. The inclusion of Noble at Brennan's expense was significant. Shay was a footballing full-back in traditional Busby style. Bobby Noble was more the defender: tough tackling, quick, with fire in his belly.

This small compromise was Busby's only material concession to the orthodoxy of those times, the view that destroyers were essential if you were serious about winning. But Busby's mood had changed. He accepted that United had been a soft touch, too easy to play against when they didn't have the ball. The notion of keeping 'clean sheets' and getting a point away from home, the tenets of the new rational age were foreign to him. However, the change from Brennan to Noble reflected a shift of emphasis which was psychologically more profound than the new name on the team-sheet allowed. As a result United were a sterner proposition away from home.

The Manchester United team of that season will be remembered as long as football is played. Those who saw them rejoice in the memory of spectacular goals, defences torn apart by the glorious virtuosity of Denis Law, George Best and Bobby Charlton. The defences humbled by United's attacking play bore no resemblance to their counterparts of previous generations. The most revolutionary development in the post-war game was in the art of defending. Teams defended in numbers. Defenders were athletes, terriers where once they'd been collies. The area defenders set out to protect remained the same size; they were more numerous and infinitely more formidable than their predecessors who had faced the 'Red Devils' a decade before. The balance of football power had shifted in favour of the negative. History proves that this change was fundamental and irrevocable.

Set in this context, Manchester United's Championship victory in 1966/67 ranks as one of the greatest achievements in the history of the game. In a new world they won in the old style. They lost 2-1 away to Sheffield United on Boxing Day, but after that they remained unbeaten in the League for the rest of the season, conceding only twelve goals in twenty matches. The decisive Championship game was played against West Ham at Upton Park where United won 6-1 against a team that contained three World Cup players, Moore, Hurst and Peters, had won the European Cup Winners' Cup in 1965 and reached the final of the same competition in '66. After this performance Busby paid tribute to his team: 'This was my greatest hour.' United had taken a 3−0 lead after ten minutes. The title was theirs. What followed was described by the critics the following morning as the finest display of football seen in England since the war. Of the team which produced this perfect celebration of all the disciplines in the game only three cost real money. Alex Stepney, Paddy Crerand and Denis Law were the exceptions. The others − Best, Sadler, Dunne, Stiles, Foulkes, Brennan, Aston and Bobby Charlton − had graduated from Busby's School of Excellence, the car-park at Old Trafford. Bobby Noble, another from the academy, missed the last three games of the Championship season. A car crash, two hundred yards from his Stockport home, had brought his career to a tragic end. He survived, alas disabled for life. Bobby was a lovely, typically earthy Manchester lad, whose fate cast a shadow over United's season.

A fortnight after United's Championship victory, Glasgow Celtic beat Inter Milan to become the first British club to win the European Cup. Celtic's manager, Jock Stein, had much in common with Matt Busby. He had worked down the mines until his mid-twenties and shared Busby's romantic vision of football as played by James and Gallacher and their Wee Wembley Wizards. Jock loved the horses too. He gambled less furtively but with no more success than Matt. Their shared success in the summer of 1967 seemed a good omen for the kind of football Busby and Stein adored with equal passion.

For Manchester United the final emotive challenge awaited: Europe. Winning the European Cup was not, as many claimed, an obsession for Matt Busby. He didn't like the inevitable references to the past whenever United were engaged in Europe, and Munich was never mentioned in the Busby household. According to Sandy Busby he got annoyed when people mentioned the crash. Not even Jean could raise the spectre of that dreadful day. 'He never talked about Munich or the lads who were killed,' Sandy confirms. 'We never knew if he blamed himself.'

Europe was not a crusade for Matt. United initially accepted the challenge of the Champions' Cup for pragmatic reasons.

First he wanted experience for his young team. He believed in playing matches, practice matches, five-a-sides, friendly matches, all were better than training. There was no substitute for games. That's where you learned your craft. The better the opposition, the more you were tested, the more you learned. For that reason more than any other Matt defied the Football League in 1956. There were other reasons. He had a large squad with more quality players than he generally needed. European Cup football allowed him to blood young players in real competition, the better to prepare them for the First Division. Money was another incentive. The great European club sides packed Maine Road and Old Trafford. Seventy-five thousand people watched United play Borussia Dortmund at Maine Road on 17 October 1956. The 'Red Devils' had drawn 20,000 fewer people to their League game at the same venue the previous Saturday.

Those were the football reasons for Europe. There was, however, something else: Matt's own love of style, the kind of grandeur offered by the floodlit setting of a European night, the pomp and circumstance, the graciousness, the mutual respect, the contrast between all of this and the drab unction of an English Saturday afternoon. To this ritual Matt was attracted, the ceremony attending his beloved football.

The reasons for going to Europe were many, Matt's taste for adventure not the least significant of them. If he felt guilty about the crash, this was why. In his character there were conflicting spirits, always. One was responsible, modest, conforming to the everyday necessities of ordinary life. This fellow lived in Kings Road, Chorlton, in semi-detached comfort, an extraordinary place for a man of his spiritual dimension to be confined. This modest Matt continued to live in Kings Road when most of the journeymen professionals who drifted through Old Trafford in years, shortly to come, inhabited small mansions in fashionable Cheshire. The other Matt, more circumspect, but no less real, was a snappy dresser, a gambler, fascinated by the larger stage, the glamour of Hollywood, at ease in the luxury of a great ocean ship or a grand hotel, attracted to the exotic in that peculiar Scottish way. Those closest to him respected him as he really was. They never imagined he was simple.

United conceded just one goal on the way to the semi-final of the European Cup in 1968. They played it tight away from home against Hibernians of Malta – a 0–0 draw being enough after a 4–0 victory at Old Trafford – and the same scoreline was sufficient in Sarajevo to ensure progress if they beat the Yugoslav champions at home. Goals from George Best and John Aston saw them through to the quarter-final against Gornik Zabrze of Poland. Brian Kidd, an eighteen-year-old Collyhurst lad, scored for United in the home game, the Polish defender Florenski knocking another past his own 'keeper to give them a two-goal cushion for the second leg. Kidd, from St Pat's, the same school as Nobby Stiles, Wilf McGuinness and Paddy McGrath, was in the side for Denis Law who had been suspended for six weeks in October 1967, his third lengthy suspension since returning from Italy. Denis had been sent off along with Ian Ure for fighting in a League game against Arsenal at Old Trafford. He and Best were particular targets for the assassins without whom no First Division team felt properly equipped to counter the great attacking players of that age. Ure, in fairness, was no kicker. But Denis had a tendency to strike back at the enemy and ask questions afterwards.

United had a poor disciplinary record, the most common of their crimes being retaliation. Busby was criticised for not dealing with this problem, criticism that was generally accompanied by a claim that in Nobby Stiles United possessed their own hit-man. The reality as viewed from Busby's office was that Nobby's aggressive posturing could not be compared to the clinical wickedness of men like Peter Storey of Arsenal, Hunter of Leeds and their less renowned counterparts in the First Division, Duncan Forbes of Norwich being one such dangerous character whose crimes escaped back-page opprobrium. As for Law, Busby didn't approve but there was no way he was going to inhibit a player whose combative spirit was the essence of his game.

Law had another more pressing problem. Although it was not yet apparent, Denis was to miss most of United's critical games that season with knee trouble that was defying diagnosis. He would contribute only seven League goals as United attempted the historic Double of Championship and European Cup.

Gornik managed only one goal on an icy surface in the return leg of the quarter-final, and United progressed to meet Real Madrid in the semi-final. The League Championship had, by the New Year, developed into a four-club contest. In early January, United led Liverpool by three points at the top, with Leeds and Manchester City also in contention. That lead stretched to five points before injuries to Bill Foulkes and Nobby Stiles allowed the chasing pack to close on United. The most remarkable aspect of United's season was the confirmation of George Best as perhaps the greatest player the post-war era had produced. He was more tightly marked than ever. The euphoria of his early seasons had dissolved. This left Best's pure genius. In Law's absence he grew to occupy the large void the Scot no longer filled with his inspiring presence. Taking the number 10 shirt for much of the season, George scored twenty-eight League goals and made as many. He was now dating Miss United Kingdom and the hassle was increasing by the week. But his football was unaffected. When people question George's place in the history of the game, a video of the football he played in season '67/'68 will show all that is best in soccer brought to spectacular realisation, grace and athletic purpose forming an exquisite blend.

United beat Real 1–0 at Old Trafford. Denis Law played; Best scored the goal. Francis Burns, another Scot from the car-park who had established himself at left-back, played in this game but was dropped in favour of Shay Brennan for the return leg in Madrid. Denis Law was not fit to travel. A one-goal lead seemed insufficient.

The team United fielded in the Barnabeu Stadium contained only two bought players, Alex Stepney and Paddy Crerand, if you discount Tony Dunne who was a boy reserve when first acquired from Shelbourne for £6,000. In an attempt to protect the one-goal lead Busby played David Sadler as an extra defender in midfield. Brian Kidd and George Best played alone up front. Overwhelmed by a brilliant Real performance, United were 2–0 down, defending desperately when Zoco put through his own goal to give them heart. The relief was temporary. Amancio, Real's brilliant international forward, responded to the unique rhythmical fervour of the Madrid audience by teasing United's defence, a dying, desperately flailing bull to his matador, to score contemptuously. Real left the field, regally, at half-time, 3–1 ahead and sure of their place in the final.

United's dressing-room was like a morgue. It was the old story, Lisbon and Belgrade, a different script, the same denouement. Busby said little. He was sick. Having seen Benfica beat Juventus 2–0 he believed that this semi-final tie against Real would decide the destiny of the Champions' Cup. The final against Benfica at Wembley would surely not be lost.

Bobby Charlton recalls those moments: 'They had won the game. I'll always remember going in at half-time and the old man was speechless. I'd never known him speechless before, even Jimmy said nothing. We were gutted. Hardly anybody said anything, I remember thinking there must be something, someone must talk but nobody did. We were waiting for the Boss or Jimmy but they were down. I was trying to convince myself that it wasn't the end of the world, all the things you try to dredge up to console yourself when you know you've gone. Then someone said, "We only need one goal to get a replay in Lisbon." Someone else said, "Let's have a go." That was all.'

Busby told David Sadler to get forward whenever he could. George Best was having a hard night: 'The guy marking me, Sanchis, was a great defender. I could beat him but he always got back goalside. I was having a stinker really. Sanchis was only a kid but he was one of the best defenders I've ever played against.'

United got back to level terms in the tie when David Sadler made it 3–2 on the night. Charlton explains: 'Dave half headed it, the ball clipped his heel and crept over the line. But really the second half was down to them. I think Real thought teams don't come back from 3–1 in Madrid. After Dave scored they started to panic. This gave us heart. They started moaning at the ref, appealing for everything. They were gone, different players from the first half. I remember thinking of a few of them, "You wouldn't get in our side, not for attitude." '

Morale decided this game. United simply wanted it more. There was no inspiring half-time oration from Busby or Jimmy

Murphy, no telling words of wisdom. They were 'gone' in the vernacular of the game. But they had done their work over the previous twenty-three years. The esprit de corps of the car-park, the deep unarticulated sense of values and experience shared, bonds first formed in the 'A' and 'B' teams, the FA Youth Cup and similarly daunting moments in Zurich where the 'bottle' factor often saw them through against European opponents who wilted at a certain temperature, these were the resources which in the end proved decisive on this historic night. The commodity now brought into play could not be bought.

With less than fifteen minutes to go George Best received a throw-in from Paddy Crerand. United had their replay, in Lisbon, but it was no longer enough. Real, a different breed, had packed it in. Best ran at Sanchis and Zoco. George was back in the car-park. So was Bill Foulkes who loved to get among the goals in five-a-sides. Bill strode into Real's penalty area. Bobby remembers wondering what the hell Foulkesy was doing running past him: 'I couldn't believe it. Bill had never gone into the other team's box except for dead-balls.'

George was past Sanchis, past Zoco. Now from the goal-line, he laid the ball in the path of a red shirt: 'I just remember seeing a red shirt,' George recalls, 'I pulled the ball back, looked up and saw big Foulkesy – of all players – and he hit it in the top corner.' Nobby Stiles organised the resistance in the final twelve minutes.

Busby cried in the dressing-room afterwards. His players had honoured him. For many lesser men than Matt football was only a game. For him it was his life. Football had rescued him from grief in childhood, from the filth of the coalface in adolescence. Football had not been, for Matt, about winning or getting rich. The game was a glorious escape from loneliness and squalor. Football was his faith. Defending his divine conviction Matt Busby was hard, ruthless and, when necessary, cunning. He was no intellectual, rather a man of instinct. He was a loner, always had been, behind the various façades . . . genial . . . team player . . . club man . . . *pal*. He never used the word friend. There was a difference between a pal and a friend. Harold Riley, the most perceptive of Matt's pals remarks: 'Pal is a word he used very often . . . and in the most affectionate way.' Pal is a loner's word. Nobody, except Jean, Sheena and Sandy, was closer than a pal. Jean was his friend. The rejected child, the most poignant of life's outsiders. Matt had understood her in Bellshill when they met as kids, because the death of his father had left him outside too.

Matt understood one communion – only one – which reached the core of men's spirits bringing them together for a while: football. For all the talk of camaraderie among miners the General Strike of 1926 had brutally unveiled a shocking truth about the brotherhood of friendship. His trust in football never wavered. The ruthless enforcement of the Manchester United ethos was necessary because he knew how ephemeral the bonding process was.

And he knew that all the great players were that because football meant as much to them as to him: everything. The task of managing such men had consumed him. His was an outsiders' club. The individual mattered, could find sanctuary in his club. Most of United's great players had been loners . . . Edwards, Carey, Rowley, Whelan, Viollet, Charlton, Law and George Best. He was what they had in common, he and United. Football.

The goal created from the disparate gifts, and spirits, of George Best and Bill Foulkes in the Barnabeu Stadium can be regarded as good fortune or a mystical fusion of all the instincts and experiences of Matt Busby's life. For a few extraordinary seconds when he was 'gone', Best, the genius imp, and Foulkes, the dour coalminer Busby had plucked from the pits of St Helens, came together to rescue United. Popular Bill, the quintessential loner didn't have a pal, much less a friend, at Old Trafford. Bill was not one of the lads, too dour, too bluntly honest, no glib sense of humour. He'd seen too much of the coalface to laugh easily.

George was less obviously but more profoundly alone. His was the magic of Busby's childhood dreams. Two outsiders, beauty and filth, George and Bill: Busby's life in microcosm. It was a strange glorious night.

Denis Law was forced to miss the European Cup Final. His knee problem had been diagnosed at last, revealing that he had a piece of cartilage in there, the residue of an operation he'd undergone at Huddersfield ten years earlier. He watched the Wembley game from his hospital bed. United fielded the same side as in Madrid against Benfica:

Stepney

Brennan   Foulkes   Stiles   Dunne

Crerand   Charlton   Sadler

Best   Kidd   Aston

George Best remembers little of the game, except the feeling of disappointment: 'I was looking forward to the match. I'd imagined ninety minutes of pure magic, I thought we would hammer them. But I only played in snatches. Bobby scored a header to give us the lead but we still weren't playing well. I don't know if it was the tension.'

Neither team played well. Charlton's glancing header was beautifully judged, though he could never remember scoring with his head before. It was weird. The night was weird. John Aston was the outstanding player on the pitch, producing a memorable performance he would never again match. Ten minutes from time Benfica equalised. The goal was curiously predictable. Torres, the giant Portuguese centre-forward climbed above United's defence to glance the ball to Graca who levelled the scores.

Lying on the pitch waiting for extra-time, Nobby Stiles remembers Busby: 'He said exactly the same as Alf in '66, "If you pass the ball to each other you'll beat them." It was desperately humid. The other thing that lifted us was the sight of them. They were like the Germans, knackered.' Nobby had known the worst moment of his football life in the closing minutes of normal time: 'I'd been man-marking Eusebio but I got drawn towards a loose ball which was poked past me leaving Eusebio clear on Alex. He went for the glory, tried to break the net.' Had he remained composed, Eusebio would have finished United. Alex Stepney held Eusebio's powerful blast.

George won the European Cup for Manchester United with a classic street-game goal. Fastening with razor reflexes onto a

317

loose ball twenty-five yards from goal, he beat one man, then another, then rounded the desperate 'keeper before gliding the ball deftly across the turf into the empty net: 'It was like something from *Roy of the Rovers*,' he recalls, a smile of wonder lighting his face. Brian Kidd and Bobby Charlton scored two more goals to finish the Portuguese. Charlton's goal, a delicate touch, the ball spun on a teasing curve, beyond the 'keepers pawing reach, was, like the story it brought to a climax, incredible.

No coherent memory of that night exists. George can't remember where he went or what he did in the hours after the game. Bobby Charlton had fainted after the semi-final in Madrid. Now he collapsed again in his hotel bedroom: 'It was worse this time than in Madrid. When we got back to the Russell Hotel, Johnny Berry and Kenny Morgans were there, and the families of the Munich lads, and I thought, great, this is going to be brilliant. I went upstairs with Norma to get ready. I was sitting on the bed waiting for her and she said, "Right, let's go down." When I stood up the blood seemed to drain out of me. I tried five times but I couldn't get up. I lay on top of the bed in my clothes and felt fine, but every time I reached the door I was gone again.'

Downstairs, Joe Loss and his Orchestra played for the guests at the banquet. Nellie Busby and Jimmy and Agnes Matthie were there from Old Orbiston. Matt's sisters, Delia, Kathy and Margaret as well. So were Duncan Edwards's parents. Duncan, someone said, would have been thirty-one on this night. Matt Busby sang 'What a Wonderful World'.

David Sadler's memory is the clearest: 'I remember back at the Russell looking at Bobby and the Boss, they both looked drained. The Boss looked very old, which he had never seemed. There was a sense that this was the end of something momentous, there really was a sense of that and it was almost immediate, not something that came days or weeks later.' Another thought struck Sadler, a notably cool and observant man: 'I wondered if there was anywhere to go from here, even in defending the cup . . . I don't know . . .' his voice, for once uncertain, trails off. John Aston thought it was 'a strange night'. Glorious, but strange.

16

Wonderful World

'Matt had a phobia about the family.
He was too loyal to old employees. I
think that was his weakness.'

Billy Behan

Matt Busby was knighted by the Queen in the summer of 1968.
The previous autumn he'd become a Freeman of Manchester.
In February 1969 a Gallup poll identified Sir Matt as the seventh
most admired man in Britain, though the people who voted in
the poll didn't know very much about him. He had never been
on a chat show, books and profiles of him offered no clues to his
real character because he simply told the same few ancedotes to
everyone who came looking for his story. When pressed he
would refer to Manchester United and the achievements of his
teams: that, he would say, was the only memorial he wanted.

So it was for a notion of Sir Matt Busby that Gallup's
interviewees voted. There was a montage of images, the story
of his club by which he was known: Munich, Bobby Charlton,
George Best, the gracious, genial image of Sir Matt himself and
the grand style of his teams. Courage, tragedy, style, achievement, an admirable decency of behaviour – that was what
people voted for. Reality was unusually faithful to the image.
But not by any means the whole story.

By February 1969 Britain's second football knight (Sir Alf
Ramsey had been honoured in 1966) Manchester's first sporting
Freeman and Britain's seventh most admired man was in a trap.
Professional soccer had produced many outstanding men, but
Sir Matt Busby was the only *great* man, in the fullest sense of
that description, ever to emerge from a sport that had changed
little since Billy Meredith's time.

The circumstances Busby now found himself in illustrate

319

professional soccer's endemic sickness. He had announced his retirement from team management in January eight months after Wembley. Speculation raged as to who would succeed him. He had decided that question but not yet announced the name. The most immediate dilemma was what to do with himself.

Sir Matt was touching sixty. Although he looked old the night United won the European Cup he possessed a strong constitution. He felt vigorous by any standards, remarkably so for a man of his years who had been through so much. Alas, for all he'd achieved he owned nothing except his semi on Kings Road, Chorlton. Busby had always earned good money. Since 1967 he'd been on £10,000 a year with a ten-year contract. But he was generous to his family, his mother in Scotland, his son Sandy whom he'd helped set up in a bookmaking business, and daughter Sheena whose husband, Don Gibson, had just eighty-eight League games in six seasons after leaving Old Trafford. Matt had also gambled quite heavily.

On retirement to the position of General Manager of United, Sir Matt was assured of a salary for the foreseeable future. He would be treated like any other employee, better perhaps, but still an employee. He couldn't become a director of the club he had built as Football League rules decreed that directors couldn't be paid and shareholders were restricted to a dividend of five per cent which yielded a mere £100 a year to Louis Edwards, by now in effect United's majority shareholder. So, you could wield power in football *or* earn money. This was professional football. Power could only be vested in the game's ruling class, the small-time merchants who liked the reflected glory and petty boardroom politics which enlivened the otherwise dull existence of a breed of very dull men. This was 1969, yet professional football had stood still since the Edwardian era, as deformed in the new Britain as in the old.

Sir Matt Busby was a professional. If he wanted to wield power in the institution he had created he would have to live without income. If he wanted material reward, Football League rules determined that some kind of sinecure be devised for Sir Matt Busby, Freeman of the City, Britain's seventh most admired man.

Power was what interested Sir Matt. A clever man, he had

devised his own means of keeping control of Manchester United. He had 'his' director, Louis Edwards. 'Champagne' Louis was Matt's surrogate, groomed from the time they'd first met backstage at the Opera House. Louis was, Matt thought, perfect for the role. The butcher wasn't as close to Matt as Paddy McGrath, Johnny Foy or Willie Satinoff, but his closest pals were unsuitable for one reason or another. Paddy the nightclub owner was wrong for the same reason as Johnny the bookie. The images, nightlife and gambling, were wrong for Manchester United. Willie Satinoff was clever and popular, but he was his own man and Matt wanted someone who would belong to him. Louis was perfect. Amiable, willing to listen, anxious to serve the man he so admired.

In the Manchester United saga Louis Edwards has traditionally been depicted as the villain, but Louis was no villain. He was a nice man, a classic 'Billy' in the argot of the dressing-room. Billy Bunters, Punters, there were good ones and pains in the arse. Louis was OK. He was a bit gauche and physically clumsy, but Louis was generous, bought the lads a drink, and he wasn't a snob. Depending on who you talk to, Matt's director was 'a big soft lump', the Boss's 'lap-dog' who 'hung on Matt's every word'.

Most importantly, Louis was not Harold Hardman. Hardman, Busby's chairman, was of the Gibsonion school of directors. Straight as a die, bright as a button, tough as they make them. Hardman never succumbed to Matt's charm. He respected his manager, but expected respect in return. Hardman always unsettled Busby. Basically the chairman questioned things in a rigorous manner. For Matt, a creature of impulse and instinct when it came to football matters, the boardroom as debating chamber was a nuisance. The Tommy Taylor transfer illustrates the point. Taylor had played only forty-four League games when Busby decided to break United's transfer record to buy him for £29,999. Hardman was uneasy about the gamble. He demurred again when Albert Quixall arrived for £45,000, another record-breaking purchase.

Harold Hardman had been a player, and *that* was the problem in Busby's view. He had an opinion. The worst kind of director was the man who thought he knew.

Louis Edwards came along at the right time. In the Fifties when Matt and he became acquainted, Hardman was proposing to bring a new director on the board, claiming that United needed fresh blood at boardroom level. Gordon Gibson was the name Matt heard. He knew Gordon Gibson, and he was horrified. Gibson was a former referee, a sometime visitor to Old Trafford to train with the players on a Sunday morning. He had opinions about the game. Harold Hardman multiplied by two. No thanks. Enter Louis Edwards.

Louis did as he was told. The expensive players bought after Munich: Quixall, Cantwell, Setters, Law, Crerand, Herd, were all gambles. This was not the Gibson/Hardman way. Louis tipped the boardroom balance in Matt's favour.

They did a deal. Their pact was made in the early Sixties, the 'Bollock Chops' era when Busby was at his lowest ebb. At Busby's bidding Louis set out to gain a majority shareholding in Manchester United. This was a tricky business, time-consuming, a touch delicate, but by no means impossible if tackled the right way. There were just over 4,000 shares of which Harold Hardman owned twelve, the Gibson family 1,762, the rest scattered around Manchester in small batches – sometimes a single share – belonging to people whose forebears had contributed in United's hours of need in past decades.

In 1962 Louis began his task by getting a copy of United's share register. Then he employed a rather dubious local Conservative councillor, Frank Farrington, to knock on doors, many of them, buying up the shares. Alderman Farrington had form. Louis knew him through dealing with the Council to supply meat to schools and other municipal institutions. In respect of this the Edwards meat empire was, like all other municipal suppliers, dependent on the good will of fellows such as Alderman Farrington. Good will came at a price. Louis was a nice merchant. But he was a merchant.

Within eighteen months he'd bought enough shares – forty-four per cent – to give him effective control of United. Hardman made a half-hearted attempt to resist. But the straight-as-a-die solicitor knew he was beaten. Through his brother Douglas, and brother-in-law Danzil Haroun, Louis stitched up the business the year United won the FA Cup at Wembley.

In the year of 1963 owning Manchester United was about power not money. It was, indeed, a costly indulgence. Louis Edwards spent £41,000 in the service of his old pal Matt. Louis Edwards was a most unusual 'Billy'. Lap-dogs don't come more obliging. Matt was in the driving seat. Other professionals, his pals, Bill Shankly and Joe Mercer, marvelled at his shrewdness. The old fox had beaten the system.

When Harold Hardman died in 1965, Louis Edwards became chairman. He had no power or influence, but he was chairman of Manchester United. As part of their deal Louis and Matt agreed that their sons, Martin Edwards and Sandy Busby, would in time become directors of the club.

This was how things stood when Sir Matt Busby decided to retire in January 1969. Louis suggested Sir Matt take a testimonial game. Busby thought not. No professional manager had ever had a testimonial. Players on the odd occasion availed themselves of this windfall. But Busby's natural modesty set him instinctively against the unprecedented celebration which a testimonial match would inevitably entail. Besides it might rain on the night. Power mattered far more than money.

The solution to the money problem was agreed; Sir Matt was given a twenty-one-year-lease on the small souvenir shop United had opened in 1967. He paid £2,000 for the Red Devils shop with a nominal rent of £5 a week to keep things right. The deal was to be kept quiet.

When Sir Matt Busby announced his retirement in January 1969 the football world buzzed with speculation about his successor. Don Revie, Jock Stein, Jimmy Adamson, Dave Sexton, these were among the more credible names mentioned. Revie had no chance. The Leeds manager's much advertised visit to Busby when he first got the job at Elland Road was a source of deep embarrassment to Matt. Leeds were the antithesis of everything Busby believed in.

He was interested in Sexton who'd taken over from Tommy Docherty at Chelsea two years before. Sexton was decent, modest, intelligent and dignified, but tentative inquiries

323

revealed that he wasn't interested. His kids were at school. He was a family-first man.

Guided by instinct, Busby had always favoured one of his own kind. Years before he'd thought about this moment, thus, Johnny Carey and Noel Cantwell were offered coaching jobs at Old Trafford. Both Irishmen chose managerial power elsewhere. Busby briefly considered Paddy Crerand, his own type in almost every respect, a Scot, a Catholic, a family man and a lover of good football, but Crerand was still playing and had no experience.

That left Wilf – a Collyhurst lad with coaching experience who loved the club and understood its values. Wilf McGuinness's record as United's youth team coach was excellent. True, he'd won only one FA Youth Cup, but the players kept coming through: Best, Sadler, Noble, Burns, Kidd, Aston, all had been nurtured by Wilf. But there were two reservations about Wilf: his lack of experience and his temperament. On the first count Busby was reassured by the fact that he would be around to cope in areas Wilf knew nothing about: players' contracts, transfer market dealing and meetings of the Board. The question of Wilf's temperament was less easily resolved. McGuinness was a very passionate man. He was not cunning. On the contrary he was an open book. Well, almost open. For nearly ten years Wilf had run with the hare and hunted with the hounds. Always one of the lads at heart, he had tried to reconcile his ladmanship with his coaching job. He played in five-a-sides, drank in the 'Quad', played cards on the coach and involved himself in the banter and pranks of dressing-room life.

This was a balancing act of considerable proportions, and sometimes Wilf fell off the highwire. There was the occasional 'incident' in the car-park five-a-side when Wilf got stuck in. He wanted to win. He'd been a digger as a player. He was still a digger on the car-park. Sometimes people dug back, fists were raised. The conduct was unbecoming of a coach. However, within the family this was a minor matter. Wilf was a good lad – unquestionably in the young players' minds, less certainly to certain influential older players.

First team players in the 'Quad' were wary of Wilf. Some

thought he was a sneak. He wasn't, but that's what they believed. Busby knew this. He knew everything.

Wilf lacked the gravitas of a Carey or Cantwell, but he didn't lack courage. He'd tried to make a comeback in United's Championship season '66/'67: 'I was training with the Laws, Charltons and Bests, I got involved in the five-a-sides, that was my outlet. I still had the dream. I thought I could play again. After the World Cup I went to the Boss and asked him if I could have a go.' Busby consented.

'We worked the insurance thing out,' Wilf explains, 'If I got in the first team they would pay the money back.' His first reserve team game was at Maine Road. United won 4–1. He played thirty games in the reserves that season, and was selected as twelfth man for the first team at Leicester: 'None of the buggers would get injured. I put the Championship down to me,' he jokes. 'I was pushing them from behind.'

One day Matt called him into the office. He was keeping a good young player, John Fitzpatrick, out of the reserves. It was make-his-mind-up time: keep playing but quit your coaching job, or give up and stay on staff. 'There was no way I was going to risk leaving Old Trafford, so I quit.'

McGuinness had been courageous to the point of foolhardiness. His leg had never been right – you could see the tortured gait when he ran – the comeback was fuelled by astonishing courage and will power.

The bookies opened a book on Busby's successor. Revie was favourite, Wilf 6/1 fourth choice. The appointment was not made efficiently. When Busby announced his retirement in January, United were sixth from bottom of the First Division. No successor was appointed at that time. Busby allowed two months to pass. He wanted to be sure United avoided a relegation struggle. Once survival was assured, McGuinness would get the job. He said nothing to Wilf.

Billy Behan knew six months before that Wilf was the man. Behan was one of Matt's closest confidants. Ireland, a special place, was where he felt most at home. 'Matt had a phobia about outsiders,' Behan confirms. 'He didn't trust anyone outside Old Trafford. It really was a family to him.' The period during the early to mid-Sixties, when he all but lost control of

United, reinforced a deeper mistrust of outsiders in the family. Harry Matthie had come as just such an outsider into young Mattha's cottage half a century before. Power vested in Mattha, shared with his first pal, old Jimmy Greer, had, thus, been lost. His fascination with power was almost as old as he was.

Wilf's first clue about the job came in the form of a pointed remark made by Billy Behan. The next inkling came on 8 April 1969 when Les Olive joked that he should wear a tie the following morning. Sir Matt Busby had called a press conference to announce the identity of Manchester United's new manager.

Wilf told a few of his mates to take the 6/1. He thought he was in 'with a shout'. Just a shout. Two hours before the press-conference Sir Matt sent for him: 'He didn't ask me whether I wanted it, he just said "You're the one." He even made it sound as though he'd picked me.'

'We will call you Chief Coach for a start,' Sir Matt informed McGuinness. Busby would be General Manager. Wilf's salary would be £80 a week from £36 a week as youth team coach. The title Chief Coach would protect him from the media, but all team business would be in his control. His contract would be for three years. Wilf was in a daze, but the words 'three years' were the most important Sir Matt uttered. Three years was enough time to do the job. A couple of hours later the eyes of the football world focused on him. Wilf McGuinness was the new Boss of the most storied football club in Europe, in the world. The torch had been passed on. Wilf grasped the lighted end.

He was completely unprepared. He wasn't sure of anything – except the three years. Who would discuss contracts with players? Who would buy and sell? He understood he'd pick the team and run the day-to-day playing business, but the rest was fog. At thirty-one he had his heart's desire, the details could be sorted out later.

Busby, then plain Matt, had defined the modern manager's role. Now he redefined it to create in the club he'd made great the kind of circumstances for his successor which he would never have tolerated. Nobody understood better than Sir Matt Busby the ultimate truth of football management: *everything* in a football club reflects on the field of play. If the manager doesn't control everything the job can't be done. That was why he confronted James Gibson and Harold Hardman early on in his time as manager. You pay me to manage, you must therefore allow me the power to do so. No interference was the founding principle of his successful career at United.

The new Chief Coach soon discovered the limits of his powers. He could select the team and organise training. Everything else was grey, negotiable. Sir Matt could attend board meetings, no need to trouble Wilf with that. Players' contracts they could do together. When Wilf sat down with Sir Matt at the end of the season to look at contracts he learned that several first team players were earning more that he was. Nine years after the removal of the maximum wage, Law, Charlton and Best were just over the £100-a-week margin. There were some anomalies on the salary sheet. Denis was the top earner. Bobby didn't know or really care, except for the deal he'd done with Busby after Law's row in '66. 'I told him I'd play for United for nothing,' Bobby recalls. 'All I asked was that nobody should get more than me. I didn't want more than anybody else . . . but with all the rumours flying around about this figure and that, I wanted to get the top wage whatever it was.' Busby assured him that no one would get more. Bobby never doubted 'The Boss'.

All kinds of things which had been unimportant when Wilf was one of the lads now began to assume significance. Minor matters, doubts about the Sneak, old sparring matches, the vulgar pranks, such things were now reassessed. The new Boss was a distinctly human man. He had no mystique, one of many rare qualities Matt Busby had brought to the job of management.

Wilf made his own calculations. He had never lacked confidence, even as a kid he'd been cocky. He'd even confronted Roger Byrne, insisting on equal rights with the club captain as a teenage tyro. He was a Collyhurst lad, brave, streetwise, unafraid. Don't be afraid was Wilf's first vow to himself. His second concerned old friendships. That was a nettle he was anxious to grasp. Too anxious.

Shay Brennan, Bobby and Jimmy Murphy were Wilf's closest friends at Old Trafford. Jimmy was the most difficult to know how to deal with now. Despite his brash persona, Wilf was a sensitive lad. He was emotional, could be hurt and was conscious of people at a human level. Thrust suddenly into the biggest job in football, now determining the fate of great footballers whom he'd known intimately all his working life, the problems seemed to overwhelm him. Every decision he made was big, every nuance of his behaviour assessed to see what it *really* meant. Given his free-spirited ways . . . the barbed joke thrown away without any vicious intent . . . the vulgar 'Did you give her one last night' type of banter favoured in most male bastions . . . these staples of dressing-room life had new resonance. What did he mean? . . . He shouldn't be talking like that. Wilf was determined *not* to change, become *a manager* in this respect. He was going to be himself; continue to play cards on the coach, for example.

But as far as Jimmy, Shay and Bobby were concerned he took a different line: he would be tough, overcompensating for any undue warmth he felt for old friends. Everyone would be treated the same. Especially old pals.

Wilf had always been Jimmy's protégé. He was Jimmy's type of player, all heart and guts, *desire*. Now Wilf blanked his mentor. Jimmy was hurt. Badly. The last thing Jimmy Murphy needed at this time was blanking.

He had mellowed through the Sixties. Of all those left after Munich Jimmy had suffered most. The pain he experienced was different to Matt's, more personal, more everyday. For the rest of the '57/'58 season Jimmy had allowed himself to be consumed by work. Manchester United had gone on, driven by his spirit, thoughts of what had happened buried so that the club could carry on its business. He worked twenty hours a day, he never stopped to reflect. The Cup Final, the quest for results, the blooding of new signings, and kids, getting Bobby motivated again, to these tasks Jimmy turned. Away from the thoughts of the awful tragedy.

Then, the Cup Final over, the long painful close-season weeks beckoning with no distraction, it hit him with desperate force: his golden apples were gone. His boys had been killed. Duncan, Eddie, David, Billy, Mark, Roger, Geoff, Tommy . . . he used to call them his 'golden apples'. Used to tell Matt we've got another one 'ripe', ready for the first team.

Jimmy loved music, could play Chopin, Bach, Mozart or Cole Porter, but the way the 'Red Devils' moved him as they grew from boys arriving with their little suitcases to men strutting arrogantly across the great stadiums of the football world moved his Welsh soul the way no music ever had, lifted the melancholy from his spirit. They were magic. They were his.

Jimmy was the ultimate football man. He saw the poetry in the game, also the prose. He was a teacher. The poetry was theirs, he would make them pros. Little things: throw-ins, marking, winning the ball back, the grim detail without which all the talent in the world counted for bugger all, that was his job. So, he'd bollock them, affect – and often feel – anger. The more gifted they were the more he would ram the message home: give it to a red shirt, keep it simple, get the basics right.

Nobby gives an example: 'Jimmy knew the game, the detail that could make the difference. In the European Cup winning team Shay and Tony Dunne were neat and clever round the ball. They'd track the winger down and instead of knocking him onto the track or hoofing the ball into the stands, Shay and Tony would just poke it out of play. Jimmy would have a go at them: "Put it into the stand, give yourself an extra ten or fifteen seconds to get organised for a throw-in. If you just touch it out of play they've got it back straight away and before you know where you are they're in your goalmouth and you're under pressure." It seems nothing, but football is all about that kind of professionalism, if you like, at one level.'

Jimmy knew this other, uncelebrated essence of the beautiful game. The brilliance was understood by everyone, but the real player did all the business, the hard detailed persevering bit, competing, that was about concentration, the unspectacular, the foundation on which the glorious is built. People said he didn't see the larger picture – Matt was the one. Players who grew up with him, the lads who died, Nobby, Bobby, Shay, Wilf, all knew that the larger picture wouldn't exist without the other properties of the professional game, passion for the cause being, perhaps, the most important thing, Jimmy inspired.

Murphy's life revolved around the dressing-room and training ground at Old Trafford. Matt's perspective was necessarily

329

broader. They were a perfect team because they brought such different qualities to the task of building a football club. Alas, since Munich Jimmy had never really had a role. Wilf, Johnny Aston and Jack had done a lot of the work he used to do. He was very much involved but the old fiery intensity was significantly diminished. He found himself often in a suit, reflecting rather than looking forward.

The club changed when the buying started. You could hardly call Setters, Quixall, and the other expensive signings 'golden apples'. There was no time to grow 'golden apples' now; Jimmy's simple gospel seemed trite to the new men. 'Give it to a red shirt.' Oh yeah! So what's new?

Through the 'Bollock Chops' years Jimmy would think back. He missed Bert, old Bert his closest friend. The Methodist preacher and the devout Catholic, different but the same, caring, tending their lovely orchard. And old Tom Curry, he missed Tom badly too. Tom, Bert and he would have their lunch together most days, beneath the stand in the old hut they called an office. Bill Inglis and Arthur Powell, the five of them were friends . . . not pals . . . friends . . . football men . . . not politicians. This was the soul of the old club. This simple life such a contrast to the glorious fervour of Old Trafford on match days, no clamour, no glamour, just the stuff of an ordinary day in Manchester United life.

Matt existed on another level. He had created this environment but wasn't of it. Jimmy was. This wasn't an academy. This was a home, a human place. The big idea was to shape the character of gifted young men, to teach the seemingly humdrum lessons required to be a professional. You didn't have to teach them how to play, they knew that before they arrived. What you had to do was gently remove the layer of schoolboy conceit, keep your eye on the bullies and blackguards, make sure that the environment was hospitable to lads with good character who wanted to be footballers, who were willing to learn the simple lessons. The big idea was that men of good character, honest, determined, and dedicated, would grow in human terms and thus a natural gift would blossom, be fertilised by a healthy spirit. The idea was to create a sense of human values so that men wouldn't spit in young fans' faces.

The agenda changed. Jimmy and Matt, never close, grew further apart as time went on. Matt was in another kind of business, necessary but different. Jimmy had only been in the Cromford Club once, for Roger Byrne's wedding. He took his leisure in the Throstles Nest in Whalley Range, in the bar rather than the lounge. He drank too much. To kill the pain of disappointment. Often after games he'd talk with the old boys Bobby, Wilf, Shay, Harry Gregg and the best of the new men, Denis, Paddy, long into the night in a hotel on the road after a game Jimmy would reflect on what had made United great . . . *great* . . . and lovely. His eyes would fill with tears: 'What's happening?' He meant to the club. The old lads loved him in a very special way. They respected Matt, were in awe of him; they *loved* Jimmy. Because, as Bobby often said – still says – Jimmy made it what it was. He made them.

This was what Wilf determined to ignore. Not callously, but the better to deal with new realities. Jimmy was hurt. Why? He could help. Now it was Wilf and Sir Matt. When Sir Matt retired Jimmy was gone as well. Nobody asked him. Something would be organised for him. Jimmy had six children and he'd never earned. Sir Matt told him he would talk to the Board. Jimmy was not just in spiritual limbo, financially he was in a hole as well. He'd turned down the Arsenal job, although tempted, early in the Sixties, and many others, some offering financial security. Now he was adrift, uncertain, dependent on the board! Jimmy knew the score. Sir Matt *was* the Board.

Wilf got Jimmy's office; Jimmy moved in to share with Joe Armstrong. Wilf changed the training pre-season. More short, sharp stuff, Wilf's ideas, new ideas illustrated on the blackboard. United had a great pre-season. The spirit was good on the training ground, they won the friendly games handsomely. Then the real stuff began.

They drew at Crystal Palace on the first Saturday. Then lost 2–0 at home to Everton on the Wednesday, and 4–1 to Southampton at Old Trafford on Saturday. It was time to grasp another nettle: two nettles, a handful. Bobby. And Denis. Bobby had played poorly in the first three games. People were running past him in midfield. The arrow-like passes weren't

331

reaching the target. He was thirty-one coming up to thirty-two. Maybe he was gone. Maybe not. Wilf dropped Bobby and Denis for the return midweek fixture at Goodison. Harvey, Kendall and Ball had strolled through the previous week's game. The Chief Coach didn't consult the General Manager. Popular Bill was left out as well. He'd played his last game for United.

The omission of Charlton and Law was a big story. Wilf replaced them with two home-grown lads, Don Givens and John Aston, who'd been in the wilderness since Busby bought Willie Morgan for £105,000 in August '68. Morgan was the new George Best. That was his claim, which the papers took up. He had long hair, a pretty face, wore the gear, and was tricky on the ball. Wilf didn't fancy Willie: 'Willie was not as good as he thought he was, but to be fair to him he was not as bad as I thought he was either.' But he didn't drop him. Paul Edwards, another youngster, replaced Bill Foulkes.

Everton took them apart, 3–0, could have been more. Everton went on to win the Championship, but in these early days of '69/'70 their quality was not proven. The result looked worse that it was. The morning after Goodison, Wilf went to see Sir Matt: ' "What took you so long?" he asked me. I told him we needed a couple of players. We talked about Bobby and Denis. You could see Denis was struggling, but Bobby would have to be put back in the side.'

Sir Matt agreed about new players. He came up with a name: Ian Ure, Arsenal's Scottish international centre-half. 'I didn't fancy him,' Wilf admits, 'now this is what happened. Don't forget I love this man. If you look at the video of the Benfica game at Wembley you'll see me clapping *him*. *Not the team*; him. So we're in the office and he says, "I'll give Bertie Mee a ring." He picks up the phone and says, "Bertie, it's Matt here again." Hello, I thought . . . *again!*'

Wilf was confused. 'I thought I must be imagining this. All of a sudden they've agreed a price, £80,000.' That afternoon, Wilf, Jimmy and Sir Matt travelled to London to clinch the deal. Wilf consoled himself by reasoning, 'Well we needed players, the old man's not a bad judge. Jimmy didn't offer an opinion then or afterwards. So I got Ian Ure, and funny enough we went eight games unbeaten after that.'

332

Doubts about Denis's fitness proved to be well founded. He played only ten League games, scoring one goal that season. Wilf had to manage without Nobby Stiles as well in those first trying months. Nobby, always plagued by cartilage trouble, had undergone another knee operation. Wilf's plan was to blend experience – Bobby, Paddy, Alex Stepney, George, Tony Dunne and Dave Sadler – with youth – Brian Kidd, Don Givens, Carlo Sartori and John Fitzpatrick. This, plus a bit of organisation and a couple of new players, would see him through.

A number of problems arose. The new players were the most obvious difficulty. Buying players was a grey area. Soon the picture became clear. He told Sir Matt he'd like to buy Malcolm McDonald from Luton to provide the goals Denis couldn't now score. Sir Matt, Jimmy and himself went to Luton. Matt and Jimmy went on the terraces with caps and dark glasses: 'I'm sure they didn't fool anyone,' Wilf laughs. He wanted McDonald. Sir Matt agreed to do the business. The news was bad. Liverpool had an option on McDonald, Wilf was informed. United had second option. One morning Wilf read in the papers that McDonald had gone to Newcastle!

Wilf wanted Colin Todd from Sunderland: 'I'd worked with Colin with the England under-23s. I thought he was the best young defender I'd seen for ten years. The price was phenomenal, £320,000 or something. Matt poo-pooed it. 'We can't afford him. That's an outrageous price' Wilf was told. What about Mick Mills of Ipswich. 'Sorry.'

Wilf got the message. Frustration built up. He was in a hole and didn't know the way out. Football was a bloody hard game. The fans expected, newspapers blabbed on. Little did they know. They had their own perceptions. So did the players who didn't know the story either. The buck stopped with Wilf McGuinness who had the responsibility but not the power required to do the job the way he wanted to. Frustrated, he occasionally lashed out. He still played cards on the coach. One day he and Willie Morgan had a noisy disagreement over a hand of cards. Tut-tut, the senior players thought. It wasn't good for the young either. There were gulfs in the camp, significant gulfs of a kind Sir Matt would have recognised from his playing past.

333

The senior players didn't 'stop playing for Wilf' as stories had it; these were great pros – Bobby, Denis, Paddy – they weren't kids about to sulk. Two things happened: the inspiration Busby had provided couldn't be artificially induced. That was singular, his magic, which could not be manufactured. Alas, it was that thing that had made them great players. They were gifted of course but the spiritual side of greatness, the Other Side, had been the essence of Manchester United magic. Intangible, indefinable, potent beyond imagining. Busby.

Wilf offered organisation, a poor substitute for Busby's potion. Denis Law explains: 'It is wrong to say we didn't try for Wilf. There was a vacuum when Matt packed it in. Nobody could replace him. All of a sudden we've got blackboards, team-talks become very complicated. We are worried about the opposition, *their* free-kicks, *their* throw-ins, *their* corner-kicks. People started to worry before games. We didn't flow any more. Fear crept in.' This was Denis's perception. Wilf's was that Denis couldn't flow any more.

Paddy thought Wilf was a good lad who got the job too early: 'He was very excitable. The kids he brought in weren't good enough. I felt sorry for Wilf. He was too close to some of the players – Bobby, the Bomber [Shay Brennan so-called because he *wasn't* a bomber type defender].' Paddy's perception is that Bobby was Wilf's biggest enemy at Old Trafford: 'Bobby talked behind his back to the Boss and Louis,' Paddy says. There's no real evidence to support that view, although there is evidence that Bobby did get involved later.

Nor is there any reason to suppose, as many do, that Wilf was being undermined in another way by Sir Matt's socialising with senior players. Not Bobby who had too much respect for 'The Boss' to dream of drinking with him, but Paddy, Alex Stepney and Willie Morgan who played golf with Sir Matt at Davyhulme on a Sunday and often shared a table with him at the Cromford on a Saturday. This bothered Wilf: 'I once dropped the three of them and they were golfing with the Boss on Sunday morning. That was something, a little obstacle. For one thing everyone still called him "Boss". I was supposed to be the boss.'

Bobby Charlton, still a leading player in the Manchester United story, is cautious about those times. An injudicious word or comment could have consequence beyond meaning. Bobby is a good man, a great football man, United through and through, a curious, singular man, part Busby seeing the big picture, part Jimmy, the best of both his mentors, with a special stubborn vision of his own. 'Wilf is a good lad,' Bobby shrugs. 'It was the wrong time for him.' Although he doesn't say so, or even hint, it's clear that Bobby didn't approve of Wilf's appointment. Nothing personal, they're blood brothers from the days of Friday fish'n'chips and pictures in Town. But both have seen the world, the world of power, fame and glory; the bloody hard world of professional football that vanishes you as ruthlessly as an Air Crash if you're not watchful.

A certain toughness is required if you are to survive. Bobby had it, so did Denis. Jimmy didn't, Giles did. Matt invented it. Wilf never really had that hardness. '*World*,' he smiles, 'I'm a dreamer, at least I was. You learn later that the world is a big place but at the time Manchester United was my world, that was it; mainly because of all the lads who'd died in the crash, we'd grown up together, you can see how easily that could bind you to the club. When John Giles said to me, "Maybe Matt will change his mind, but I won't," it shocked me, I couldn't believe he wanted to go. These feelings clouded a lot of things; unrest with the players, my dealings with the Boss. I was sure of one thing, he'd stand by me. I had three years.'

George Best was the other constant: 'George was brilliant,' Wilf recalls, 'some days when it was bad I used to just pray for George to do it. And he did. At Sheffield we're two down with five minutes to go and up he pops, makes one, scores one. Thank God, I thought.'

George was better than ever those first few months. Stunning. Goals, he ended the season leading scorer with fifteen League goals, and all the rest of him: competitive, tormenting the kickers, lighting up United on the bleakest afternoons. 'I still loved playing,' George explains. He was dating Miss World by now, beginning to become disenchanted. One of the reasons was the absence of new players. 'Good players were needed. The team was starting to grow old. They had opportunities to sign players and I couldn't figure out why a club as great as Manchester United that had five great years from '63 to '68 wouldn't spend whatever was needed.' George blamed Wilf. He also saw the other things: 'I felt the back-stabbing going on. The dressing-room was unhappy. Playing used to be the greatest high in life, especially for the Boss, I never felt the same respect for Wilf, although I liked him.' George's uneasy feeling about the game dated further back, to '66: 'Football started to become a chore at some stage during this period. Kickers and systems. I was coming off the pitch with mixed emotions when Wilf took over. I knew I was playing well but we were losing. I was training hard but I wasn't enjoying it like I used to. The fun went out of it, people started bickering, slagging each other off, then there were fights, fists-up jobs. From my point of view I wanted to do it for Wilf, he deserved it because of all he'd been through for a club he loved. Most of the young lads felt like that but the older ones didn't.'

Despite all the difficulties Wilf did well in his first season, thanks mainly to George. United finished a respectable eighth in the League and reached the semi-final of the FA and League Cups. They lost to City in the League Cup. The FA Cup run really took off after they beat City 3–0 at home in the fourth round. In the boardroom afterwards Wilf was so excited he vomited on the floor. That's how much it meant to Wilf.

The semi-final of the FA Cup against Leeds United went to two replays. Leeds were still wicked but quality was emerging, with Giles replacing Collins in midfield and Lorimer, Eddie Gray and Terry Cooper maturing. The first game ended 0–0. The replay was at Villa Park on Monday 23 March 1970. A fateful day.

They had lunch at a hotel in Worcester. The plan was to have a sleep after lunch. George had a different plan. She was a doll, sitting at the bar as they ate. 'Everyone could see him clocking her,' Nobby recalls, 'It was obvious what was going to happen.' Things were bad at the club as George remembers: 'We had started drawing lots to see who we'd room with. I refused to do it.' So he was booked with Dave Sadler.

The lady at the bar was about thirty. She looked what she was, a businessman's wife. He was at a conference in another part of the hotel; she sent the right signal to George. They disappeared. Semi-final afternoon. This was bad form, and someone blew in Wilf's ear. He went hunting. George wasn't in his room, but the lady's room was next door to Bobby and Nobby who were sharing. Wilf knocked them up. They thought he'd gone daft, for he didn't tell them what he was up to. Instead, hushing them to be quiet, he put his ear to the bedroom wall. Nobby thought he knew. Bobby claims he's forgotten the incident. They looked at each other, wondering has this guy gone or what?

'The bastard,' Wilf screeched. He now knew where George was. George wouldn't open the door, so Wilf went down for the pass-key. He threw George out, stared *her* down and went downstairs to have a whisky at the bar: 'I needed a drink while I figured what to do. Here's my best player, he's done great for me and he's in bed with a bird a few hours before playing Leeds. Leeds! So, I went to Busby: "What should I do?" '

'What do you want to do?' Sir Matt asked him.

'Play him,' Wilf replied. 'Do the players know?' Busby enquired. Wilf didn't think they did. 'Leave it to me,' 'The Boss' told him. 'To this day I don't know what Matt said to him,' Wilf declares. The players soon found out. Dave Sadler knew anyway: 'It was not the first time, but he always did the business. He was amazing. The atmosphere was fraught on the way to Villa Park. The Leeds players found out about United's trouble: 'We knew,' John Giles confirms, 'we thought it was a disgrace. Even though it might work in our favour, we still thought it was serious, out of order.'

Nobby wonders: 'I think it might have been a set-up by Revie,' he asserts. Leeds were thought to be capable of anything.

'It was a classic match,' Giles recalls. Wilf agrees: 'We really played. George had a nightmare. And he got the chance.' He missed it: 'Any day of the week you'd fancy George to do it especially on the big night,' Wilf ruefully explains.

Leeds won the second replay. Chelsea won the FA Cup. Wilf's lifespan shortened by a considerable distance. The older players blamed him. George admits: 'I'm ashamed of many things and that is one of the worst. But I'd been doing it for years.' He was sick of 'the cliques, the bickering, I was longing for someone to come and sort it out'. Nobody came.

At the end of the season Wilf McGuinness and Sir Matt sat down to work out the retain and transfer list. Shay Brennan was getting a free transfer. They could have looked for a fee but a 'free' would enable Shay to make a few quid. Shay was a gambler. He needed the money. Because he was fond of a bet – to say the least – United wouldn't give him a testimonial match but a pension for life: £20 a week. Before inflation, before the oil crisis in 1973 this was decent. Giving Shay a 'free' was part of Wilf's nettle-grasping operation. Shay was best man at Wilf's wedding; Wilf best man for Shay.

Shay loved United. He didn't want to go. At thirty-one he felt he was OK for a couple more seasons. That summer the club were off to America on tour, and Shay had been fitted for his suit. The end of the season was always a tense time at a football club – judgement day. Shay was well pleased, his fitting for a suit was a good sign, and Jimmy had marked his card. 'I'd never been Jimmy's type of player,' Shay explains, 'but we'd often spent the small hours together. I was one of those who understood. The day before the list came out, Jimmy, sensing I was on the borderline, said, "Don't worry, they're putting Denis on the list, that's the only big move." So I thought, great, I'm OK.'

They were at the Cliff, training finished, when Wilf called him over: 'The Boss wants to see you.' Sir Matt broke the news. Wilf sat beside him stonefaced. Bang.

'I'd known for days, I should have told him,' Wilf admits, 'but there was so much going on. It was stupid, but I thought I was doing the business the right way.'

Shay was sick. The world fell in on him. *Leave the club*! Where would he go? Was it Wilf's decision? The Boss's? Hurt, scared and confused, Shay went back to Old Trafford. Jimmy was there. 'Come on, come upstairs,' Jimmy said. They went up and sat at the back of the stand. Jimmy was consoling. He'd been blown out himself, and he knew what Shay was feeling. Suddenly Jimmy's anger and hurt burst out: 'He'd never had a go at the Boss before, but now it poured out,' Shay recalls. 'I think *he* needed someone to talk to more than I did. He pointed to the ground, "Look at this . . . all of it, *I* built this fucking place, we built it: Bert, Tom, with our bare hands . . . and now." ' Tears flowed. Jimmy's and Shay's.

During the summer Wilf McGuinness was given the title of Manager. Nothing changed except the title. He tried again to sign Mick Mills from Ipswich, but he couldn't persuade Sir Matt. This is why he feels he failed. 'I should have been stronger but I was in awe of him,' Wilf admits. With two years of his contract left, Wilf felt he could afford to experiment, blood the youngsters. Jimmy Rimmer replaced Stepney in goal. Paul Edwards got a run at right-back. Denis was in and out through injury. Bobby played every game. George was still doing it.

Two days after Christmas Wilf was sacked. He was destroyed. There had been some noise in the newspapers, speculative stuff, nothing serious: 'I wasn't worried. I knew Sir Matt would stand by me no matter what. No two ways about that. It came as a hell of a shock.' United reached the semi-final of the League Cup, losing the two-legged tie to Third Division Aston Villa: 'We were due to play the first leg at Villa Park but there were power-cuts so that was switched to Old Trafford. We drew. They beat us 2–1 in the second game.' That was 23 December.

Wilf looked terrible, Paddy Crerand recalls: 'The change in his appearance was unbelievable. He'd come in on a Monday morning with his eyes down around his cheekbones. He looked as if he had the world on his shoulders.' Sir Matt got more involved in the final few weeks: 'I welcomed that,' Wilf says. 'I felt a closeness between us. He was helping me. We went over the team together for the Villa games. He said a few words in the dressing-room before the second match. I thought he was trying to help not hinder. I was quite happy to let him help.'

United drew 4–4 at Derby on Boxing Day. The following day Sir Matt sent for Wilf: ' "Wilf," he said, "things haven't been working out. The Directors have asked me to take charge again." I couldn't believe it. I said, I've got a three-year contract. He said, "We'll end up in Second Division." I had a go at him. I wasn't going to give up easily. I wasn't a quitter. I must have swore at him. We were in there about an hour.'

Wilf was told to report to the ground at six o'clock for a board meeting. He could have his old job back. He can't remember much about the next few hours. Before the meeting, at which a draft of a statement was to be agreed, Wilf found himself in the boardroom. It was four o'clock: 'I phoned my wife Beryl. I told her it was over. She was pregnant with our third child. My father-in-law had cancer. To me it was the end of the world. I looked around for the whisky bottle. All I could find was sherry. I had several glasses. I remember getting up and actually banging my head against the wall. I thought I was going insane. Jack Crompton came in as I was hitting my head off the wall. He said, "What are you doing?" I told him it was all over. The Boss had sacked me. I was heartbroken. I didn't want to cry in front of Jack. I was in a daze, everything was blurred at that moment. I called my dad.' At six o'clock Wilf attended the board meeting. 'It was the first time I'd attended a board meeting. I left that to Sir Matt.'

His mood changed: 'I loved the club. I didn't want to hurt United, people like Alan Gibson, he'd cried when we lost at Villa. He was upset for me. So I said, I'm sorry it didn't work out. Then I thanked them or something daft, there were handshakes all around. We agreed that the statement would say I'd asked to have my old job back. I was home by seven o'clock.'

At home with Beryl, and his father who came to comfort him, Wilf's mood changed again: 'I thought, this is not right, this isn't me, I wouldn't give in. People knew I wouldn't give in, I wasn't like that. So I phoned Sir Matt. Jean answered the phone. I told him I'd been thinking and talking to my family. I wouldn't resign, they'd have to sack me. He said OK, come in at nine in the morning and we'll draft a new statement.'

The players were told in the gym at the Cliff before training. Sir Matt made the announcement. When he'd finished, Brian Kidd, a Collyhurst lad like Wilf, turned to the senior pros: 'You lousy bastards, you've let him down.'

'I said, now now Brian, come on, we're all United here,' Wilf ruefully remembers. 'The press came in. "How do you feel?" they asked. I said, I'm still United, if you cut me I bleed red. And I thought, what am I saying, that's crap. But I was still trying to protect them. Really I would have done a better job if I'd been more myself.'

Sandy Busby was a close friend of Wilf's: 'Sandy was great. He came round to see me and said, "Have a holiday on the club, take Beryl and the kids and just get away for a while." He was feeling for me. I didn't know what I was going to do. Every time I thought about it I filled up. I was still in love with the club.

'Bill Foulkes had the job I'd been doing with the reserves. Sir Matt said, "Do it together." I thought, Oh no, you can't do that. He said, "Give it a try." I tried it for a couple of weeks. It was a disaster. Bill was giving half the team-talk, then I'd come in. It was a joke. One day at Burnley, he's talking and I'm waiting to have my say. There was a kid called Kevin Lewis and Bill was steaming into him, too strong. So I said, you can't talk to a Manchester United player like that.'

Wilf went looking for Sir Matt: 'He tried to avoid me but I caught him on the stairs one day. Am I having my old job back or not? I said. He said, "Oh Wilf, bloody hell lad, don't you think I've got enough on my plate?" '

Wilf left. He was offered the job as manager at Bolton with Nat Lofthouse as General Manager: 'I thought, no thanks, not that again.'

Sir Alf Ramsey, football's Public Enemy Number One, called Wilf: 'He was a gentleman of the highest order, Alf. He said, "Don't mind the bastards, come down and have dinner with me." He offered me the job of managing the FA XI going on tour to Australia, and playing Ireland at Lansdowne Road. It would put me in the frame, get me going again while I was looking for work. Alf was magnificent.'

Wilf eventually took a job in Greece with Aris Salonika: 'He started as a boy and left United as an old man,' Tony Dunne remarked. In Greece Wilf's hair started falling out. It grew again, little white tufts, before falling out again. The doctor told him it was delayed shock. In the end he was completely bald. He was thirty-three, United through and through, and he thought Busby was a bastard. For a while.

17

The Outsider

'It seems to me that someone from
the real world came in to Matt's
fantasy world, at Old Trafford. They
were all part of the same family
circle. Really the club was a mess.
There was no reality to the myth.'

Frank O'Farrell

Sir Matt resumed his post. Results improved dramatically.
United finished eighth in the League. George Best, who had
scored four goals during the first half of the season, scored
fourteen for 'The Boss' between January and May. Denis Law
also enjoyed a purple patch ending the season second top scorer
with fifteen goals. Busby was back on a temporary basis. The
search for a new manager was on. According to conventional
wisdom the next man would have to be 'big enough to manage
Manchester United'.

Jock Stein was considered suitable. Dave Sexton's name was
also flagged, as was Don Revie's. Paddy Crerand approached
Stein, known as the 'Big Man' in the game. Celtic had
dominated Scottish football for several years as well as claiming
a European Cup. Paddy made the approach in Stein's Glasgow
home. Jock's son was a United fanatic, but Jock himself was less
enthusiastic. Jock was wise in football's ways, and he understood Busby. He, Matt and Bill Shankly all came from the same
part of Scotland, the west, mining villages where football was
religion. They were great football men, but fly men also. Busby,
Stein and Shankly, each built great teams, great clubs. Each
was different. Each knew about the other, the man behind the
myth. 'Shanks' was a fanatic, hard, passionate, a believer in the
glory. As John Giles puts it: 'If Bill hadn't been Liverpool's
manager he'd have been on the Kop roaring the team on.'

Shankly always came onto the pitch when Liverpool were parading an FA Cup or Championship trophy round Anfield. He'd have a red and white scarf around his neck: 'Other managers would be fannying,' Giles allows, 'Shanks wasn't. He was a fan.' He was no man-manager in the Busby mould. Ian St John recalls: 'If you were injured he wouldn't talk to you. He took it personally. You didn't exist. You were no use to Liverpool Football Club. He lived for the game.'

Shankly wasn't a worldly man. Sometimes he'd tender his resignation to the Liverpool board to force them to accept his view on something or other. This was a game to Bill; they couldn't do without him, he *was* Liverpool Football Club. In 1974 the board accepted his resignation, and Bill Shankly never recovered. Within a couple of years he was dead. They say he died of a broken heart.

Shankly wasn't fly enough. Busby and Stein, though, were different propositions, more worldly men. They knew the difference between glory on the pitch, beautiful football played by great players and the clamorous noises from the terraces and fame in the press or television. One was real, one was fake. This distinction was important. You could be done without. The only glory that mattered was the football on the field.

Asked once if he and Matt ever discussed the game, Stein replied, 'Och, no I would nae embarrass the man.' This was a reference to Busby's presumed ignorance of the game in a technical sense. He was *only* a manager of people. Jock could talk you through a game, intricate move by move, telling you who should have been doing this, that or the other when the goal was scored or conceded. This was – is – called, Knowing the Game. In that sense Jock knew the game, Jimmy Murphy also. Matt didn't. But he knew something more important.

Sir Matt knew Jock. He knew that Jock was fly. But he respected the football Stein's teams played. It was Matt's kind of game. They met in a motorway café, and terms were agreed. The only problem in Stein's mind was the prevailing mood at Old Trafford – the shadow of Sir Matt. He put a proposition to Busby. Bobby Charlton and Denis Law were over the hill. Jock felt it would be a bad start if he was the one to give them the hard word. So if Matt would sort that out, then Jock would come down. Sir Matt demurred. Still, Stein appeared willing to take the job and they shook hands. The following day Stein rang to turn the job down on the grounds that his wife didn't want to leave Glasgow. Paddy Crerand believes this was true. Matt didn't. He thought Jock used the approach to up the ante in his negotiations for a new contract with Celtic.

Dave Sexton was next on the list. Sexton took a while to reflect on the offer. In the end he said no, and Busby turned to Frank O'Farrell. The Irishman had done a good job with Leicester, before that he'd been successful with Torquay. He was the right type. Tough and impeccably behaved. Peter Shilton had given O'Farrell a hard time when Leicester were in the Second Division and Shilton wanted away to further his career. O'Farrell made the goalkeeper honour his contract, leaving him sitting in the stand when Shilton started uttering threats. Busby was impressed.

Frank O'Farrell's integrity was well known in the game. In this age of dodgy deals [like all the other ages!] and Flash Harrys, O'Farrell played by the rules and eschewed big talk. He was at this time negotiating a new contract with Leicester. He was free and interested, not desperately interested, just interested. Busby explained about Stein letting him down and said he would like a quick decision. O'Farrell, he said, would have a five-year contract and no interference. Aware of the prevailing view that his presence had inhibited McGuinness, Sir Matt assured Frank that he would no longer be involved in team affairs in any way as he intended becoming a director.

' "The job is yours if you want it," he told me,' O'Farrell recalls. 'I was flattered, I told him, but I asked for a day to think it over.' The salary was £12,000 a year plus bonuses for winning trophies. After discussing the offer with his wife, Anne, Frank accepted. He arranged to meet Sir Matt and Louis Edwards to complete discussions. Secrecy was important to United, with the Stein sting still fresh in Busby's mind, so they agreed to meet at a hotel in Derbyshire.

Frank O'Farrell was forty-five, an experienced football manager who'd started out with Weymouth in the Southern League after a good career as a wing-half with West Ham and Preston. From Weymouth he joined Torquay where he achieved promotion from Fourth to Third Division for this small club. When O'Farrell arrived at Leicester the club was on the way to relegation from the First Division. He inspired a Cup run which took Leicester to Wembley in 1969 where they lost to Manchester City. They were relegated, losing their last match of the season at Old Trafford. O'Farrell rebuilt, selling Allan Clarke to Leeds, keeping Shilton and introducing some excellent young players like David Nish and Rodney Fern to the team. When United came for him Leicester had just won the Second Division impressively.

As a player at West Ham Frank had been a member of the Academy, a group of players led by Malcolm Allison who began discussing the new ideas of the mid to late Fifties. Dave Sexton, John Bond, Ernie Gregory, Noel Cantwell and Ken Brown belonged to this group, Frank was a junior member, Allison the guru. 'Malcolm had served in Austria on National Service, he'd seen the Continental way of doing things, we knew the English game was years behind in terms of training and technique,' Frank explains.

'After training every day we'd go to this Italian café/restaurant round the corner from Upton Park and discuss the game. Over steak and chips we'd move the salt and pepper pots around the table devising new ways to play the game.' This group did influence English football, for good and bad, in the coming decades. Moore, Hurst and Peters, nurtured in the West Ham style, formed an essential element in England's World Cup winning team. Later Allison coached Manchester City to a Championship, Dave Sexton and Ken Brown became successful managers and Cantwell brought the new thinking to Old Trafford. John Bond also rose to prominence.

Frank O'Farrell was his own man. He listened but was never likely to be convinced by the likes of Allison and Bond who, whatever he thought about their academic analysis of football, were in human terms unappealing characters to this serious-minded Catholic from Cork. Frank O'Farrell is a staunch Catholic, though his is a different form of Catholicism from that widely practised in Ireland, the Latin countries and in Manchester by men like Busby and Paddy McGrath. O'Farrell's Catholicism is more commonly found elsewhere in

England and is more disciplined, less worldly than the norm for this faith. Subtle deals with conscience are out. Sin is not so easily dissolved in the confession box. The slate can't be wiped clean by the few prayers offered to God in penance for sins committed. Your faith is taken seriously, is the foundation of your character. Catholics like O'Farrell do not, as most do, regard their faith as some kind of convenience food for the soul. Their Catholicism is a way of life, its values inherent in everything they do. They don't commit adultery, lie and cheat or otherwise play fast and loose with the tenets of their religion. The Pope *is* infallible. Sin is *not* negotiable. Birth control is *not* practised and priests who tell you that 'the pill is a matter between you and your conscience', who are 'progressive', are compromisers selling out on true Catholicism.

Frank O'Farrell's character was formed by this rigorous interpretation of God's intentions. He is a man of absolute honour, unworldly to a degree. Everything must be done 'the right way'. Thus, he conducted the leaving of Leicester. The Board were informed. When they offered to match United's offer, better it even, he explained that he had given United his word and wasn't prepared to renege on that promise. Mr Len Shipman, who was at that time chairman of Leicester City and President of the Football League, the principal enforcer of football law, was disappointed with O'Farrell, didn't understand this fastidious observance of unwritten agreements. Frank O'Farrell was widely respected in professional football, *despite* his honourableness. This belief in integrity, this fetish for doing things right was regarded as a kink in his make-up. Of course there were compensations; Frank wouldn't fuck you. The problem was he wouldn't fuck anyone for you either.

He met Sir Matt and 'Champagne' Louis in Derbyshire. The hotel was full of people, so they drove out to the countryside and stopped at a lay-by. Frank got into Edwards's Rolls Royce and Sir Matt introduced his chairman. Frank thanked Louis for the offer, repeated that he was flattered and sought confirmation of the terms. 'So Matt repeats £12,000 a year plus bonuses,' Frank remembers. 'Big Louis interrupted . . . "No, Matt, it's £15,000 basic salary." "Oh, yes, I forgot," Matt says.' It was a small chink, but O'Farrell felt uneasy: 'It must have been providential my asking,' he declares. 'It bothered me a little bit. He could have forgotten the bonuses . . . but the basic salary? They were a big club, looking for a manager, and they weren't sure of the basic salary. I thought it was odd. I went back to Anne and told her it was £15,000 not £12,000. She said that's not a bad start, you've got a £3,000 rise before you begin!'

Old Trafford was big. That was the first thing that struck Frank. He stood on the pitch on his first day and looked around. 'I was impressed by the size of the place. They were building a new stand with Executive Boxes. There were big cranes all around, it was like a building site.' The building was incomplete so United's early season games would have to be played away from home. Sir Matt introduced O'Farrell to Johnny Foy his bookmaker friend: 'Johnny was a nice man, sincere, did a lot for charity. We had dinner. I liked him.'

That first day Frank decided to grasp his first nettle: 'Sir Matt took me up to the offices. His was large and well appointed, it was clearly the Manager's Office. He showed me my office which was small, down the end of the corridor. Alarm bells started ringing.' Frank understood the symbolism of the Manager's Office in a professional football club: 'Another fella might have "bottled" it, but I thought I've got to do this now. So I said, Matt this is not right, and he was a bit taken aback. I was impressed but not overawed by him. I was quite a confident person myself.'

O'Farrell argued that it wouldn't be right for Sir Matt or for him to allow these office arrangements to stand. He reminded Sir Matt of the common perception that it was still his club: 'I said if you stay in that office it makes my position look very bad, it reinforces their belief that you are the real boss.' Sir Matt explained that he was keeping an office to deal with correspondence and other bits and pieces unconnected with the game: 'Well, I said, Matt, the Manager's Office should be recognised for what it is . . . the Manager's Office. I said it in a respectful way. He couldn't argue . . . so he said, "All right, I'll move my things out." It was a tough moment but I proved I had the courage to face it. I was nobody's puppet.'

Jimmy Murphy was one of O'Farrell's first callers: 'Jimmy says to me, "How did you get him out of here?" ' The sardonic tone in Murphy's voice rang another bell in Frank's head.

347

Jimmy's role at United had been clarified, unhappily from his point of view. After a long wait he was offered £20,000, five years' salary, as a retirement settlement and a scouting job at £25 a week. The scouting post was really a sinecure during the McGuinness/Busby regime just ended. Life would now be financially difficult. In football terms he'd been pushed to the margins of the club he loved. He was almost a non-person. This uncomfortable existence was made worse by the decisions taken by the Board which Jimmy knew was really Sir Matt. He'd never driven a car. For several years he'd made the journey from Whalley Range to Old Trafford and back in a black taxi provided at the club's expense. The fare was £3 each way. Jimmy had recently received a letter from Les Olive informing him that this arrangement was being discontinued. He was also informed that United could no longer pay his telephone bills. The year before, his son Nicky had left United after four seasons as a reserve player. Nicky recalls his father's hurt: 'My dad was never interested in money, but the football side of things meant everything to him. He never said anything against Sir Matt or the club, but he was very hurt. He couldn't understand it. He had a lot to contribute.' Without the taxi Jimmy turned to British Rail: 'I know it sounds unbelievable,' Nicky confides, 'but for years after, Dad used to make the trip without a ticket. The railway guards knew him so they never asked to see his ticket. He'd just wave and walk through the barrier.' Nicky's emotions are aroused as he tells this story.

Frank O'Farrell rearranged the furniture in Sir Matt's office: 'There were low easy chairs for visitors which meant you looking down on them from behind the desk. I created a little sitting area in the corner of the room where you could sit together with people when they came in.' He was particularly conscious of this when Sir Matt called as Frank had invited him to whenever he wanted: 'I didn't want to appear to be looking down on him, so whenever he came in we would sit together in the corner. I thought this was just good manners.'

O'Farrell got off to a flying start. United lost just once in the first thirteen League games. By December they were top of the First Division. Everyone was happy. United were back. Frank thought the revival was 'an illusion'.

'When I looked at the team I realised their reputations were better than their performances.' The results were due to one man: George Best. 'He was fantastic,' O'Farrell declares. 'He really was.' Before the end of November Best had scored fourteen goals, including two hat-tricks. Not a man to indulge in rhetoric, Frank O'Farrell says simply: 'George was a genius.'

But O'Farrell believed Best was 'covering up a multitude of sins. After some games we won when we shouldn't have I used to say, Thank God for George.' When O'Farrell looked at the wage-sheet he saw that Denis Law and Bobby Charlton were earning significantly more than George: 'I called him in and improved his wages out of respect for his ability. I didn't think the situation I found was fair.' O'Farrell reported this and other matters to the board: 'Johnny Aston was the chief-scout, he was using his own car and being paid mileage. Nothing depreciates quicker than a car. I thought a club like United should provide a car for the chief-scout.' So another item went on the agenda for the board.

'I was conscious that these things were a reflection on Sir Matt and I didn't want to hurt him but the club had to have decent values.' O'Farrell had no doubt about where power truly lay in the boardroom: 'Louis Edwards was the chairman, but Matt had him in the palm of his hand.'

In January results began to reflect football reality as O'Farrell had suspected they would. 'That's when the friction really started,' he says. O'Farrell had redesigned the team when he arrived. Malcolm Musgrove had come with him from Leicester as coach. They believed in working on the game during the week, practising functional play in training, adopting a rational team structure rather than sending teams out to 'play it off-the-cuff'. In O'Farrell's opinion this organisation, allied to Best's genius, explained the good results early on. He thought Bobby and Denis were past it and he didn't rate Alex Stepney. Paddy Crerand was too slow for Frank's taste and was never selected during the O'Farrell period. Frank sent him to train the youngsters 'to get him out of the way as nicely as possible'. Willie Morgan was another iffy item in Frank's view: 'Morgan would sometimes say, "Let's go out and play football," implying that what I was asking for was not real football.

349

Then a ball would arrive at the far post and he'd duck. I used to think, Get your head to the ball, *that's* football.'

Looking objectively at Manchester United, Frank O'Farrell saw a mess that resembled a bad soap-opera. It was, he thought, some family all right. So he decided to go to work. He told the Board he wanted to buy Peter Shilton. This didn't go down very well. There was money available for players but nobody would tell him how much. He said it would cost £1 million to reconstruct the team. He would have to replace Law, Charlton and Stepney. United needed a central defender. And Frank O'Farrell firmly believed he needed a captain, a leader, someone, ironically, like Roger Byrne or Johnny Carey. Bobby was the captain but O'Farrell didn't believe that leadership was Charlton's forte. He admired Bobby as a man and a footballer, but the Stepneys and Morgans were the dominant influences at Old Trafford and Bobby seemed unable or unwilling to set a different tone.

Of course Stepney and Morgan were more than mere players. They were Sir Matt's golfing and drinking companions. There was a joke going the dressing-room rounds at this time about Sir Willie and Matt. O'Farrell didn't find this funny but it did prove that the values he thought essential to a football club were irreconcilable with the ethos of the family of which he was now the head – at least as far as the public were concerned. Musing aloud to Paddy Crerand one day about such things as the relationship between Sir Matt and certain players, O'Farrell was advised to 'get out and play golf on Sundays and Mondays'. He didn't play golf.

Denis Law was another problem. In Frank's view his fitness was questionable. The Law of old, the great player, was now a shadow. He'd flash in and out of games, still splendid but only in patches, his knee never right after '68. But Denis still thought he had a lot to offer. Midfield was where he wanted to play, he told O'Farrell. The manager said no, he wanted Denis where he was most effective: up front. Denis also wanted a long-term contract. Again O'Farrell disagreed. A one-year deal was all he was prepared to offer. United collapsed in the second half of the season to finish eighth in the First Division. After good runs in the two Cup competitions they departed without disgrace in the

FA Cup sixth round and the fourth round of the League Cup, replays being necessary in both instances.

'They couldn't see what I could see,' O'Farrell says of the United Board. Here another serious problem lay buried from the public's view. The relationship between manager and chairman is one of the most important in a professional club. Protocol demands that the Board be kept informed about football matters through the chairman. The corollary is that, when seeking day-to-day guidance about transfers and other things requiring expenditure, the chairman be the conduit of club policy. O'Farrell therefore dealt with Louis Edwards, United's chairman, whom he would telephone on a daily basis. Although the *realpolitik* of Manchester United seemed clear – that the chairman was 'in the palm of Busby's hand' – Frank felt quite properly that it wasn't for him to make assumptions as to who was really running the club.

One day Les Olive, United's secretary, told O'Farrell that there had been complaints about him 'not keeping the Board informed'. O'Farrell was bemused. He had been in constant contact with Louis Edwards. Louis would immediately call Sir Matt for advice before offering the definitive boardroom opinion. So, Frank's crime was the observance of football protocol. Sir Matt was the source of the complaints. 'Sir Matt hadn't told me at the beginning to ignore the chairman,' O'Farrell explains, 'if he had I might have acted differently.'

In March 1972 Frank O'Farrell paid Aberdeen £125,000 for Martin Buchan. Having assessed the situation at Old Trafford, nine months into his tenure O'Farrell decided that the club needed new players *and* a new image: 'I wanted professionals with different values. Martin was an intelligent fellow with the right attitude. Thank God, I thought, at last someone I can relate to and talk to.' The following week Ian Storey-Moore was signed from Notts Forest for £185,000. Over the next few months he bought Wyn Davis and Ted McDougall, the latter from Bournemouth for £200,000. George Best played forty League games scoring eighteen goals that season.

Reflecting during the summer, Frank O'Farrell realised he had one hell of a job on his hands. He found it difficult to reconcile the image of Manchester United with the pathetic reality he'd found. Frank was a tough, experienced pro but this place was incredible. It seemed to him that he had 'arrived from the real world to disturb Sir Matt Busby's fantasy world. They were all part of the same family circle.' The atmosphere was hostile. Frank could feel it. His consolation was the five-year contract in his desk. Martin Buchan was another ray of hope, Frank's Johnny Carey, his Roger Byrne, cast out of the same mould as Busby's two great captains. Not one of the lads in the accepted sense, Buchan preferred to read rather than play cards. He enjoyed a joke, knew the day-to-day nature of a professional club, had, indeed, grown up the son of a professional player. Buchan not only resembled Carey and Byrne, he bore himself in the manner of the young Matt Busby. Thus, O'Farrell felt it all the more ironic that those from the dressing-room who now appeared to influence Busby most disliked Buchan the model professional. O'Farrell believed that he and his captain were being undermined by the relationship between Busby, Morgan and Stepney. This was a reasonable conclusion. Busby's contradictory nature was beginning to catch up with him to the detriment of dressing-room morale.

Instead of playing golf, or socialising in the Cromford Club, Frank O'Farrell did his duty: 'If I had free time I'd spend it promoting Manchester United, giving talks to Supporters Clubs, presenting prizes and generally projecting what I believed was the right image for the club in the community.'

Season '72/'73 began badly and things deteriorated from there. Bobby Charlton, who had played forty League games the season before and scored ten goals, was club captain. Like George Best and Denis Law, Bobby was in a curious position. None of these great players was a confidant of Sir Matt's. Law, Charlton and Best respected Busby too much to glibly invite him for a drink, a meal, or a game of golf. Paddy Crerand, on the other hand, was close to the Busby family in a natural way, being regarded as Jean and Matt's 'adopted' son. O'Farrell had alienated each of those men for different reasons.

George Best was sick of carrying the team on his back, and was becoming increasingly blatant in his disregard for the norms of professional football's discipline. The slide from misdemeanour to outrage was not as rapid as is commonly perceived. George lived for football. Although disenchantment set in during Wilf McGuinness's period as manager, he continued to perform magnificently. He was leading goalscorer for United for four seasons after the European Cup win of '68, missing only a handful of games. George was not deemed to be *living* like a professional should, but he was certainly *playing* like a pro.

David Sadler had by now married and left Mrs Fullaway's. He and George remained close. Sadler explains dressing-room reaction to Best's initial adventures: 'Well, it was difficult. Around the time of the Villa Park incident I started to get a bit resentful of George. I thought he was wasting that great talent and sticking two fingers up at the rest of us who were less gifted but more diligent in our approach to training and preparation for games. We had words. He reacted, more or less saying sod-off, I'll live my life the way I want to. And to be fair to George he was putting bonuses in our pockets and he was probably the only one doing it. That goes back to Wilf's time.

'I remember Tony Book writing an article in the *Evening News* saying George was shitting on his team-mates etc. and we all thought, hold on a minute, it's all right for us to have a go at him, but not an outsider. So there was a paradox there.'

A more significant paradox was that during the McGuinness/O'Farrell years George Best was the best player in the club, doing his stuff in style while senior professionals, who were consciously or otherwise undermining the two managers, used George as a scapegoat for United's troubles. McGuinness and O'Farrell thanked God for George. *He* wasn't the problem, but he was a convenient target for journalists and senior players at United who sought to explain the club's downfall in terms of one man's unprofessional behaviour. The illusion thus created persists.

Frank O'Farrell thought George 'a likable lad'. Martin Buchan contrasts Best with his putative clone 'Sir' Willie Morgan: 'George was a wonderful player. They all made a good living off his back, the poor lad never had a youth really. When I arrived the press had him marked as a villain, it was nearly over for him. But George was coming in after the games every Saturday with his legs black and blue from the kickings he was getting and he wouldn't even report to the physio, just go out and do his training and go his own way. And there would be Willie Morgan in the corner mouthing off . . .'

O'Farrell remembers George at this time as 'a kind of lost soul. He'd stay out training longer than anyone, he was a good trainer, obviously loved the game and would still be out shooting in with the apprentices long after the others had gone home. I don't think George had anywhere to go.'

Shortly after Dave Sadler left Mrs Fullaway's, George moved into a new house designed to his tastes. The dream home became renowned in Manchester. Life within was nightmarish: 'I was becoming a loner,' George recalls. 'About 1970 things started to get worse. It was gradual. I was drinking more, staying out later. When Wilf was manager I would go off on my own on a Friday night in London. I started going to the theatre. Some of the lads would stay in the hotel or go to the movies. I preferred the theatre, see a play, have a couple of lagers. But I always got in before eleven o'clock.'

Girls were his only indulgence at the beginning. Girls rather than women. Most of them were just good-looking. For George women didn't simply equal sex, although if that was how it looked from the outside that's how he preferred it to look. Girls were an escape. At first he used them to live the fantasy most men grow up with. Then the novelty wore off, the loneliness grew worse, and the girls started using him. A date with Georgie Best guaranteed front-page coverage, a spread in the gossip section being second prize. He was a male 'bimbo'. He was bored.

'I started having a few quid on the horses and going to casinos. Not because I was particularly interested in gambling, just for the buzz.' The boredom was personal and, worse, professional: 'I was bored with football, with all the nonsense at Old Trafford. I'd been in love with the game all my life, now it felt like I'd lost something; as if you'd been married for twenty years, then all of a sudden it's over.'

The scene in Manchester offered endless opportunity for a famous man seeking temporary relief from boredom. George's life began to revolve around a pub called the Brown Bull on the Salford/Manchester border. This was a high-life, low-life scene,

354

reflective of Cottonopolis as it had remained through the passage of the decades. A fun town. The Brown Bull was a home for those who didn't belong anywhere else. Actors from the nearby Granada Studios joined villains, dodgy bank-managers, gamblers, journalists and other refugees from suburban conventions. Jimmy Greer would have felt at ease in this milieu. Sir Matt Busby and his pals – the less conventional ones – would not have been offended by the scene in a bar where human vulnerability was not frowned upon, was, on the contrary, celebrated. Being flawed or, to put it more colloqui-ally, slightly fucked up, was deemed essential to membership of the Brown Bull's inner circle. George was happy here. He was left alone, accepted for what he was perceived to be, Jack the Lad. A mythical monster had been created. George Best was a prisoner of Georgie Best.

At first the monster was a media creation. Then insidiously, through the years '65 to '71/'2, the intelligent, gentle athlete known to David Sadler and me and the youngsters he'd grown up with at Old Trafford, lads like John Fitzpatrick, Bobby Noble and Jimmy Ryan – the real George Best – was isolated from the people he was fondest of and the game he loved. Fame allowed him to indulge some fantasies but it also detached him from the friends of bowling-alley, snooker-hall days. Others got married and settled to suburban existence, George hung out in Town. A first team player, he was not ever really regarded as a senior pro. He fell into a void somewhere between the factions at United. The younger players, his old buddies, found it hard to identify with the legend Georgie, yet at the same time the senior players didn't take him seriously in terms of his opinions about important matters. George Best was carrying them every week for four seasons yet he was never in on the politics of Old Trafford the way 'Sir' Willie and Alex Stepney were. A 'bimbo' outside, George was something of a 'bimbo' within as well.

He was only the greatest footballer in the world, European Footballer of the Year in 1968, yet nobody consulted him about training or tactics. And George was too timid to get involved without invitation: 'I knew the club was a mess. It was burning me up inside but I suppose I didn't have the guts to tell the great man to his face.'

During his slow descent George kept hoping that the club would sort itself out. The worse the mess became, the more he despaired, until in the end he was part of the problem, a symptom, rather than a cause of the sickness. The world didn't see things that way, neither did Sir Matt or Bobby Charlton.

Bobby was alienated from Frank O'Farrell because the manager wouldn't do something about George. O'Farrell tried but he was faced with a real dilemma: 'We were an inadequate team without him,' O'Farrell explains. 'The first time George went missing was before a cup-tie at Southampton. I fined him but didn't drop him. We got a draw down there. In the return at Old Trafford we were struggling. All of a sudden George scores two great goals and we've won.' O'Farrell also felt an obligation on a personal level: 'I thought I could help him or at least try. If I failed that would be too bad, but I didn't think he was my most serious problem, I felt for him in many ways.' Even when George lied to him O'Farrell sympathised.

'One day he came in after a spell on the run and told me he was concerned about his parents in Northern Ireland. He said they'd been threatened and so on. He claimed he'd been to Ireland to comfort them.' O'Farrell checked and discovered this was untrue. Reassured by his five-year contract, O'Farrell resolved to sort George out when 'the time was ripe'. O'Farrell now concedes that he might have acted sooner: 'I was anxious to get rid of the George Best problem, it was a real distraction and time consuming.' It was also terminating Bobby Charlton's faith in O'Farrell.

'It was unfortunate for Frank to come into this situation,' Bobby admits. 'There was no way he could win. If he dropped George he alienated the fans, at the same time the players were complaining to me as club captain.' Bobby took the complaints to the manager. George was not only failing to turn up, he had started messing on the training ground. At this stage O'Farrell was rarely at training. Malcolm Musgrove was popular with the players but helpless, surrounded by a family at war. When Bobby Charlton talked to O'Farrell he got little satisfaction. The manager, growing more exasperated by the day, told Bobby that he should sort George out himself if training was being disrupted. 'I didn't think he was a good captain,'

O'Farrell explains. 'They'd be practising set-pieces and George would do something to cock everything up. And Bobby would come in, "Why are we practising if he's screwing things up?" I told him not to come moaning to me. You're the captain with one hundred odd England caps, if you can't control the situation and work as planned don't come bloody moaning to me. Push George out of the way and get on with it.'

Bobby had been dropped by O'Farrell earlier in the season. O'Farrell admits that Charlton never stopped trying but simply wasn't playing well, and though he had no ulterior motive for dropping his skipper, Bobby thought otherwise: 'It was the Wilf thing all over again. They all seemed to think that if they dropped me it would prove something.' Left out, Bobby sulked, or so it seemed to the Morgan/Stepney tendency: 'Bobby trained on his own for a while,' O'Farrell recalls, 'just running endless laps of the pitch, talking to nobody. Stepney came to me and said, "What's the bloody matter with him?" As you can imagine, it was some club to try and manage.'

Denis Law was angry because he had been refused the four-year contract he'd sought. Nor was he able to play in midfield as he wished to. Paddy Crerand knew he was being sidelined with the youngsters. Paddy describes the atmosphere in the club that autumn as 'dreadful'.

Crerand thought O'Farrell a 'very, very, nice man, but totally lost. Looking at it from Frank's point of view he was working with ghosts really. The great man Matt Busby's still there, Jimmy's still there, Bobby and Denis are around and George has gone.' According to Paddy, Busby should never be blamed for O'Farrell's downfall, which was rapidly approaching: 'Anybody who claims Matt was involved in anything is telling a lie,' Crerand insists. 'Matt never interfered with Frank O'Farrell. Bobby was the one who got Frank the sack. Bobby was running to Louis Edwards all the time. If Frank wants to have the needle with anyone it is not Sir Matt, but Bobby Charlton. Matt didn't even know what was going on,' Paddy Crerand claims.

Bobby Charlton is equally loath to blame Sir Matt; 'I don't think the old man wanted to get involved. I was as much to blame as anyone for Frank's dismissal,' Bobby says.

The truth revealed by the denouement to this wretched saga is that Sir Matt Busby was intimately involved and well aware of everything that was happening. Bobby *had* gone to see 'The Boss' in his Kings Road house, the first time Charlton had ever been inside the Busby home. The visit was at Sir Matt's invitation. Bobby's concerns were genuine, those of the great professional he was. He could see that he was as helpless as anyone else to halt United's decline: 'I complained about George,' Bobby admits. 'I told Sir Matt the football world was laughing at us and asked him to do something about it. "Bobby," he said, "to err is human, to forgive is divine." '

Bobby Charlton's hostility towards George was evident to all at Old Trafford. The consummate professional was deeply offended by Best's apparent contempt for the rules by which his colleagues were governed. Reflecting on his mood at that time, Bobby admits that in human terms he felt sorry for George: 'Sometimes I'd seen him looking as if he'd been out all night and part of me would be outraged yet at the same time I often wanted to put my arm round his shoulder and offer him advice. But everyone was doing that and I just couldn't bring myself to make the gesture.'

Busby had been monitoring events on the field and off. On 28 October United lost 4–1 at home to Spurs. That night the club held its Annual Dinner Dance for the staff. O'Farrell and his wife Anne went along: 'You don't feel like socialising after a result like that, but it was part of the job,' Frank explains. Anne went to the toilet just before the function ended. As she passed Sir Matt on the way back O'Farrell claims a remark was passed: 'Anne only mentioned it on the way home. He'd said that I was, "an independent sod. Why don't you get him to come and talk to me? I used to be like that but Frank shouldn't be that way with me." I was annoyed. Why wasn't he man enough to come and talk directly to me, I thought. I'd always invited him into the office for a cup of coffee so he had ample opportunity to give me advice if he thought I needed it.'

O'Farrell tackled Busby on the Monday morning after training: 'I waited behind and asked him in for a coffee. What's all this about me being an independent sod?' O'Farrell asked as politely as he could. Busby ventured that Martin Buchan wasn't playing well. He'd been at fault for one of the goals against Spurs. He also indicated disapproval of the omission of Bobby Charlton a few weeks before. O'Farrell challenged him on the Spurs goal: 'I probably sealed my fate that morning,' Frank speculates. 'He said Buchan should have been on the cover when Chivers scored for Spurs. In fact, it was Buchan who jumped with Chivers, and someone else who put the ball in the net. David Sadler was the one who ought to have been covering if anyone. Oh, he said, I must have got that wrong. Then he questioned me for dropping Bobby. So, I thought, I've got to defend myself here.' This O'Farrell did, respectfully, but firmly.

Then George Best took his most spectacular liberty to date. He disappeared with the actress Sinead Cusack. Ms Cusack, a member of the famous theatrical dynasty, was a cut above the usual Best 'bimbo'. She was an intelligent self-possessed young woman with whom George fell madly in love. According to Sinead's television producer brother, Paul, the romance was just 'an adventure' for his sister: 'She got lots of publicity and her career took off from that point,' Paul explains. This wasn't the scenario projected to the world via the national press and television who covered the story as if it were a matter of international importance. The couple were eventually dis-covered and siege was laid on what was described as 'Georgie's Love-Nest.'

Manchester United had had enough. Not Frank O'Farrell, but the real power behind the scenes: Sir Matt Busby. At a specially convened board meeting the Best scandal was the only item on the agenda. Busby spoke. He thought Best should be placed on the transfer-list. Bobby Charlton's opinion that the club had become a 'laughing stock' was being vividly borne out. O'Farrell, the manager, objected, politely as usual: 'I told them not to do it. I still needed him. I said what will happen if Manchester City try to buy, which I suspected Malcolm Allison would do . . . and did. I also knew that this would be seen as my response. I objected as strongly as I could but I was over-ruled. From then on my position was weakened.'

City did bid for George. As O'Farrell feared, he was blamed for the decision. Newspapers talked about O'Farrell's patience finally snapping' . . . and of the manager 'facing up to the Best problem at last'. United valued George Best at £300,000. Newspapers editorialised about The Boy Who Couldn't Handle Fame. On the feature pages, where he'd once been lionised, George Best was now analysed. Agony aunts and uncles sought meaning in the superstar's sad – yet newsworthy – decline. Some told Georgie to 'come off it', some called him a 'spoiled brat', the hero who died of self-indulgence. Best had been 'given too much, too soon', and the results were, many wrote, 'inevitable'. For the conventionally wise, George Best was a gift from the gods. Virtually all involved in this orgy of self-righteousness agreed that Sir Matt deserved a slap on the wrists for being too lenient with his prodigious star: 'Sort him out, Sir Matt' was another favoured solution.

The one man who stood to benefit from the Best saga was, ironically, Frank O'Farrell. Had he chosen to, O'Farrell could have billed United's troubles to George, taken the credit for 'facing up to the problem' and sought a fresh start. Alas, Frank was too honest to adopt this ploy. He knew that having covered up a multitude of sins in the team for four seasons Best's fall from grace was but the symptom of a deeper malaise at Old Trafford. A modicum of low cunning might have served O'Farrell at this point, but alas, Frank was a straight shooter, 'lost' as Crerand explained.

Amid the media hysteria of the time one piece of journalism stands out, a model of reasoned assessment, an objective, informed insight into the reality behind the scenes at Old Trafford. David Meek has been covering the Manchester United story for the *Manchester Evening News* for almost thirty-four years. David, son of a sports writer on the *Yorkshire Post*, was pressed into service on a temporary basis when Tom Jackson died at Munich. He'd joined the *News* as a political correspondent and leader writer eighteen months before the Munich Air Crash. As he had done some football reporting at weekends on his father's newspaper David was asked to fill the vacancy on Jackson's death. He had no desire to be a football correspondent and accepted the job initially as a stop-gap until the end of the '58 season. United was, as he explains, 'a news story as well'. So he stayed with it: 'It was always going to be just another season.'

'Like many footballers I found Manchester United very hard to walk away from, there was always something happening, even in the unsuccessful years.' Reflecting, David vouches that every year has been different. Sometimes he feels embarrassed to admit that he'd been doing this job for over thirty years: 'People say, "What a terrible rut watching the same team every week for thirty-four years," but I must admit I never felt like that. The politics of Old Trafford,' he concedes, 'intrigued me.'

After a couple of seasons Matt Busby wrote to the editor of the *Evening News* expressing satisfaction with Meek's work: 'Old Tom Henry was the editor. He and Matt were pals. I was congratulated and given a rise.' The message was unmistakable: don't rock the boat.

David Meek's assignment was one of the toughest in journalism for paranoia is endemic to professional soccer and journalists are mistrusted, at best servile, at worst inventors of stories designed to do the football man down. Few within football understand the journalist's role, those who do are usually bullshit artists. Chronicling football's affairs at close quarters, for a local rather than national readership, is a tricky business. A delicate balance between conflicting interests must be preserved. The reporter must serve his readers while maintaining a working relationship with the subjects of his copy. Achieving this, in a civilised yet incisive manner, as David Meek invariably did over a period of three decades, requires the instincts of a good reporter and the skills of a diplomat.

Meek belongs to the school of gentleman journalist, the old school. His work reflects his personality, urbane, objective, sympathetic. The style is literate, the tone even. There are few theatrical flourishes, no hint of behind-the-scenes intimacy. The occasional scoop is welcome but by and large Meek's work involves keeping his readers informed and the club reasonably happy. Access is important.

Busby was usually pleasant in his dealings with David Meek, though a certain distance was maintained. Meek travelled with the team on coach or train and was privy to many things he couldn't report without breaching the unwritten rules which governed his difficult task. David sat on the coach and never broke the rules, passing up many juicy stories down the years.

361

Busby remained 'affable on the surface, but he was suspicious of journalists and I was always kept at arm's length,' Meek explains. This disappointed him slightly. He was anxious to learn more about the game, thought he might benefit from the great man's knowledge. 'I was raw in terms of football knowledge at the beginning,' he recalls. Alas, no tutorials were offered.

Ten years on Meek was still as he puts it 'a second-form boy. I regarded Matt Busby as the headmaster, he had that aura about him. When you are around for so long you might expect to be treated like a sixth-former, a prefect. You know the head-master starts to talk to you man-to-man.' But David never became a prefect. Even when he was in his forties Busby was still calling him 'David lad'. Conflict was rare but not unknown. In 1963 when there were rumours about Busby's position at the club Meek sought an interview with Harold Hardman expecting confirmation that the manager's job was secure: 'I thought it was inconceivable that United would dismiss him five years after Munich. It was that confirmation I was seeking to nail the speculation,' Meek remembers. Hardman somewhat grud-gingly gave the assurance Meek was seeking. 'Before I had time to write the story Matt was on the phone. He said he wanted to see me.' The meeting in Busby's office was terse: ' "I know what you're trying to do," he said, "you're trying to get the Chairman to say my job is on the line." I was shocked and disappointed. I'd always been supportive in general terms, and the idea that I would go behind his back to do a story undermining him was to misunderstand me completely. He had obviously made the wrong assessment of me.'

Meek found Busby an intimidating figure. 'I didn't like to cross him. It wasn't that he would shout or make threats, but one sensed an inner strength. When you were face to face with him he was extremely formidable. I mean one could have said, "How dare you, I'm doing my job without being unduly vicious or unfair," but I don't know a single journalist who ever responded in that way.'

After fourteen years covering Manchester United David Meek knew the score. So when the Best/O'Farrell story reached its frenzied climax he was best placed to serve the reading public. This he did by penning a piece for the *Evening News* which attempted to place the lurid events depicted elsewhere in some perspective. Meek liked O'Farrell whom he found 'personable and thoroughly decent'. Having witnessed the sacrifice of Wilf McGuinness at the same altar Meek wrote that if blame were to be apportioned for United's failure then the buck should not stop with Frank O'Farrell or indeed George Best. 'I felt that sacking Frank was too easy. So I wrote a piece pointing out that everybody at Old Trafford ought to share the responsibility for United's problems. Of course the manager must accept some blame but the players also had to answer for their performances.' And Meek added 'the directors made a mess of handing over from Busby to McGuinness without preparing the young coach adequately.' O'Farrell, he went on, had 'inherited a mess. Sacking him was no solution. Now was the time to clear the air, issue a statement supporting the manager and resolve that all at the club would work together to solve the problems.'

This article, filed in mid-November, was unfortunately timed from the club's point of view. Two days previously the Board had decided to sack O'Farrell. Meek had no knowledge of this decision, but Sir Matt thought he had and was, as Meek puts it, 'deliberately defying the club. He thought I was trying to embarrass them.' For this crime Meek was banned from travelling with the United party, a sentence that stands to this day.

The letter delivered to the *Evening News* offices was signed by Les Olive on behalf of the board. 'Mr David Meek is no longer welcome to travel on the team coach.' The letter was addressed to the editor, Brian Redhead, a journalist of the new school: 'Brian was a tough character. He was outraged and quite prepared to go to war on my behalf. "You write exactly what you want," he told me. I thanked him for the support, there was no need to go to war,' Meek recalls.

Behind the amiable, urbane exterior David Meek was a courageous reporter. On 'a point of principle' he continued his normal working routine. He dined in the same hotel restaurants and travelled on the same trains as the United team. He had a job to do and wouldn't be cowed by the hostility now focused on him. Busby and the other directors affected not to see him. The players, with one notable brave exception, ignored him. All but Paddy Crerand, who made a point of hailing him fondly when they met. 'I will always remember Paddy for that,' Meek says. 'It was a difficult time and he spoke out and didn't care a toss about whether it was politically acceptable or not.'

O'Farrell was courageous as well. He would make a point of leaving the table in the restaurant to go over to David and inform him of team news.

David Meek's article suggesting that the directors get behind O'Farrell forestalled the move to sack him. Having insisted that George Best must go a couple of weeks earlier, Busby now made the extraordinary decision that he must be forgiven and brought back to Old Trafford. Frank O'Farrell wasn't consulted: 'The first I knew of it was when a journalist rang up to tell me, "George is coming back," ' O'Farrell recalls. O'Farrell, still observing protocol, rang his chairman. Edwards was unavailable so he called Busby. Sir Matt confirmed the news. O'Farrell argued that this U-turn was completely out of order: 'I told him you can't do that without informing me. I'm the manager, what's going on? Busby replied: "We need George Best at Old Trafford." ' O'Farrell believes on reflection that this blatant disregard for him was an attempt to force his resignation. There were by now three and a half years left on his contract. If he resigned United would save over £50,000. He didn't panic, but the writing on the wall was becoming increasingly clear.

Best recalls his meeting with Busby: 'He was always giving me advice. People would phone up to tell him stories, he knew everything that was going on in town. This time he started going on about the Brown Bull, except he kept getting the name wrong. First he called it the Brown Cow, then the Black Bull, but he always got the colour – or the animal – wrong. I nearly laughed but I thought I'd better not.' Their relationship was odd, intimate on an emotional level, practically non-existent in terms of conversation: 'He was always good to me, no matter how badly I'd behaved. I remember once going to London for an FA disciplinary hearing. I'd had a few drinks but I wasn't drunk. I got suspended and on the way downstairs in the lift I got sick. It wasn't booze, just emotion. He put his arms around me and just held me. He didn't say anything, he just seemed genuinely sorry for me despite the trouble I caused him.'

O'Farrell's execution was only postponed. Busby consulted Denis Law and Willie Morgan about Tommy Docherty, Scotland's manager. This controversial character had been rehabilitated by outstanding work with the Scottish team which he had already virtually assured qualification for the 1974 World Cup Finals. Law and Morgan had toured Brazil with Scotland the previous summer. Both vouched that 'The Doc' was a reformed character.

On 16 December United travelled to London to play Crystal Palace. The result, a 5–0 humiliation, was the excuse Busby needed. Tommy Docherty attended the game. In the Palace boardroom at half-time he was offered the United job. Getting rid of Frank O'Farrell was the next item on the agenda. United were second from the bottom of the First Division.

O'Farrell had arranged a Testimonial match against Celtic for Bobby Charlton in October. Celtic travelled from Scotland attracting 60,000 to Old Trafford. A dinner to celebrate Charlton was arranged for Monday after the Palace game. Louis Edwards rang O'Farrell that afternoon to ask him to go on Granada Television to explain the Best situation. O'Farrell refused. There had been enough hysteria about George, we should cool things down, O'Farrell advised. He remembers someone asking him that day if he felt secure? His answer was, 'Yes.' He thought the outside world, the real world, could see the truth of his circumstances: 'David Meek was great. They went insane over his article. Brian James also wrote a supportive piece in the *Sunday Times*. They were angry about that as well.' James, one of the most distinguished British sports writers of that period was, O'Farrell believed, voicing the majority opinion. If United *had* become a laughing stock Frank O'Farrell was not to blame.

At the Charlton dinner United's manager was not seated at the top table. The room was ablaze with rumours of the imminent sacking. Johnny Carey came over to Frank offering words of solace: 'He told me I'd done a good job but he said, "you've got a few problems." ' Martin Buchan also talked to

365

Frank: 'I'm going to tell the chairman that if they get rid of you I want out as well,' Buchan said. O'Farrell urged him not to do anything.

The following morning O'Farrell was instructed by Les Olive to attend a board meeting at four p.m. Johnny Aston and Malcolm Musgrove were also summoned. Aston picked O'Farrell up at his Salford home. It was a glorious summer-like day: 'Nice day for an execution,' O'Farrell quipped to his chief-scout. It was 19 December, one week before Christmas Day.

Louis Edwards broke the news: 'We are relieving you of your duties,' he told his manager. O'Farrell asked why.

'No reason,' Louis replied.

'Mr Chairman, I am not leaving this room until you give me a reason for my dismissal,' O'Farrell retorted. Louis looked across at Sir Matt. Busby's head was down, avoiding eye-contact with his pal. Louis then admitted that O'Farrell was being sacked because of United's 'League position'. O'Farrell asked that this be recorded in the minutes. Wise in the ways of professional football, Frank was thinking ahead to settlement of his contract. As always, he was being correct. The meeting concluded. Sir Matt had not spoken.

The headlines the following day reflected the scale of the massacre. As well as O'Farrell, Aston and Musgrove were dismissed and it was announced, 'George Best will never play for United again.' United promised to honour the remaining years of his contract in full. Frank went home.

Christmas would be bleak for Frank, his sacked colleagues and their families. That evening a lorry pulled up outside O'Farrell's home in Eccles Old Road, Salford: 'The lorry-driver knocked on the door. He said, "I've just heard the news on the radio and I've come to say how sorry I am. I'm a United supporter and I'm ashamed of them now." It was a lovely gesture,' Frank recalls. The following day there was another knock on O'Farrell's door. Johnny Foy, Busby's close friend had arrived with Canon, another of Sir Matt's intimates: 'They said we're sorry for what's happened, Frank. We think you've had a raw deal.' This coming from Johnny who was as close to Busby as anyone, who played cards with him in his house, I really appreciated it.' Johnny Foy had come bearing more than condolences: 'He said you have a mortgage to pay and children to bring up, let me give you £10,000 now to tide you over until you get your settlement. This was the nicest thing that happened to me during this period,' O'Farrell explains. He refused the offer but promised to avail himself of it if the need arose.

Manchester United had not finished with Frank O'Farrell just yet. The torture continued. He received a letter requesting that he return the club car, a Jaguar. He offered to buy the car out of his compensation money. The next letter was from United's solicitors: 'They offered me £20,000 odd in settlement.' Frank consulted a leading Manchester solicitor. He felt in a desperately weak position. He'd seen judges and barristers drinking champagne in Manchester's boardroom, what chance a fair hearing if he went to court? His advisor reassured him: 'Don't worry, I'm a City supporter.' Frank was also told, 'You will have to sign-on at the Labour Exchange to show that you are looking for work.'

'I had been working since I was fifteen, I had never had to sign on in my life. That hurt.'

Eleven months later, after his case has been listed for court hearing, Frank settled for £45,000, less £2,300 for his 'Jag'. His career in club management was finished, apart from a short period at Cardiff where he went as troubleshooter to save the Welsh club from relegation. Finally he went abroad to manage the Iranian national team, successfully, winning the Asian Games and qualifying for the Olympics.

O'Farrell determined never to be at the mercy of professional soccer again: 'I thought if Matt Busby and Manchester United are the good guys, what are the bad guys like? In the boardroom after matches you'd see showbiz celebrities, prominent businessmen, priests, lawyers and judges all enjoying lavish hospitality. At the same time they had taken Jimmy Murphy's taxi and telephone off him, and Johnny Aston the chief-scout was driving his own car, the contradiction was sickening.'

Sir Matt Busby never contacted O'Farrell again: 'I didn't want him to contact me, I never wanted to speak to the man again. I have no time for that man. He hired me and he fired me, despite the fact that he'd told me at the beginning that the job would take a long time.'

Some people in Manchester will tell you that Frank O'Farrell is a bitter man. According to Paddy Crerand, O'Farrell has 'a poison against Matt. Frank was too nice to be a football manager,' Crerand believes. Another point of view was expressed to Jean and Sheena Busby by a Catholic priest acquainted with Sir Matt and Frank O'Farrell: 'That's a very wicked thing Sir Matt has done sacking a good man like Frank O'Farrell.'

18

'The Doc'

'I never did anything, I fell in love.'

Tommy Docherty

In a work of fiction Tommy Docherty would serve as an ideal villain. He is one of the most notorious characters in professional soccer. Busby chose Docherty to succeed Frank O'Farrell because he seemed 'big' enough for the job of managing Manchester United. Denis Law and Willie Morgan were consulted. Martin Buchan, who also played for Scotland during Docherty's reign, was not consulted. In similar circumstances in eras past, Matt Busby would surely have sought advice from Johnny Carey or Roger Byrne.

There were sound reasons for appointing 'The Doc'. He had an impressive track record in football management. At Chelsea in the Sixties he'd built a brilliant young team from such talents as Peter Osgood, Terry Venables, John Hollins and Peter Bonetti. This side had class, the same kind of wit and elegance, distinctly Scottish, that Matt Busby valued. One night in Blackpool, coincidentally in the same hotel United used, Docherty caught eight of his team breaking the midnight curfew. As they made their way up the the fire-escape 'The Doc' nabbed them and the following day sent them home in public disgrace. He was impulsive. But he could nurture talent. With Scotland he had shown himself courageous enough to defy the parochial bigots who controlled the game up there by selecting 'Anglos' – Scots exiled in England, like Denis Law – to represent their country. Moreover, Docherty allowed his players to express themselves. In that sense he was big, or at least bigger than most. So one can identify Busby's football rationale for turning to Docherty in his hour of need.

Docherty got off to a bad start with United being relegated to the Second Division eighteen months after he took over. Since enough blood had been shed over the previous three years, however, he was not sacked. The following season United won the Second Division playing scintillating football while averaging crowds of over 50,000 at Old Trafford. In 1976 Docherty led his team out at Wembley to face Southampton in the FA Cup Final. United were long odds on to win. They lost 1–0, the goal scored by Bobby Stokes against the run of play. In 1977 United returned to Wembley, this time as underdogs, to face Liverpool. A fluke goal credited to Jimmy Greenoff was enough to give them victory. Six weeks later Tommy Docherty was sacked. He had fallen in love with Mary Brown, wife of Laurie Brown, United's physiotherapist.

While understandable in football terms, Docherty's appointment is difficult to reconcile with the values Busby had always sought to promote within Manchester United Football Club. 'The Doc' was famous for many things before coming to Old Trafford, observing the rules by which professional soccer is governed was not one of them.

Since Busby's retirement Manchester United had, in Bobby Charlton's view, become the 'laughing stock of the football world'. Under Tommy Docherty the next five years would read like a cheap novel. All was revealed, as they say, when Docherty and Willie Morgan became embroiled in a legal battle which was triggered by a television interview screened by Granada eighteen months after 'The Doc' left Old Trafford. Commenting on Docherty's performance, Morgan described him as 'about the worst manager there had ever been'. Docherty sued for libel. This he would later describe as 'the biggest mistake of my life'.

Morgan spent two years preparing his defence, during which he gathered enough evidence to level twenty-nine separate allegations of misconduct against Docherty, covering the years prior to the manager's dismissal for having an affair with Mary Brown. A number of players from the club were due to give evidence on Morgan's behalf at the Old Bailey, among them Paddy Crerand, Denis Law and Alex Stepney.

To an eye untutored in professional football's ways, the charges laid against 'The Doc' were damning. He was alleged to have sold Cup Final tickets on the black market, two before the 1974 Final – for £100 each – and two hundred for a total of £7,000 when United reached Wembley in 1977. Docherty was also alleged to have demanded a personal payment of £1,000 to allow George Best to play for Dunstable Town in August 1974. Barry Fry, Dunstable's Manager and a former United player, testified that he had agreed the payment and was satisfied that the money was for Docherty's personal use.

Many other incidents of this nature were recounted when it was expedient to discredit Tommy Docherty. He had muscled in on players' commercial activities, carving a piece of the action for himself whenever possible, as in an advertisement for Gillette razors originally offered to Steve Coppell which eventually featured Gordon Hill, and 'The Doc' as well. On a tour of Australia in 1975 he committed the United players to a head-tennis tournament in a deal agreed with an agent in Manchester before leaving England. The United head-tennis squad would consist of three relatively junior players – Brian Greenhoff, Sammy McIlroy and Steve Coppell – and 'The Doc'! The fee was £1,000 with more to come as the tournament progressed, the money to be shared amongst the head-tennis squad. The inference was that Docherty would get the lion's share of this money, the younger players a nominal fee. When members of the first team learned of this arrangement, a row ensued for the form was to distribute such money among *all* the players through the players' pool.

In Michael Chick and David Smith's book *Betrayal of a Legend* this dispute is described as coming to a head in 'an extraordinary scene more appropriate to gangland than to Britain's most prestigious football club'.

One evening after a game in Sydney, Docherty called a meeting of all the players. He sat at a table in front of them, a full bottle of brandy on the table beside him. Each player was allowed to speak. They aired their grievances. Then it was his turn. One by one he laid into them, telling them what he thought of them as footballers and people. This tirade was prefaced by an admission that he had arranged the head-tennis tournament with an agent before leaving Manchester. It was a rough encounter, as Docherty knew it would be, for he had insisted that seventeen-year-old Arthur Albiston remain outside the room on the grounds that the kid was too young for this kind of thing. The confrontation lasted an hour, by the end of which, Alex Stepney claims in *Betrayal of a Legend*, the bottle in front of 'The Doc' was empty. There is no doubt that Busby and his fellow directors were aware of scenes like this.

Willie Morgan's libel action was subsequently heard at the Old Bailey. Questioned by the player's barrister about apparent discrepancies in his evidence, Docherty was forced to admit that he had told 'a pack of lies'. Docherty was tried on two charges of perjury in the same court in 1981, then acquitted on the grounds that the lies were not deliberate. But mud sticks, and, sadly and rather unfairly, Tommy Docherty's notoriety has entered football's folklore, the suggestion being that his conduct was an affront to values prevailing in professional soccer. Which begs the question, why wasn't he dismissed by Manchester United during the five-year period when his conduct was supposed to be at odds with the ethos of this great club? After all, those who would later accuse him of notorious behaviour were close friends of Sir Matt Busby, then the most influential voice in the boardroom. There can be little doubt that Busby and his fellow directors knew of Docherty's activities all along. They weren't shocked or minded to dismiss him, because, lurid though his conduct may seem to the outsider, many of 'The Doc's' alleged crimes were as old as the professional game itself. And of course, after a bad start, his team delivered on the field. Losing is the only crime in football, as Frank O'Farrell and Wilf McGuinness had both learned.

When Docherty felt the time was right to declare his love for Mary Brown he sold the story to *The People*. He thought he was safe. He had just won United their first major trophy in almost a decade. The team that won had done so in the cavalier United tradition, or so it could be argued. There was the scent of old glory in the air. Tom felt secure. For another reason: adultery was not unknown at Old Trafford. Wondering who might cast the first stone, 'The Doc' thought and thought again and concluded he would be OK.

His instincts were correct. If you grow up in the Gorbals, Glasgow's legendary tenement district, your 'suss' is usually pretty good. On the day this tabloid scandal broke, Docherty phoned his chairman and close friend, Louis Edwards, to mark his card. 'Champagne' Louis was still celebrating the Cup Final win and was asleep that Sunday afternoon. His son Martin now a United director, took the call. He promised to inform 'Father' and told 'The Doc' not to worry. The next day Manchester United issued a statement confirming that their manager's love-affair was a personal matter. 'The Doc' remained sanguine.

Paddy Crerand was outraged. The club's name was being dragged through the mud. Sir Matt Busby was on holiday in Ireland when the story of Docherty's affair broke on an indifferent nation. Sir Matt was staying in the beautiful Downhill Hotel in Ballina, Co. Mayo, in the west of Ireland. He was on a golfing holiday with two of his pals, Peter Molloy and Martin Flynn, both wealthy Manchester Catholics, both fond of the 'ould sod'.

Crerand phoned Busby at the Downhill: 'What's he done now?' Sir Matt began. Paddy provided the details. Sir Matt booked his return flight.

Laurie Brown had been reflecting too. His life had been shattered in the most appalling public manner. What about his two daughters? What about his job? How could he continue to work at Old Trafford for the man now living with his wife? Oddly, Brown came to the same conclusion as 'The Doc'. Adultery was par for the course at United. This thought had reassured 'The Doc'. Now Laurie Brown also drew some comfort from it.

'The Doc' was sacked on 4 July. The following day's *Daily Express* headlined the story: 'CLUB WIVES OUST DOC'. Under the joint byline of John Roberts/James Price this article explained that 'Directors' wives at the club, which is proud of its family image, helped force Docherty out'. Docherty was the source of this news claiming, 'I've been punished for falling in love. This is the most shattering experience of my football life.' The wives, the *Express* added, 'had acted from shock and embarrassment over his love affair'. This news broke two weeks after the club's statement asserting that Tommy Docherty's love life was a 'personal matter'.

Between times one cannot say for certain what these 'club

wives' did or did not do. Lady Jean Busby and Mrs Muriel Edwards were the ladies concerned. Both were extremely decent, reasonably worldly people. There is no proof that their influence was decisive in the sacking of Tommy Docherty.

On Monday 4 July the United Board met twice at Louis Edwards's Alderley Edge home. First in at nine a.m. was Laurie Brown. What happened at *this* meeting depends on whose tale you believe. The conventional account is that Brown offered numerous stories about Docherty's conduct of club business, the kind of evidence Willie Morgan would later gather for his defence in the libel case. On hearing this we are assured the Board was shocked and promised to sack the villain of the piece and give Laurie a wage rise.

Some people around Old Trafford tell another story. In this version Laurie Brown was informed that *he* would have to go, 'The Doc' would stay and a golden handshake would be paid to Laurie to ease his hurt and shame. All the speculation of the previous fortnight had prepared Laurie Brown for this verdict so he had taken certain precautions. If he must go, then, Laurie informed the board, he would sell *his* story about adultery at Old Trafford to the tabloids. Hence the need for a second board meeting. At which Tommy Docherty was given the bad news.

Tommy Docherty's affair with Mary Brown had been going on for three years. They were discreet. There was nothing cheap or lurid about their romance. Today, thirteen years on, Tommy Docherty and Mary Brown live happily in Hyde, Cheshire. They are clearly in love. She is a charming woman whose misfortune it was to find herself in this soap-opera setting.

What is really rather cheap about the Docherty Affair is the way it was conducted and presented to the public. Manchester United were certainly entitled to sack him, indeed another man might have chosen to resign. If one discounts the official reason given for his dismissal and believes the alternative account, it appears that Docherty was sacked not for his behaviour but because Laurie Brown threatened to create an even bigger scandal by going to the tabloids with even more lurid tales of life at Old Trafford. By and large the public has accepted the official account of this affair which portrays Manchester United as a 'family club', shocked by adultery and *worse*, it seems, the touting of blackmarket Cup Final tickets. When the business of selling cup tickets to spivs was raised as a determining reason for dismissing him 'The Doc' smilingly retorted, 'Are you sacking me for selling tickets on the black-market? I've been doing that since 1950!' The hypocrisy shocked even this street-fighter.

Commenting approvingly on the decision to rid United of this disreputable character, one newspaper observed: 'Sir Matt Busby had created a club with high standards of public conduct.' Keeping Docherty would, it was claimed, 'fly right in the face of United's traditions'. However, the hypocrisy of Docherty's years at Old Trafford, ironically reflected in the furore surrounding his demise, is extraordinary by any standards. One might seek a perspective on Docherty's life and times at Old Trafford by reflecting on the fate of his predecessors. When United's Board of Directors – the same men now lauded for upholding decent standards – had sacked McGuinness and O'Farrell nobody mentioned integrity and tradition.

Billy Meredith would have understood the moral of Docherty's five years at Old Trafford; the crime in professional soccer is not to breach the regulations, but rather to be found out. Life, as Meredith had observed it seventy years previously, had not changed. The Wizard knew all about intergrity, he possessed it. Until he entered professional football the Welsh Methodist had been a man of principle. Forced to tarnish himself, to lie and cheat and break the rules in order to get just reward for his labour, Meredith insisted on speaking out, pointing to the hypocrisy of the merchant class who ran the professional game, spelling out, chapter and verse, how preposterous their idea of integrity was. Meredith was a crusader. Penury was his reward. Honesty was his virtue. Unlike Catholics, Manchester Catholics in particular, Methodists live by their principles. Most do anyway. Methodism is not convenience food. Meredith took under-the-counter payments, illegal signing-on fees and when necessary represented the crooks on his Board by offering a bribe to Alec Leake, the Villa captain, in order to try and fix a game. Why not? As Meredith saw it integrity was like virginity – you either had it or not. Methodists are like that, there are no subtle deals with conscience. You live by the book or you don't.

There was more than a touch of Billy Meredith about 'The Doc' during his Manchester years. A rogue renowned for his wheeling and dealing he was unapologetic for his various breaches of football law. Tickets? Everyone sold to touts, including directors. Under-the-counter payments illegal? Come off it. Everyone in professional football was involved at some stage or another in 'backhanders'. As in Meredith's time, club chairmen, the upholders of football integrity were 'at it' themselves as soon as they were out the door of the League Management Committee. Illegal approaches to players – and managers – contracted to other clubs, who didn't do it? Selling stories to the tabloids was custom and practice in the game. 'The Doc's' stories were simply better. If they wanted fiction he was their man. The jokes were good as well.

'The Doc' had tried integrity – at Chelsea when he was naive enough to send eight of his best players home for breaking the curfew he had imposed at the hotel in Blackpool. That cost him his job. He learned a bitter lesson and decided to conform to football's perverse notion of integrity, and being the impulsive fellow he was– and fundamentally honest – he was less inclined, as the years wore on, to conceal his roguishness.

When Sir Matt came to reflect on a successor to Frank O'Farrell – the man of real intergrity as victim – Docherty's notoriety may have made him pause. Briefly. Busby had never been a crusader like Billy Meredith. He had never been indiscreet like 'The Doc'. But he had long since been tarnished by professional soccer, as had everyone else at Old Trafford. The 1957 Cup Final team, the 'Red Devils', had received many times the number of Final tickets allowed for by Football Association law which restricted each of them to an allocation of twelve. Matt knew about this for *he* had sanctioned this breach of regulations. Some of the players in the pre-Munich era had bartered enthusiastically on the black-market. Matt could not have been unaware of this. Those players were on an artificial wage of £17 a week so who could blame them if they doubled their annual salary by flogging a few tickets to the spivs? Within the context of professional soccer Tommy Docherty was an imaginary villain. The truth is that given the nature of the game Manchester United was bound to confront reality sooner or later.

Insidiously, year by year the reality of professional soccer seeped into Old Trafford in the post-Johnny Morris/Charlie Mitten era. In 1963 the players were given 100 FA Cup Final tickets each, a spectacular breach of Football Association rules. By then a slush fund existed – as at every club – to bribe young players to join United. This tarnished everybody from Busby to Jimmy Murphy and the club's coaches and scouts. Great people, lousy game.

The myth of United's integrity suited Matt Busby. When players came looking for rises, the big money available elsewhere, Matt could always point to the interests of Manchester United Football Club, its ethos, which was vaguely, increasingly vaguely, to do with integrity. Thus Denis Law could be made to feel guilty about asking for a salary journeymen were earning elsewhere. Thus, Bobby Charlton felt he was conforming to United's ethos when declaring that he would play for nothing. Why should a great *professional* player play for nothing? Nobby Stiles was the classic victim of the psychology of 'integrity' as promoted at Old Trafford. Having initially signed for a Miraculous Medal from Lourdes, turning down £4,000 'dirty money' from Wolves, Nobby, one of the most beautiful spirits ever to serve the United cause, returned from the World Cup realising that his wage, £35 a week, was outrageously low. He was under contract and Matt Busby reminded him that contracts must be honoured. After fourteen years' outstanding, cheaply bought, service, Nobby was transferred to Middlesbrough for £22,500 in the period after the McGuinness sacking when Busby was back in charge. When I discussed the Busby story with Paddy Crerand a short while ago he said, alluding to his own departure from United during Docherty's time, 'I know I got a testimonial but I'd been there thirteen years, everyone got a testimonial.' Paddy is as honest as the day is long. He's a Busby loyalist, sadly he is wrong about a number of things: testimonials for instance.

Nobby Stiles never had a testimonial. He wasn't fly enough.

Like Paddy, Nobby believed the myth of integrity. Jimmy Murphy never got a testimonial. Jimmy ended up doing a 'bunk' on British Rail. These scandals are down to integrity as it is understood in football and as it was enforced by Matt Busby at Manchester United after 1945. Billy Meredith would have laughed, as Tommy Docherty did. James Gibson and Harold Hardman would not have seen the joke.

Until the Mary Brown affair Tommy Docherty had been acclaimed as a worthy successor to Sir Matt Busby. They got on well together.

Sir Matt Busby was no fool. He knew what 'The Doc' was like. He knew what the game was like. He had done his best to administer professional football's so-called laws, and they had served him well, in fact you could argue that he might not have been able to create the wonders he had done in a world where integrity was real rather than fake. Now that his beloved United was in trouble, staring relegation in the face, Matt was desperate. Tommy Docherty was not the choice of Prudent Matt, rather Matt the Gambler.

'The Doc' thought he had been employed to do the dirty work. To him Manchester United was 'the best football club in the world'. But the team he found on arrival at Old Trafford 'weren't giving a hundred per cent, they were not interested in how they played, only how long they played'.

'Bobby Charlton did me a great favour,' he explains. 'Bobby came to me one day at Stoke and asked permission to speak to Matt and the chairman. He'd decided to retire. I knew that was a decision I would have to make one day, and I knew it wouldn't be a popular one.'

Bobby recalls that decision: 'I'd always wondered what it would be like when you had to make a decision that you were not going to play any more. I played in the World Cup in Mexico in 1970, that was my last international. At the club we really struggled for a couple of years and I began to feel mentally drained as much as physically drained. And the matches were getting hard, we nearly got relegated. I realised I wasn't looking forward to getting up on a Saturday morning any more, I'm not wanting to play, so I thought maybe this is what it feels like. So I said to Norma one morning, I think I'll pack it in at the end of the season.

'There was no ego or any of that rubbish about getting out at the the top, because I wasn't going out at the top. We were playing bloody awful. I'd only had one full close season off since I was seventeen. With playing for England, going on club or international tours, the most I'd ever had off was four weeks. I knew it was over for me.'

Charlton thought he would give 'The Doc' a couple of months' notice. The board accepted his decision and on 28 April 1973, one of the greatest footballers ever to grace the game played his last match against Chelsea at Stamford Bridge.

Bobby was the last 'Red Devil'. He had made his début against Charlton in 1956 on a day when he had been desperate to play and had done so with damaged ankle ligaments which rendered his right foot useless. On one leg he scored two goals. Seventeen years later he departed the professional game the most honoured player in its history. Bobby won every honour, but his place in football history owes more to what he stood for than what he won: the power, grace and competitiveness will never be forgotten. He did it in a certain style, as understood in the *barrios* of Rio as the slums of Glasgow. Charlton the footballer symbolised Englishness in a way that was unique to him, in a way that brought honour to his people and to the professional game as well. He was a sportsman, his dreams nurtured in the 'paradise' that was Mrs Watson's circa '53/'55. Few professionals remain untarnished, Bobby was one the few, Pele perhaps the other.

Forty-four thousand people filled Stamford Bridge to pay tribute to Bobby that April day. The *Daily Mirror* devoted its front page to him, sending a message to 'Britain's greatest sports ambassador as he plays his last League match'. The message was in the headline 'HAVE A NICE ONE BOBBY!'

The Chelsea game was Bobby's 751st appearance for Manchester United. Chelsea won 1–0. At the end of the season he left Old Trafford to become Manager of Preston North End. Of Tommy Docherty, Bobby says: 'I didn't spend a lot of time with him, just six months. I have no complaints about 'The Doc' – none at all – he had nothing to do with me finishing playing. On the contrary he was good to me. Occasionally I'd have to go off to London or somewhere to do a promotion or something and I used to feel guilty for asking for time off other players weren't getting. I'd always hated that even when I was playing for England but Tommy never embarrassed me. People say Tommy Docherty told a load of lies and did this and that but he was great with me.'

Charlton was no mythic figure. He *was* a great pro. The tribute that would probably please him most is offered by Nobby Stiles: 'Bobby Charlton is everything that's good in this game. He's an ordinary working lad is Bobby. My relationship with him is the same as it always was. People say he has changed, he will never change. He was a pro. After Munich when he was only a boy everything hung on him. I have great respect for Bobby as a man, as a footballer and as a friend.'

The only place in professional football where the word integrity has any meaning is on the field. Docherty's treatment of Bobby Charlton suggests that, rogue though he was, 'The Doc' understood this truth.

Denis Law was next on the list of immediate business. Docherty thought Denis was 'a world class player coming to the end of his career'. So 'The Doc' and Denis did a deal: Denis would get a testimonial and bow out gracefully. Docherty broke the agreement, giving Denis a free transfer and announcing this to the press before informing the man who sponsored his appointment at United. Law learned of his fate watching the news on television. He went to Busby. He got no joy. Busby refused, on this occasion, to interfere. Denis was disappointed in 'The Boss'. He'd wanted to retire, instead he joined Manchester City, returning to Old Trafford to score the goal that sent United down to Division Two: 'That was my last kick in League football,' Denis recalls.

Paddy Crerand was now top of the Docherty agenda. A tricky one this, Matt's 'adopted' son. This time Busby did intervene to suggest that Crerand be appointed assistant manager. Docherty reluctantly acquiesced. There is no doubt that Busby hoped Paddy would manage Manchester United one day. Alas, managing life as it unfolded during the coming months proved impossible for Paddy.

Tommy Docherty knew the professional game inside out, every stroke in the book. One trick was getting rid of dangers to your job, such as Paddy Crerand represented. Within six months Crerand was gone. Docherty went to the board and complained that Crerand was disorganised, unpunctual and drinking heavily. Crerand remembers Sir Matt coming to him one day: ' "Paddy, I believe you're drinking a lot and never at the ground when you're supposed to be," he said to me.' This was completely untrue. On another occasion 'The Doc' arranged to take the playing staff to watch a big game at Derby. Everyone was told to report to Old Trafford at three p.m. Then Docherty ordered his secretary to contact everyone and tell them that the coach would be leaving Old Trafford at two p.m. Everyone except his assistant Crerand. He'd do that himself, 'The Doc' proposed. He didn't. Crerand arrived at the ground an hour after the coach departed. Paddy left to manage Northampton. Another problem solved in Docherty's distinctive style.

He wanted to get rid of Alex Stepney. Peter Shilton was his preferred alternative. Sir Matt was consulted. 'The Doc' had no inhibitions about seeking advice from Busby: 'Why not, when the greatest football manager of all time is sitting in the office down the corridor?' he says. Sir Matt was not against signing Shilton, but he *was* against distorting United's wage structure, as Docherty explains: "They were on £300 a week, the lowest paid players in the First Division. Shilton wanted £400 a week. End of deal. When I signed Jimmy Greenhoff from Stoke in 1976 he took a £50 a week pay cut to come to United.'

By then much had happened. Lou Macari had arrived. George Best came back briefly, but sadly it did not work. 'The Doc' met George socially. It was autumn 1973. George hadn't played for almost a year. His life without football was desperate. He drank more than ever, his business interests were sinking fast, and gambling compounded his money problems. George had never cared about money. In the good years he'd been a soft touch for old friends in need. He would play in testimonials for old, failed, United players, taking no fee or even expenses. The great player had never been conceited, never forgotten the lads in the reserve team dressing-room with whom he'd first got pissed in Zurich, danced in the Plaza, hung around with in snooker-hall and bowling-alley. On the contrary, his grief, the disease from which Georgie Best of tabloid myth now suffered was twofold: he missed the simple pleasures of his early years in Manchester and he missed his football, the one thing which made him feel fulfilled.

At a meeting in Paddy McGrath's house, Sir Matt, 'The Doc' and George agreed to give it another try.

'I knew I would never get back to full fitness,' George explains, 'but I thought if I could get back to seventy-five per cent physically my skill and experience would be enough.'

George trained mornings with the first team, afternoons with the apprentices. He only missed one session. 'I could feel it coming back. At first when I went past players I'd get caught. But we played at Tottenham and I scored and I was able to go past people again.' That game at White Hart Lane was the fourth in George's comeback. He played twelve consecutive games, the last on 1 January 1974, a 3–0 defeat at QPR. Four days later Docherty dropped him for the FA Cup Third Round tie against Plymouth.

'He looked frightened,' Docherty recalls, 'there was fear in his face before games, he wasn't enjoying football, it wasn't the George Best we'd known. I picked him to play against Plymouth but he turned up at 2.40 and knocked on the dressing-room door. I told him he wasn't playing and I never saw him again.'

George had always turned up at 2.40. Busby understood, 'The Doc' was not willing to accommodate this idiosyncrasy. 'The other players didn't like it when they had to conform to the rules and George did whatever he liked.' United were relegated that season.

George Best was finished. He was twenty-seven. 'My life became total madness,' he recalls. 'I stayed in bed all day. getting up at four or five in the afternoon and having a drink. The gambling got worse.' George has no coherent memory of the months immediately after he played his last game for United. He was gone, his heart, like all football's heroes, 'still full of it'. George was unlikely to prosper in the Old Trafford dressing-room which was an unhappy place once more. 'The

Doc' fell in and out of love with his players depending on his mood. Morgan was captain for a while. Then he and 'The Doc' fell out. The same thing happened with Stepney. And Macari.

When success arrived things went from bad to worse. Stan Flashman arrived at Old Trafford. Once he would have had to hang around in the car-park. 'The Doc' brought him up to the director's lounge to pass on the Cup Final tickets. The barman who witnessed this outrage was so angry he punched the tout – now a Football League chairman – and made to whack United's manager.

For five years all professional football's vices were brazenly practised at Manchester United, the club renowned for the 'high standards of its public conduct'. Tommy Docherty played as enthusiastically as anyone. He muscled in on lucrative product endorsements originally intended for his stars. He behaved as most professional football people do, breaking the rules with exceptional relish. He was also impulsively generous when the mood took him. After the '77 Cup win he gave the players £5,000 out of his own pocket. Martin Buchan who had been in and out of favour was given the money. As the players had dispersed for the summer Buchan gave it back to 'The Doc' for safe-keeping until the lads returned for pre-season training. Meanwhile Tommy got sacked and decided to keep the 'readies'.

What Tommy Docherty did at Old Trafford was to open the gates to the culture of professional football, the squalid reality of everyday life in the English game. He banished hypocrisy.

I went to see him in Hyde in the autumn of 1990. He and Mary live in style on a few pleasant acres of lovely Cheshire with a paddock out the back for Mary's daughter's horses. Tommy Docherty earns a living as a broadcaster and after-dinner speaker. In private he is not the notorious man of tabloid repute. He talks sense about the game, his opinions the product of a sharp mind doused in a sardonic spirit. A certain innocence remains not about the business of pro football, rather about the game on the field. He played with Finney. Talking about this great old footballer, 'The Doc's' hardened Gorbals face, pock-marked and fleshy in middle-age, softens as he reminisces: 'Tom was a great player, the best ever, better than George – he turned up more often – no, seriously, you could toss a coin between Finney and Best. George was a genius, Finney was more reliable. He had the perfect temperament. If you kicked Tom he just walked away. Off the pitch he was a gentleman, didn't drink or smoke and wasn't a bird man or anything like that. I used to train with him. He was an animal for fitness.' This Tom Finney was Nat Buck's Slave, you will recall. 'The Doc' belonged to a generation of football men who had learned from the Finney experience.

'The Doc' also eulogises Stan Matthews and Gordon Milne's father Jimmy, who was Preston's trainer in his time: 'A lovely man, old Jimmy.' He recalls with regret the unfulfilled promise of his first team, the Chelsea side he more or less finished by sending eight of them back home from Blackpool: 'I was too impetuous, too much of a disciplinarian. I could have handled it better, got the same results in a different way.'

This team was, one senses, his great opportunity to be what he wanted: 'I wanted to be the best, to win the Championship the way Busby had won it with United in the Fifties. My philosophy about how the game should be played was simple: good passing, quick wingers, an attacking, entertaining side. I have always believed that football must be entertaining. If you entertain the public, the ground won't be big enough to hold them. If you don't, you've got no chance. I had great players at Chelsea: Osgood, Venables, Charlie Cooke, Eddie McCreadie. When they broke the rules I had to make a decision. In hindsight it was the wrong one.'

Football cynics will smile at the idea that one might seek to explain 'The Doc' by reference to the team he impulsively destroyed. People prefer the simpler image of Docherty, the one he has traded on over the period since he left Old Trafford. He is the sum of his experience. He has been in professional soccer all his working life. Everything that is objectionable about the game as it has, inevitably, evolved from its deformed beginning can be perceived in the persona of 'The Doc'. Behind his mask there is a sadness too; a heart that once was full of football.

Going to Manchester United was another chance. He failed without honour. One might conclude that if he did not possess the strength of character to manage Chelsea he was unlikely to discover it four jobs and several years on.

Tommy Docherty loves Sir Matt Busby: 'He's a lovely man. He never once interfered, apart from the Shilton business, if I wanted a player I could go out and get him.' Docherty believes Busby's concern about wages was prophetic: 'Matt told me he could see the future of our football, players' salaries would become so inflated that it would be the ruination of the game. He was right. He had great vision.'

Docherty brought Jimmy Murphy back to Old Trafford. Again his instincts were sound: 'Jimmy was a wonderful man. He went to see Steve Coppell play for Tranmere and told me to buy him. "Sign him," Jimmy said. So I rang Bill Shankly and "Shanks" confirmed Jimmy's opinion. I bought Coppell without seeing him play.' Docherty understood that things were strained between Sir Matt and Jimmy. 'I knew something was wrong, that Jimmy hadn't been looked after. United were a big club and they should have done things in a big way.'

At first 'The Doc' socialised with Sir Matt, Crerand, Paddy McGrath, Peter Molloy, the Kennedys and all the other members of what he calls 'The Manchester Mafia'.

'We'd go out with the wives on a Saturday night to the Cromford or the Queens for a meal and a few bottles of wine. Matt, Jean, Sandy and Sheena were lovely people, we'd have a sing-song, the company was great. But then players like Willie Morgan and Stepney would be joining in and I thought this is wrong, so I backed away from that.'

'I was getting home at five and six o'clock in the morning from the Cromford or the Queens, players would be chipping in with opinions about other players, things would be said. I wanted to be judged as a football manager rather than a socialiser.'

So 'The Doc's' life at United was lived on a number of levels; after a while he became a successful manager. He fought with players, behaved as venally as was necessary to survive, socialised with the Busby family one day, dealt with Stan Flashman the next. Manchester United had become just another football club, run on the same principles as all the rest. Nobody objected. Until Tommy Docherty fell in love with Mary Brown.

Sir Matt knew about 'The Doc's' wheeling and dealing at Old Trafford. He stood for it because, for all his wretched spivery with tickets, Docherty was not cynical about the game on the field. For his first eighteen months at United he tried to play a negative game to avoid relegation. Now, for the first time since the war, Manchester United had 'ball-winners' in midfield. Tommy Cavanagh, Docherty's coach, spouted the jargon of the Second Division and beyond, jargon that in the 1990s is the universal language of English soccer. Sir Matt dropped by to see Docherty one day when they were doomed to relegation. Assuring him that his job was safe, Busby pleaded: 'Play the Manchester United way, if we're going to go down let's go in style, with a bit of class.' 'The Doc' obliged.

Sir Matt had fought a long war for his kind of football. He created three great teams, in three separate sets of circumstances. Glorious flowing football and a certain decency of behaviour were their common denominators. But the dressing-room beneath the Old Trafford stand was a different place now. Gulfs were endemic. It was no place for a young lad to grow into greatness. United was no longer the club of Mattha's dreams.

19

The Merchant and the Professional

'Nobody is bigger than the club.'

Matt Busby

After he retired as team manager Sir Matt had a brief tussle between reason and instinct. Reason argued that his presence at Old Trafford would be a problem for those attempting to succeed him. Instinct replied that the club was where he belonged. Instinct won.

Manchester United was still the family home, the club and its people, old players, the office staff, the groundsmen and the laundry ladies, the focus of Sir Matt's life. That was why he kept an office at the ground. He did not want to interfere, but he could not walk away. Old Trafford was his home, his life, his family; it had replaced the one terminated by a sniper's bullet at Arras in 1916. United was Lady Jean's family too, the one that a warm, loving fosterchild had never really had. Yes, the Busbys had a phobia about family, it was understandable. Sir Matt was still living in Kings Road, 'Sir' Willie in more lavish circumstances. But the Busbys were a happy family, with a contentment of the spirit that meant more to them than material possessions.

Manchester United was his dream given life and substance. Without Mattha and the dreams inspired by Alex James and Hughie Gallacher the glory of Manchester United would never have existed. Manchester United is not merely a football club, it's a beautiful memory: the '48 team – Carey, Cockburn, Rowley, Pearson, Mitten and Jimmy Delany; the 'Red Devils'; then, post-Munich, Law, Charlton, Best, Nobby. Football as never played before on England's grounds. There is no doubt about the source of this wonder: Sir Matt 'Mattha' Busby.

Matt and Louis Edwards had their deal about Martin and Sandy going on the Board. In 1970 Martin Edwards was made a director. The following year Sir Matt himself joined the board. The souvenir shop was beginning to go nicely.

Matt began to smell a rat round about 1974. Sandy knew his 'old fella'. Something's going on, Matt told the family, his instincts alerted by a subtle change in Louis's manner. Sir Matt had hoped to be elected chairman, just for a couple of years, a final symbolic recognition of his contribution. So he waited and waited. Nothing happened. Now it was time for part two of the deal: Sandy to go on the Board. A reason had existed for delaying Sandy's appointment: he was in the bookmaking business. Football League regulations prohibited bookies from being directors of clubs. They were the wrong type. Merchants were the right type. Men like Louis Edwards.

Louis had never sought power or influence. He just wanted to be around, to buy the champagne and bathe in the reflected glory. But by the mid-Seventies he was in trouble. His business empire was beginning to crumble, partly because of his extensive involvement in football, and also the fact that Local Authorities with whom Edwards & Sons did most of their business were cleaning up their act after the Poulson/T.Dan Smith scandals. Soon the Edwards family meat business would be on the verge of bankruptcy.

But Louis had a new pal: 'The Doc'. He had always been in awe of Matt, the lap-dog nature of the relationship understood by both. Louis knew Matt's other pals laughed at him behind his back. 'The Doc' did not laugh at Louis, they laughed with each other. The boy from the Gorbals and 'Champagne' Louis got on famously. They had both been laughing stocks in their time, both were strangely lonely characters behind the bonhomie. Martin Buchan talks of glimpsing 'The Doc' at odd moments looking rather sad and vulnerable. 'The Doc' himself remembers Louis with affection, a big, generous man, 'a lonely soul really.'

Between 'The Doc' and Louis there was a measure of mutual respect which neither man easily found elsewhere. They were rogues, free spirits, whispered about and scorned when the party went wrong. They dined together, shared many a bottle of Dom Perignon and chewed the best cigars.

When 'The Doc' called Louis 'Mr Chairman' he meant it. Louis had done a lot for Manchester United without ever getting the credit. Until now.

Who had bought the worthless shares for forty-one grand to give Matt Busby control of United? Who had joined forces with Matt to solve the Harold Hardman problem? Who had supported Matt when he needed to buy all those players after Munich? Who went with Matt on the Quixall deal, the Setters deal, the Cantwell and Herd deals? Who helped clinch the Paddy Crerand transfer? And who went to Switzerland to bring home Denis Law?

Johnny Foy? Paddy McGrath? The Catholic Mafia? The people who sniggered at Louis The Lump, Matt's lap-dog?

No. Louis Charles Edwards was the man who served the Busby Cause, Manchester United's cause.

'The Doc' understood his chairman. He had had a great chairman in Joe Mears at Chelsea in the old days.

Sir Matt waited patiently. He knew he was not going to be chairman. But Sandy was no longer in the bookmaking game. Sandy could go on the Board now. Louis avoided the subject. Sir Matt decided to confront the directors. He hated confrontation but he was angry now. The club were in Majorca on holidays. Sir Matt and the directors were sitting round the swimming pool of their nice hotel, having a few drinks. Everyone was relaxed. Sir Matt gathered them round, his board: 'While we're all here, gentlemen, I want to put forward my son to be a director of Manchester United Football Club.'

There was an uneasy pause. Sir Matt broke the silence: 'I'm going to ask you one by one.' Alan Gibson pointed out that Martin Edwards was not there so the subject could not be discussed. Bill Young thought it was not on because Sandy was a pal of Paddy Crerand. 'What kind of statement is that?' Sir Matt demanded. 'I'll have you know Paddy Crerand is a player who has given great service to this club. He helped us win the European Cup.'

Sir Matt turned to Louis Charles Edwards, the man he had invented. Louis said no. He wanted his youngest son, Roger, on the Board. Mr Secretary, Les Olive was there. Sir Matt turned to him and said: 'I want this in the minutes of the next Board meeting.' Then he turned back to his lap-dog: 'We had an a agreement, you and I, that Sandy would go on the Board.' Louis told him it would be discussed at the next board meeting.

The board supported Louis. Sir Matt and Lady Jean went round to Sandy's house that night to break the news: 'My mam was sick,' Sandy recalls. Sir Matt was too. Sandy told them not to worry, he would rather not be on a Board with people like that.

Sandy Busby was not just a friend of Paddy Crerand's. Big Duncan, Shay and Bobby, little Eddie Colman, George Best, all of them were Sandy's friends. He was one of them, a footballer, a good lad.

Next they took Sir Matt's club car from him. Wasn't he a director now? Only employees had club cars. Sir Matt bought the car from Manchester United Football Club. He stopped fighting. He'd always hated fighting.

In 1970 the Edwards family started planning a Rights Issue. Roland Smith, another United 'Billy' suggested the Rights Issue as a way of raising money for United and for Louis whose business was now in a mess. Sir Matt opposed the Rights Issue. He argued that United could raise money by other means. There were other means of raising money but these might cause the Edwards family to lose control of *their* club.

Busby's opposition created a fuss, providing a focus for discontent over the Rights Issue. Researchers from the *World in Action* television programme were attracted to this noise and began to poke around. When they came to investigate Louis Edwards's meat empire, *World in Action* discovered myriad examples of bribery and corruption. You could write a book about this kind of thing. In fact Alex Stepney's *Betrayal of the Legend* is such a book. This book is rather twisted in so far as it purports to explain Manchester United Football Club. The depiction of 'Champagne' Louis as some kind of villain unique in the history of professional football – or indeed of Local Authority transactions – is unjust and misleading. Business is business. Louis is not the villain of the Manchester United story. Louis was OK. As 'Billy Bunters' go, Louis was better than the average. He was an expansive merchant. Matt's lap-dog.

The television programme screened in January 1980 vilified Louis Edwards in classic muck-raking style. A month later he died. Louis died 'an unhappy man'. According to his son Martin he died of shame.

Dave Sexton succeeded Tommy Docherty as manager on Sir Matt's recommendation, his last influential act at Manchester United. Sexton was another Puritan, a first-class type like Frank O'Farrell, in many ways the best of his caste. But he wasn't United's style. Perhaps, more profoundly, Sexton, an English Catholic, was wrong for 'Cottonopolis' the city of extravagant rogues, men who thought anything was possible.

Ron Atkinson followed, 'Big' Ron. He was more Manchester's style, in fact, classically so: the gear, the patter, the night, the rub-a-dub-dubs. Ron was a rogue. He did well. He bought Bryan Robson and Remi Moses for £2 million. Sir Matt thought this was too much. Shortly afterwards he resigned from the Board to become President of United, a titular role, a 'figurehead', as he wryly remarked one night in Belfast not too long ago.

In 1982 Lady Jean was struck by Alzheimer's Disease. Sir Matt himself survived a cerebral haemorrhage in 1981. Lady Jean and he had moved to a flat in Wilbraham Road where he cared lovingly for her as she slipped away from the conscious world. Her final years were spent in a nursing home. Every afternoon Sir Matt, whom she no longer recognised, sat and held her hand for two or three hours. They had come a long way together from Bellshill. Harold Riley recalls seeing them having a pre-dinner cocktail in the Midland Hotel one evening in the Eighties. 'They were like lovers, great pals after all their years together.' Lady Jean died in 1986. Sir Matt visits her grave twice a week: 'He just walks up and down smoking his pipe,' Sandy says.

In 1989 the lease on the souvenir shop ran out. Sandy had made a great success of it. The business was flourishing, the legend of Manchester United growing all the time. Martin Edwards sent a letter to the Busbys explaining that the lease would not be renewed. United bought the old stock and made a settlement of about £100,000.

Although Martin Edwards doesn't actually say so, there is

391

little doubt that taking back the lease was a measure of revenge for his father's death: 'If Matt had gone along with the Rights Issue at the time *World in Action* probably would not have had a story. But the publicity from Matt opposing it got people interested and they started to dig,' Martin explains.

Martin Edwards is Chief Executive of the new Manchester United, a corporation as well as a football club. Martin, the merchant's son, is the putative villain of the piece, but to paint him thus is unfair. He is a businessman, United his business. He sits, smoothly charming, in his large office above the new souvenir shop. He likes Sir Matt because 'he has always been pleasant with me', Martin explains.

'I have never fallen out with Sir Matt, I like him and respect him for what he has achieved. I think he was one of the greatest managers of all time. He is not brash in any way, in fact he's quite a humble man, a lovely man. But I suppose there had to be a toughness in there to get the success he did.

'All the great men have to be tough at some time otherwise they get washed away,' Martin ventures.

Perhaps he is thinking of the man he calls 'Father'.

'Father and Matt did it together after Munich. Father supported Matt and I think Matt welcomed Father's involvement. They were a good partnership. They ran the club together really. Father was with Matt on the Law deal and all the other purchases at that time. Obviously the combination worked. That period from '63 to the European Cup win was very successful. It was then that Father became prominent with Matt.'

'At the end of the day we have all benefited in some way because of the traditions. In one sense tradition makes life harder.'

Martin goes on to talk about 'the lingering shadow of tradition', which, he explains, 'you can't allow to dominate you'.

'You are never going to get rid of the Best/Law/Charlton era, that is always going to be held up as an example, it is part of our history, you have to live with it. The point I am trying to make is that you have to have continued success to ever live it down, if you can live it down. The past is the past. You live with the shadow of Sir Matt. It is there.'

It would be easy to take Martin Edwards's words out of context to mock the notion of 'living down' the past. But he is a pleasant young fellow, a man of his football time, obeying the imperatives of this age. Of course, he is a businessman coming from a different place than many of us, the lads, who played another game in another age. Martin has not been notably generous to Sir Matt Busby. But as we have seen, professional soccer is a hard game and when it suited Sir Matt he played as tough as anyone. So when searching for a villain we can leave Martin out, although that is not the way many of my pals would have this story told.

Some other old players bear a grudge of a kind against Bobby Charlton. Bobby came back after seven years away to become a director of the Edwards's United. His 'paradise' has changed: 'You have to be realistic in this day and age. Oh, it was changed, it is just not the same game as it used to be, much as you would like to go back to the old days. The only way you can have the same sort of feeling is to try and have the same kind of success. That is as near as you can get. I am trying my best to maintain the standard set by Sir Matt but it is just not the same game.'

Talking to Bobby one can see that underneath the director he is, as Nobby says, 'the same lad' he always was. The problems have changed, his role is different, he serves United as best he can. He is a tough lad, is Bobby, not a sentimentalist, except about the paradise days. He has grown up, accepted professional football for the hard business it is, not become a victim.

Some Lads resent this. But when you hear Bobby speak about 'paradise', see his eyes moist at the mention of the Crash and listen to him talk about Jimmy you understand the Lads are wrong, very wrong indeed.

'I remember when I first started out as a pro,' he reflects. 'I had a cousin who owned a greengrocer's shop and I asked him how much it cost him to set himself up in business. I thought one day I'd have to do the same. I assumed it would be when I was about thirty-five. He told me it cost him two thousand and I worked it out, if I could save a hundred pounds a year I should be all right. That was all the security I wanted in those days. How it's changed for players now,' he says in wonder.

Bobby and Denis Law never really got on: 'He's mellowed

over the years,' Denis admits, 'he has become more approach-
able. I get on all right with Bobby now, probably better than
when I played. It's ironic that Bobby will almost certainly
become chairman now. I think it would be a good thing for
Manchester United.

'Bobby Charlton is a world-renowned name, respected
everywhere. A diplomat.' Denis smiles sardonically.

Jimmy Murphy died in 1989. He left a large, lovely family
behind. Sir Matt and Jimmy were strangers at the end. His son,
Jim, talks fervently and succinctly about his dad. They got to
know each other over the final ten years, sharing many a pint in
the Throstles Nest. Jimmy's heart was full of it to the end. He
found Steve Coppell for 'The Doc', later he spotted Peter
Beardsley playing for Carlisle, Paul Parker, and young
McAllister who is now at Leeds. Ray Houghton was another
Jimmy first saw playing for Fulham.

On Beardsley Jimmy was fascinating: 'My dad saw him
playing first as an out and out striker. He wasn't impressed. He
thought Beardsley should play as a sort of advanced midfield
player,' young Jim recalls. But seeing these players Jimmy had
no one to tell about them. One night in the Throstles Nest he
said to his son, 'Why should I bother my arse going down there,
nobody listens.' He was not bitter, Jim explains, just sad.
Jimmy Murphy, the immaculate dresser, did not bother in the
end: 'He'd go down to the pub in his old clothes, just sit there
and have his pint,' his son recalls.

'My dad never said anything against Sir Matt or the club. The
only thing he used to feel when he went to Old Trafford was the
loss of tradition. The souvenir shop, the museum, the basket-
ball team, the Lottery office, the Miss Manchester United
models, there were so many different ventures. My dad was a
traditionalist.'

He was a great football man. Of the many heroes of these
pages Jimmy is, perhaps, the truest reflection of the game as
treasured in our memories.

A few years before he died Jimmy was rushed to hospital.
Something had burst, his son can't remember exactly what.
'Bobby Charlton and Freddie Pye came to see him.' Pye,
another Manchester lad, was chairman of City. 'My father was

all wired up, at death's door, and he's telling Freddie whether or not to sign Paul Stewart. Lots of football people came to see him. Sir Matt never did. It was only after he died, at the funeral, I was speaking to Les Olive and Les said that Sir Matt had just been to see Joe Mercer in hospital in Rhyl. I thought, he went fifty miles to Rhyl to see Joe and he wouldn't come five miles to see my dad.' Young Jim thought it strange. A hard game.

Sir Matt Busby CBE, Freeman of Manchester, still goes to the ground every day. The hardest man in this hard game, the professional who survived the longest. He is a lovely man. The world has honoured him, but professional football never could find a way to honour its greatest man. Matt Busby was a romantic. He loved the game, more than people or possessions. Through his love he rendered professional football in England more beautiful than any other man. Yes, Frank O'Farrell was right, Manchester United was Matt's fantasy world. His greatest-achievement was to create the illusion of beauty in a craft wretchedly deformed from the beginning. As it decays now, the plaything of spivs and merchants, the glorious memories of Matt Busby's United serve to soothe the pain. His has been a strange kind of life, a strange kind of glory.

The old man is eighty-two. Yet not an old man. I've been in many large rooms with him during the course of researching this book, and any room he walks into is hushed in reverence. A great man is present. His old pal Paddy McGrath is usually with him, the two of them still impeccably dressed, handsome, imposing. You can imagine them in Blackpool, the lads in their prime. And you can understand what Big Louis fell for, why he ended up in the palm of Matt's hand.

Unlike many of those closest to him Sir Matt is not bitter. Others reflected on the disappointments: Louis reneging on the agreement about their sons going on the Board. Martin refusing to renew the lease on the club's souvenir shop at the very moment when Manchester United was being valued at more than £20 million. Smaller things rankled. At the club's Centenary Dinner Sir Matt had not been seated at the Top Table. When the smart new restaurant opened at Old Trafford the club's executives enjoyed free lunches. Nobody told the Club President. This oversight was taken as a slight. But not by him.

When Bobby Charlton became a director some regarded this as treachery, a service rendered to the new man, a betrayal of Sir Matt. He did not share that view, the old man was too wise in the ways of professional football to dwell on such matters. As he always reminded troublesome players – Johnny Morris, John Giles, Denis Law – nobody is bigger than the club. Not even the last great football man.

Index

401

Acknowledgements

I wish to thank the Busby family for their co-operation over the past two years. Also the family of the late Jimmy Murphy, Jim and Nicky in particular. Jimmy Matthie and his wife Agnes in Old Orbiston were very kind. Paddy McGrath, Harold Riley and Paddy Crerand were particularly indulgent with their time and co-operation. Among many I am indebted to are Henry Cockburn, Charlie Mitten, Bobby Charlton, Shay Brennan, Denis Law, Harry McShane, Noel Cantwell, Gordon Clayton, Harry Gregg, Jackie Blanchflower, Jimmy Shiels, George Best and Mary Shatila, John Doherty, Billy Behan, Martin Buchan, Nobby Stiles, John Giles and David Sadler.

Wilf McGuinness, Frank O'Farrell and Tommy Docherty relived some painful experiences. I am especially grateful for their time and help. A special thanks also to Martin Edwards. David Meek of the *Manchester Evening News* was extremely generous and of inestimable assistance; I am grateful to him.

During several months spent in Manchester, Ian Connelly and Terry Corless (and Kath) were kind, fun and helpful. Harry 'The Shoe' gave me a place to live and didn't complain (yet) about the mess. Jimmy Jones provided the gourmet lunches and many laughs. Thanks, J. J.

I would also like to thank John Cooney of the *Irish Times* (now at the European Commission in Brussels), whose book on Scottish Catholicism was an invaluable work of reference. My friend Colm Tóibín was a constant source of encouragement. I once again availed myself of the superb facilities at The Tyrone Guthrie Centre at Annaghmakerrig, Co. Monaghan. I simply cannot express my gratitude to Bernard Louchlin, his wife Mary and the staff at Annaghmakerrig. To Owen and Maeve as well.

Without the forbearance of Angus Fanning, editor at the *Sunday Independent*, this book would have been impossible. This debt I hope to repay. My sports editor, Adhamanan O'Sullivan, was similarly sympathetic; I am eternally grateful. Also to my colleague Sean Ryan for guidance, a special thanks.

For his inspiring professionalism and courage when the going got tough I wish to thank Tom Weldon, my editor at William Heinemann. He deserves and will doubtless acquire a better class of author.

Thanks also to Lisa Glass for her editing.

For her faith in defiance of all the evidence – and for much more than I can publicly express – I thank Imogen Parker of A. P. Watt.

My assistant Veronica Farrell has been the staunchest ally from day one – once more, words are inadequate. Jennifer's transcription of the original tapes was much appreciated.

My colleague Christy Fenlon of Independent Newspapers owns one of the most comprehensive collections of published material on the subject of Manchester United. My access to this was a priceless asset.

Maurice Quinn was incredibly diligent and wise at the final editing stage, to him and his RTE colleague Tim O'Connor my sincerest thanks.